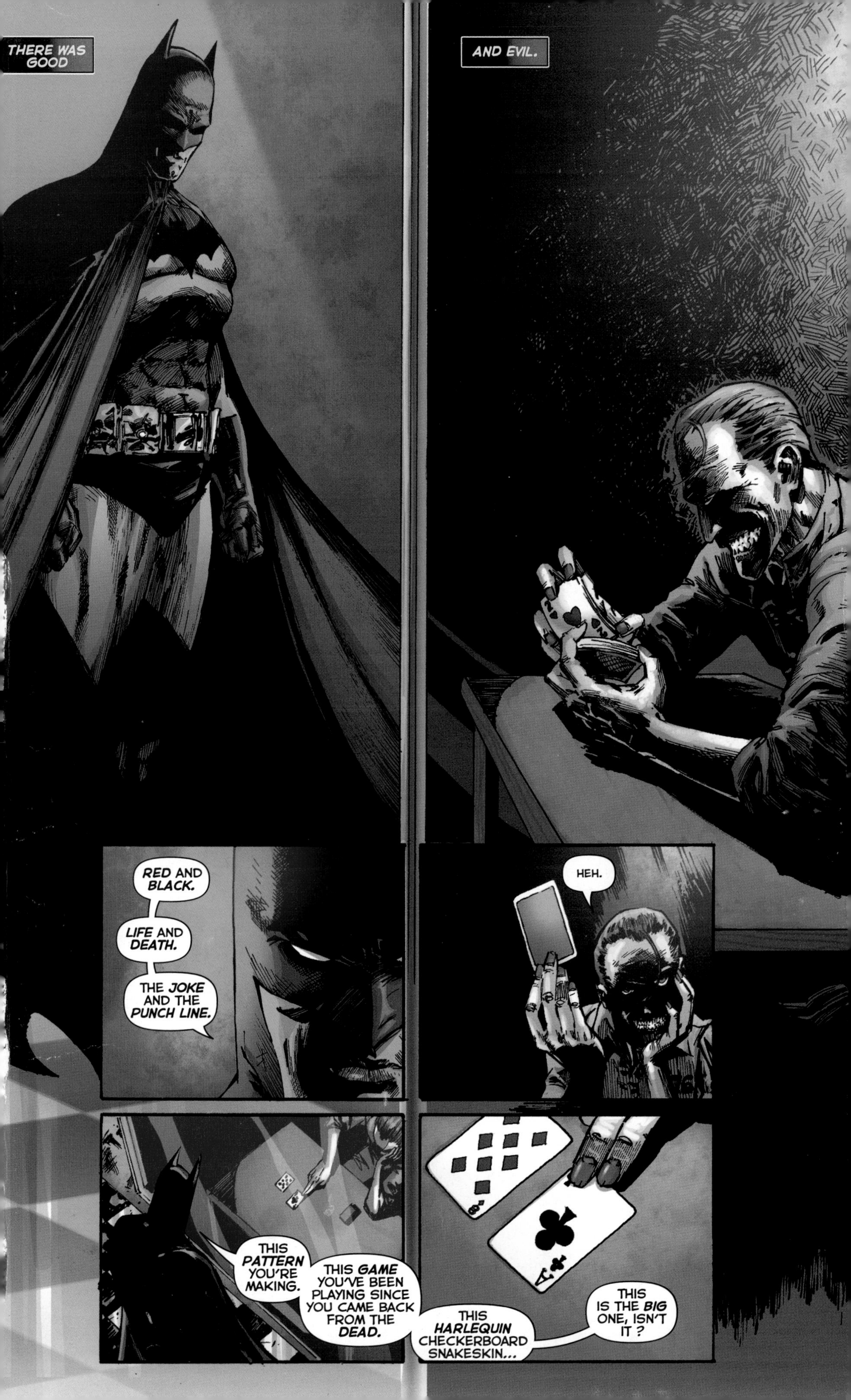
THERE WAS GOOD
AND EVIL.
RED AND BLACK.
LIFE AND DEATH.
THE JOKE AND THE PUNCH LINE.
HEH.
THIS PATTERN YOU'RE MAKING.
THIS GAME YOU'VE BEEN PLAYING SINCE YOU CAME BACK FROM THE DEAD.
THIS HARLEQUIN CHECKERBOARD SNAKESKIN...
THIS IS THE BIG ONE, ISN'T IT ?

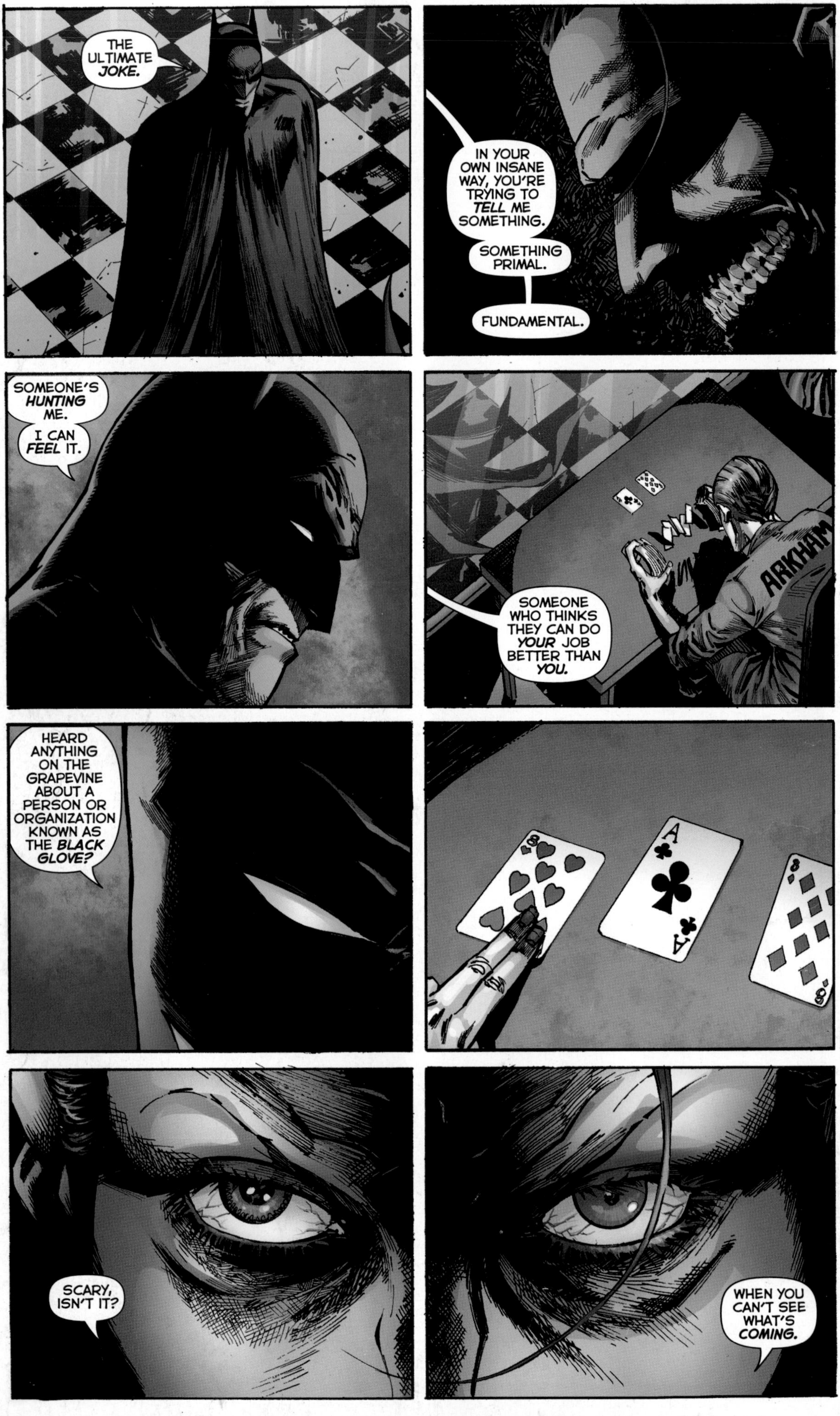
THE ULTIMATE JOKE.
IN YOUR OWN INSANE WAY, YOU'RE TRYING TO TELL ME SOMETHING.
SOMETHING PRIMAL.
FUNDAMENTAL.
SOMEONE'S HUNTING ME.
I CAN FEEL IT.
SOMEONE WHO THINKS THEY CAN DO YOUR JOB BETTER THAN YOU.
ARKHAM
HEARD ANYTHING ON THE GRAPEVINE ABOUT A PERSON OR ORGANIZATION KNOWN AS THE BLACK GLOVE?
SCARY, ISN'T IT?
WHEN YOU CAN'T SEE WHAT'S COMING.

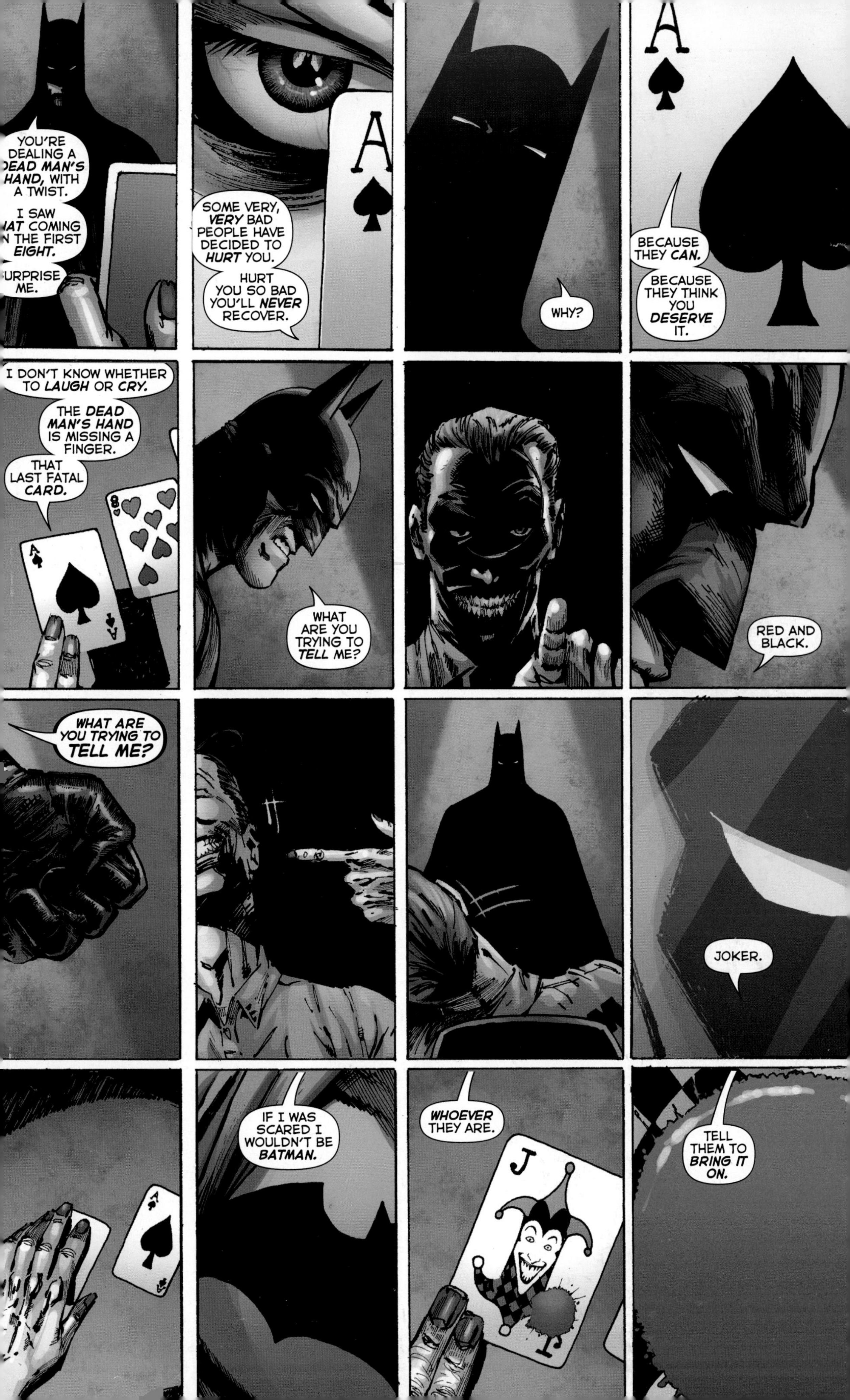

YOU'RE DEALING A DEAD MAN'S HAND, WITH A TWIST.
I SAW AT COMING N THE FIRST EIGHT.
URPRISE ME.
SOME VERY, VERY BAD PEOPLE HAVE DECIDED TO HURT YOU.
HURT YOU SO BAD YOU'LL NEVER RECOVER.
WHY?
BECAUSE THEY CAN.
BECAUSE THEY THINK YOU DESERVE IT.
I DON'T KNOW WHETHER TO LAUGH OR CRY.
THE DEAD MAN'S HAND IS MISSING A FINGER.
THAT LAST FATAL CARD.
WHAT ARE YOU TRYING TO TELL ME?
RED AND BLACK.
WHAT ARE YOU TRYING TO TELL ME?
JOKER.
IF I WAS SCARED I WOULDN'T BE BATMAN.
WHOEVER THEY ARE.
TELL THEM TO BRING IT ON.

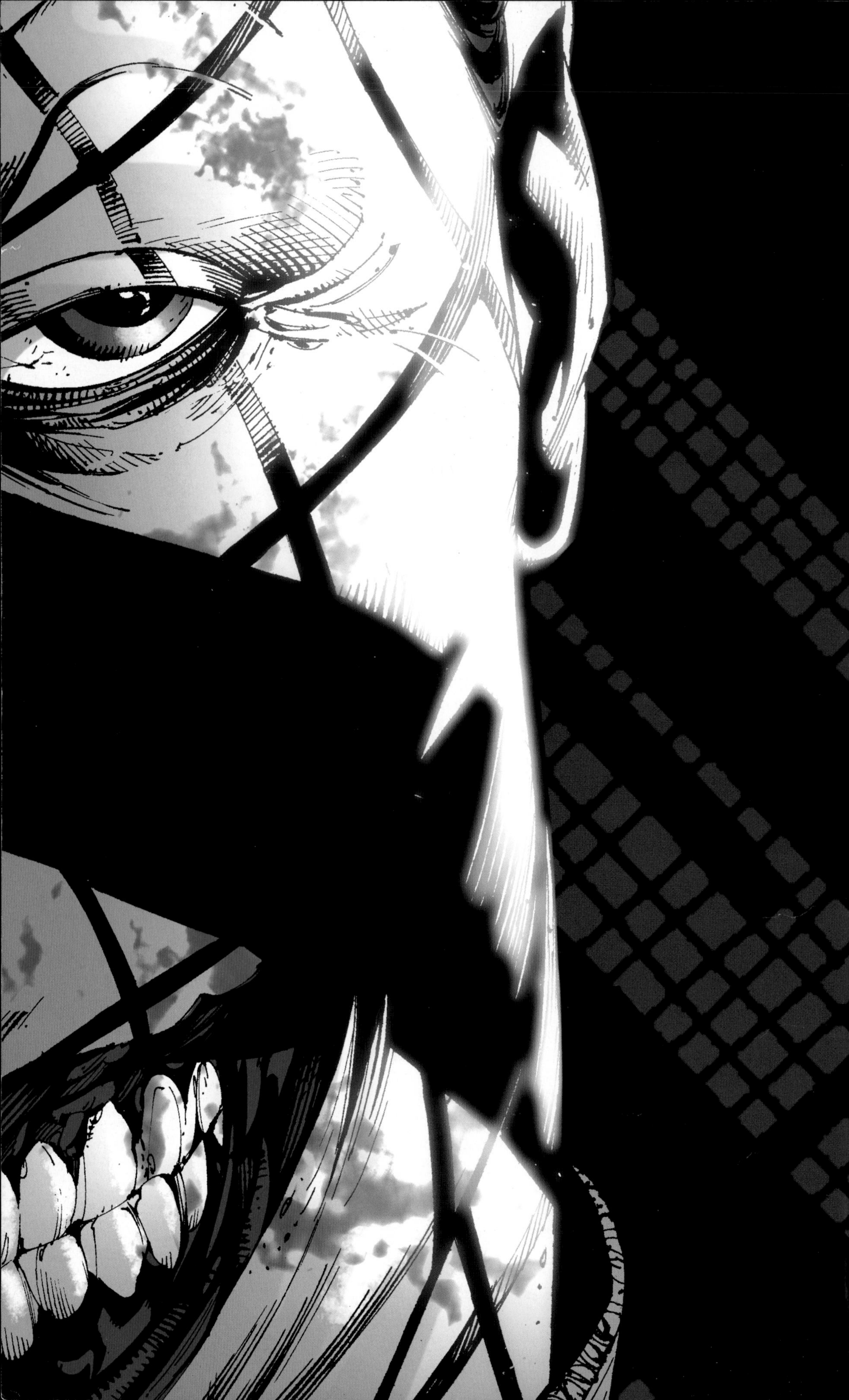

BATMAN R.I.P.

THE DELUXE EDITION

written by
Grant Morrison

art by
Tony S. Daniel
Sandu Florea
Lee Garbett
Trevor Scott

colored by
Guy Major
Alex Sinclair

lettered by
Randy Gentile
Jared K. Fletcher
Nick J. Napolitano

painted cover art by
ALEX ROSS

variant cover art by
TONY S. DANIEL

Batman created by
BOB KANE

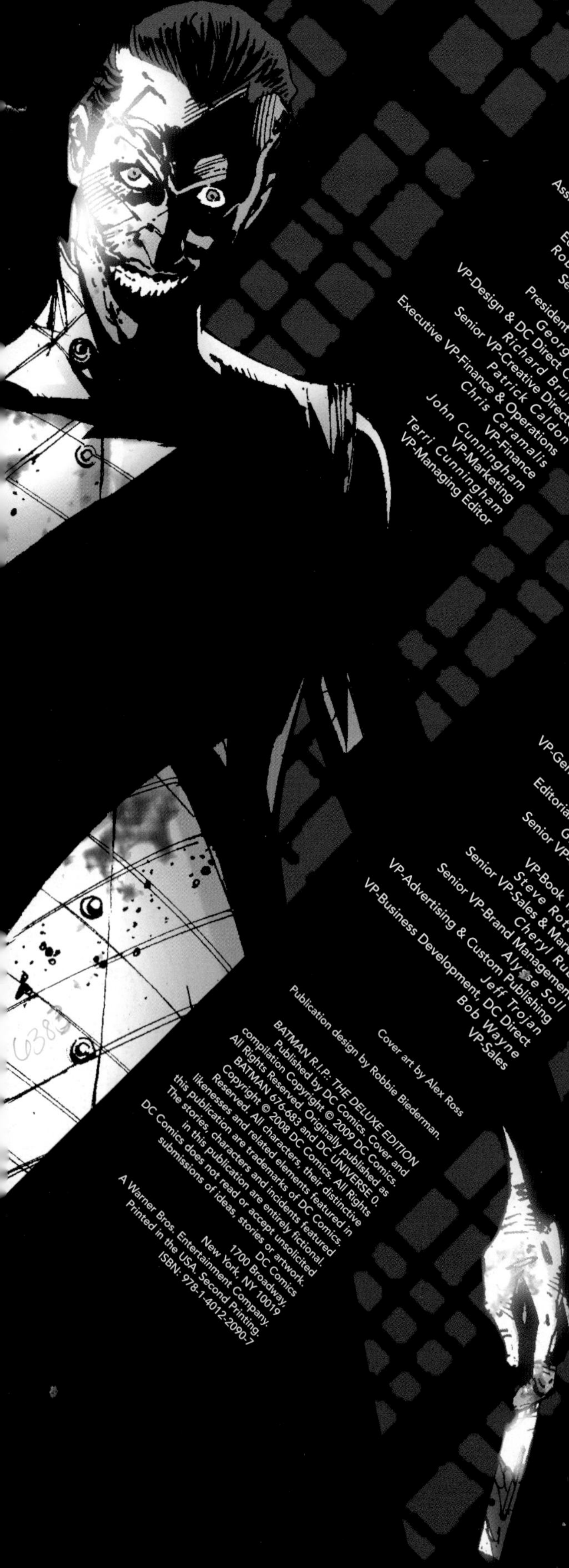

Dan DiDio
Senior VP-Executive Editor
Mike Marts
Editor-original series
Jeanine Schaefer
Associate Editor-original series
Janelle Siegel
Assistant Editor-original series
Scott Nybakken
Editor-collected edition
Robbin Brosterman
Senior Art Director
Paul Levitz
President & Publisher
Georg Brewer
VP-Design & DC Direct Creative
Richard Bruning
Senior VP-Creative Director
Patrick Caldon
Executive VP-Finance & Operations
Chris Caramalis
VP-Finance
John Cunningham
VP-Marketing
Terri Cunningham
VP-Managing Editor

Amy Genkins
Senior VP-Business & Legal Affairs
Alison Gill
VP-Manufacturing
David Hyde
VP-Publicity
Hank Kanalz
VP-General Manager, WildStorm
Jim Lee
Editorial Director-WildStorm
Gregory Noveck
Senior VP-Creative Affairs
Sue Pohja
VP-Book Trade Sales
Steve Rotterdam
Senior VP-Sales & Marketing
Cheryl Rubin
Senior VP-Brand Management
Alysse Soll
VP-Advertising & Custom Publishing
Jeff Trojan
VP-Business Development, DC Direct
Bob Wayne
VP-Sales

Cover art by Alex Ross

Publication design by Robbie Biederman.

BATMAN *R.I.P.*: THE DELUXE EDITION
Published by DC Comics.

DC Comics
1700 Broadway
New York, NY 10019
A Warner Bros. Entertainment Company.
Printed in the USA. Second Printing.
ISBN: 978-1-4012-2090-7

Table of Contents

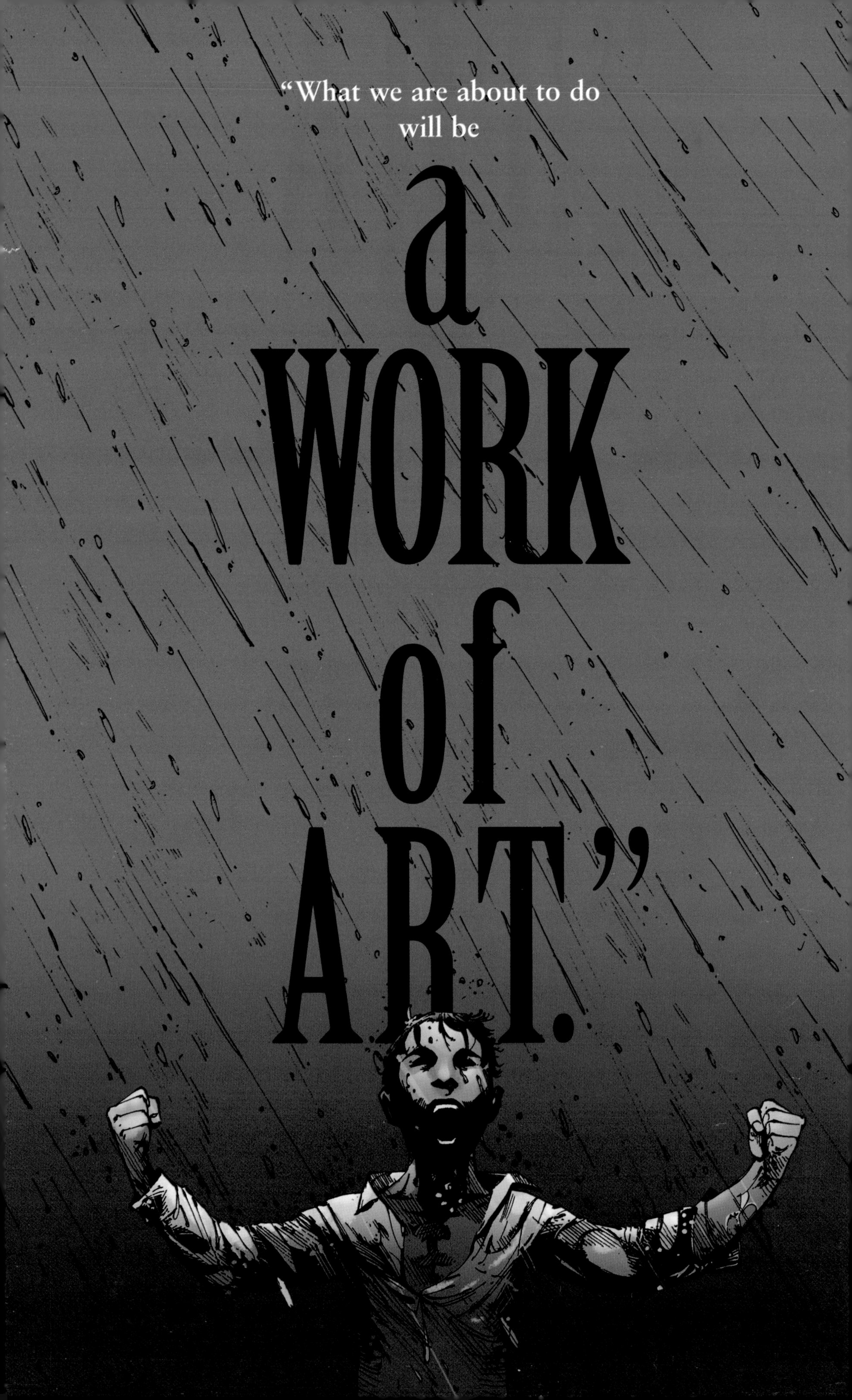
"What we are about to do
will be
a
WORK
of
ART."

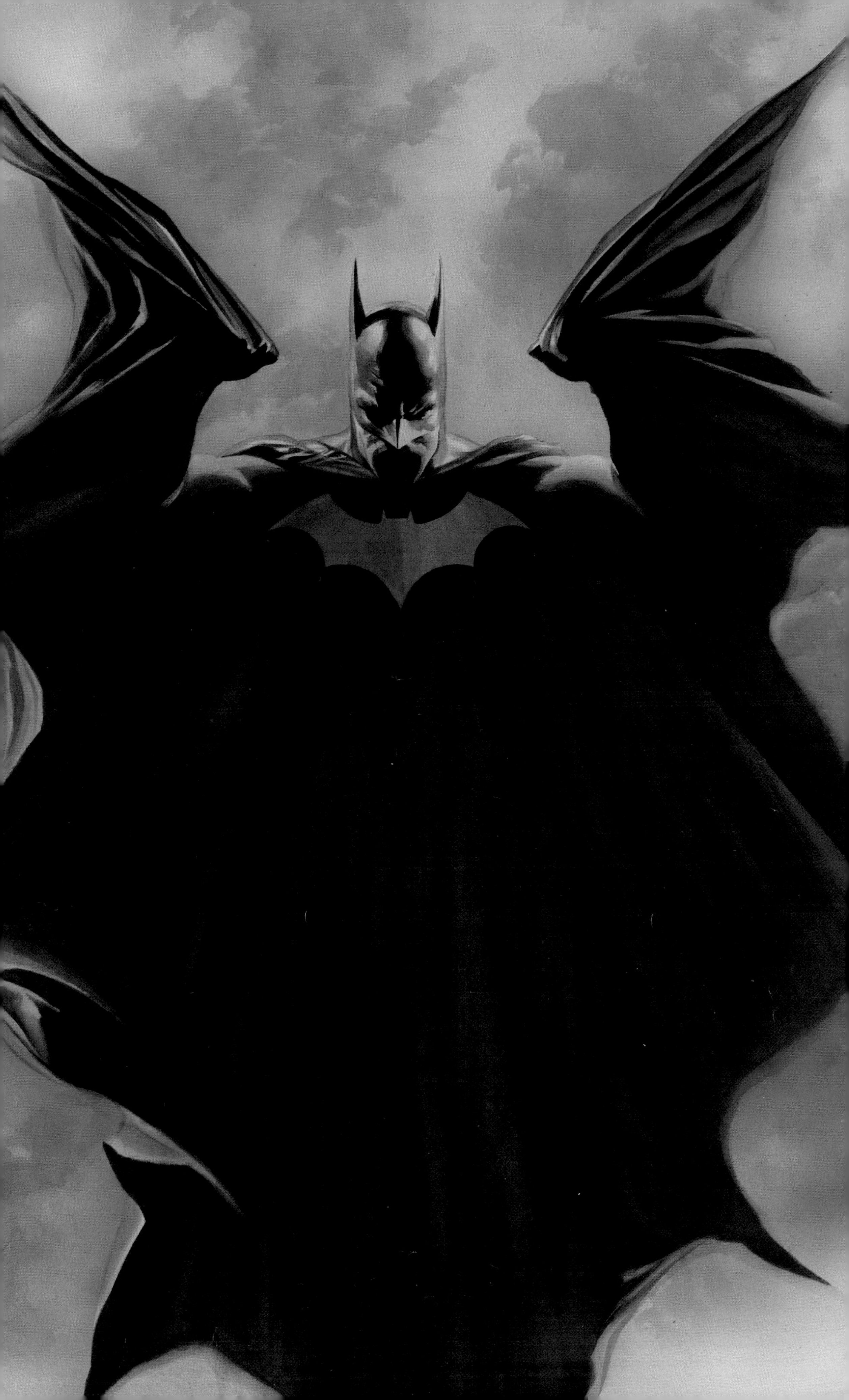

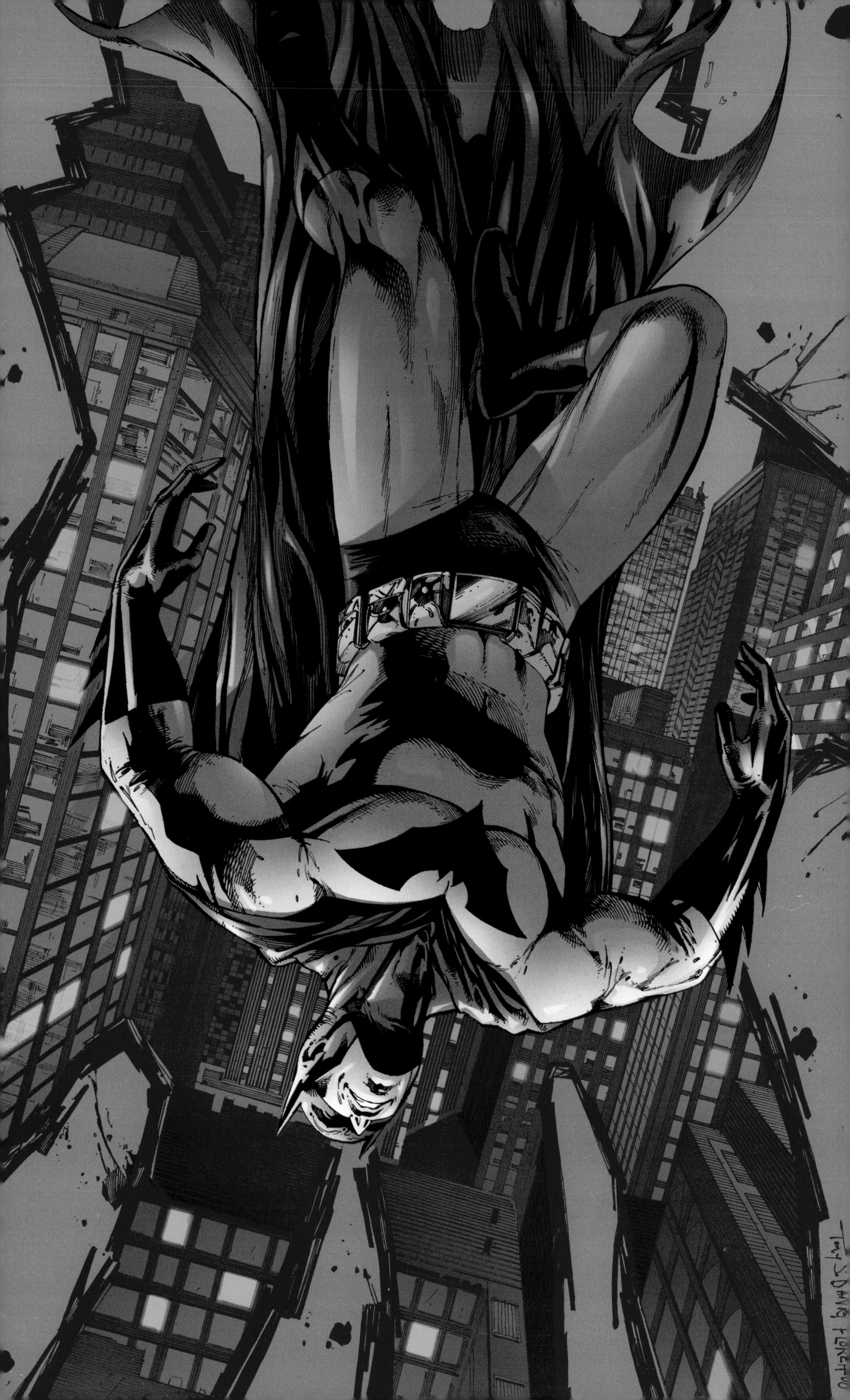

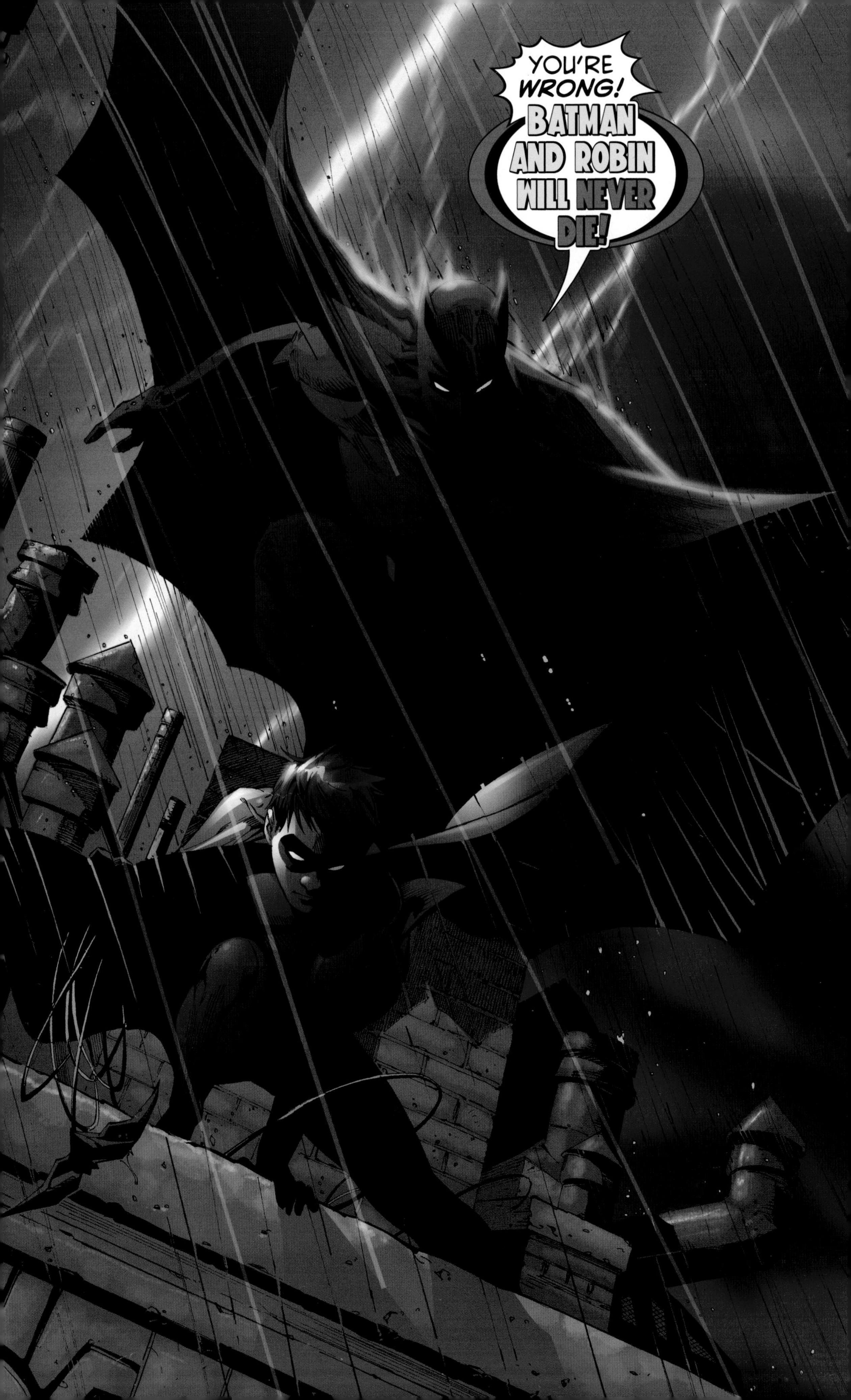
YOU'RE WRONG! BATMAN AND ROBIN WILL NEVER DIE!

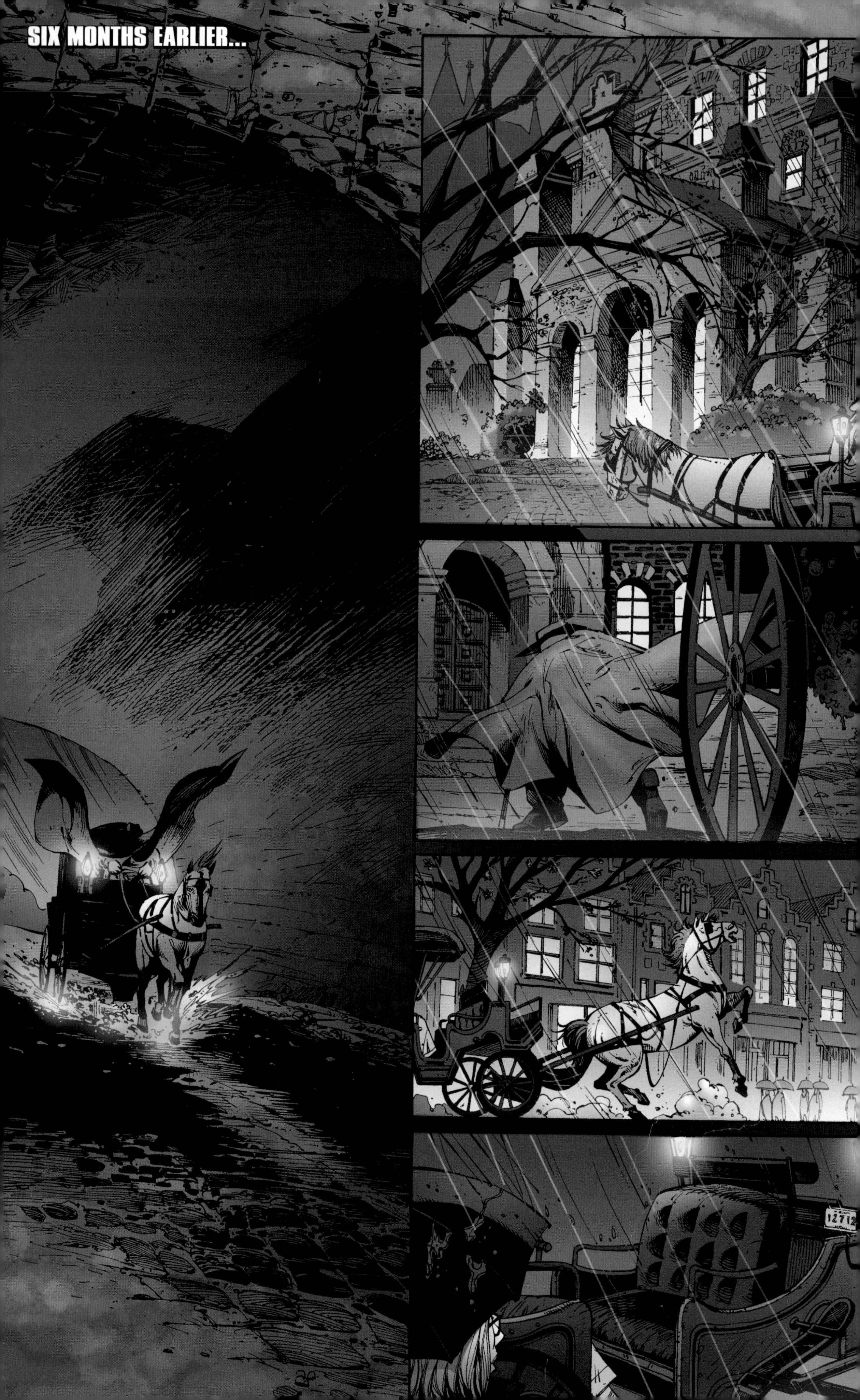
SIX MONTHS EARLIER...

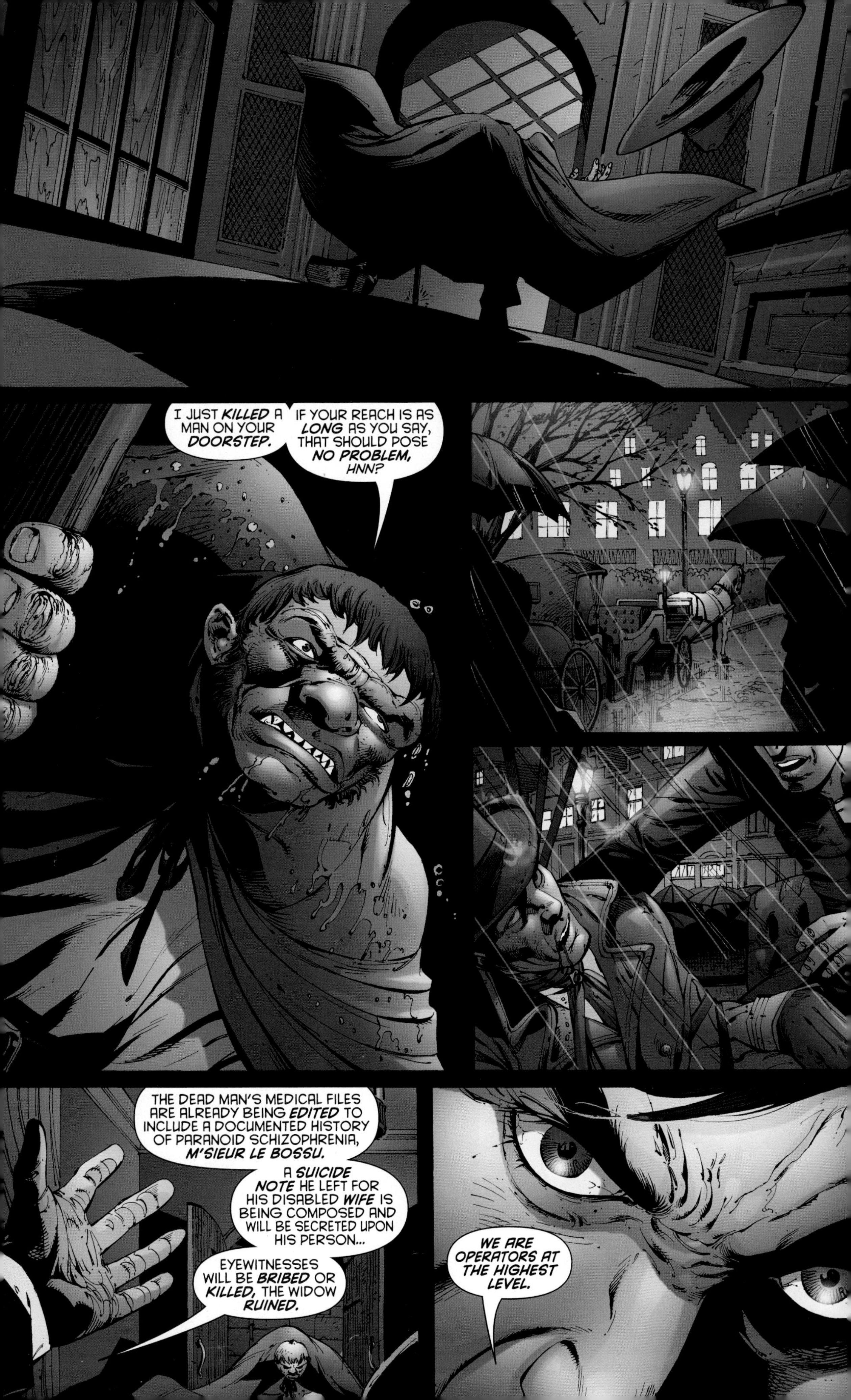
I JUST KILLED A MAN ON YOUR DOORSTEP.
IF YOUR REACH IS AS LONG AS YOU SAY, THAT SHOULD POSE NO PROBLEM, HNN?
THE DEAD MAN'S MEDICAL FILES ARE ALREADY BEING EDITED TO INCLUDE A DOCUMENTED HISTORY OF PARANOID SCHIZOPHRENIA, M'SIEUR LE BOSSU.
A SUICIDE NOTE HE LEFT FOR HIS DISABLED WIFE IS BEING COMPOSED AND WILL BE SECRETED UPON HIS PERSON...
EYEWITNESSES WILL BE BRIBED OR KILLED, THE WIDOW RUINED.
WE ARE OPERATORS AT THE HIGHEST LEVEL.

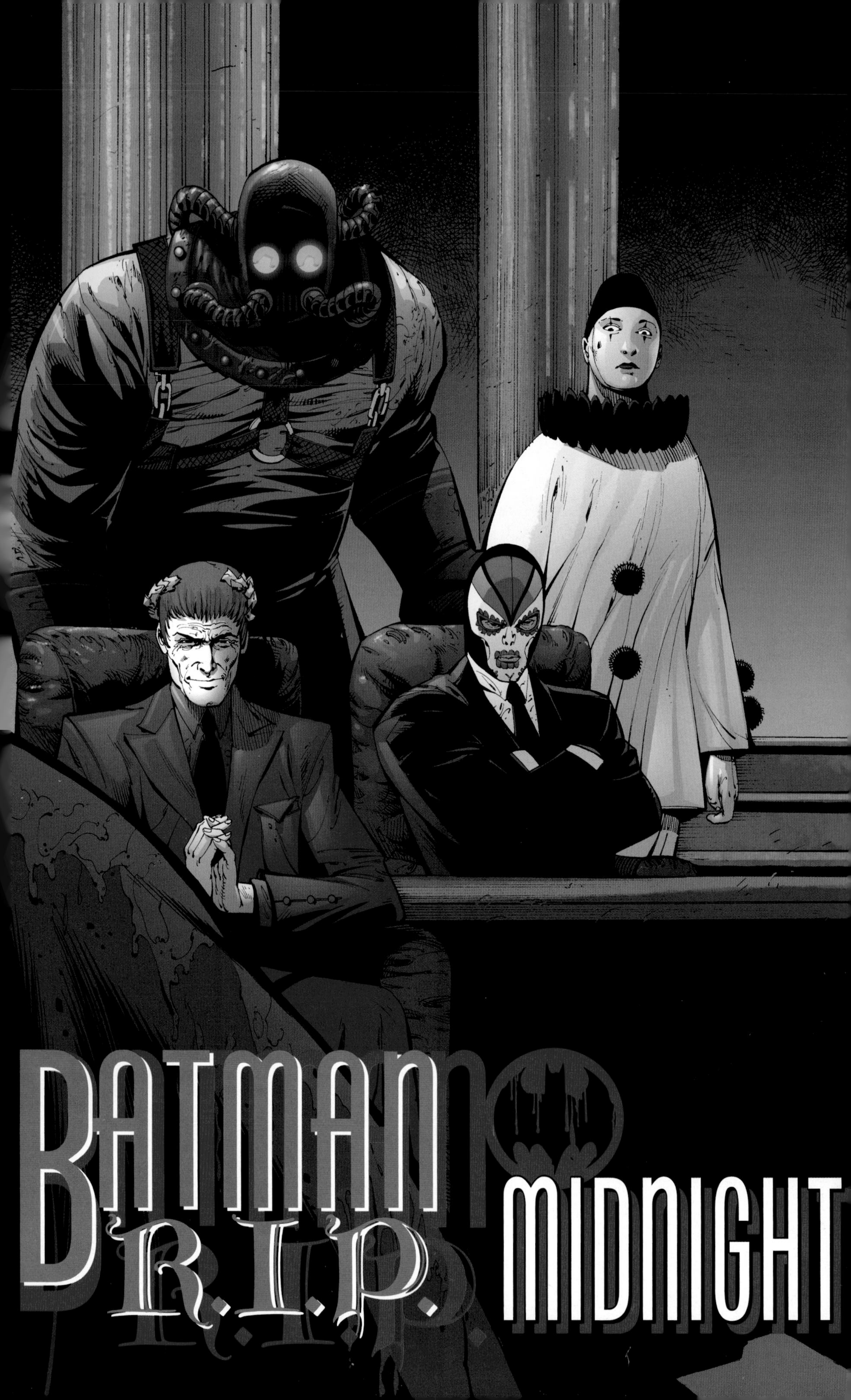
BATMAN
R.I.P.
MIDNIGHT

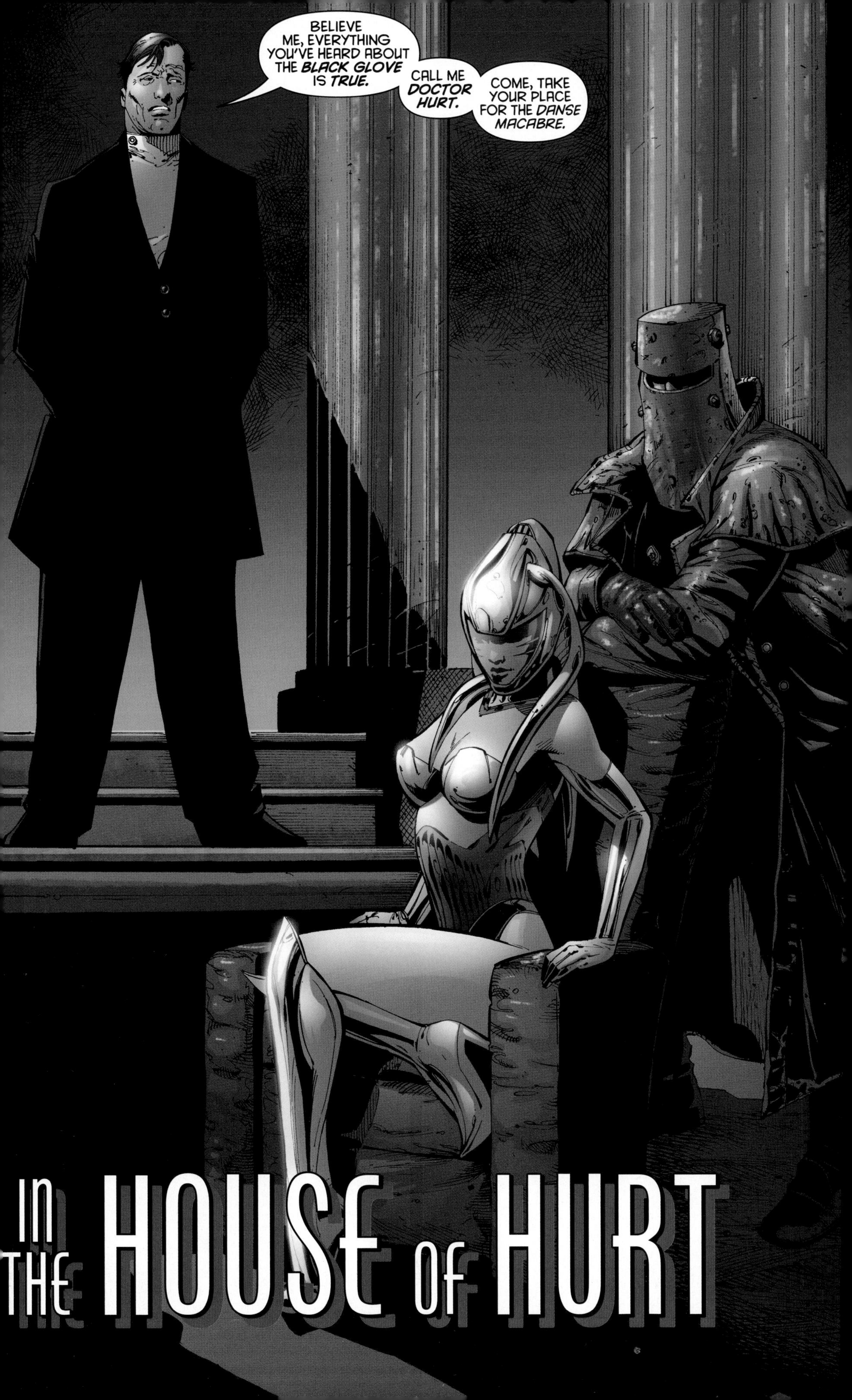
BELIEVE ME, EVERYTHING YOU'VE HEARD ABOUT THE BLACK GLOVE IS TRUE.
CALL ME DOCTOR HURT.
COME, TAKE YOUR PLACE FOR THE DANSE MACABRE.
IN THE HOUSE OF HURT

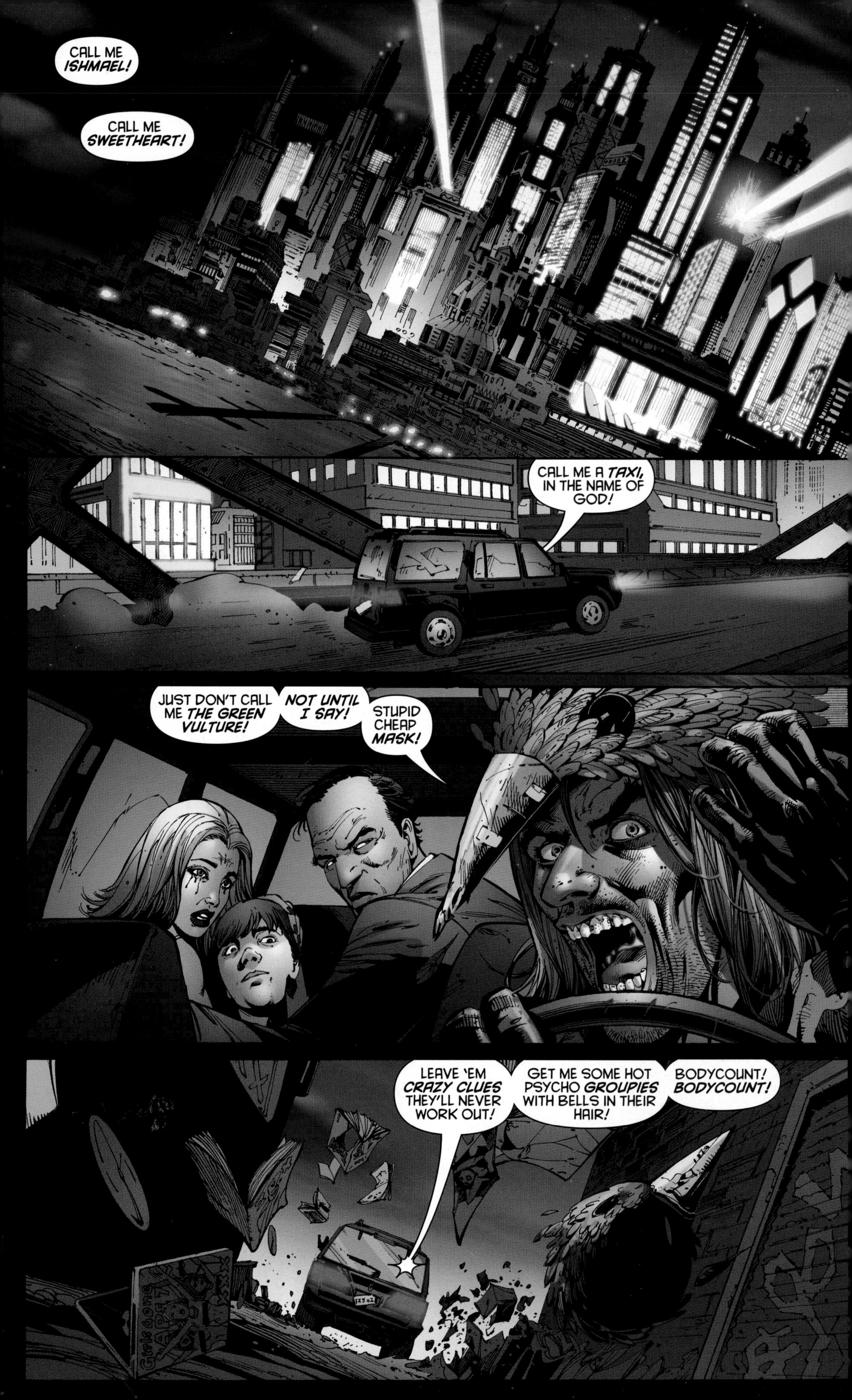
CALL ME ISHMAEL!
CALL ME SWEETHEART!
CALL ME A TAXI, IN THE NAME OF GOD!
JUST DON'T CALL ME THE GREEN VULTURE!
NOT UNTIL I SAY!
STUPID CHEAP MASK!
LEAVE 'EM CRAZY CLUES THEY'LL NEVER WORK OUT!
GET ME SOME HOT PSYCHO GROUPIES WITH BELLS IN THEIR HAIR!
BODYCOUNT! BODYCOUNT!

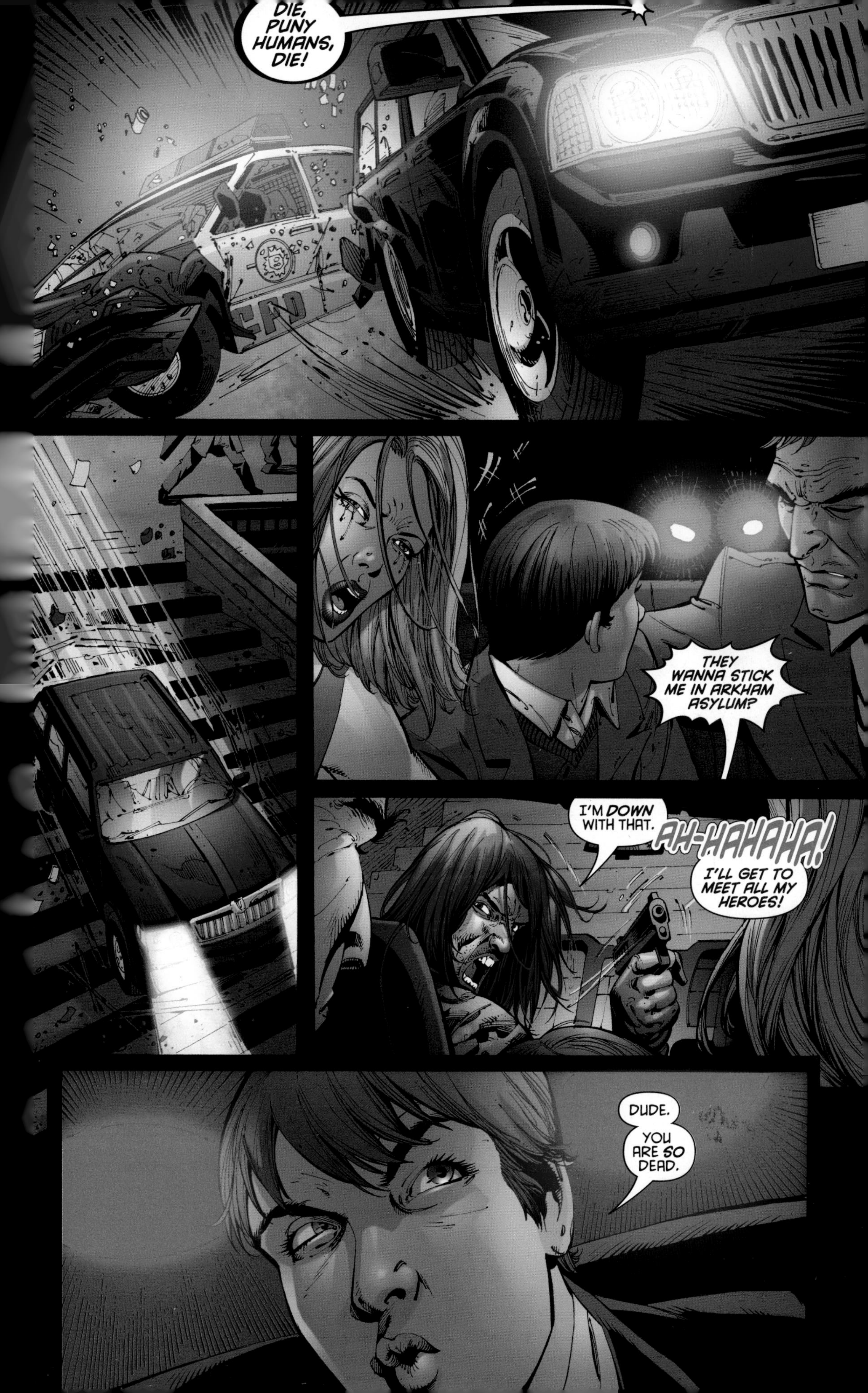
DIE, PUNY HUMANS, DIE!
THEY WANNA STICK ME IN ARKHAM ASYLUM?
I'M DOWN WITH THAT.
AH-HAHAHA!
I'LL GET TO MEET ALL MY HEROES!
DUDE.
YOU ARE SO DEAD.

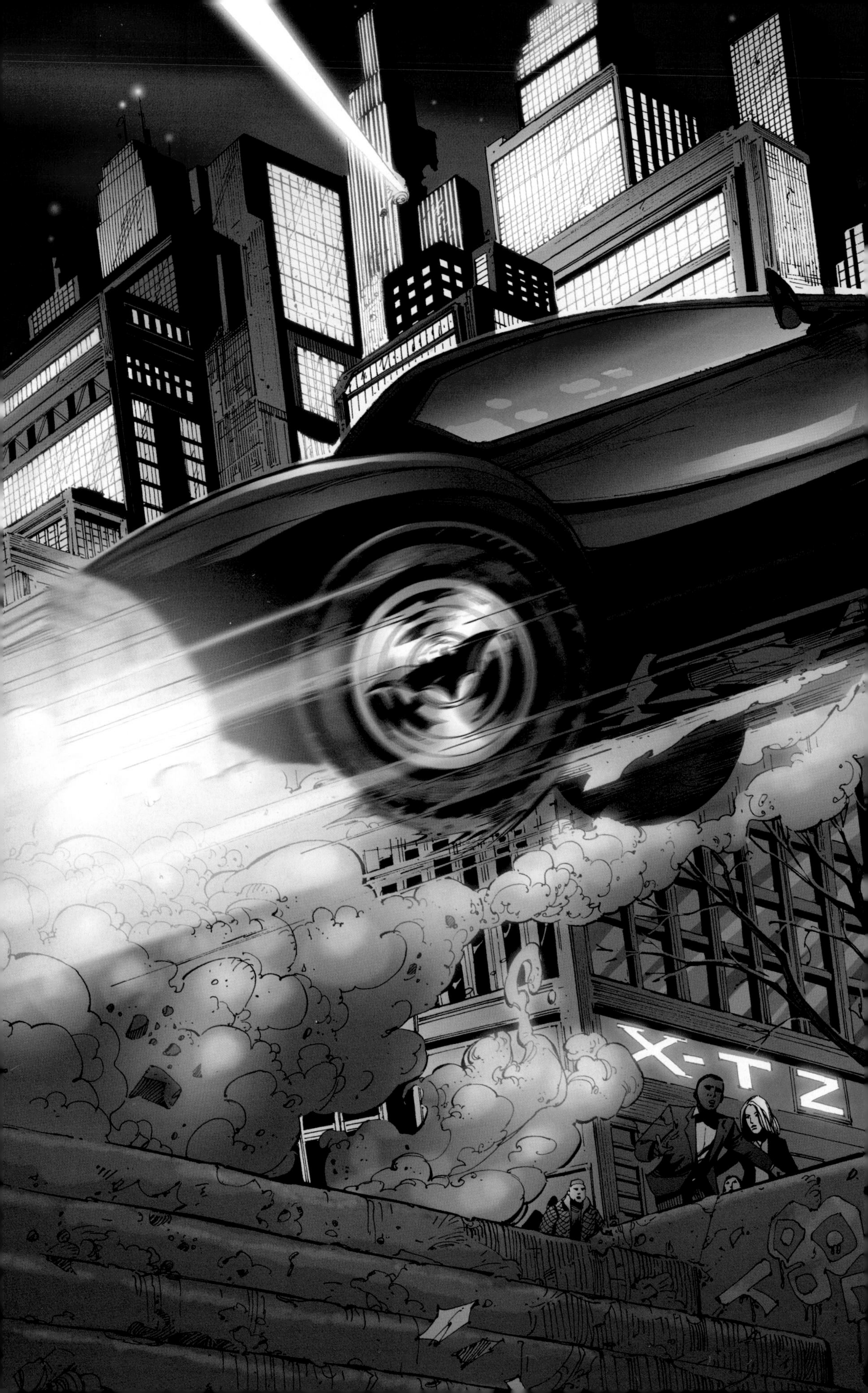
X-TZ

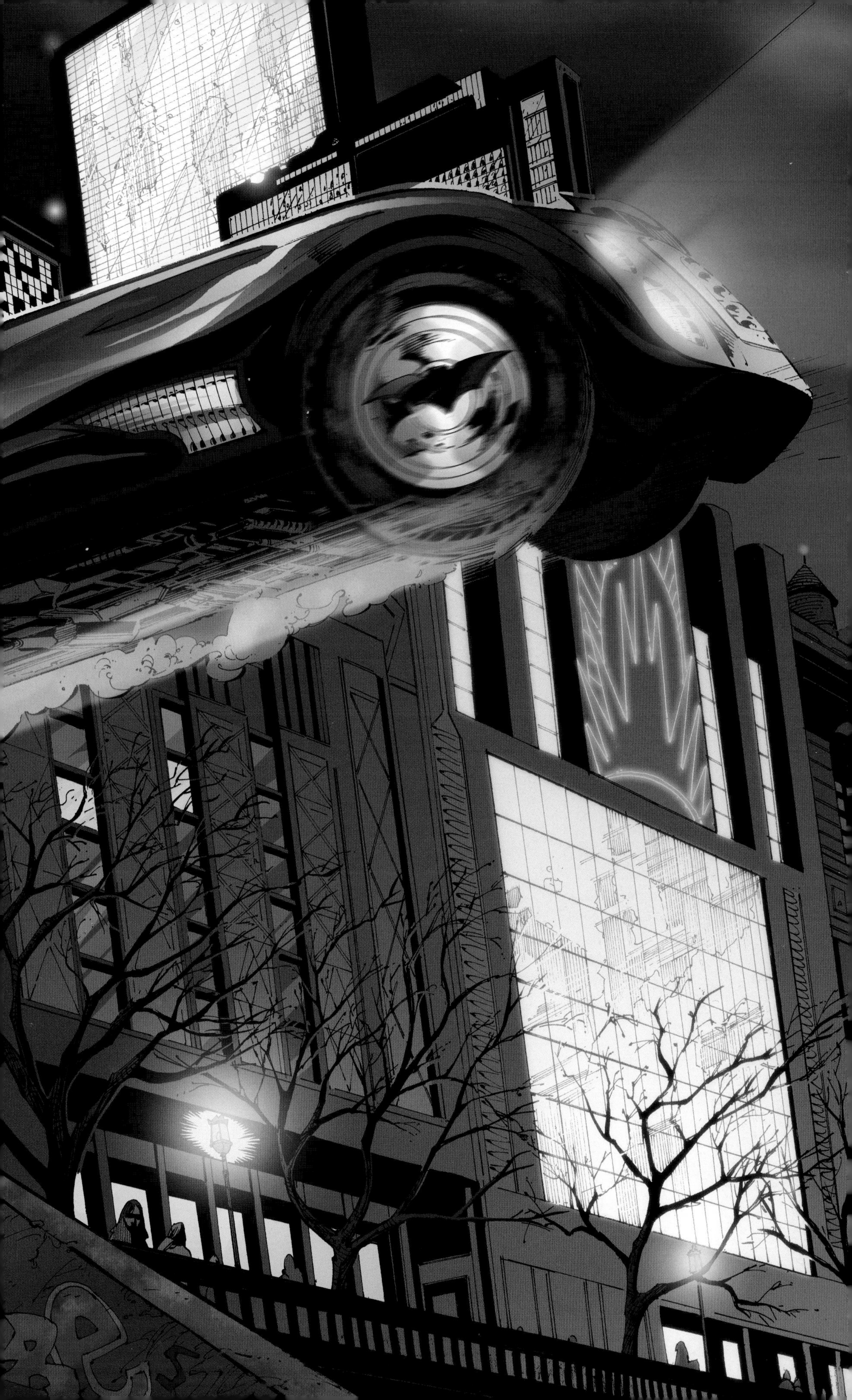

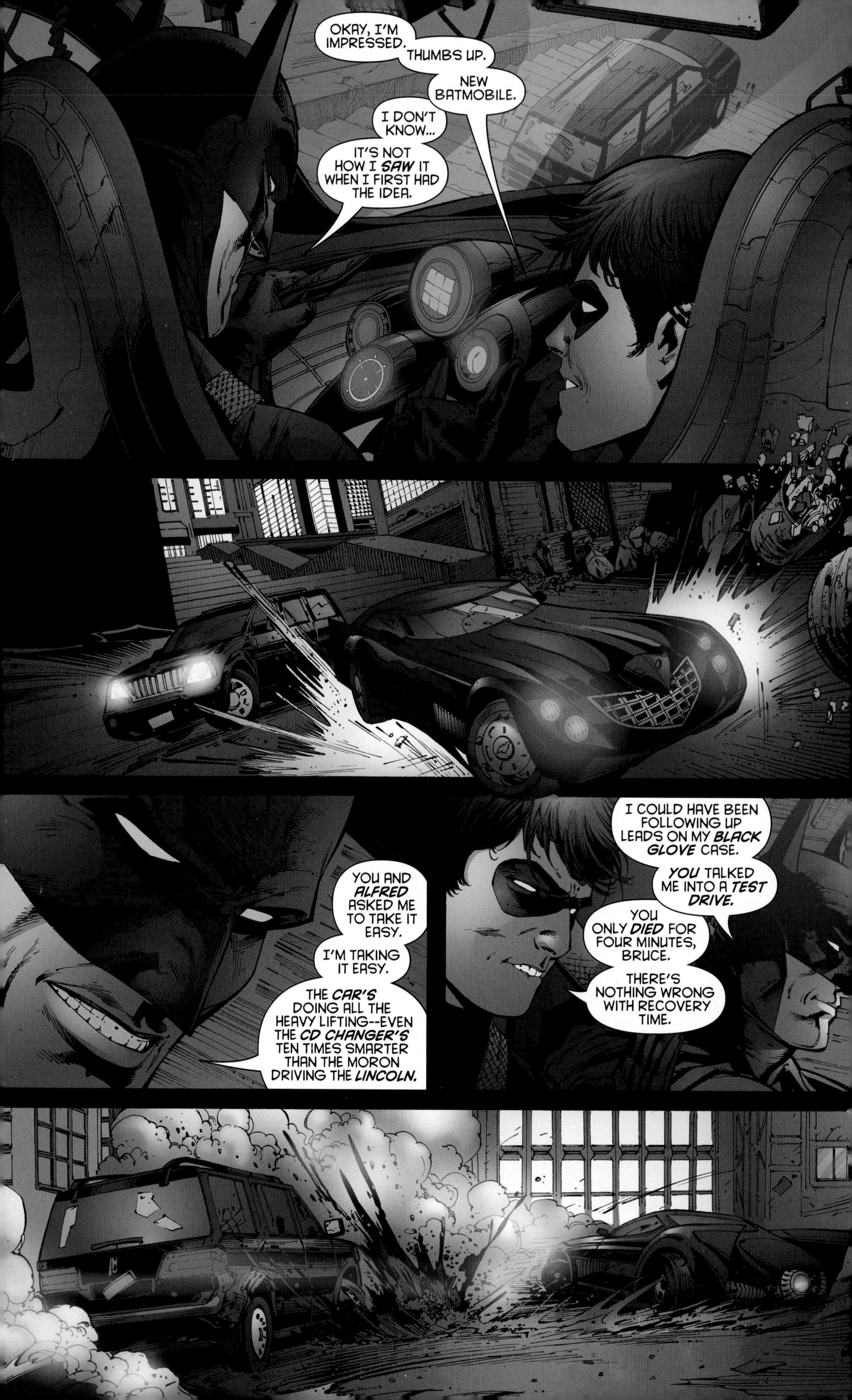

OKAY, I'M IMPRESSED.
THUMBS UP.
NEW BATMOBILE.
I DON'T KNOW...
IT'S NOT HOW I SAW IT WHEN I FIRST HAD THE IDEA.
YOU AND ALFRED ASKED ME TO TAKE IT EASY.
I'M TAKING IT EASY.
THE CAR'S DOING ALL THE HEAVY LIFTING--EVEN THE CD CHANGER'S TEN TIMES SMARTER THAN THE MORON DRIVING THE LINCOLN.
I COULD HAVE BEEN FOLLOWING UP LEADS ON MY BLACK GLOVE CASE.
YOU TALKED ME INTO A TEST DRIVE.
YOU ONLY DIED FOR FOUR MINUTES, BRUCE.
THERE'S NOTHING WRONG WITH RECOVERY TIME.

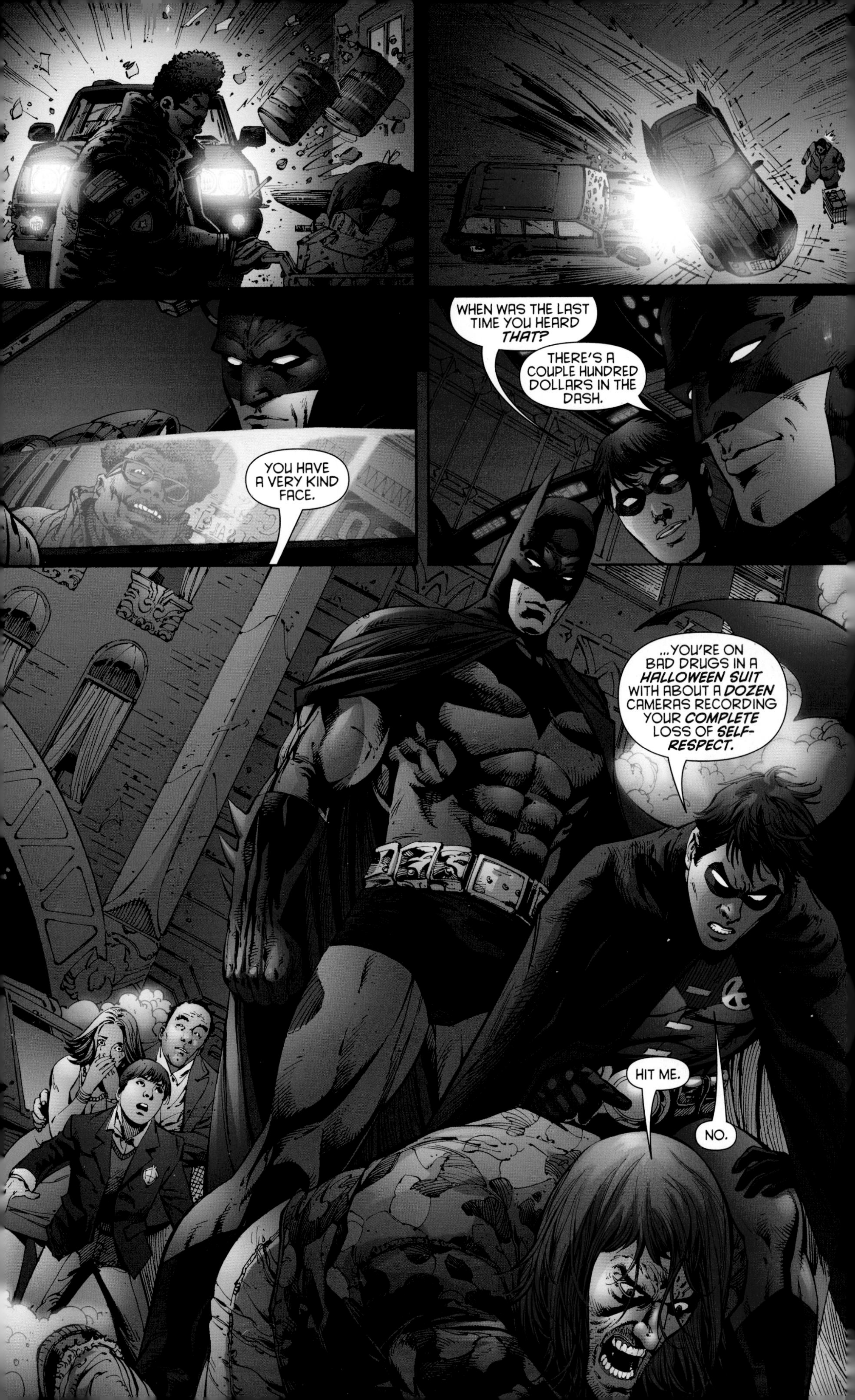
YOU HAVE A VERY KIND FACE.
WHEN WAS THE LAST TIME YOU HEARD *THAT?*
THERE'S A COUPLE HUNDRED DOLLARS IN THE DASH.
...YOU'RE ON BAD DRUGS IN A ***HALLOWEEN SUIT*** WITH ABOUT A ***DOZEN*** CAMERAS RECORDING YOUR ***COMPLETE*** LOSS OF ***SELF-RESPECT.***
HIT ME.
NO.

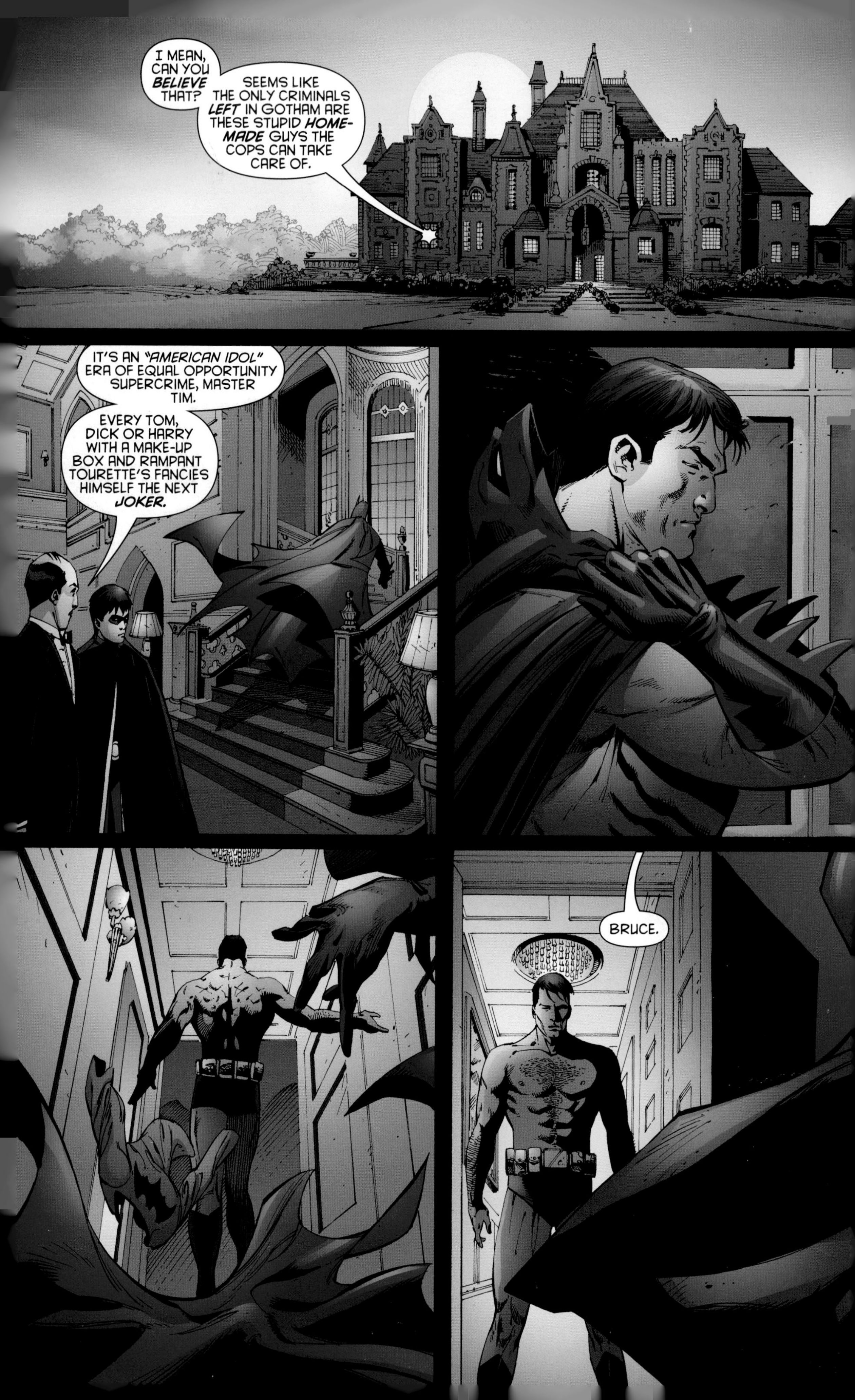
I MEAN, CAN YOU BELIEVE THAT?
SEEMS LIKE THE ONLY CRIMINALS LEFT IN GOTHAM ARE THESE STUPID HOME-MADE GUYS THE COPS CAN TAKE CARE OF.
IT'S AN "AMERICAN IDOL" ERA OF EQUAL OPPORTUNITY SUPERCRIME, MASTER TIM.
EVERY TOM, DICK OR HARRY WITH A MAKE-UP BOX AND RAMPANT TOURETTE'S FANCIES HIMSELF THE NEXT JOKER.
BRUCE.

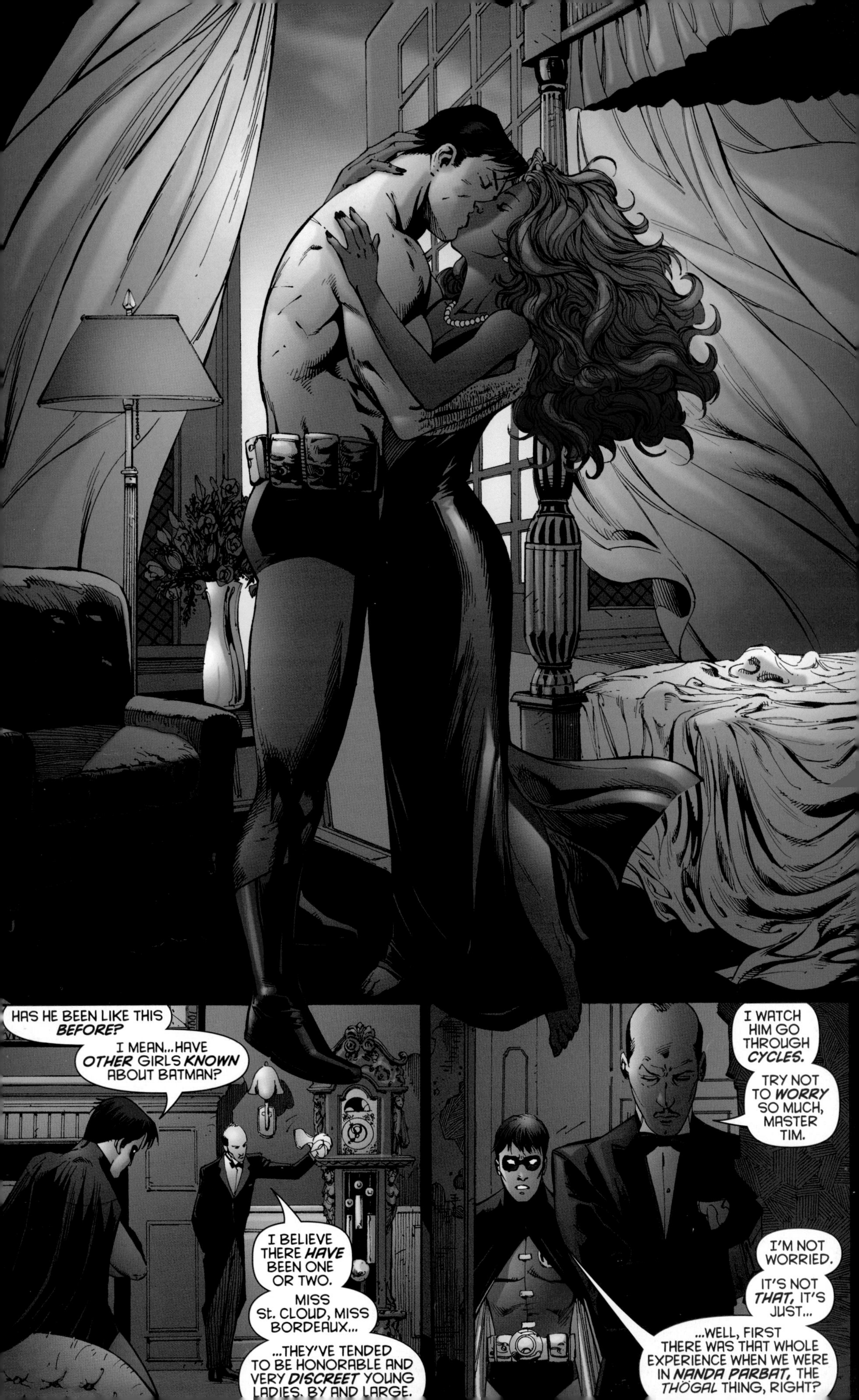

HAS HE BEEN LIKE THIS BEFORE?
I MEAN...HAVE OTHER GIRLS KNOWN ABOUT BATMAN?
I BELIEVE THERE HAVE BEEN ONE OR TWO.
MISS St. CLOUD, MISS BORDEAUX...
...THEY'VE TENDED TO BE HONORABLE AND VERY DISCREET YOUNG LADIES. BY AND LARGE.
I WATCH HIM GO THROUGH CYCLES.
TRY NOT TO WORRY SO MUCH, MASTER TIM.
I'M NOT WORRIED.
IT'S NOT THAT, IT'S JUST...
...WELL, FIRST THERE WAS THAT WHOLE EXPERIENCE WHEN WE WERE IN NANDA PARBAT, THE THÖGAL THING, RIGHT?

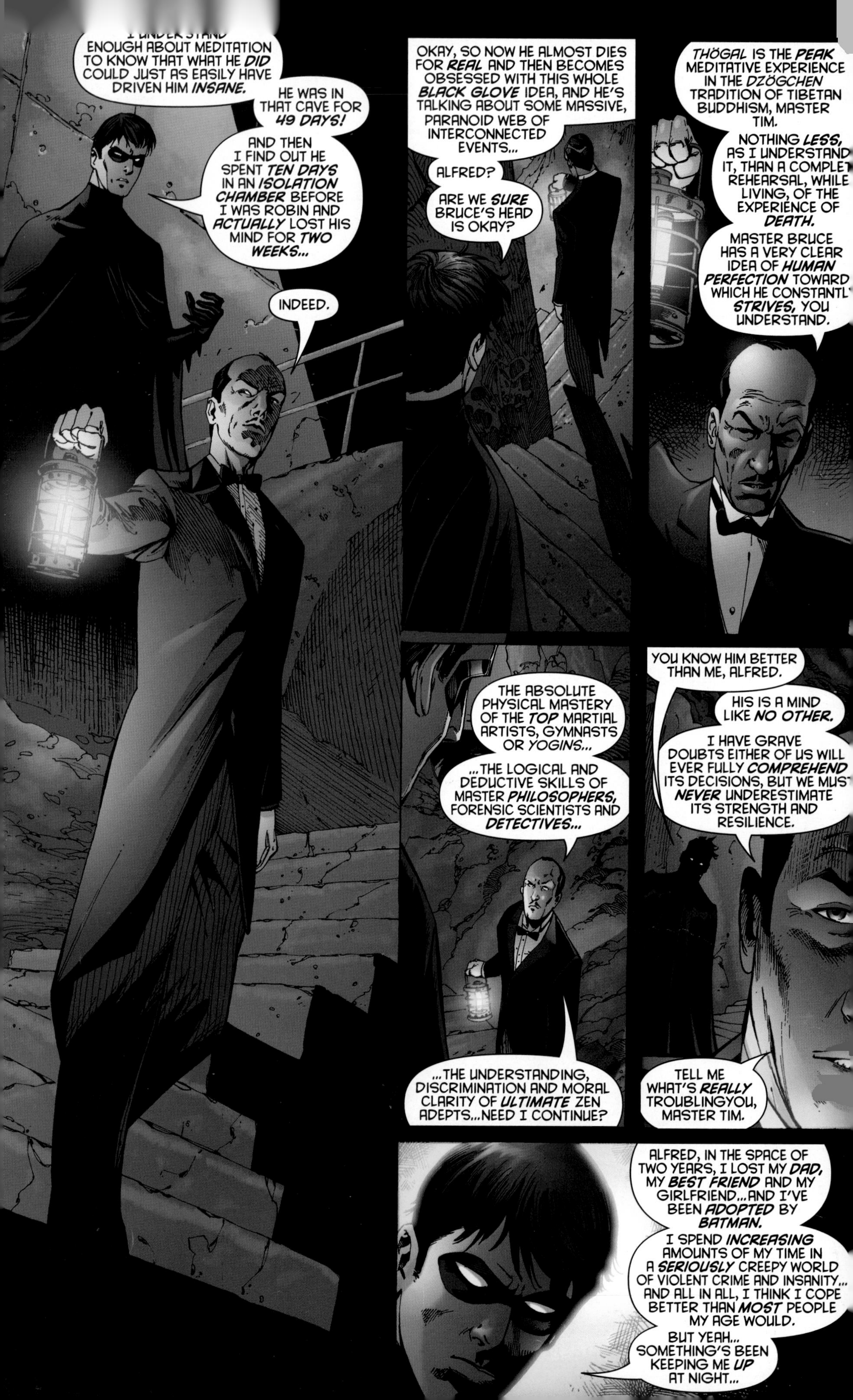
ENOUGH ABOUT MEDITATION TO KNOW THAT WHAT HE DID COULD JUST AS EASILY HAVE DRIVEN HIM INSANE.
HE WAS IN THAT CAVE FOR 49 DAYS!
AND THEN I FIND OUT HE SPENT TEN DAYS IN AN ISOLATION CHAMBER BEFORE I WAS ROBIN AND ACTUALLY LOST HIS MIND FOR TWO WEEKS...
INDEED.
OKAY, SO NOW HE ALMOST DIES FOR REAL AND THEN BECOMES OBSESSED WITH THIS WHOLE BLACK GLOVE IDEA, AND HE'S TALKING ABOUT SOME MASSIVE, PARANOID WEB OF INTERCONNECTED EVENTS...
ALFRED?
ARE WE SURE BRUCE'S HEAD IS OKAY?
THÖGAL IS THE PEAK MEDITATIVE EXPERIENCE IN THE DZÖGCHEN TRADITION OF TIBETAN BUDDHISM, MASTER TIM.
NOTHING LESS, AS I UNDERSTAND IT, THAN A COMPLETE REHEARSAL, WHILE LIVING, OF THE EXPERIENCE OF DEATH.
MASTER BRUCE HAS A VERY CLEAR IDEA OF HUMAN PERFECTION TOWARD WHICH HE CONSTANTLY STRIVES, YOU UNDERSTAND.
THE ABSOLUTE PHYSICAL MASTERY OF THE TOP MARTIAL ARTISTS, GYMNASTS OR YOGINS...
...THE LOGICAL AND DEDUCTIVE SKILLS OF MASTER PHILOSOPHERS, FORENSIC SCIENTISTS AND DETECTIVES...
...THE UNDERSTANDING, DISCRIMINATION AND MORAL CLARITY OF ULTIMATE ZEN ADEPTS...NEED I CONTINUE?
YOU KNOW HIM BETTER THAN ME, ALFRED.
HIS IS A MIND LIKE NO OTHER.
I HAVE GRAVE DOUBTS EITHER OF US WILL EVER FULLY COMPREHEND ITS DECISIONS, BUT WE MUST NEVER UNDERESTIMATE ITS STRENGTH AND RESILIENCE.
TELL ME WHAT'S REALLY TROUBLINGYOU, MASTER TIM.
ALFRED, IN THE SPACE OF TWO YEARS, I LOST MY DAD, MY BEST FRIEND AND MY GIRLFRIEND...AND I'VE BEEN ADOPTED BY BATMAN.
I SPEND INCREASING AMOUNTS OF MY TIME IN A SERIOUSLY CREEPY WORLD OF VIOLENT CRIME AND INSANITY... AND ALL IN ALL, I THINK I COPE BETTER THAN MOST PEOPLE MY AGE WOULD.
BUT YEAH... SOMETHING'S BEEN KEEPING ME UP AT NIGHT...

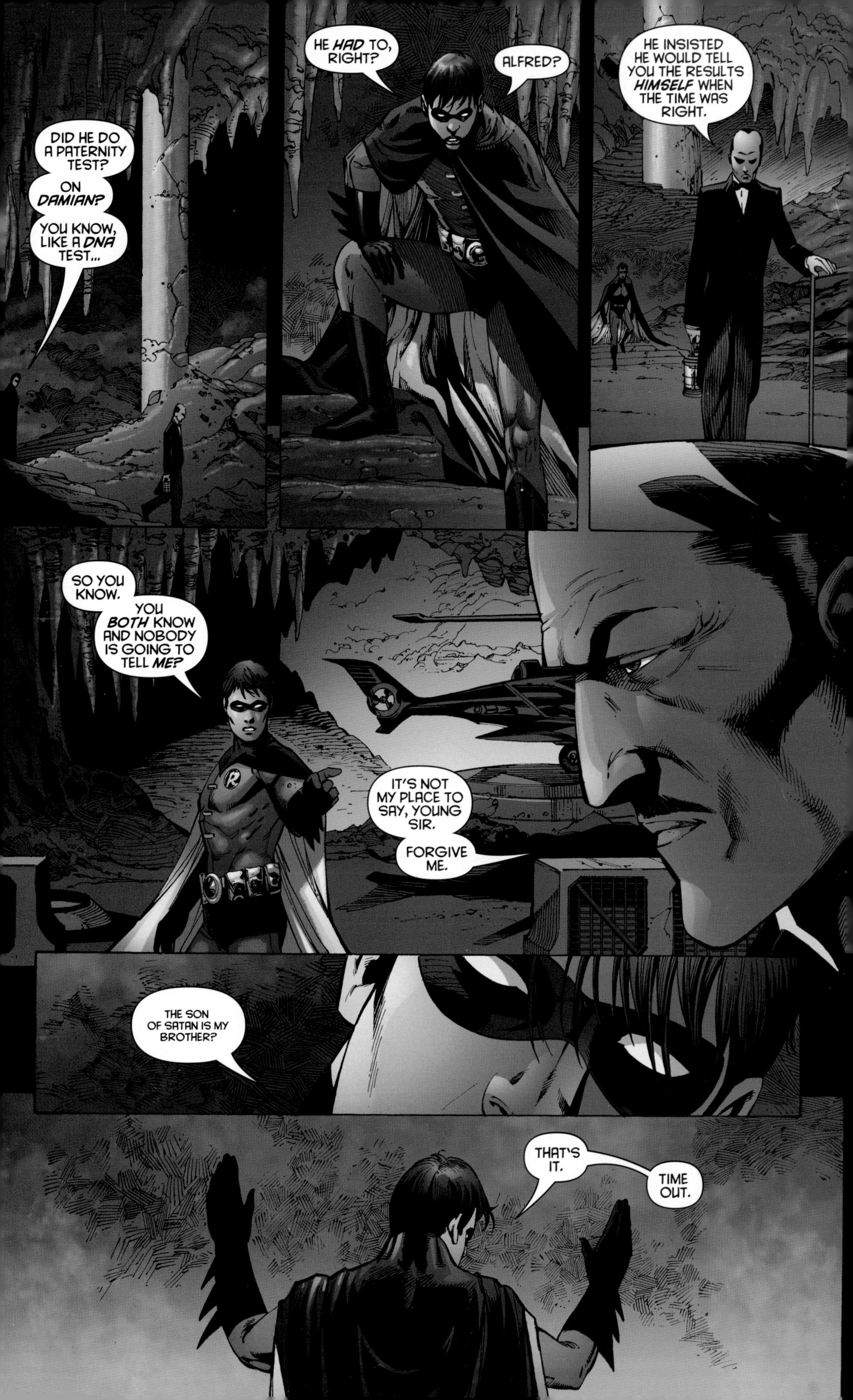
DID HE DO A PATERNITY TEST?
ON DAMIAN?
YOU KNOW, LIKE A DNA TEST...
HE HAD TO, RIGHT?
ALFRED?
HE INSISTED HE WOULD TELL YOU THE RESULTS HIMSELF WHEN THE TIME WAS RIGHT.
SO YOU KNOW.
YOU BOTH KNOW AND NOBODY IS GOING TO TELL ME?
IT'S NOT MY PLACE TO SAY, YOUNG SIR.
FORGIVE ME.
THE SON OF SATAN IS MY BROTHER?
THAT'S IT.
TIME OUT.

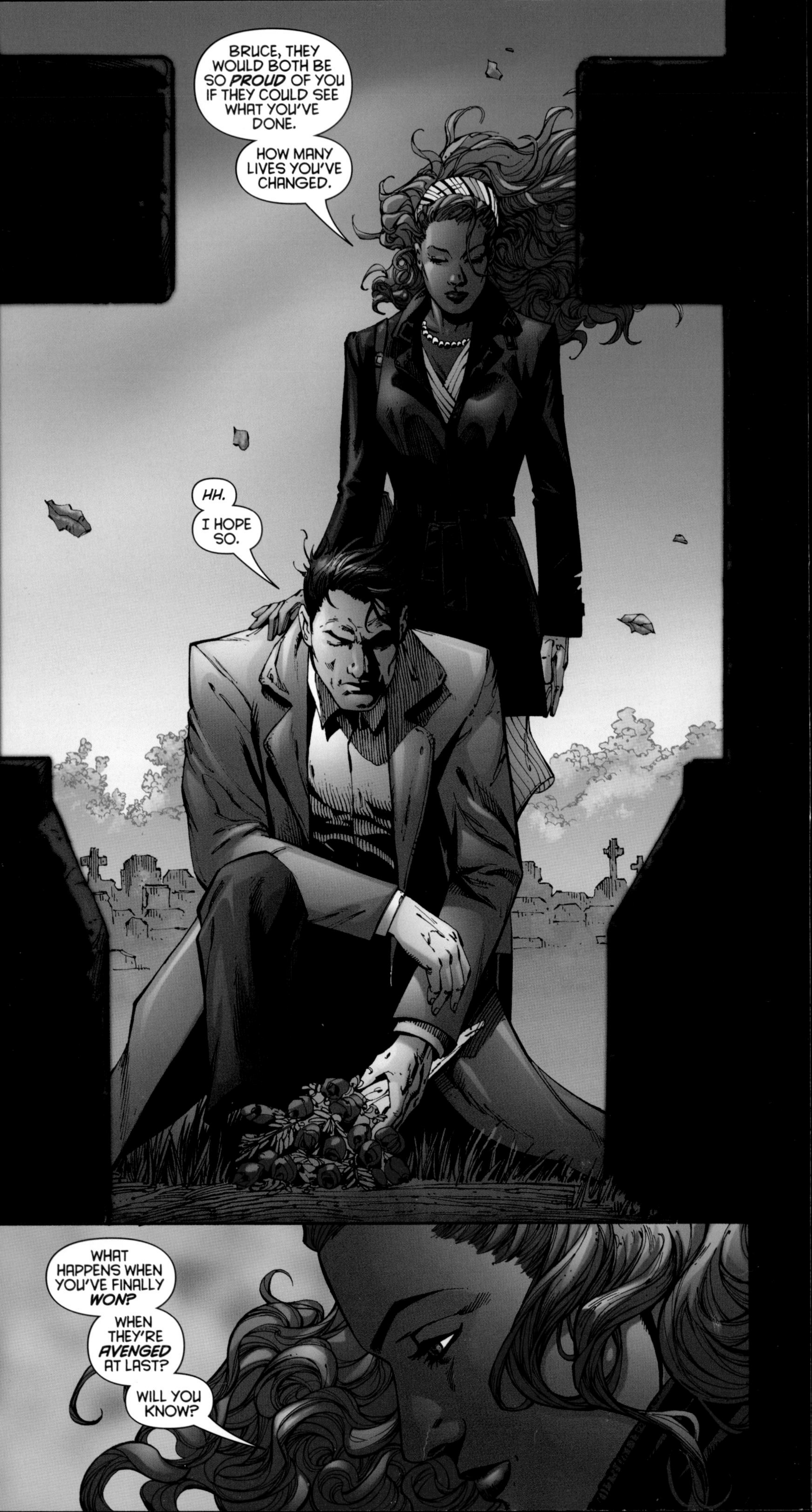

BRUCE, THEY WOULD BOTH BE SO PROUD OF YOU IF THEY COULD SEE WHAT YOU'VE DONE.
HOW MANY LIVES YOU'VE CHANGED.
HH.
I HOPE SO.
WHAT HAPPENS WHEN YOU'VE FINALLY WON?
WHEN THEY'RE AVENGED AT LAST?
WILL YOU KNOW?

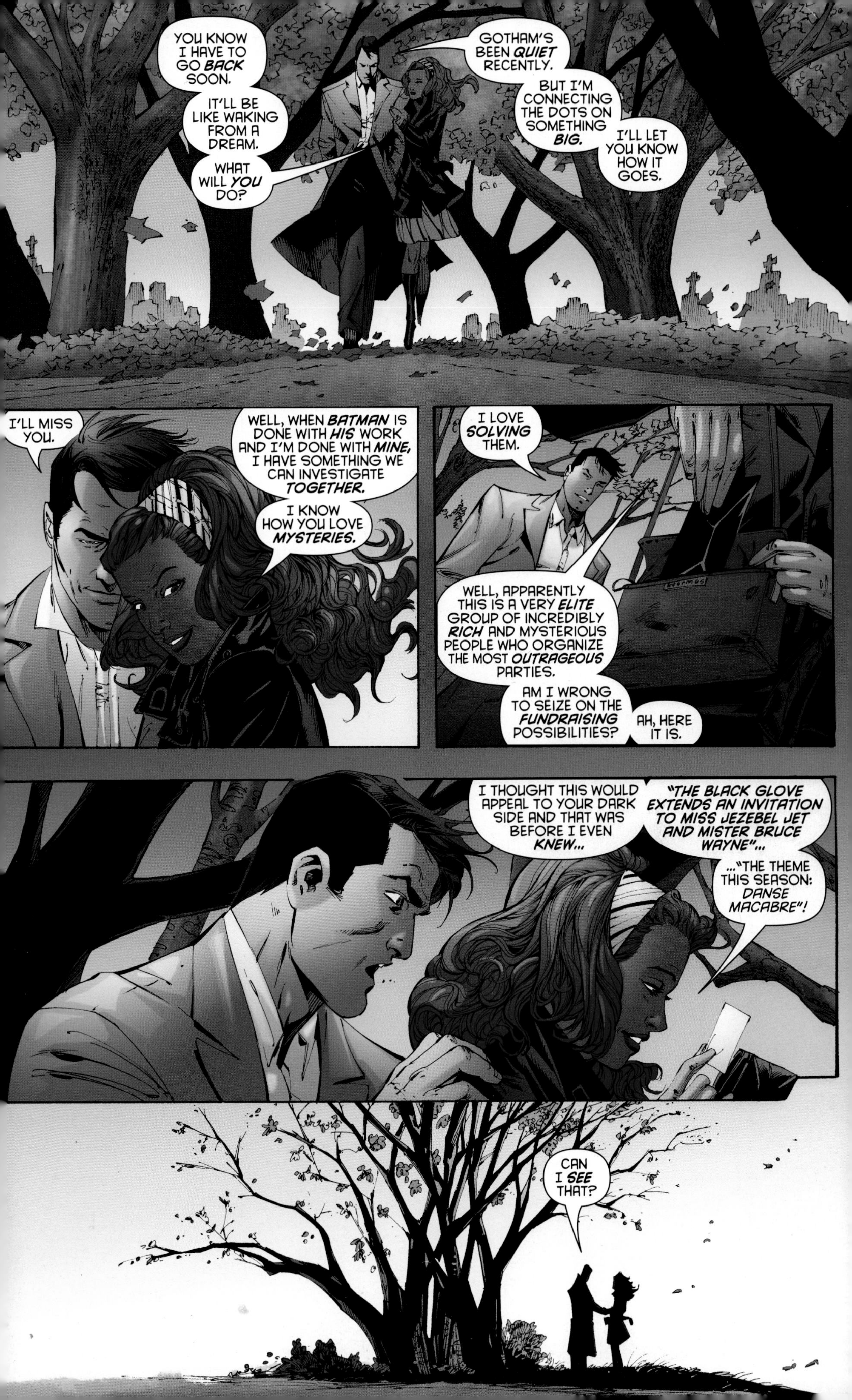
YOU KNOW I HAVE TO GO BACK SOON.
IT'LL BE LIKE WAKING FROM A DREAM.
WHAT WILL YOU DO?
GOTHAM'S BEEN QUIET RECENTLY.
BUT I'M CONNECTING THE DOTS ON SOMETHING BIG.
I'LL LET YOU KNOW HOW IT GOES.
I'LL MISS YOU.
WELL, WHEN BATMAN IS DONE WITH HIS WORK AND I'M DONE WITH MINE, I HAVE SOMETHING WE CAN INVESTIGATE TOGETHER.
I KNOW HOW YOU LOVE MYSTERIES.
I LOVE SOLVING THEM.
WELL, APPARENTLY THIS IS A VERY ELITE GROUP OF INCREDIBLY RICH AND MYSTERIOUS PEOPLE WHO ORGANIZE THE MOST OUTRAGEOUS PARTIES.
AM I WRONG TO SEIZE ON THE FUNDRAISING POSSIBILITIES?
AH, HERE IT IS.
I THOUGHT THIS WOULD APPEAL TO YOUR DARK SIDE AND THAT WAS BEFORE I EVEN KNEW...
"THE BLACK GLOVE EXTENDS AN INVITATION TO MISS JEZEBEL JET AND MISTER BRUCE WAYNE"...
..."THE THEME THIS SEASON: DANSE MACABRE"!
CAN I SEE THAT?

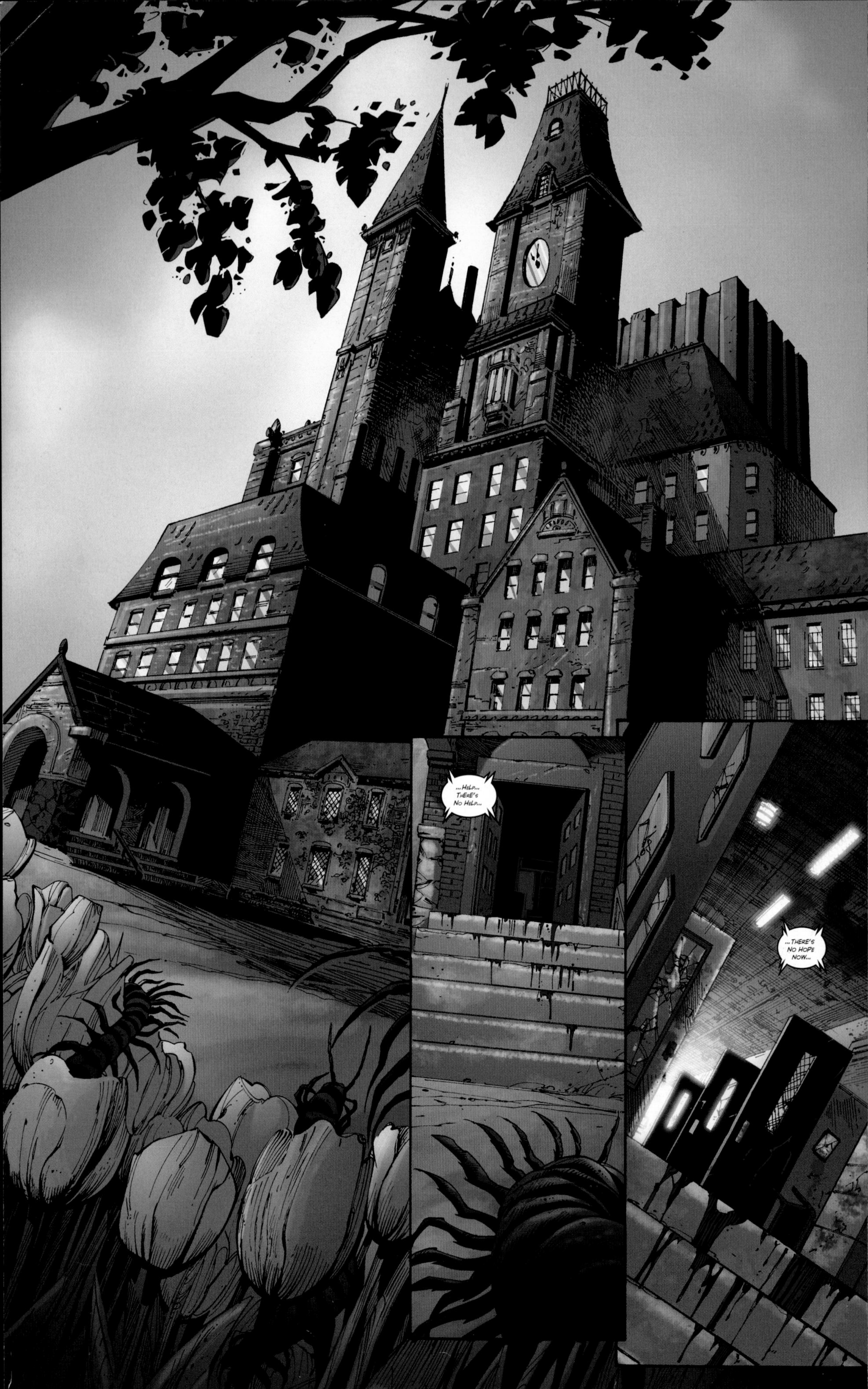
...HELP... THERE'S NO HELP...
...THERE'S NO HOPE NOW...

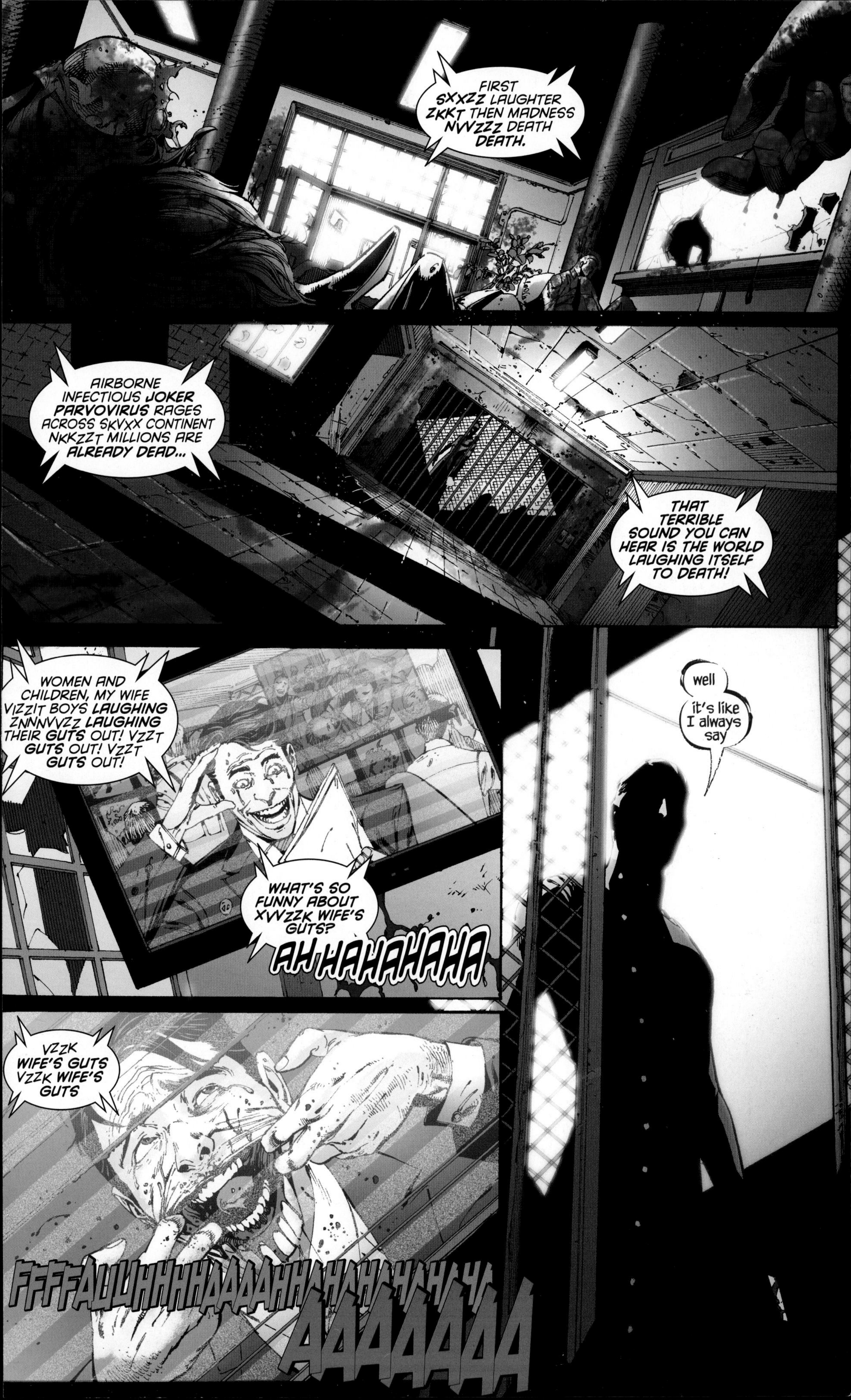
FIRST SXXZZ LAUGHTER ZKKT THEN MADNESS NVVZZZ DEATH DEATH.
AIRBORNE INFECTIOUS JOKER PARVOVIRUS RAGES ACROSS SKVXX CONTINENT NKKZZT MILLIONS ARE ALREADY DEAD...
THAT TERRIBLE SOUND YOU CAN HEAR IS THE WORLD LAUGHING ITSELF TO DEATH!
WOMEN AND CHILDREN, MY WIFE VIZZIT BOYS LAUGHING ZNNNVVZZ LAUGHING THEIR GUTS OUT! VZZT GUTS OUT! VZZT GUTS OUT!
WHAT'S SO FUNNY ABOUT XVVZZK WIFE'S GUTS?
AH HAHAHAHAHA
well
it's like I always say
VZZK WIFE'S GUTS VZZK WIFE'S GUTS
FFFFAUUHHHHAAAAHHAHAHAHAHA
AAAAAAA

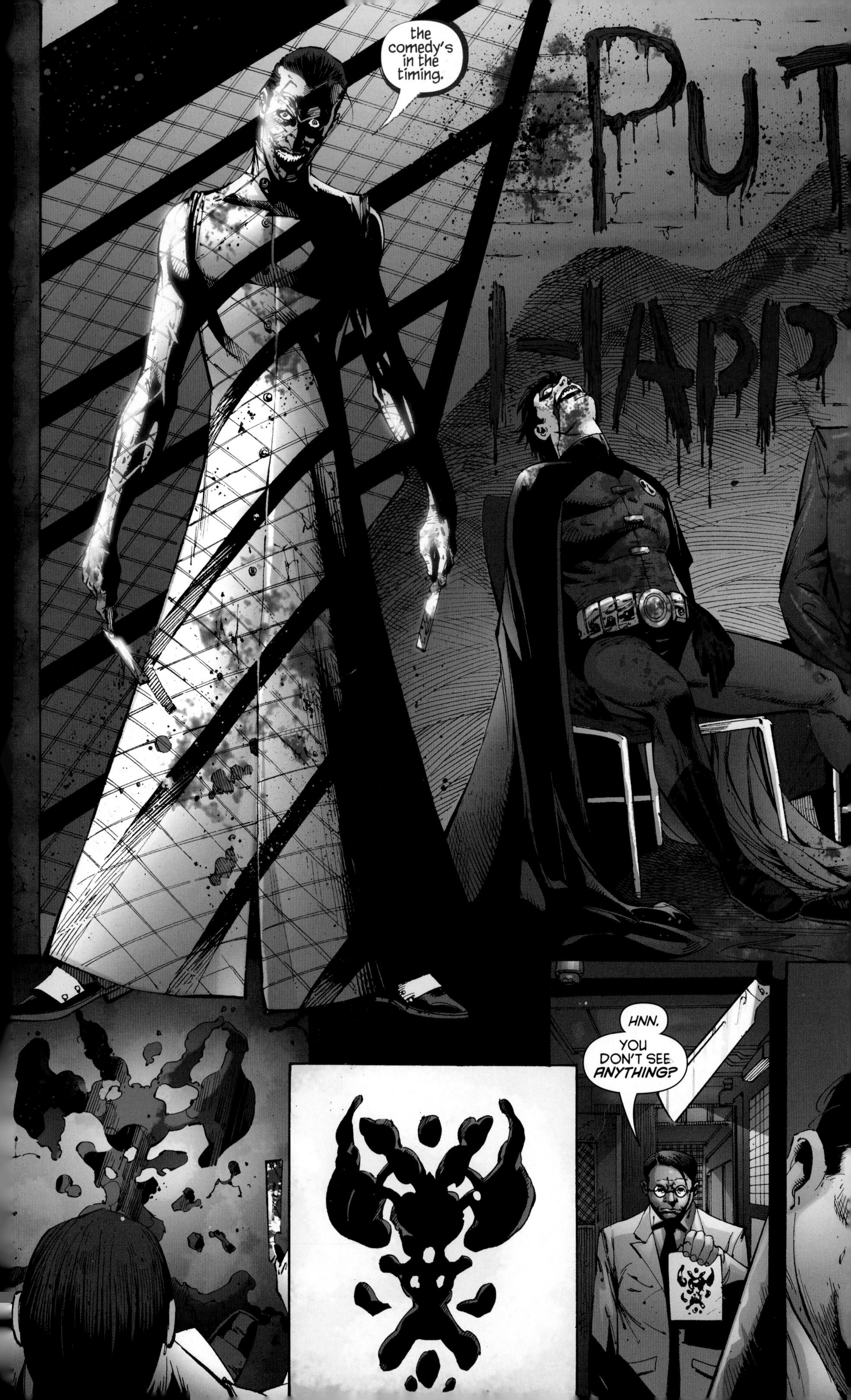
the comedy's in the timing.
HNN.
YOU DON'T SEE *ANYTHING?*

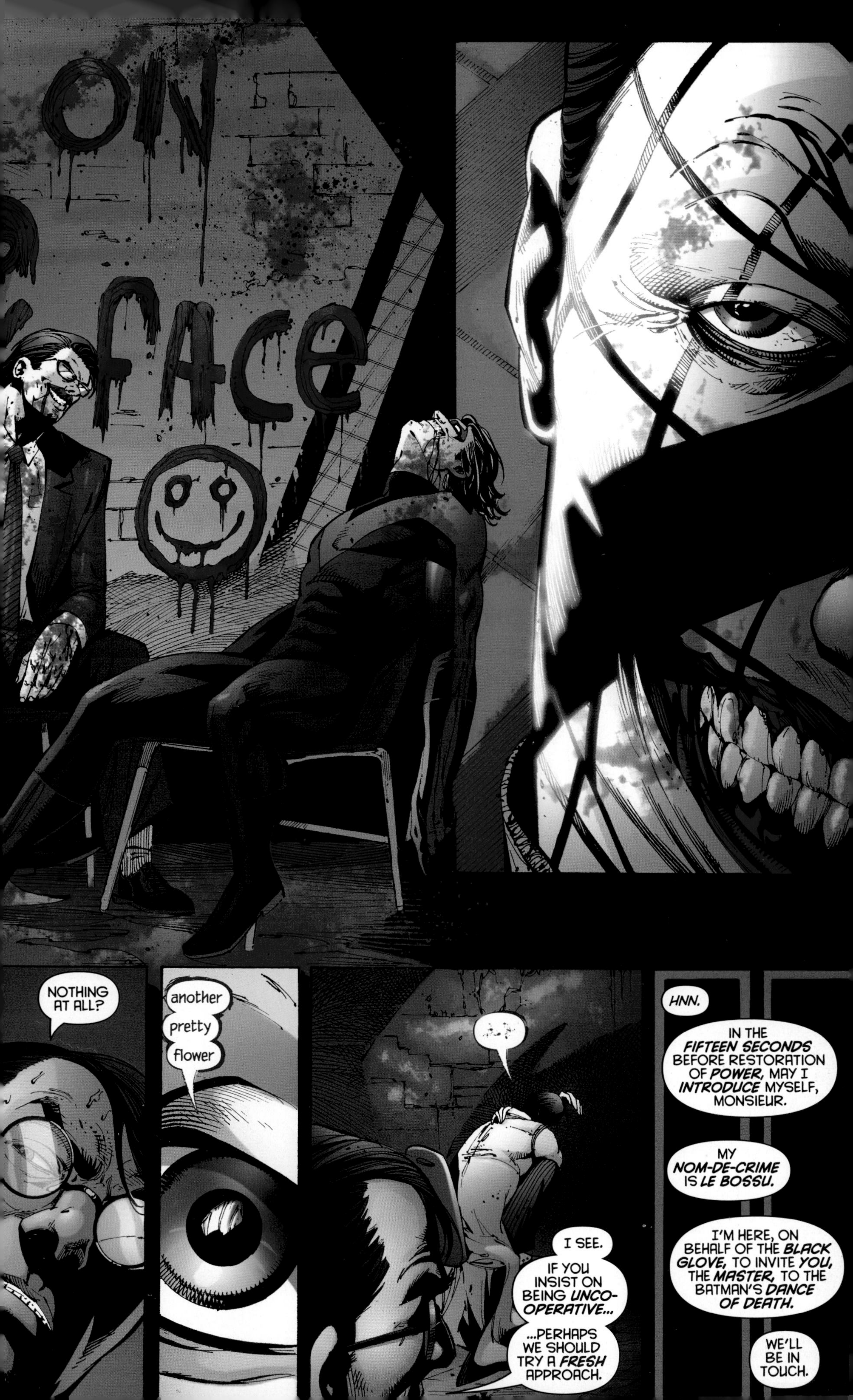

ON
FACE
NOTHING AT ALL?
another pretty flower
I SEE.
IF YOU INSIST ON BEING UNCO-OPERATIVE...
...PERHAPS WE SHOULD TRY A FRESH APPROACH.
HNN.
IN THE FIFTEEN SECONDS BEFORE RESTORATION OF POWER, MAY I INTRODUCE MYSELF, MONSIEUR.
MY NOM-DE-CRIME IS LE BOSSU.
I'M HERE, ON BEHALF OF THE BLACK GLOVE, TO INVITE YOU, THE MASTER, TO THE BATMAN'S DANCE OF DEATH.
WE'LL BE IN TOUCH.

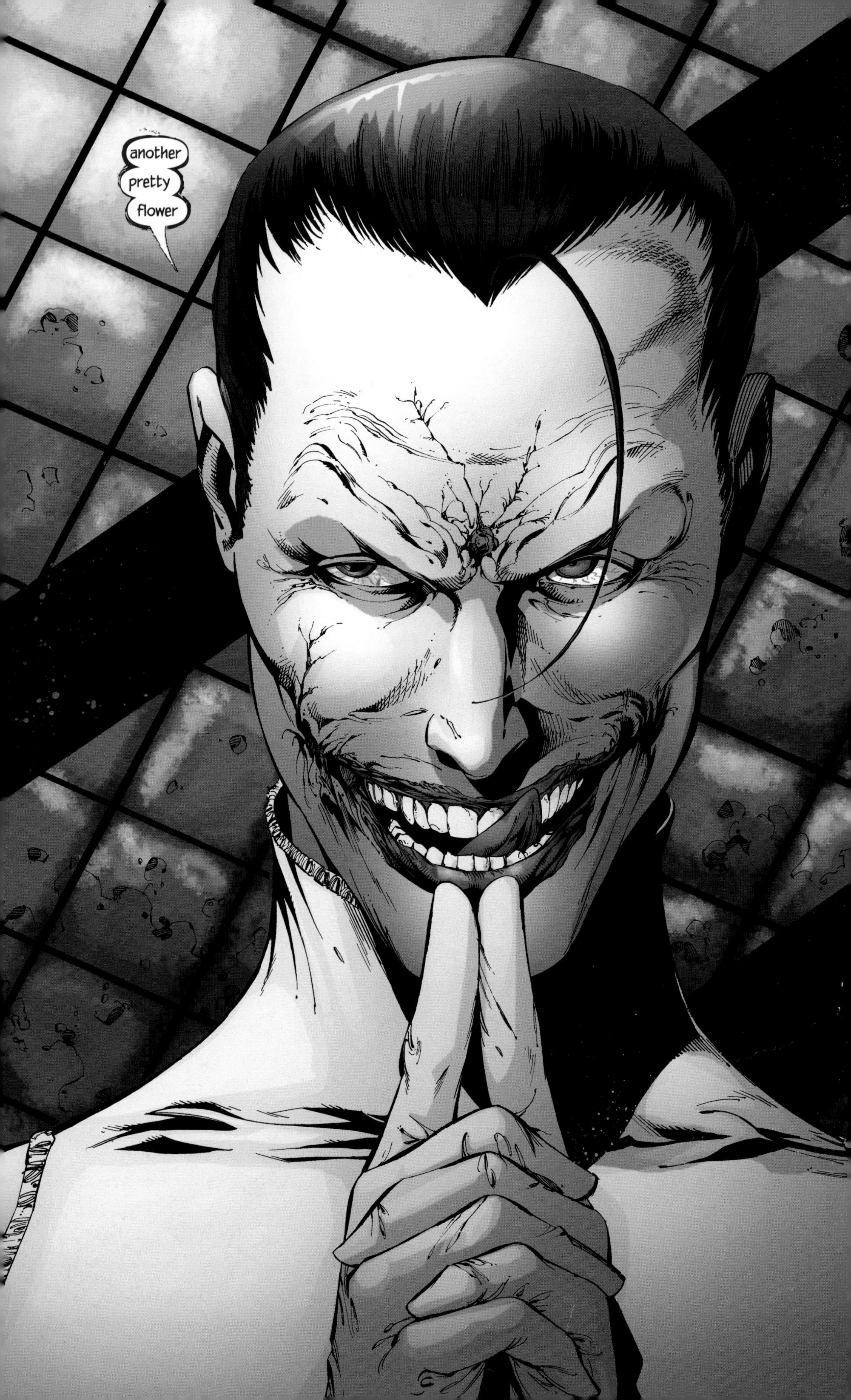
another pretty flower

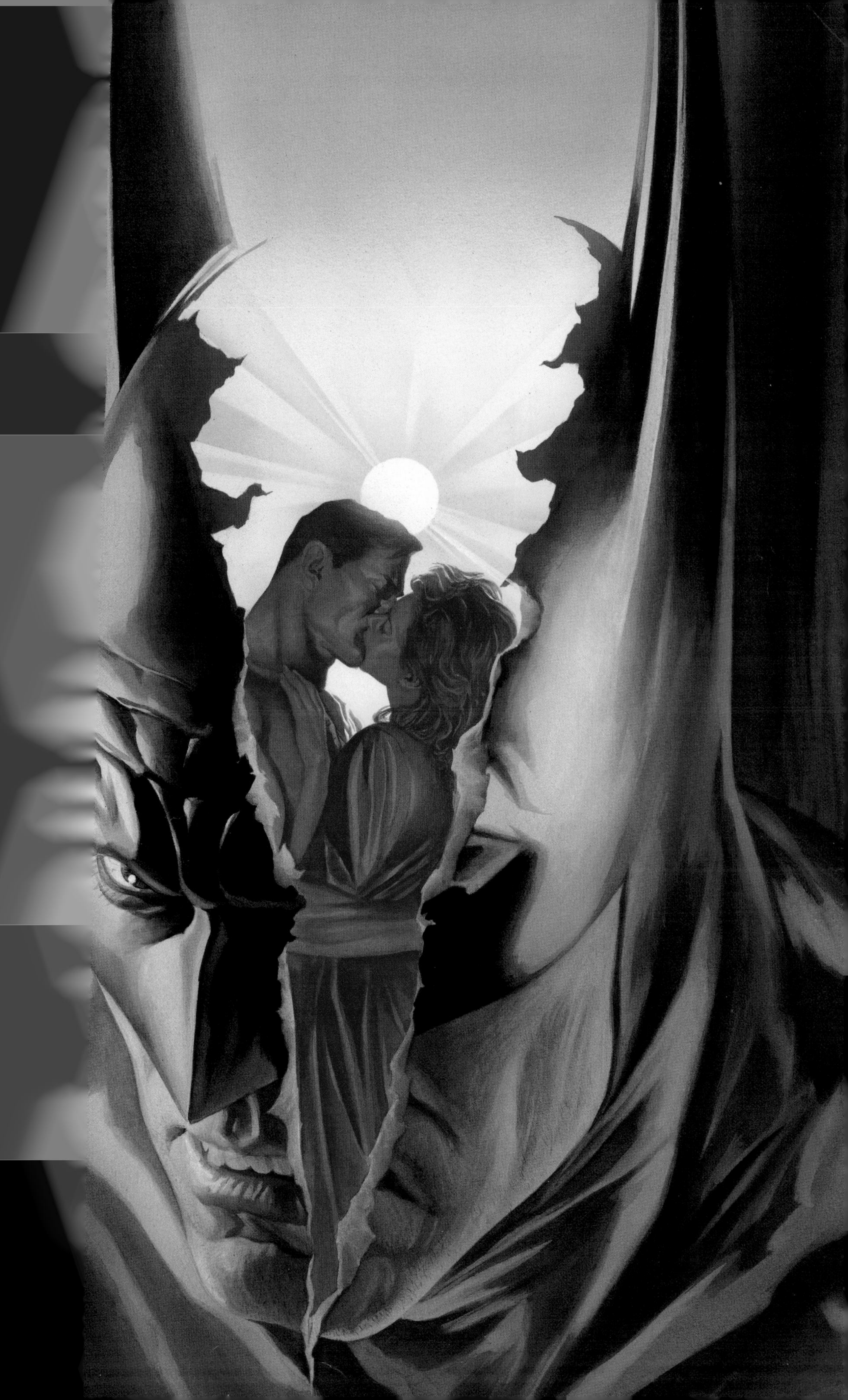

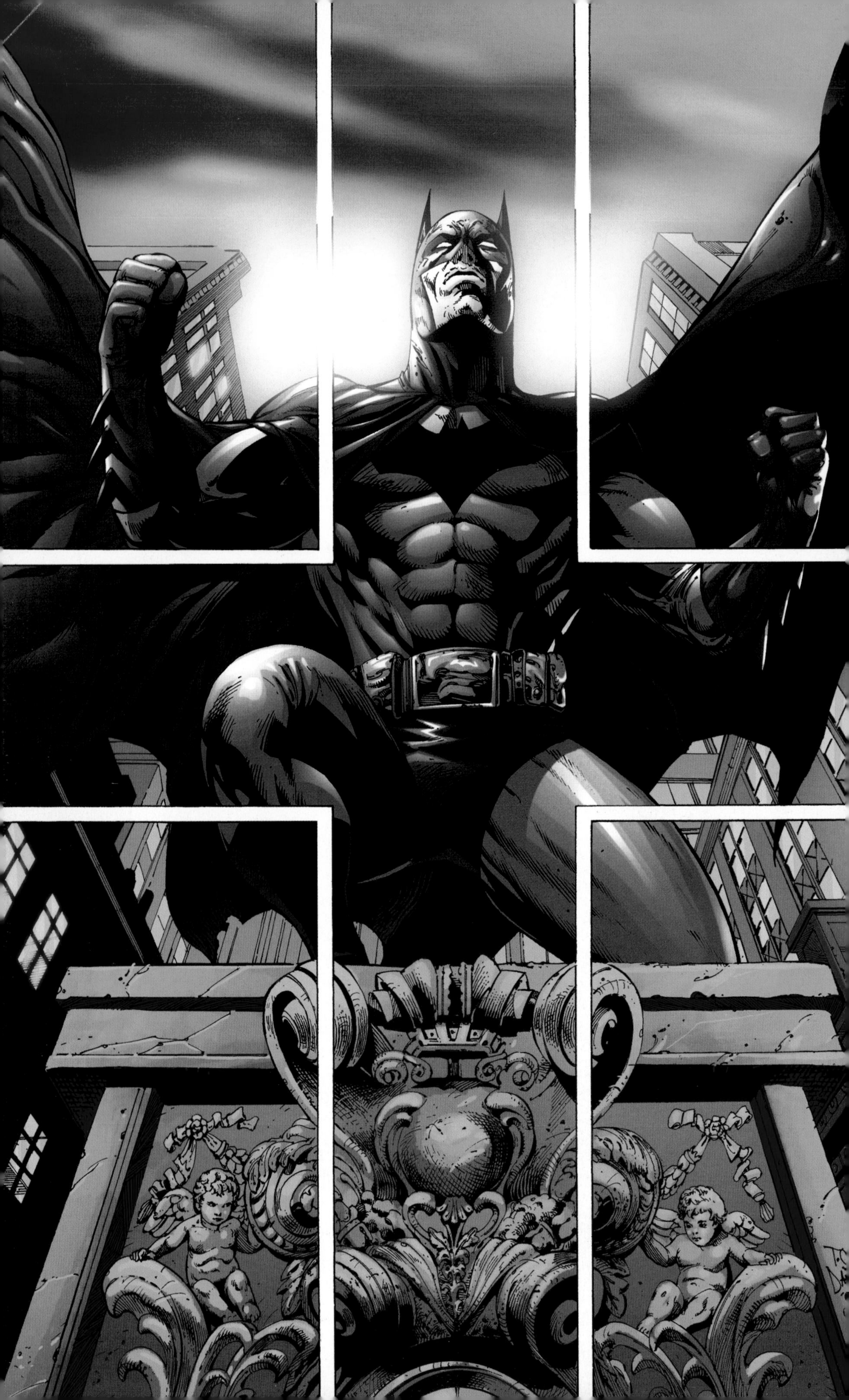

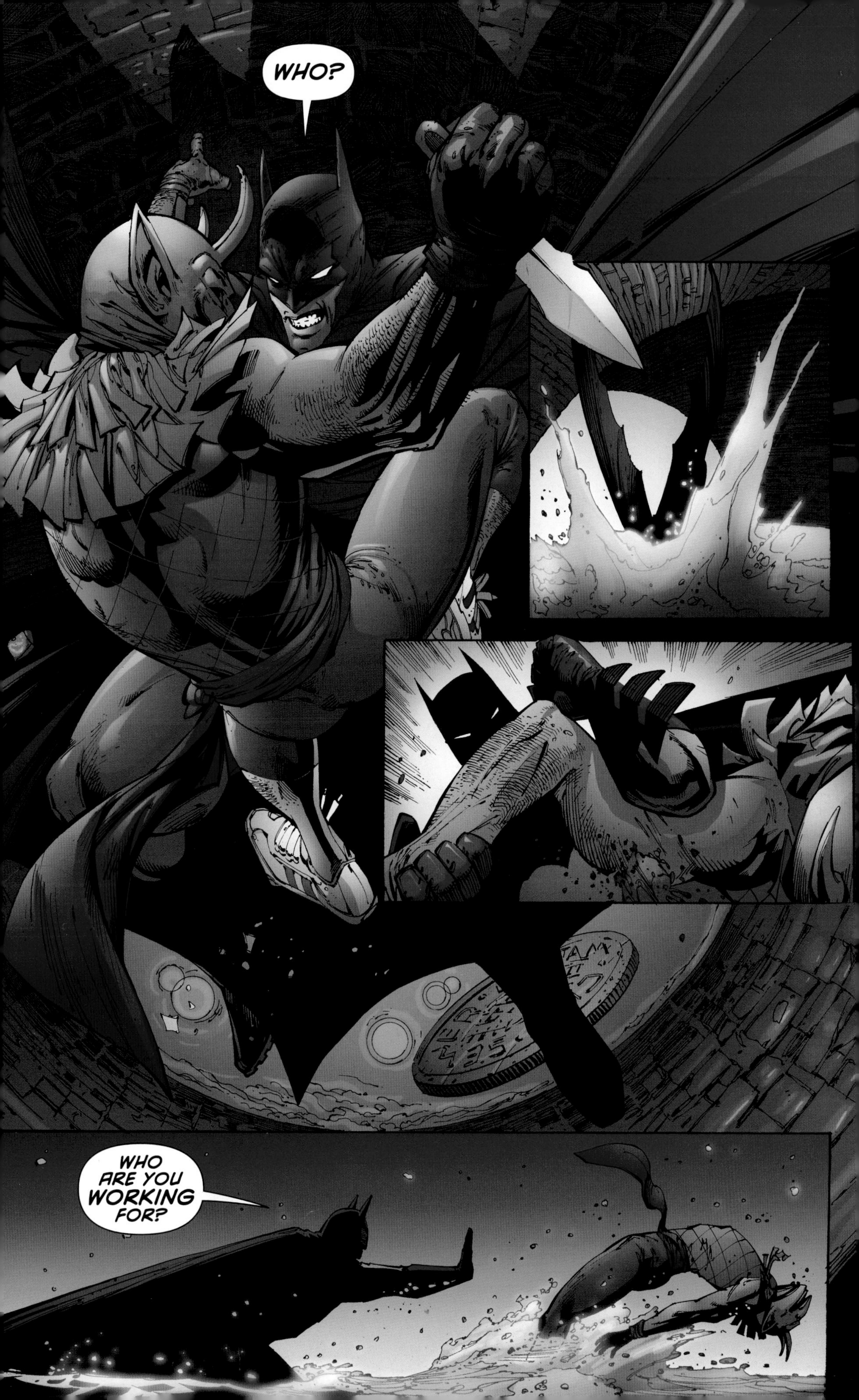
WHO?
WHO ARE YOU WORKING FOR?

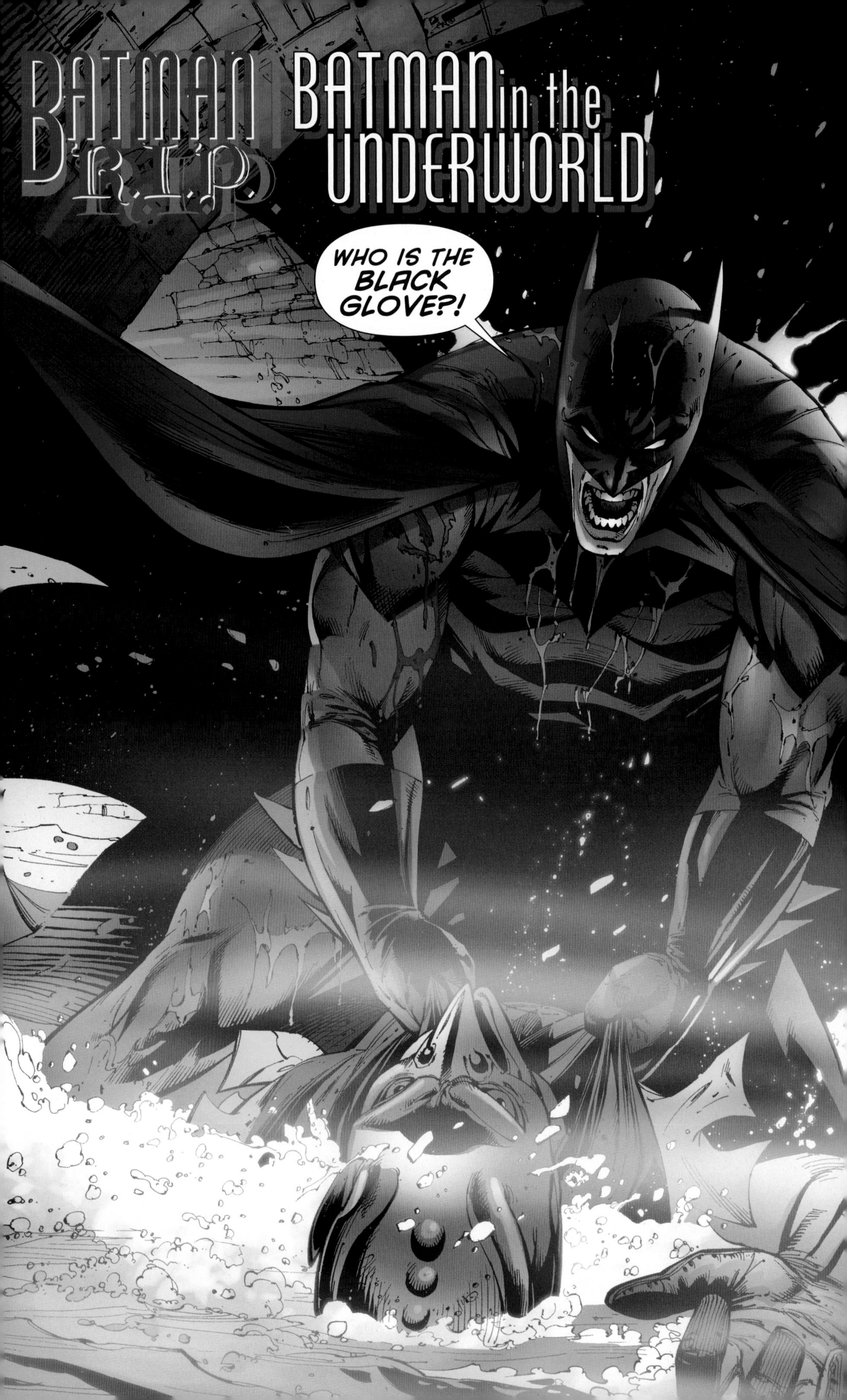
BATMAN R.I.P.
BATMAN in the UNDERWORLD
WHO IS THE BLACK GLOVE?!

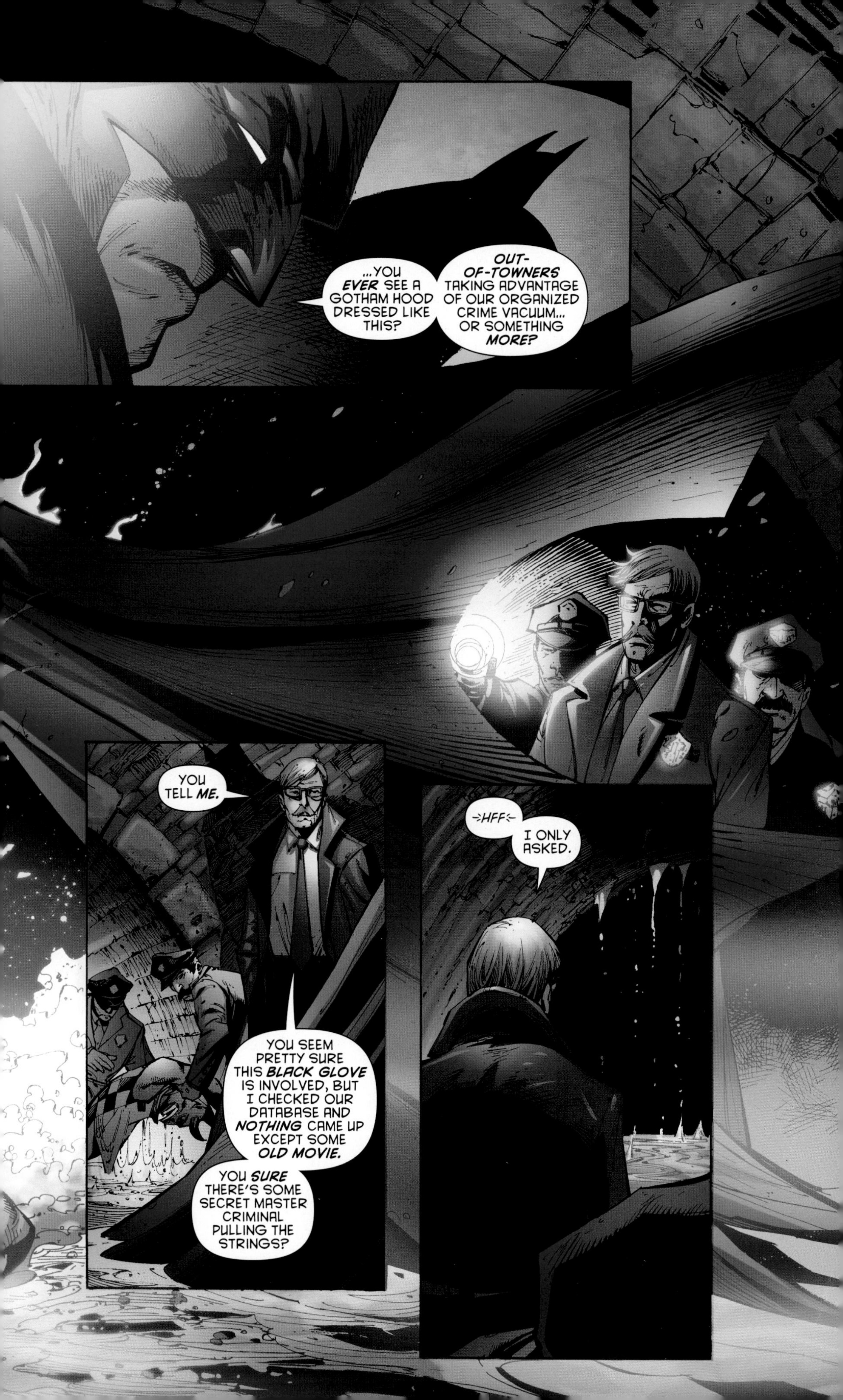
...YOU EVER SEE A GOTHAM HOOD DRESSED LIKE THIS?
OUT-OF-TOWNERS TAKING ADVANTAGE OF OUR ORGANIZED CRIME VACUUM... OR SOMETHING MORE?
YOU TELL ME.
YOU SEEM PRETTY SURE THIS BLACK GLOVE IS INVOLVED, BUT I CHECKED OUR DATABASE AND NOTHING CAME UP EXCEPT SOME OLD MOVIE.
YOU SURE THERE'S SOME SECRET MASTER CRIMINAL PULLING THE STRINGS?
-HFF-
I ONLY ASKED.

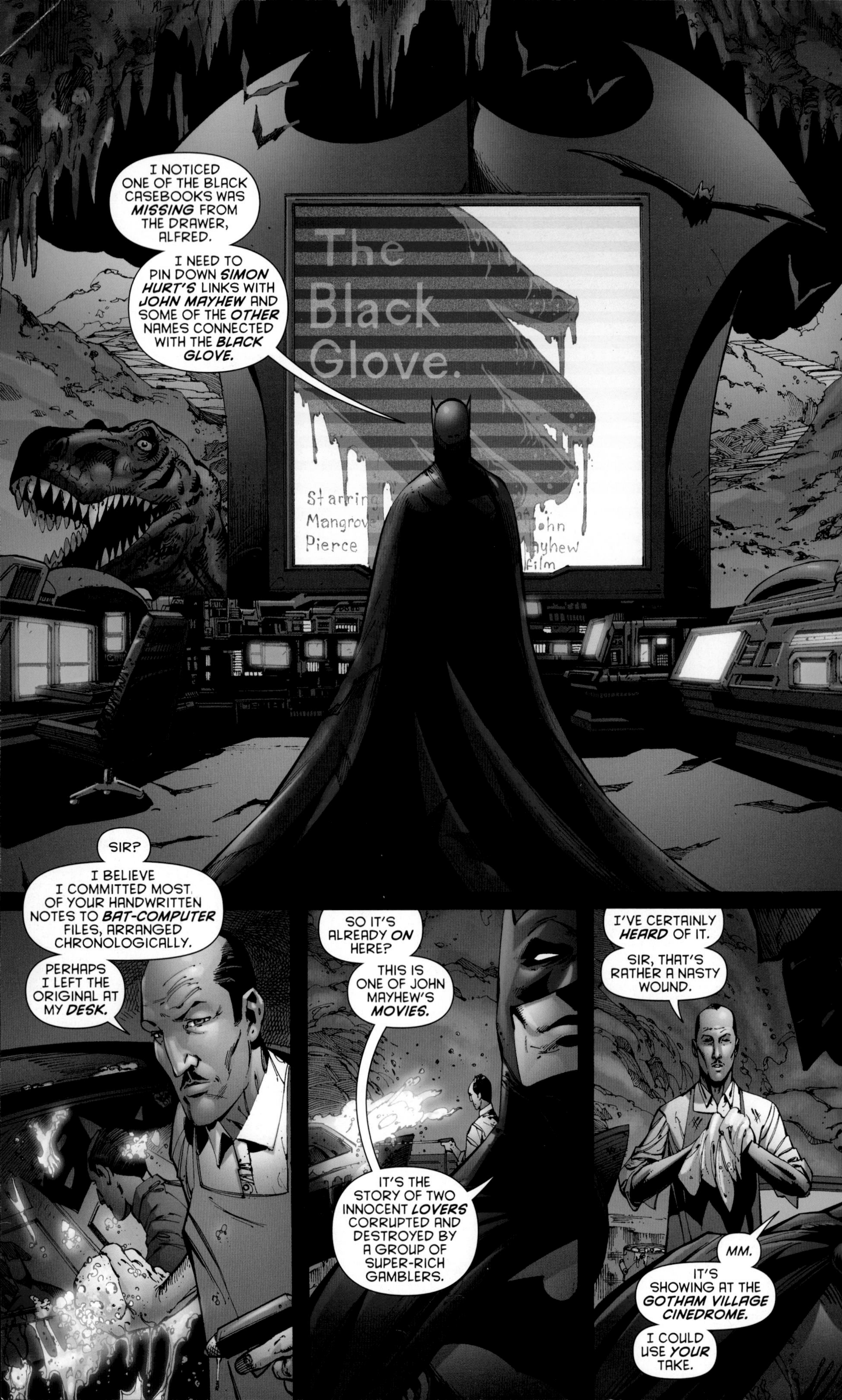

I NOTICED ONE OF THE BLACK CASEBOOKS WAS *MISSING* FROM THE DRAWER, ALFRED.
I NEED TO PIN DOWN *SIMON HURT'S* LINKS WITH *JOHN MAYHEW* AND SOME OF THE *OTHER* NAMES CONNECTED WITH THE *BLACK GLOVE.*
The Black Glove.
Mangrove
Pierce
SIR?
I BELIEVE I COMMITTED MOST OF YOUR HANDWRITTEN NOTES TO *BAT-COMPUTER* FILES, ARRANGED CHRONOLOGICALLY.
PERHAPS I LEFT THE ORIGINAL AT MY *DESK.*
SO IT'S ALREADY *ON* HERE?
THIS IS ONE OF JOHN MAYHEW'S *MOVIES.*
IT'S THE STORY OF TWO INNOCENT *LOVERS* CORRUPTED AND DESTROYED BY A GROUP OF SUPER-RICH GAMBLERS.
I'VE CERTAINLY *HEARD* OF IT.
SIR, THAT'S RATHER A NASTY WOUND.
MM.
IT'S SHOWING AT THE *GOTHAM VILLAGE CINEDROME.*
I COULD USE *YOUR* TAKE.

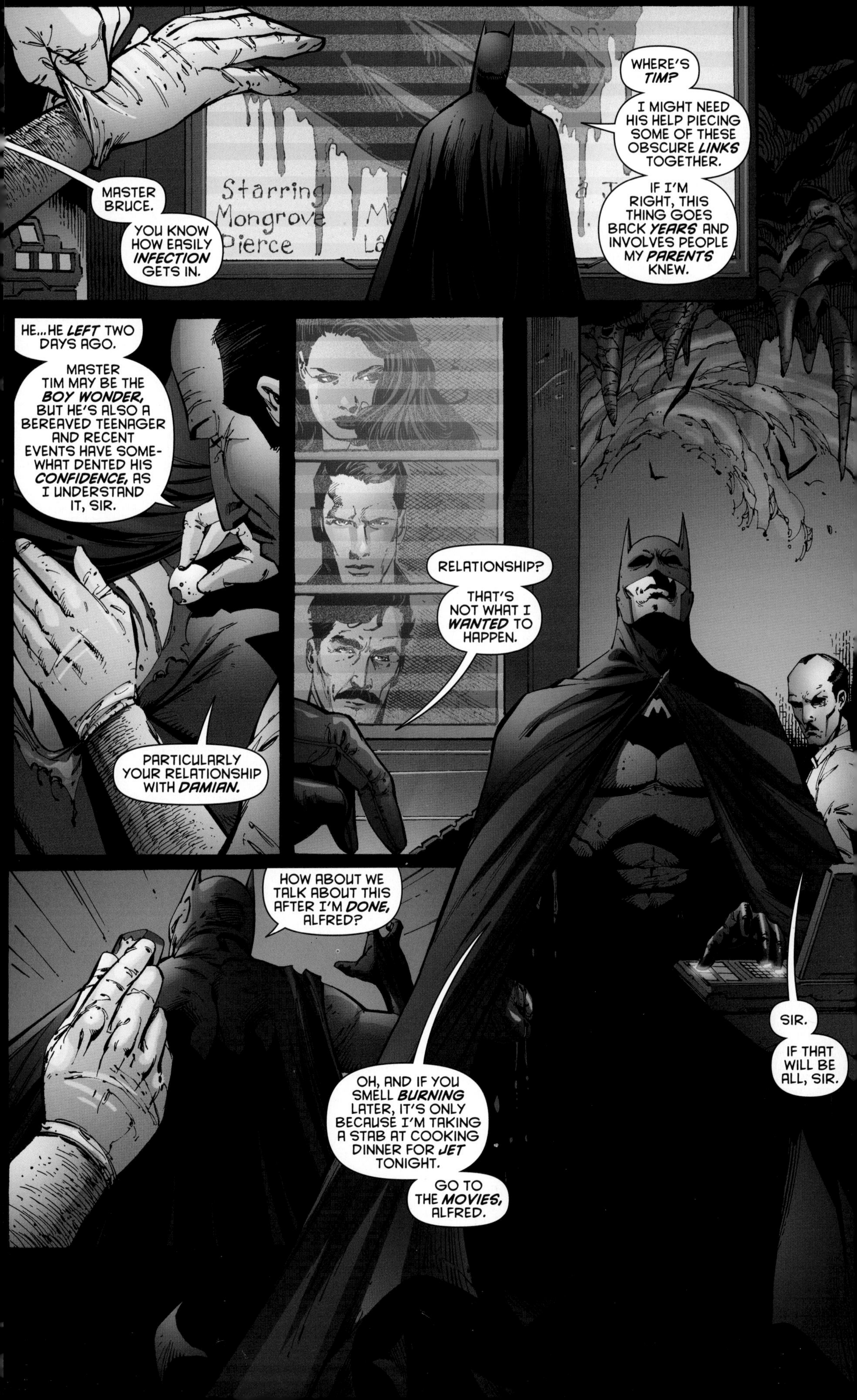

Starring Mongrove Pierce
WHERE'S TIM?
I MIGHT NEED HIS HELP PIECING SOME OF THESE OBSCURE LINKS TOGETHER.
IF I'M RIGHT, THIS THING GOES BACK YEARS AND INVOLVES PEOPLE MY PARENTS KNEW.
MASTER BRUCE.
YOU KNOW HOW EASILY INFECTION GETS IN.
HE...HE LEFT TWO DAYS AGO.
MASTER TIM MAY BE THE BOY WONDER, BUT HE'S ALSO A BEREAVED TEENAGER AND RECENT EVENTS HAVE SOMEWHAT DENTED HIS CONFIDENCE, AS I UNDERSTAND IT, SIR.
PARTICULARLY YOUR RELATIONSHIP WITH DAMIAN.
RELATIONSHIP?
THAT'S NOT WHAT I WANTED TO HAPPEN.
HOW ABOUT WE TALK ABOUT THIS AFTER I'M DONE, ALFRED?
OH, AND IF YOU SMELL BURNING LATER, IT'S ONLY BECAUSE I'M TAKING A STAB AT COOKING DINNER FOR JET TONIGHT.
GO TO THE MOVIES, ALFRED.
SIR.
IF THAT WILL BE ALL, SIR.

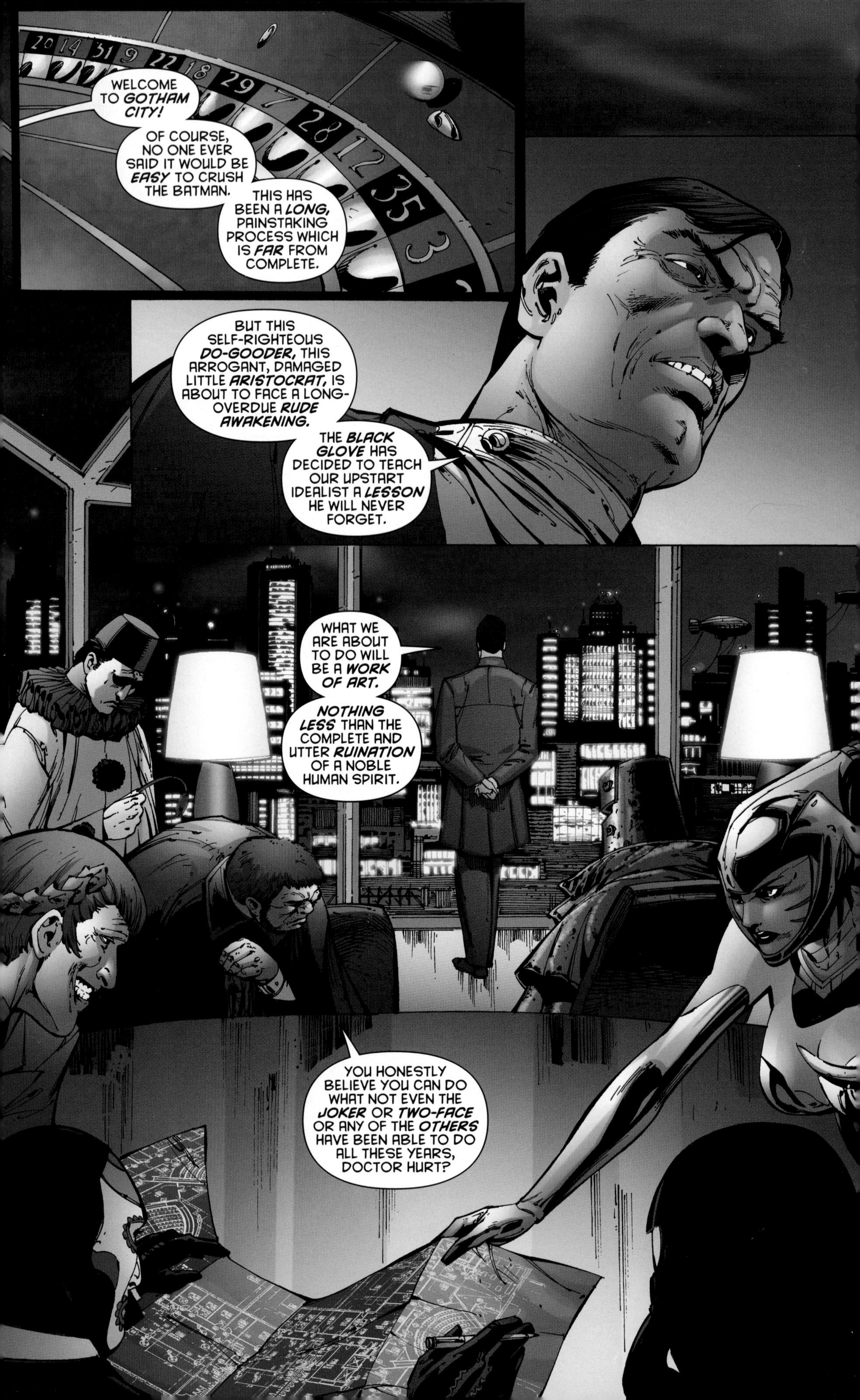
WELCOME TO GOTHAM CITY!
OF COURSE, NO ONE EVER SAID IT WOULD BE EASY TO CRUSH THE BATMAN.
THIS HAS BEEN A LONG, PAINSTAKING PROCESS WHICH IS FAR FROM COMPLETE.
BUT THIS SELF-RIGHTEOUS DO-GOODER, THIS ARROGANT, DAMAGED LITTLE ARISTOCRAT, IS ABOUT TO FACE A LONG-OVERDUE RUDE AWAKENING.
THE BLACK GLOVE HAS DECIDED TO TEACH OUR UPSTART IDEALIST A LESSON HE WILL NEVER FORGET.
WHAT WE ARE ABOUT TO DO WILL BE A WORK OF ART.
NOTHING LESS THAN THE COMPLETE AND UTTER RUINATION OF A NOBLE HUMAN SPIRIT.
YOU HONESTLY BELIEVE YOU CAN DO WHAT NOT EVEN THE JOKER OR TWO-FACE OR ANY OF THE OTHERS HAVE BEEN ABLE TO DO ALL THESE YEARS, DOCTOR HURT?

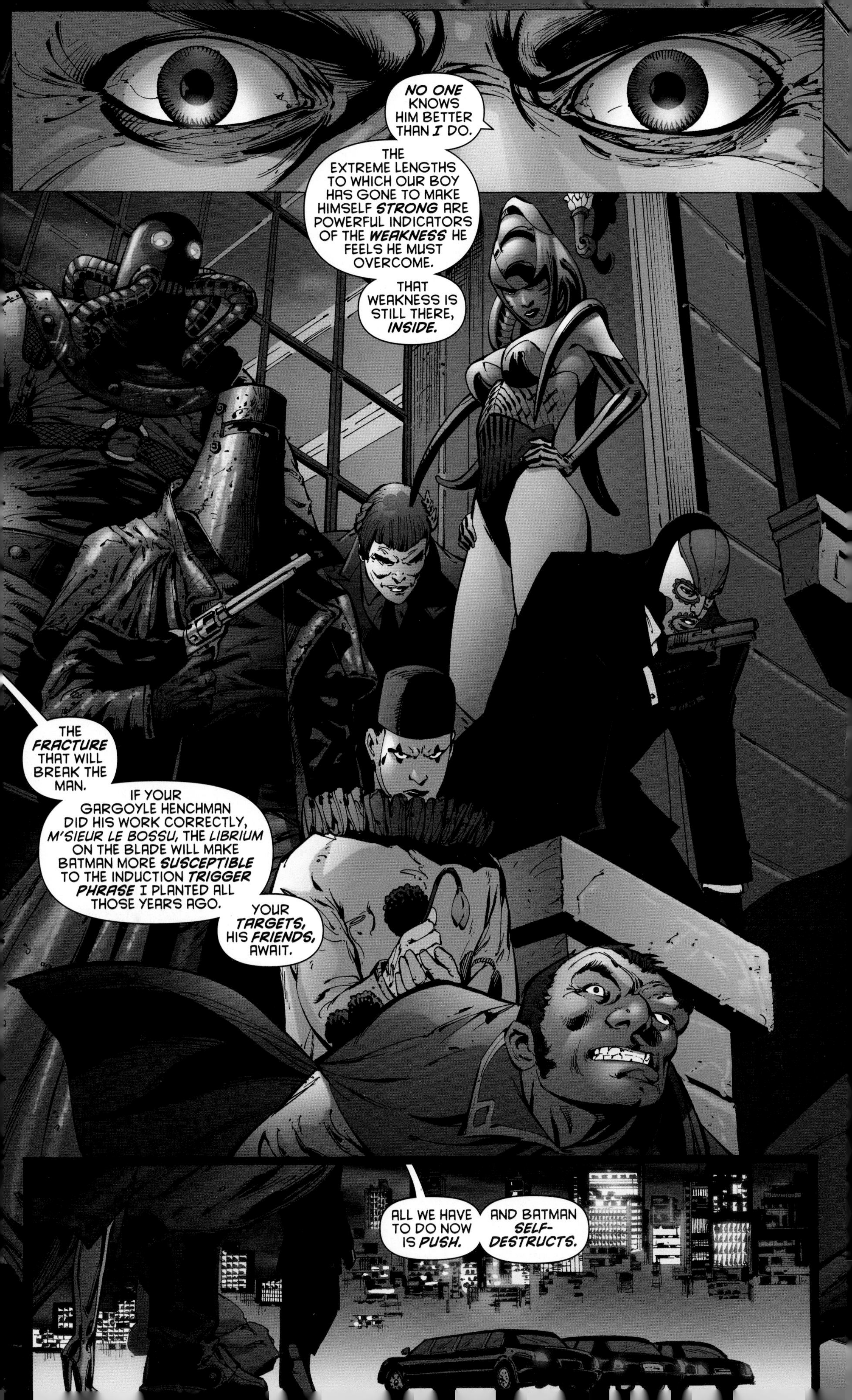
NO ONE KNOWS HIM BETTER THAN I DO.
THE EXTREME LENGTHS TO WHICH OUR BOY HAS GONE TO MAKE HIMSELF STRONG ARE POWERFUL INDICATORS OF THE WEAKNESS HE FEELS HE MUST OVERCOME.
THAT WEAKNESS IS STILL THERE, INSIDE.
THE FRACTURE THAT WILL BREAK THE MAN.
IF YOUR GARGOYLE HENCHMAN DID HIS WORK CORRECTLY, M'SIEUR LE BOSSU, THE LIBRIUM ON THE BLADE WILL MAKE BATMAN MORE SUSCEPTIBLE TO THE INDUCTION TRIGGER PHRASE I PLANTED ALL THOSE YEARS AGO.
YOUR TARGETS, HIS FRIENDS, AWAIT.
ALL WE HAVE TO DO NOW IS PUSH.
AND BATMAN SELF-DESTRUCTS.

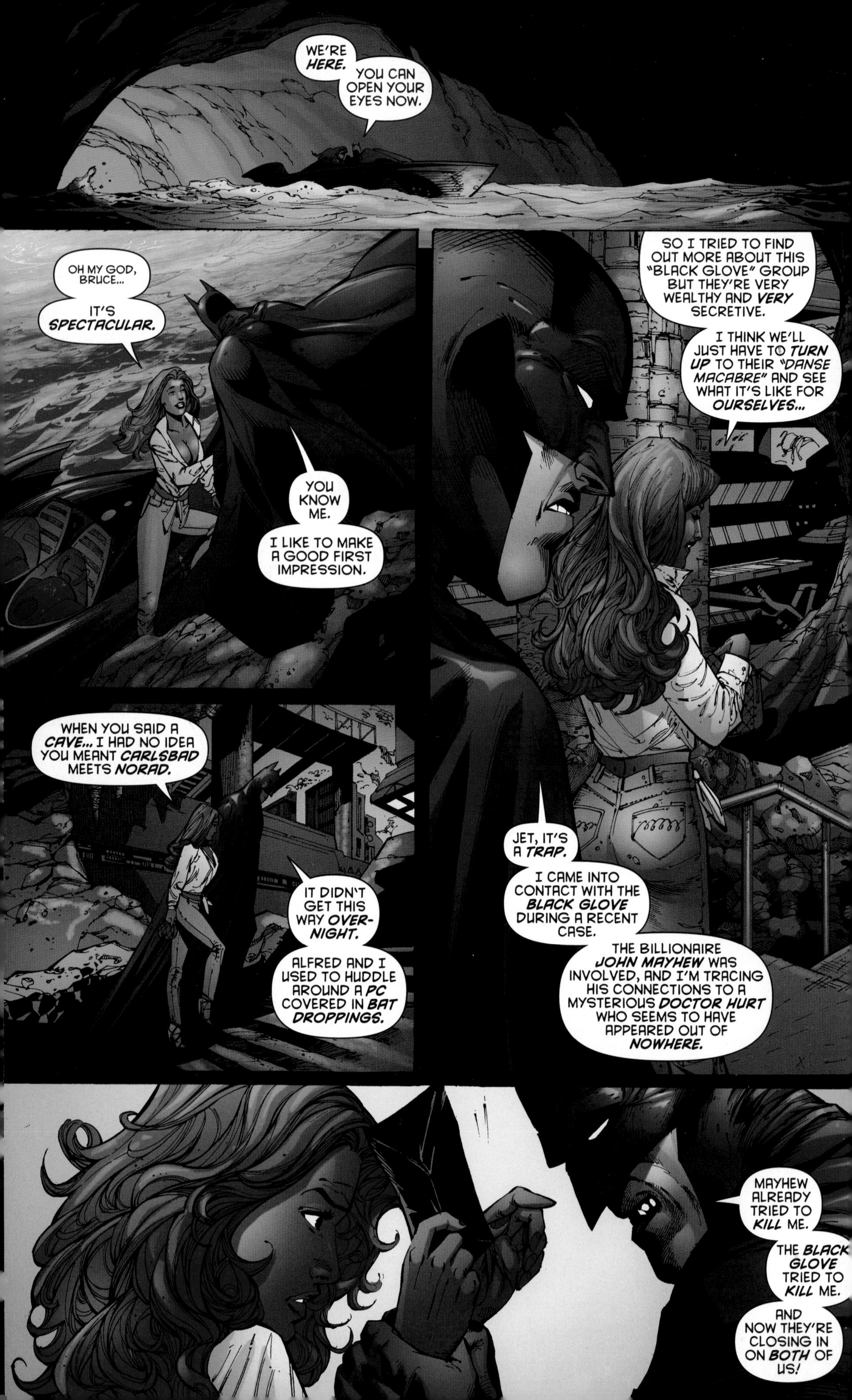
WE'RE HERE.
YOU CAN OPEN YOUR EYES NOW.
OH MY GOD, BRUCE...
IT'S SPECTACULAR.
YOU KNOW ME.
I LIKE TO MAKE A GOOD FIRST IMPRESSION.
SO I TRIED TO FIND OUT MORE ABOUT THIS "BLACK GLOVE" GROUP BUT THEY'RE VERY WEALTHY AND VERY SECRETIVE.
I THINK WE'LL JUST HAVE TO TURN UP TO THEIR "DANSE MACABRE" AND SEE WHAT IT'S LIKE FOR OURSELVES...
WHEN YOU SAID A CAVE... I HAD NO IDEA YOU MEANT CARLSBAD MEETS NORAD.
IT DIDN'T GET THIS WAY OVER-NIGHT.
ALFRED AND I USED TO HUDDLE AROUND A PC COVERED IN BAT DROPPINGS.
JET, IT'S A TRAP.
I CAME INTO CONTACT WITH THE BLACK GLOVE DURING A RECENT CASE.
THE BILLIONAIRE JOHN MAYHEW WAS INVOLVED, AND I'M TRACING HIS CONNECTIONS TO A MYSTERIOUS DOCTOR HURT WHO SEEMS TO HAVE APPEARED OUT OF NOWHERE.
MAYHEW ALREADY TRIED TO KILL ME.
THE BLACK GLOVE TRIED TO KILL ME.
AND NOW THEY'RE CLOSING IN ON BOTH OF US!

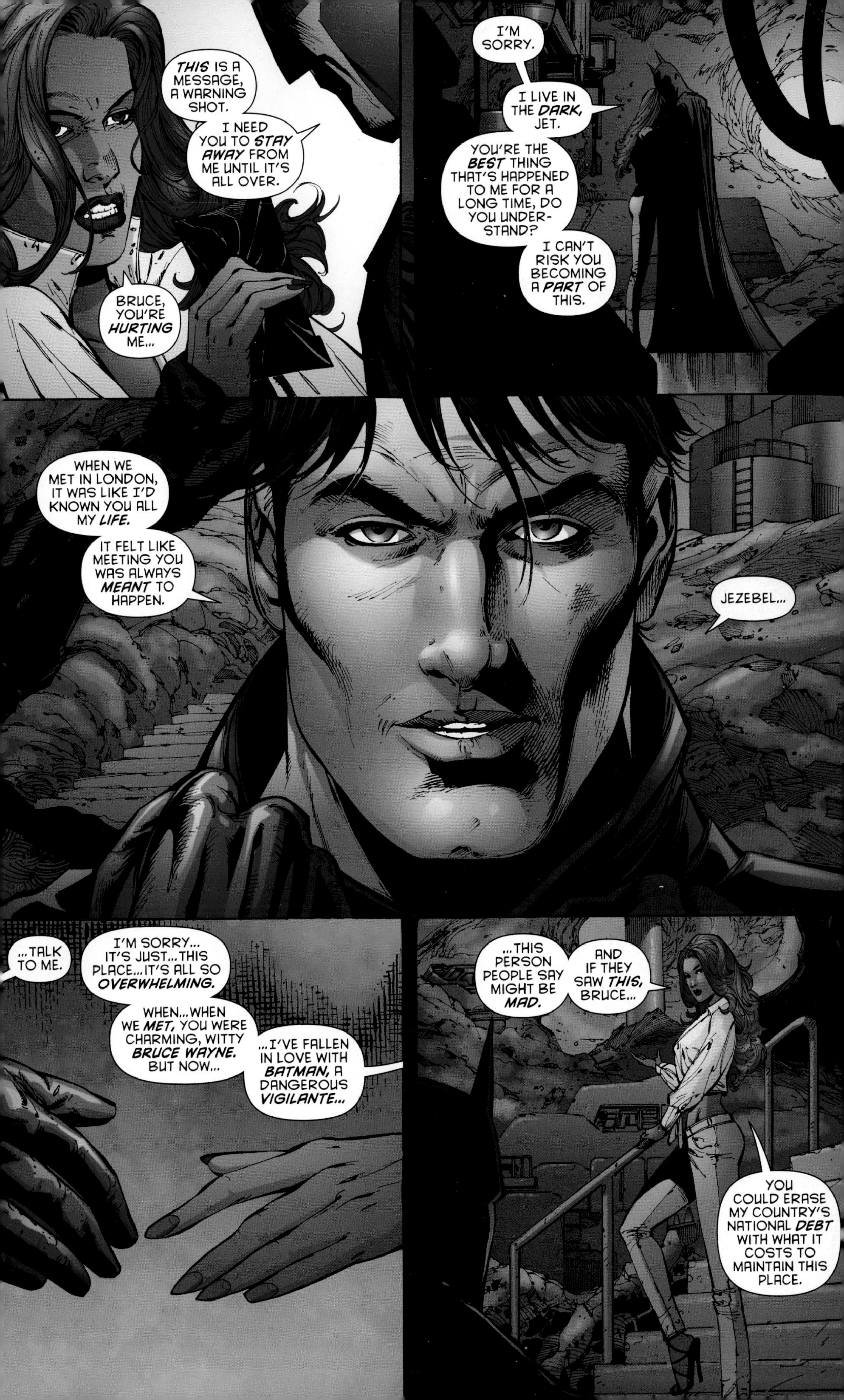
THIS IS A MESSAGE, A WARNING SHOT.
I NEED YOU TO STAY AWAY FROM ME UNTIL IT'S ALL OVER.
BRUCE, YOU'RE HURTING ME...
I'M SORRY.
I LIVE IN THE DARK, JET.
YOU'RE THE BEST THING THAT'S HAPPENED TO ME FOR A LONG TIME, DO YOU UNDER-STAND?
I CAN'T RISK YOU BECOMING A PART OF THIS.
WHEN WE MET IN LONDON, IT WAS LIKE I'D KNOWN YOU ALL MY LIFE.
IT FELT LIKE MEETING YOU WAS ALWAYS MEANT TO HAPPEN.
JEZEBEL...
...TALK TO ME.
I'M SORRY... IT'S JUST... THIS PLACE... IT'S ALL SO OVERWHELMING.
WHEN... WHEN WE MET, YOU WERE CHARMING, WITTY BRUCE WAYNE. BUT NOW...
...I'VE FALLEN IN LOVE WITH BATMAN, A DANGEROUS VIGILANTE...
...THIS PERSON PEOPLE SAY MIGHT BE MAD.
AND IF THEY SAW THIS, BRUCE...
YOU COULD ERASE MY COUNTRY'S NATIONAL DEBT WITH WHAT IT COSTS TO MAINTAIN THIS PLACE.

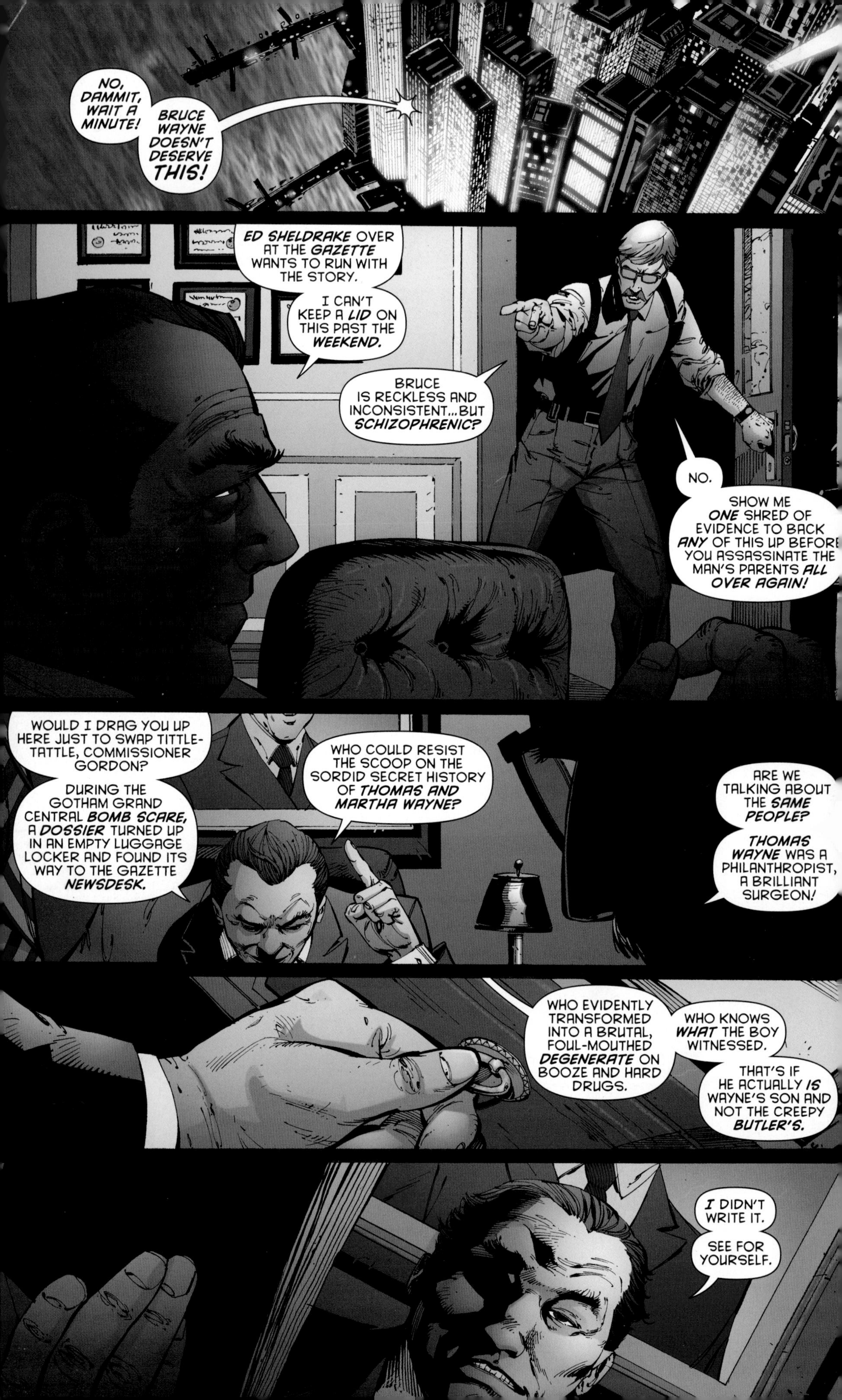

NO, DAMMIT, WAIT A MINUTE!
BRUCE WAYNE DOESN'T DESERVE THIS!
ED SHELDRAKE OVER AT THE GAZETTE WANTS TO RUN WITH THE STORY.
I CAN'T KEEP A LID ON THIS PAST THE WEEKEND.
BRUCE IS RECKLESS AND INCONSISTENT...BUT SCHIZOPHRENIC?
NO.
SHOW ME ONE SHRED OF EVIDENCE TO BACK ANY OF THIS UP BEFORE YOU ASSASSINATE THE MAN'S PARENTS ALL OVER AGAIN!
WOULD I DRAG YOU UP HERE JUST TO SWAP TITTLE-TATTLE, COMMISSIONER GORDON?
DURING THE GOTHAM GRAND CENTRAL BOMB SCARE, A DOSSIER TURNED UP IN AN EMPTY LUGGAGE LOCKER AND FOUND ITS WAY TO THE GAZETTE NEWSDESK.
WHO COULD RESIST THE SCOOP ON THE SORDID SECRET HISTORY OF THOMAS AND MARTHA WAYNE?
ARE WE TALKING ABOUT THE SAME PEOPLE?
THOMAS WAYNE WAS A PHILANTHROPIST, A BRILLIANT SURGEON!
WHO EVIDENTLY TRANSFORMED INTO A BRUTAL, FOUL-MOUTHED DEGENERATE ON BOOZE AND HARD DRUGS.
WHO KNOWS WHAT THE BOY WITNESSED.
THAT'S IF HE ACTUALLY IS WAYNE'S SON AND NOT THE CREEPY BUTLER'S.
I DIDN'T WRITE IT.
SEE FOR YOURSELF.

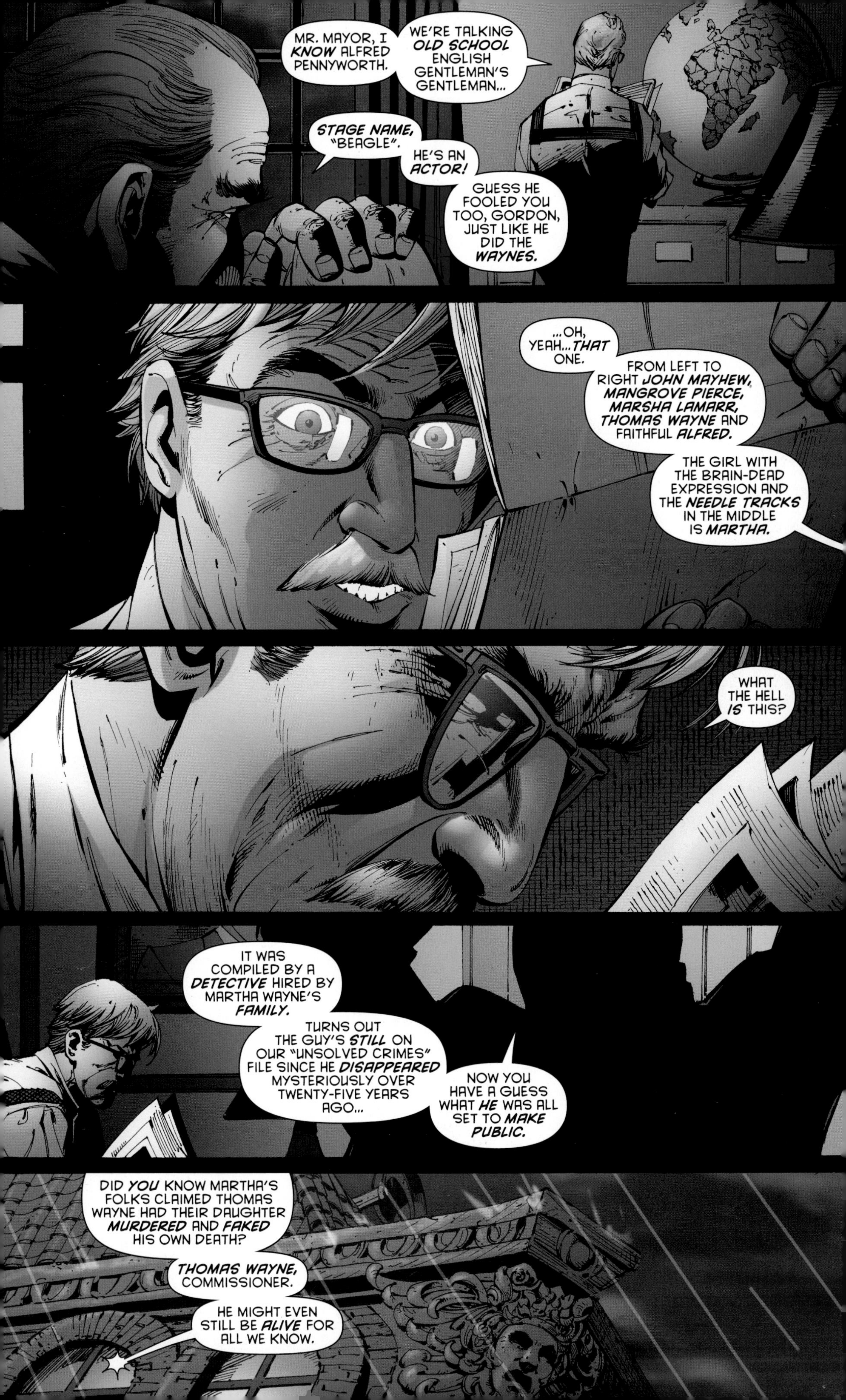
MR. MAYOR, I KNOW ALFRED PENNYWORTH.
WE'RE TALKING OLD SCHOOL ENGLISH GENTLEMAN'S GENTLEMAN...
STAGE NAME, "BEAGLE".
HE'S AN ACTOR!
GUESS HE FOOLED YOU TOO, GORDON, JUST LIKE HE DID THE WAYNES.
...OH, YEAH...THAT ONE.
FROM LEFT TO RIGHT JOHN MAYHEW, MANGROVE PIERCE, MARSHA LAMARR, THOMAS WAYNE AND FAITHFUL ALFRED.
THE GIRL WITH THE BRAIN-DEAD EXPRESSION AND THE NEEDLE TRACKS IN THE MIDDLE IS MARTHA.
WHAT THE HELL IS THIS?
IT WAS COMPILED BY A DETECTIVE HIRED BY MARTHA WAYNE'S FAMILY.
TURNS OUT THE GUY'S STILL ON OUR "UNSOLVED CRIMES" FILE SINCE HE DISAPPEARED MYSTERIOUSLY OVER TWENTY-FIVE YEARS AGO...
NOW YOU HAVE A GUESS WHAT HE WAS ALL SET TO MAKE PUBLIC.
DID YOU KNOW MARTHA'S FOLKS CLAIMED THOMAS WAYNE HAD THEIR DAUGHTER MURDERED AND FAKED HIS OWN DEATH?
THOMAS WAYNE, COMMISSIONER.
HE MIGHT EVEN STILL BE ALIVE FOR ALL WE KNOW.

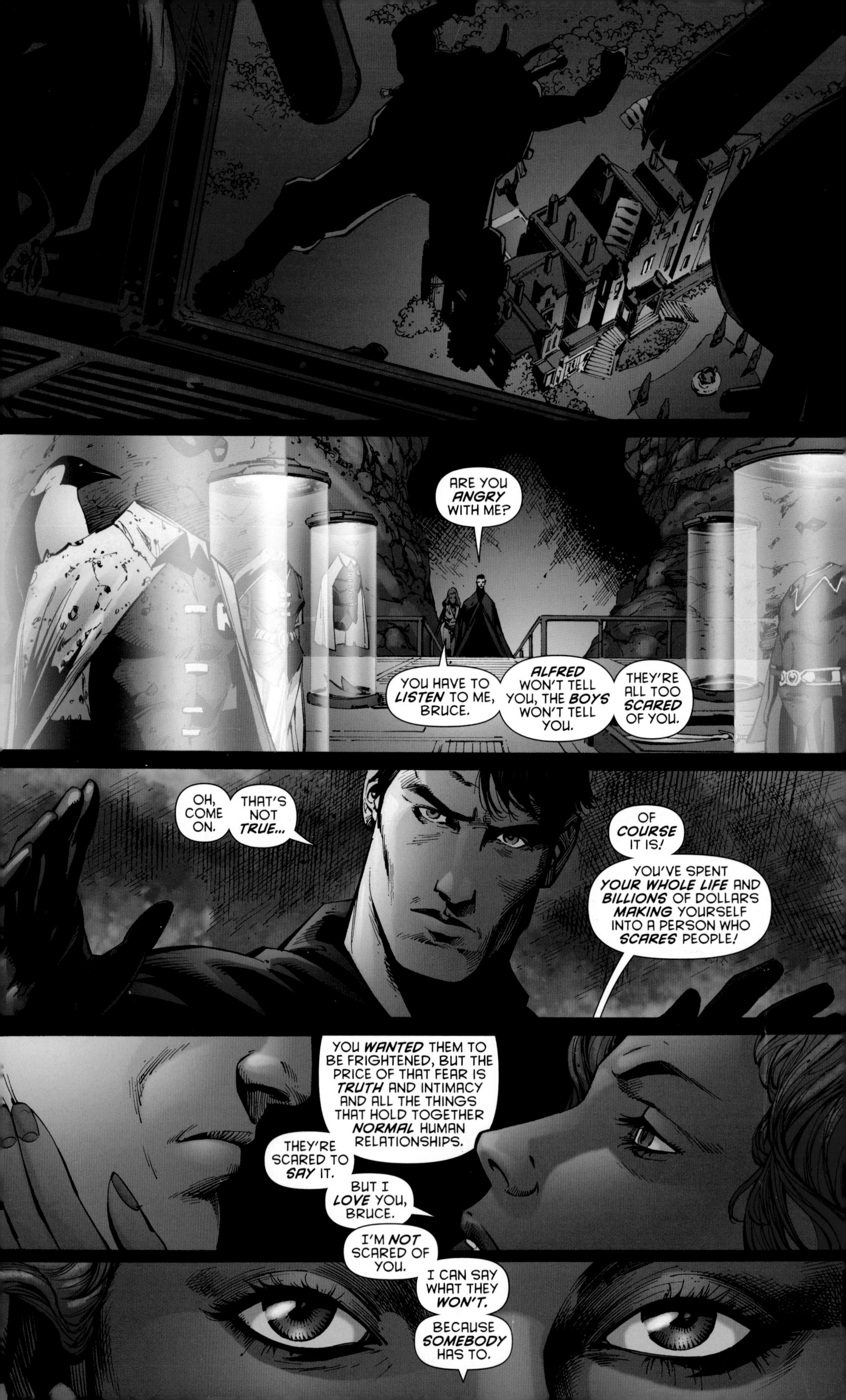
ARE YOU ANGRY WITH ME?
YOU HAVE TO LISTEN TO ME, BRUCE.
ALFRED WON'T TELL YOU, THE BOYS WON'T TELL YOU.
THEY'RE ALL TOO SCARED OF YOU.
OH, COME ON.
THAT'S NOT TRUE...
OF COURSE IT IS!
YOU'VE SPENT YOUR WHOLE LIFE AND BILLIONS OF DOLLARS MAKING YOURSELF INTO A PERSON WHO SCARES PEOPLE!
YOU WANTED THEM TO BE FRIGHTENED, BUT THE PRICE OF THAT FEAR IS TRUTH AND INTIMACY AND ALL THE THINGS THAT HOLD TOGETHER NORMAL HUMAN RELATIONSHIPS.
THEY'RE SCARED TO SAY IT.
BUT I LOVE YOU, BRUCE.
I'M NOT SCARED OF YOU.
I CAN SAY WHAT THEY WON'T.
BECAUSE SOMEBODY HAS TO.

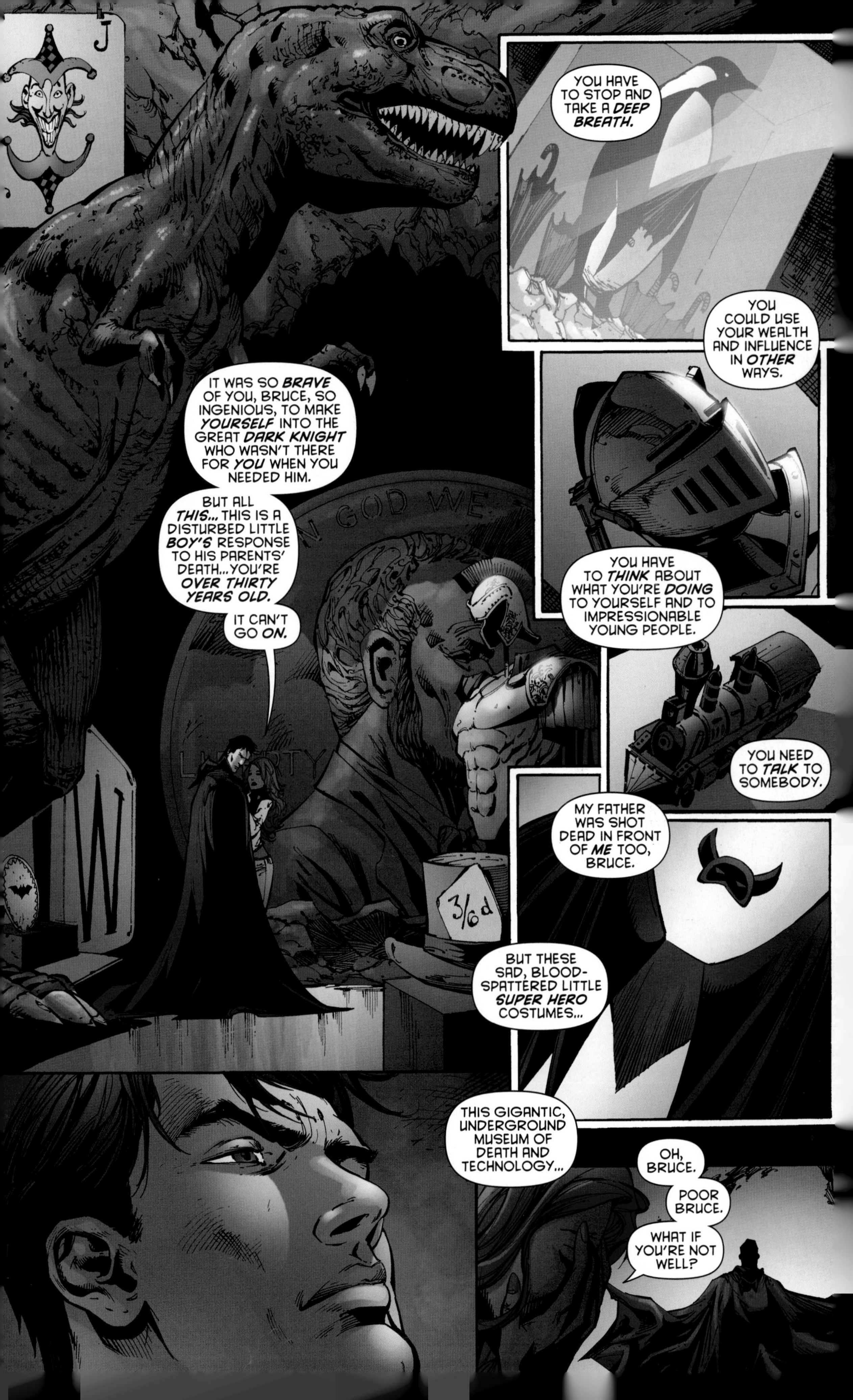
YOU HAVE TO STOP AND TAKE A DEEP BREATH.
YOU COULD USE YOUR WEALTH AND INFLUENCE IN OTHER WAYS.
IT WAS SO BRAVE OF YOU, BRUCE, SO INGENIOUS, TO MAKE YOURSELF INTO THE GREAT DARK KNIGHT WHO WASN'T THERE FOR YOU WHEN YOU NEEDED HIM.
BUT ALL THIS... THIS IS A DISTURBED LITTLE BOY'S RESPONSE TO HIS PARENTS' DEATH... YOU'RE OVER THIRTY YEARS OLD.
IT CAN'T GO ON.
YOU HAVE TO THINK ABOUT WHAT YOU'RE DOING TO YOURSELF AND TO IMPRESSIONABLE YOUNG PEOPLE.
YOU NEED TO TALK TO SOMEBODY.
MY FATHER WAS SHOT DEAD IN FRONT OF ME TOO, BRUCE.
BUT THESE SAD, BLOOD-SPATTERED LITTLE SUPER HERO COSTUMES...
THIS GIGANTIC, UNDERGROUND MUSEUM OF DEATH AND TECHNOLOGY...
OH, BRUCE.
POOR BRUCE.
WHAT IF YOU'RE NOT WELL?

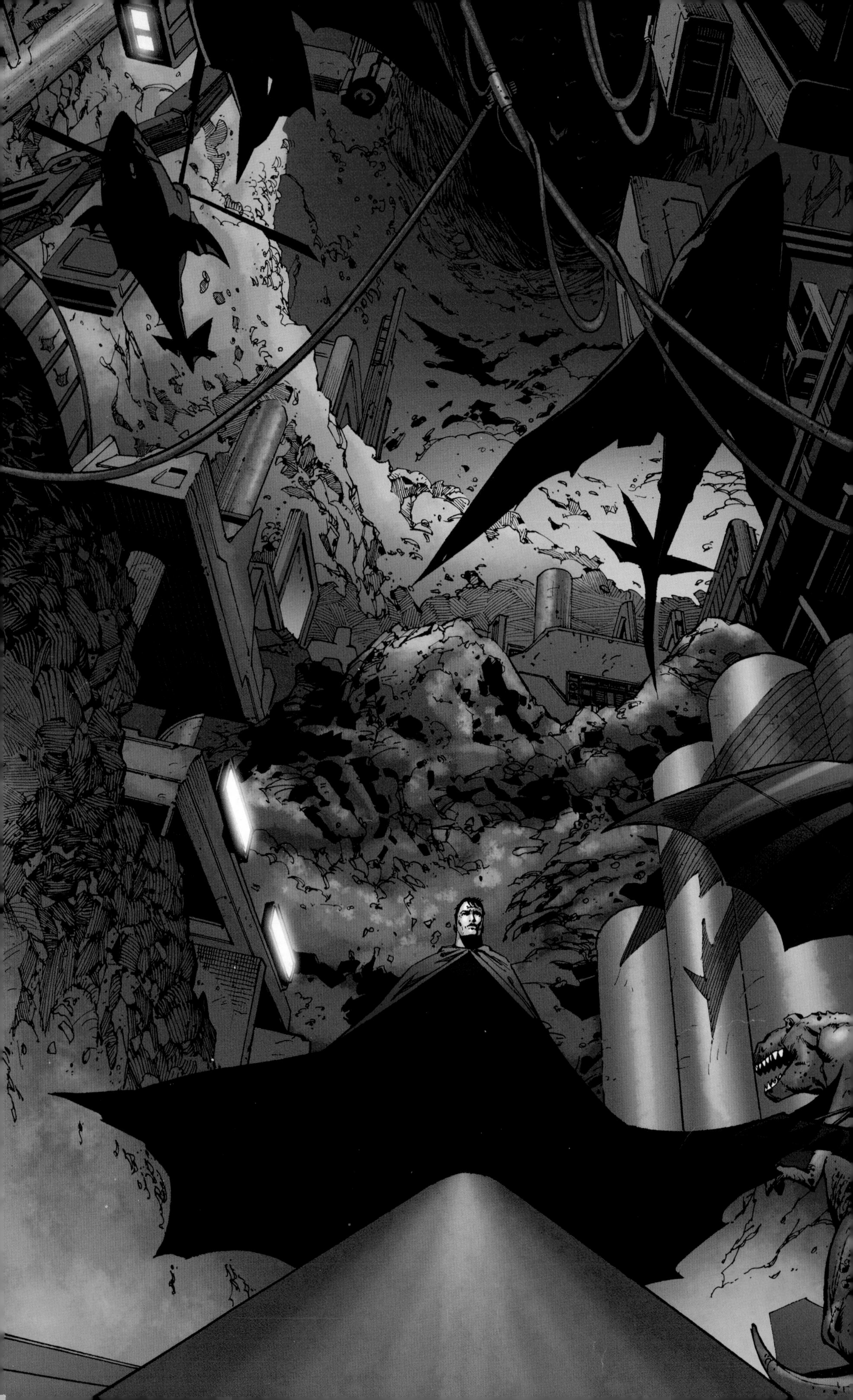

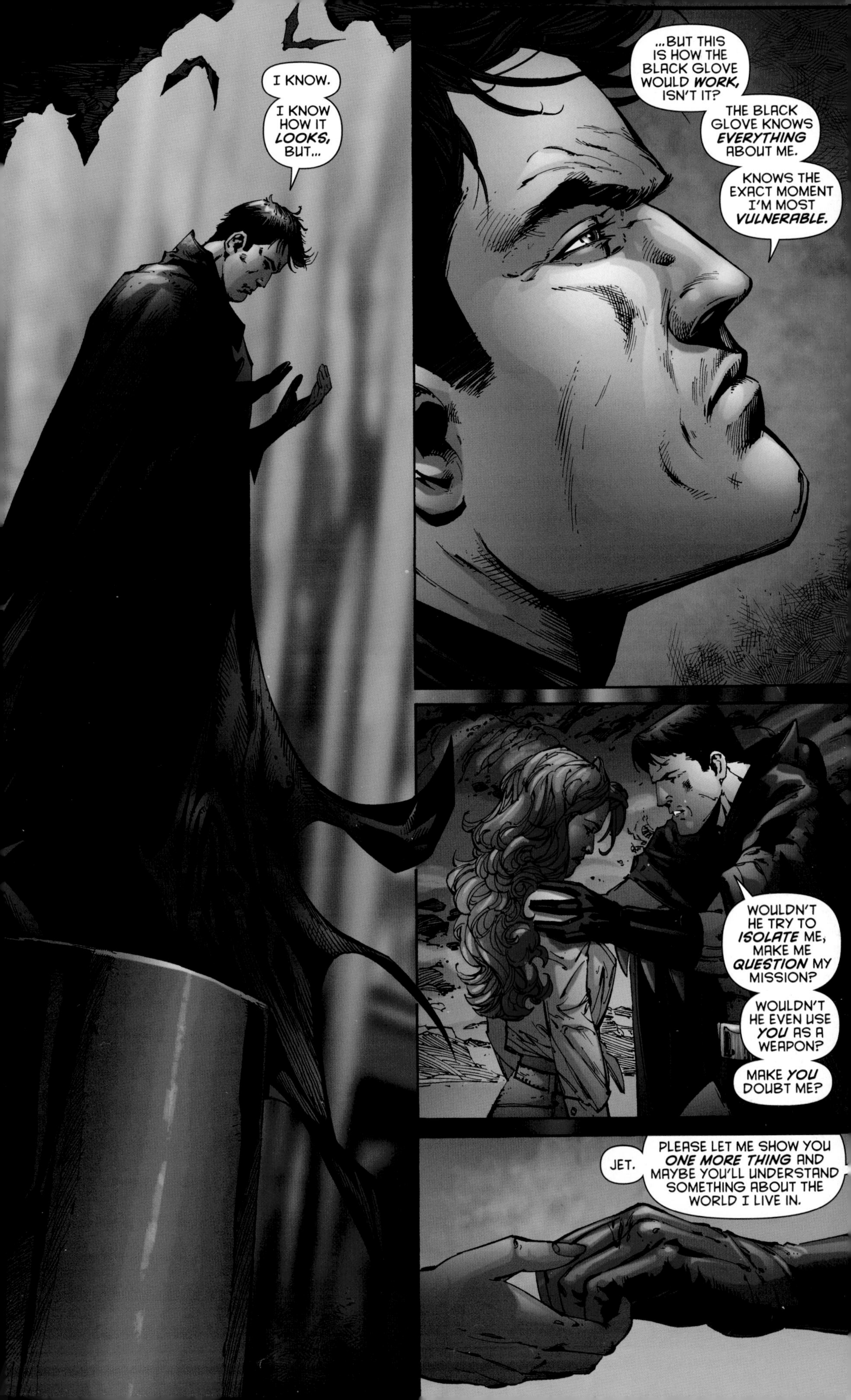
I KNOW.
I KNOW HOW IT *LOOKS,* BUT...
...BUT THIS IS HOW THE BLACK GLOVE WOULD *WORK,* ISN'T IT?
THE BLACK GLOVE KNOWS *EVERYTHING* ABOUT ME.
KNOWS THE EXACT MOMENT I'M MOST *VULNERABLE.*
WOULDN'T HE TRY TO *ISOLATE* ME, MAKE ME *QUESTION* MY MISSION?
WOULDN'T HE EVEN USE *YOU* AS A WEAPON?
MAKE *YOU* DOUBT ME?
JET.
PLEASE LET ME SHOW YOU *ONE MORE THING* AND MAYBE YOU'LL UNDERSTAND SOMETHING ABOUT THE WORLD I LIVE IN.

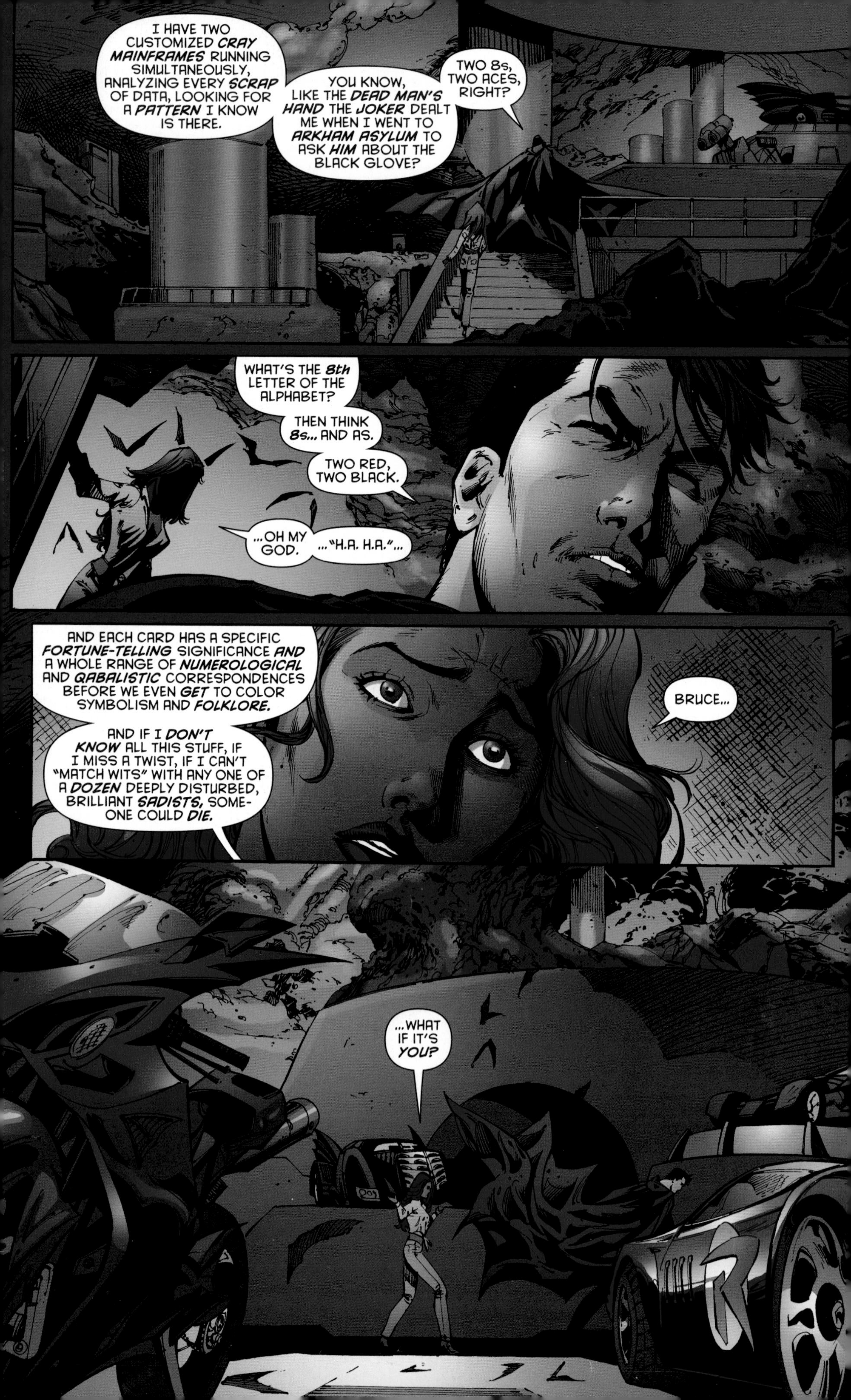

I HAVE TWO CUSTOMIZED CRAY MAINFRAMES RUNNING SIMULTANEOUSLY, ANALYZING EVERY SCRAP OF DATA, LOOKING FOR A PATTERN I KNOW IS THERE.
YOU KNOW, LIKE THE DEAD MAN'S HAND THE JOKER DEALT ME WHEN I WENT TO ARKHAM ASYLUM TO ASK HIM ABOUT THE BLACK GLOVE?
TWO 8s, TWO ACES, RIGHT?
WHAT'S THE 8th LETTER OF THE ALPHABET?
THEN THINK 8s... AND AS.
TWO RED, TWO BLACK.
...OH MY GOD.
..."H.A. H.A."...
AND EACH CARD HAS A SPECIFIC FORTUNE-TELLING SIGNIFICANCE AND A WHOLE RANGE OF NUMEROLOGICAL AND QABALISTIC CORRESPONDENCES BEFORE WE EVEN GET TO COLOR SYMBOLISM AND FOLKLORE.
AND IF I DON'T KNOW ALL THIS STUFF, IF I MISS A TWIST, IF I CAN'T "MATCH WITS" WITH ANY ONE OF A DOZEN DEEPLY DISTURBED, BRILLIANT SADISTS, SOME-ONE COULD DIE.
BRUCE...
...WHAT IF IT'S YOU?

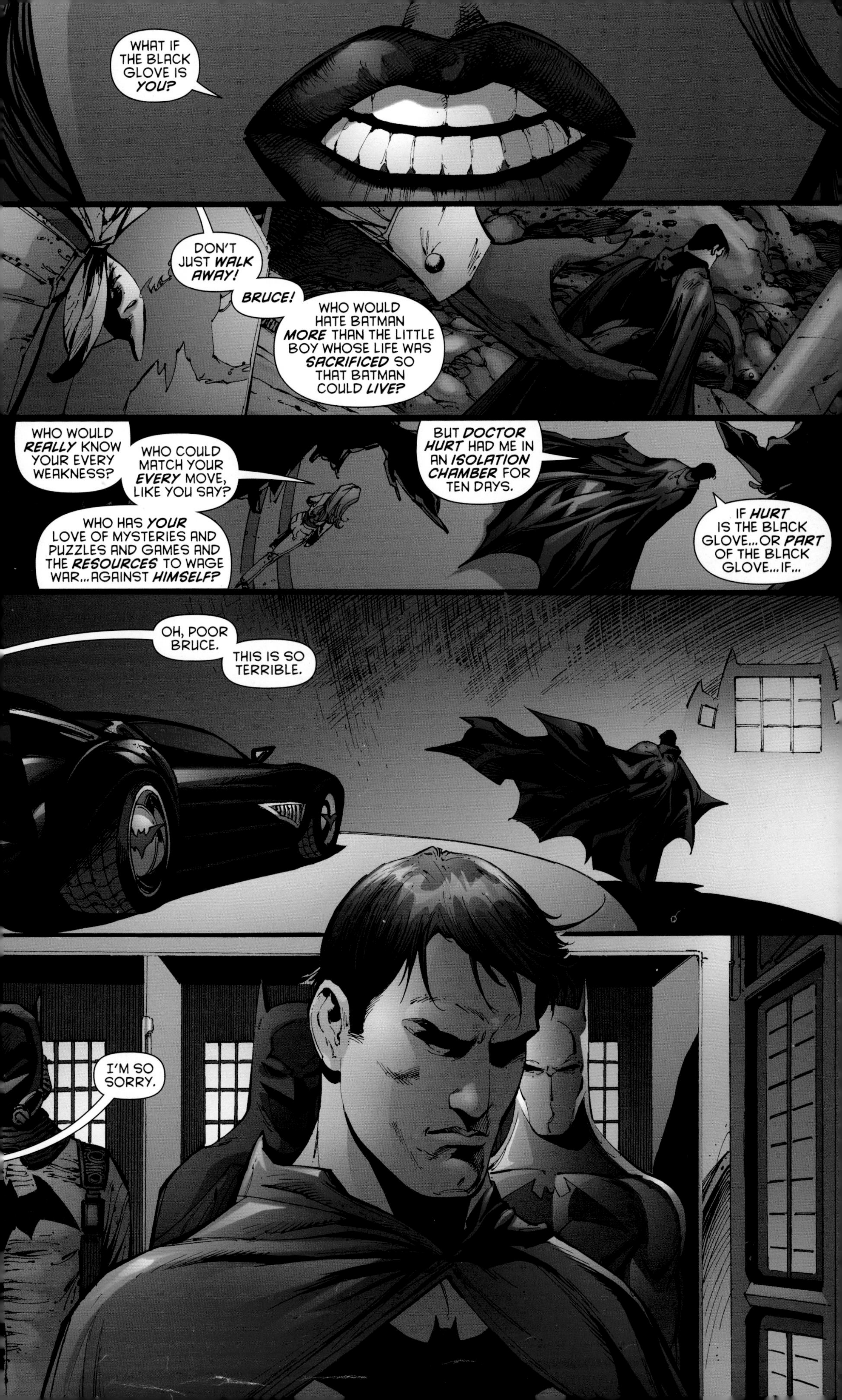
WHAT IF THE BLACK GLOVE IS *YOU?*
DON'T JUST *WALK AWAY!*
BRUCE!
WHO WOULD HATE BATMAN *MORE* THAN THE LITTLE BOY WHOSE LIFE WAS *SACRIFICED* SO THAT BATMAN COULD *LIVE?*
WHO WOULD *REALLY* KNOW YOUR EVERY WEAKNESS?
WHO COULD MATCH YOUR *EVERY* MOVE, LIKE YOU SAY?
WHO HAS *YOUR* LOVE OF MYSTERIES AND PUZZLES AND GAMES AND THE *RESOURCES* TO WAGE WAR...AGAINST *HIMSELF?*
BUT *DOCTOR HURT* HAD ME IN AN *ISOLATION CHAMBER* FOR TEN DAYS.
IF *HURT* IS THE BLACK GLOVE...OR *PART* OF THE BLACK GLOVE...IF...
OH, POOR BRUCE.
THIS IS SO TERRIBLE.
I'M SO SORRY.

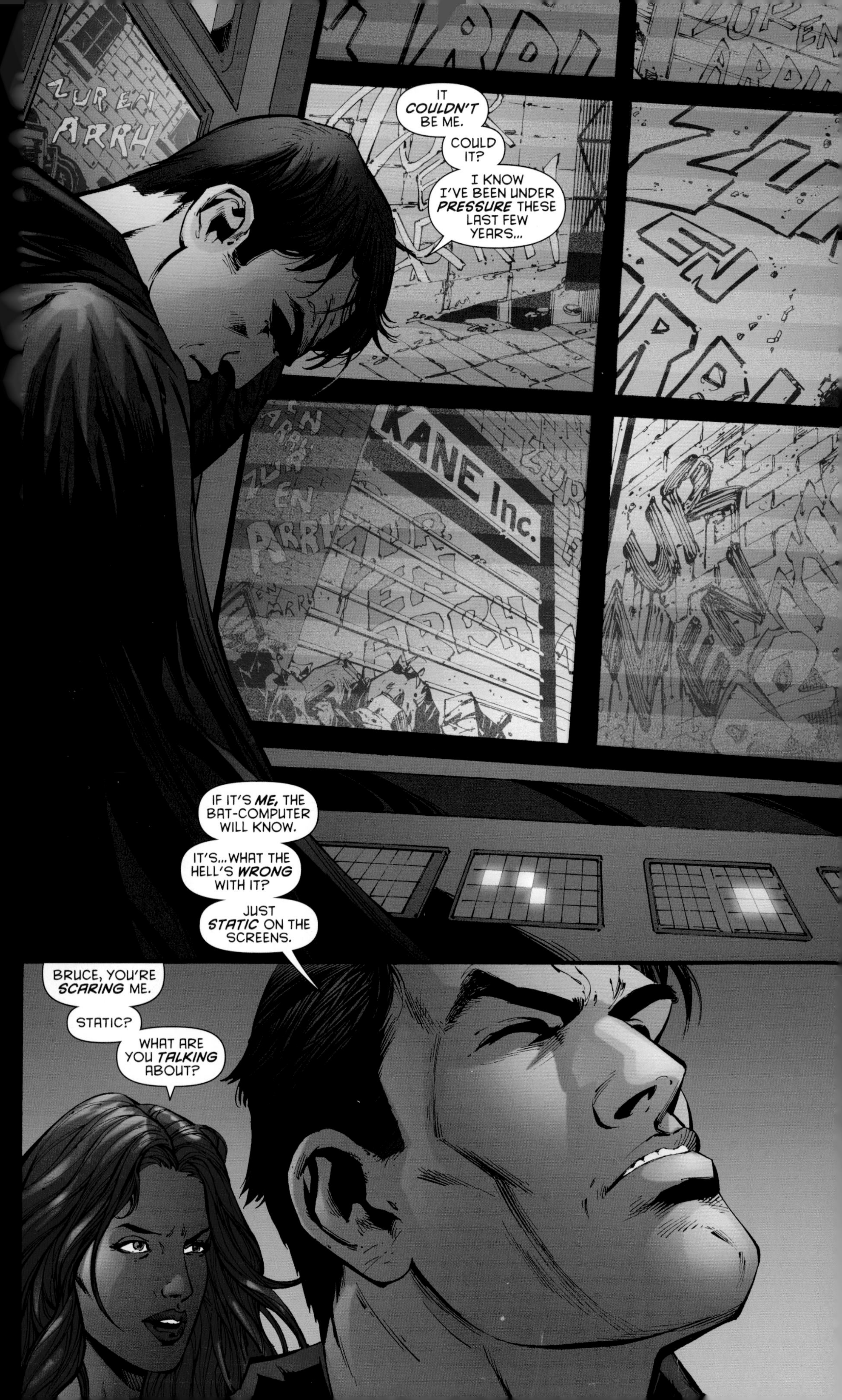

IT COULDN'T BE ME.
COULD IT?
I KNOW I'VE BEEN UNDER PRESSURE THESE LAST FEW YEARS...
KANE Inc.
IF IT'S ME, THE BAT-COMPUTER WILL KNOW.
IT'S...WHAT THE HELL'S WRONG WITH IT?
JUST STATIC ON THE SCREENS.
BRUCE, YOU'RE SCARING ME.
STATIC?
WHAT ARE YOU TALKING ABOUT?

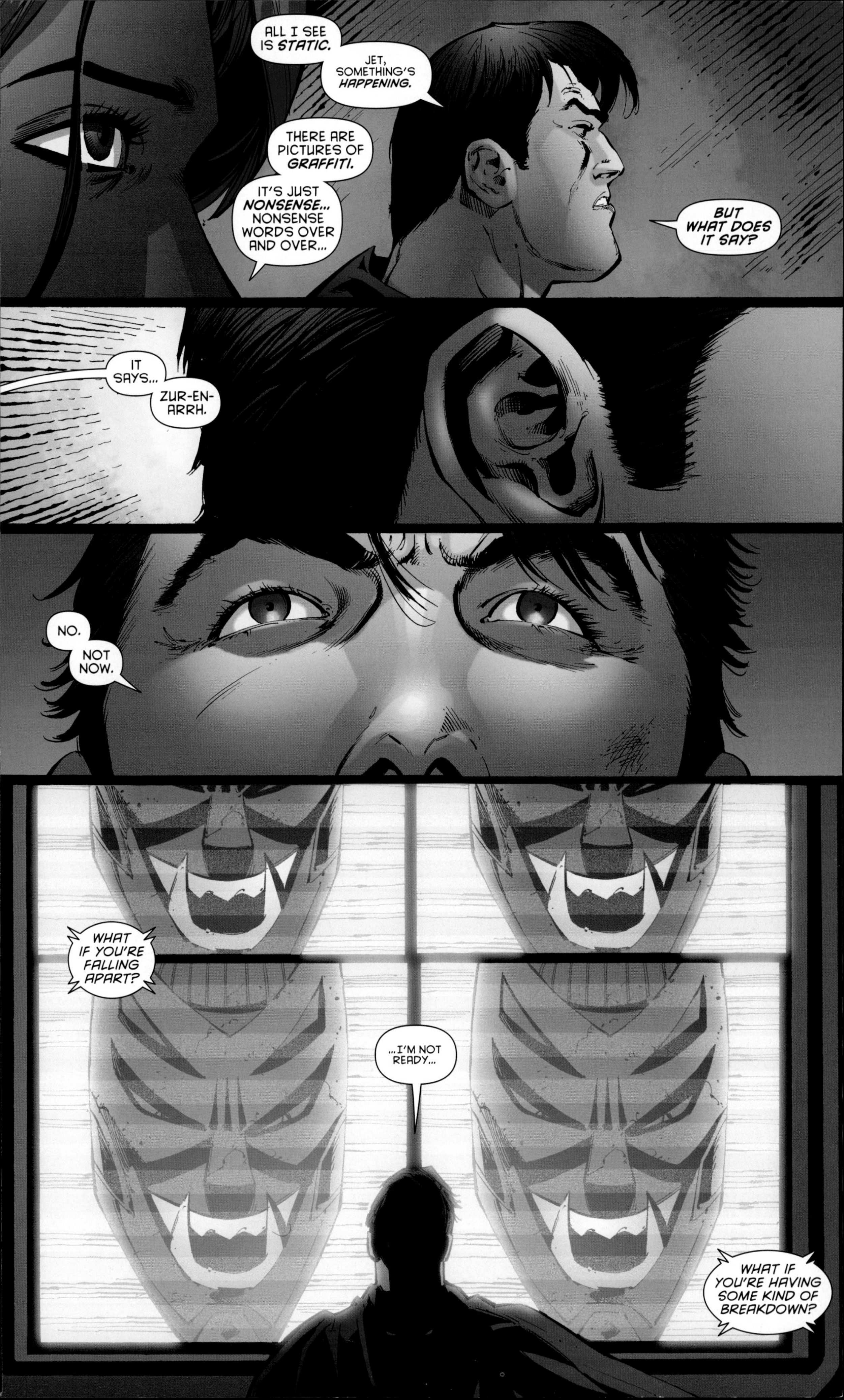
ALL I SEE IS STATIC.
JET, SOMETHING'S HAPPENING.
THERE ARE PICTURES OF GRAFFITI.
IT'S JUST NONSENSE... NONSENSE WORDS OVER AND OVER...
BUT WHAT DOES IT SAY?
IT SAYS...
ZUR-EN-ARRH.
NO.
NOT NOW.
WHAT IF YOU'RE FALLING APART?
...I'M NOT READY...
WHAT IF YOU'RE HAVING SOME KIND OF BREAKDOWN?

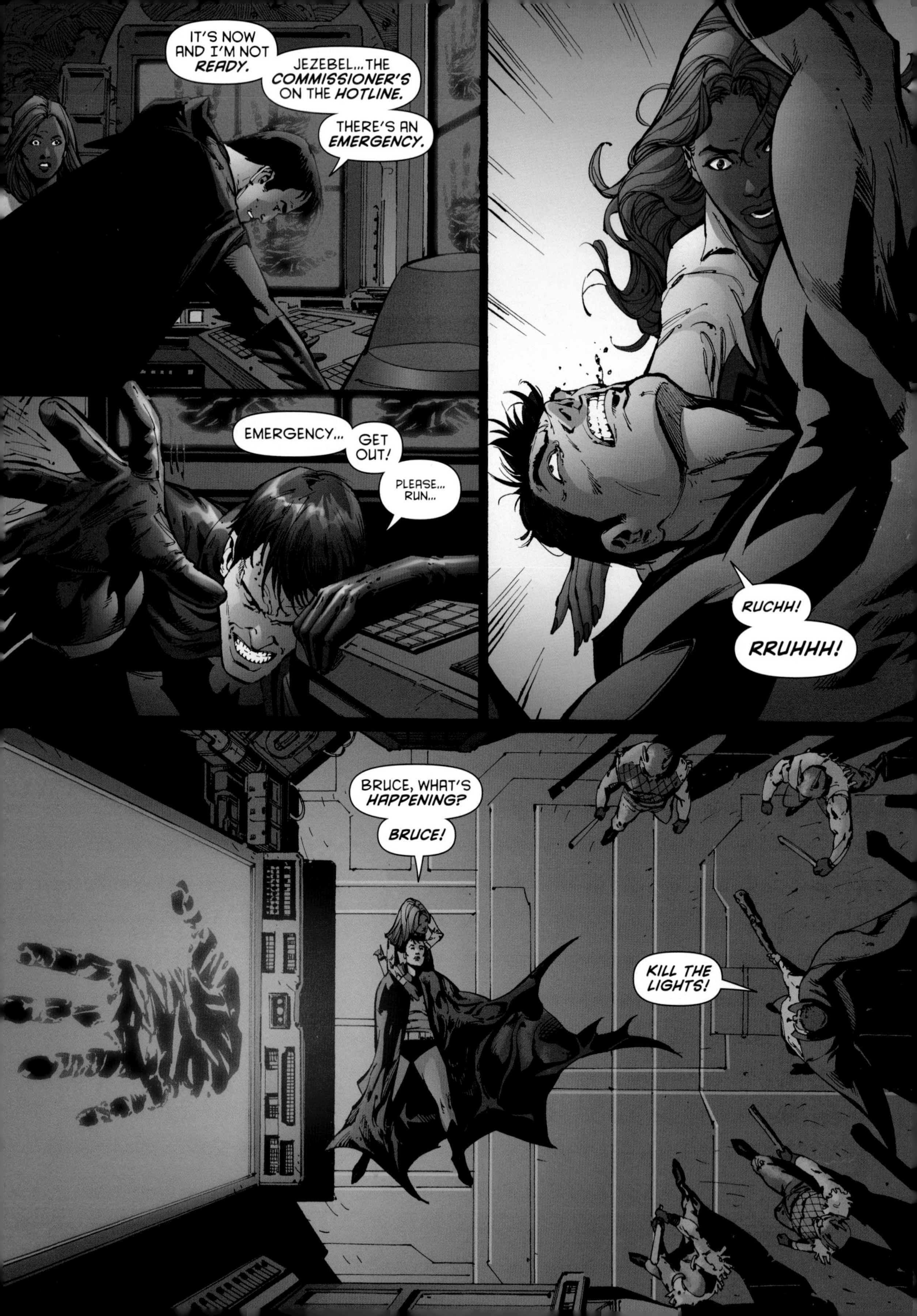
IT'S NOW AND I'M NOT READY.
JEZEBEL... THE COMMISSIONER'S ON THE HOTLINE.
THERE'S AN EMERGENCY.
EMERGENCY...
GET OUT!
PLEASE... RUN...
RUCHH!
RRUHHH!
BRUCE, WHAT'S HAPPENING?
BRUCE!
KILL THE LIGHTS!

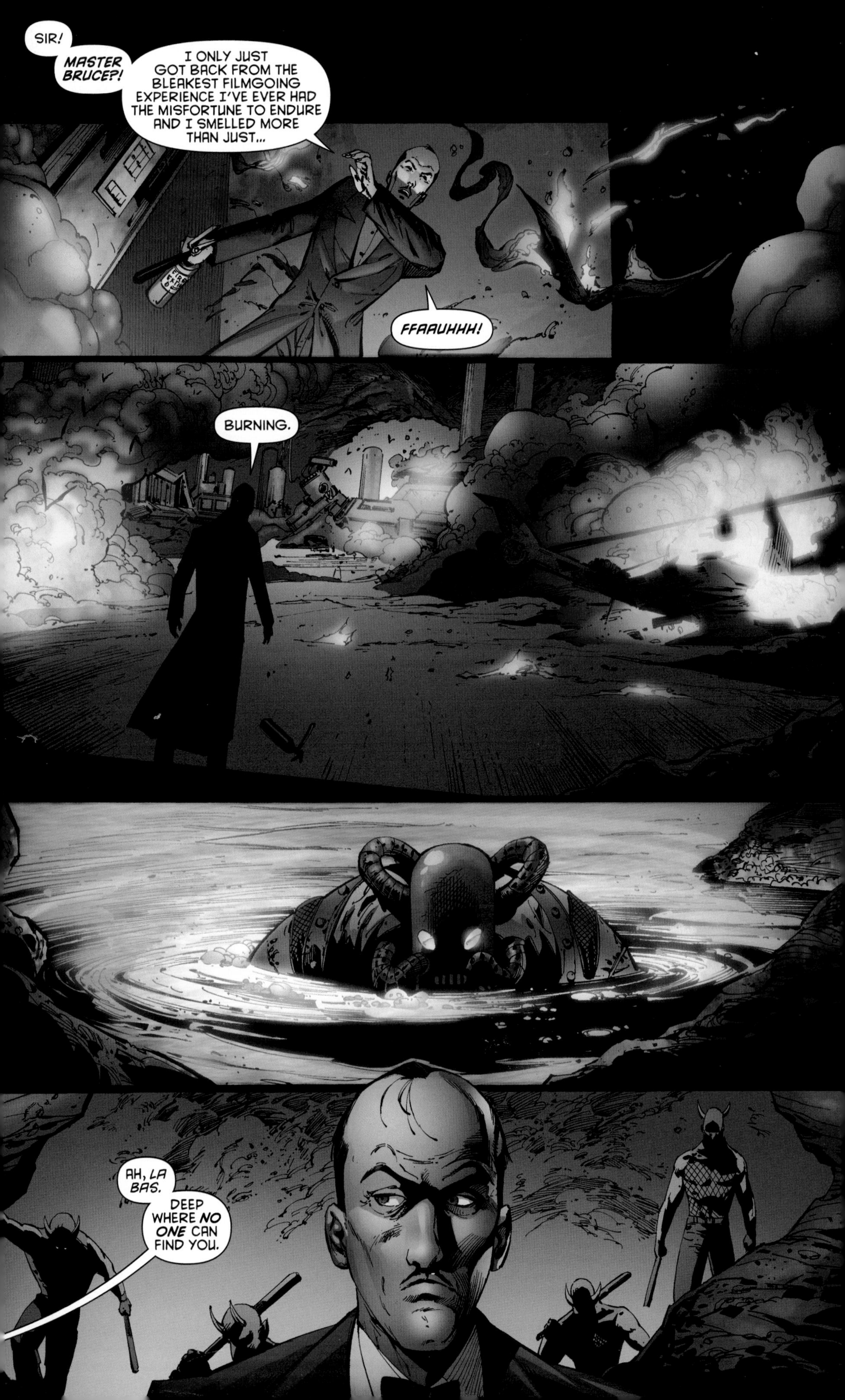
SIR!
MASTER BRUCE?!
I ONLY JUST GOT BACK FROM THE BLEAKEST FILMGOING EXPERIENCE I'VE EVER HAD THE MISFORTUNE TO ENDURE AND I SMELLED MORE THAN JUST...
FFAAUHHH!
BURNING.
AH, LA BAS.
DEEP WHERE NO ONE CAN FIND YOU.

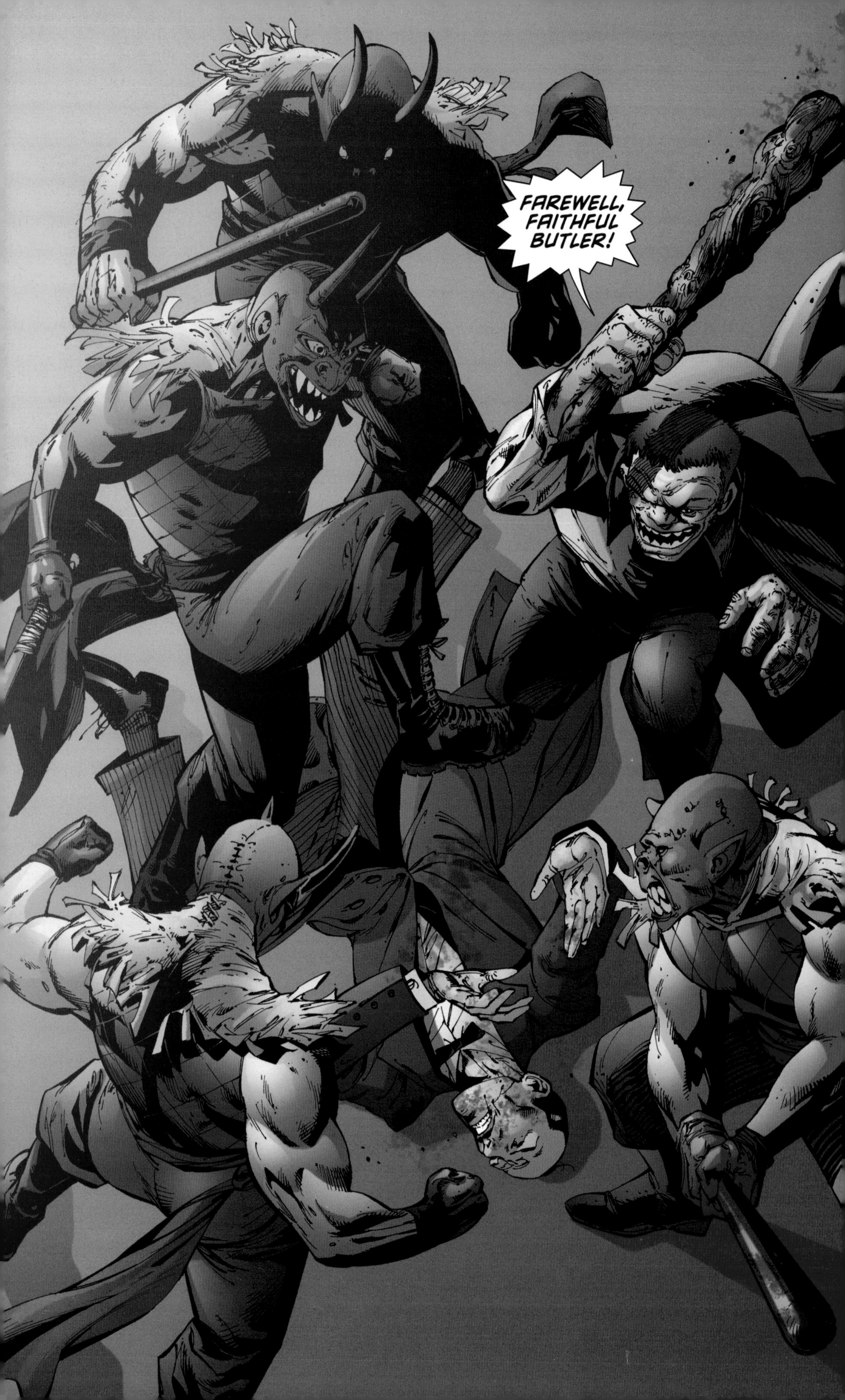
FAREWELL, FAITHFUL BUTLER!

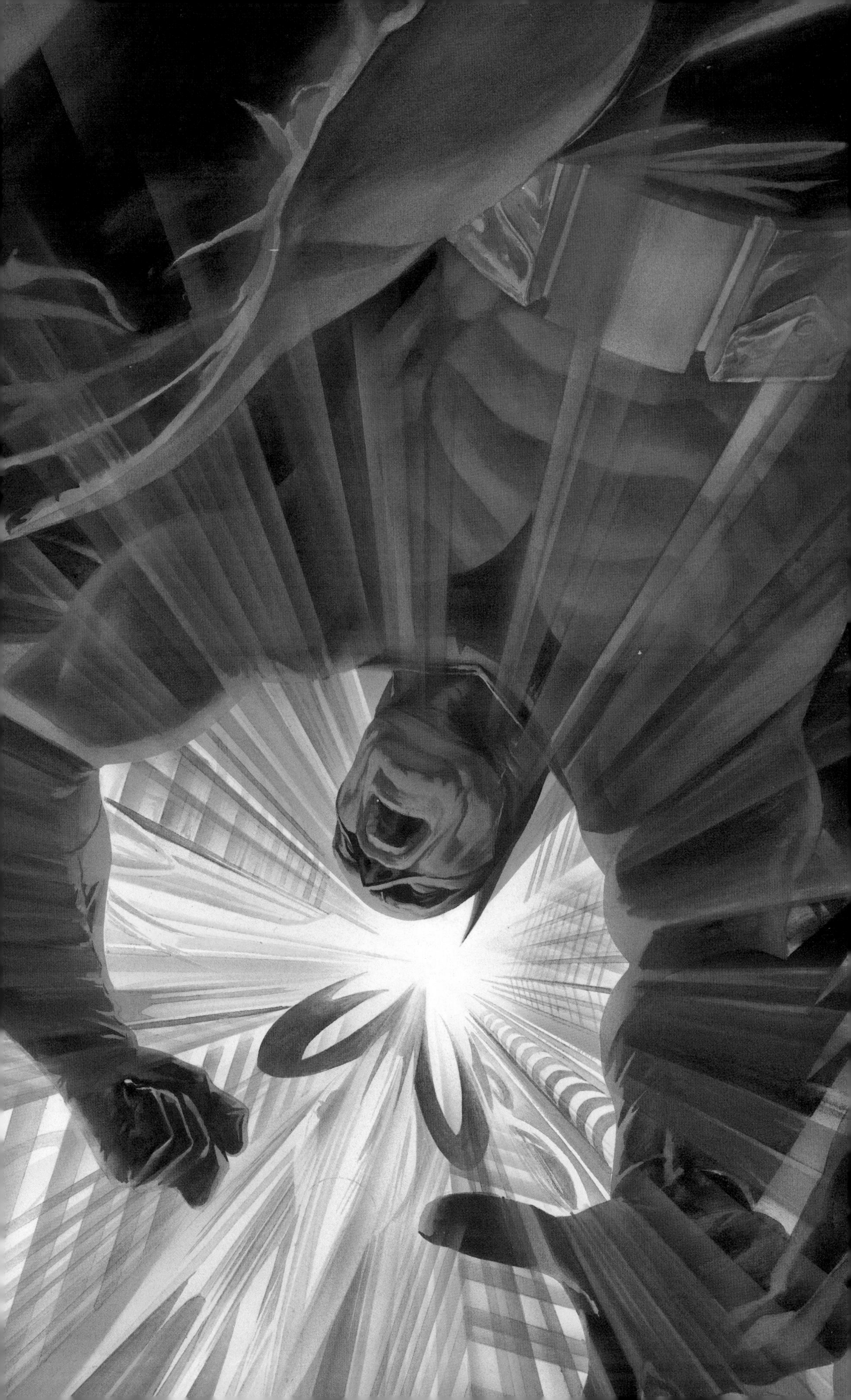

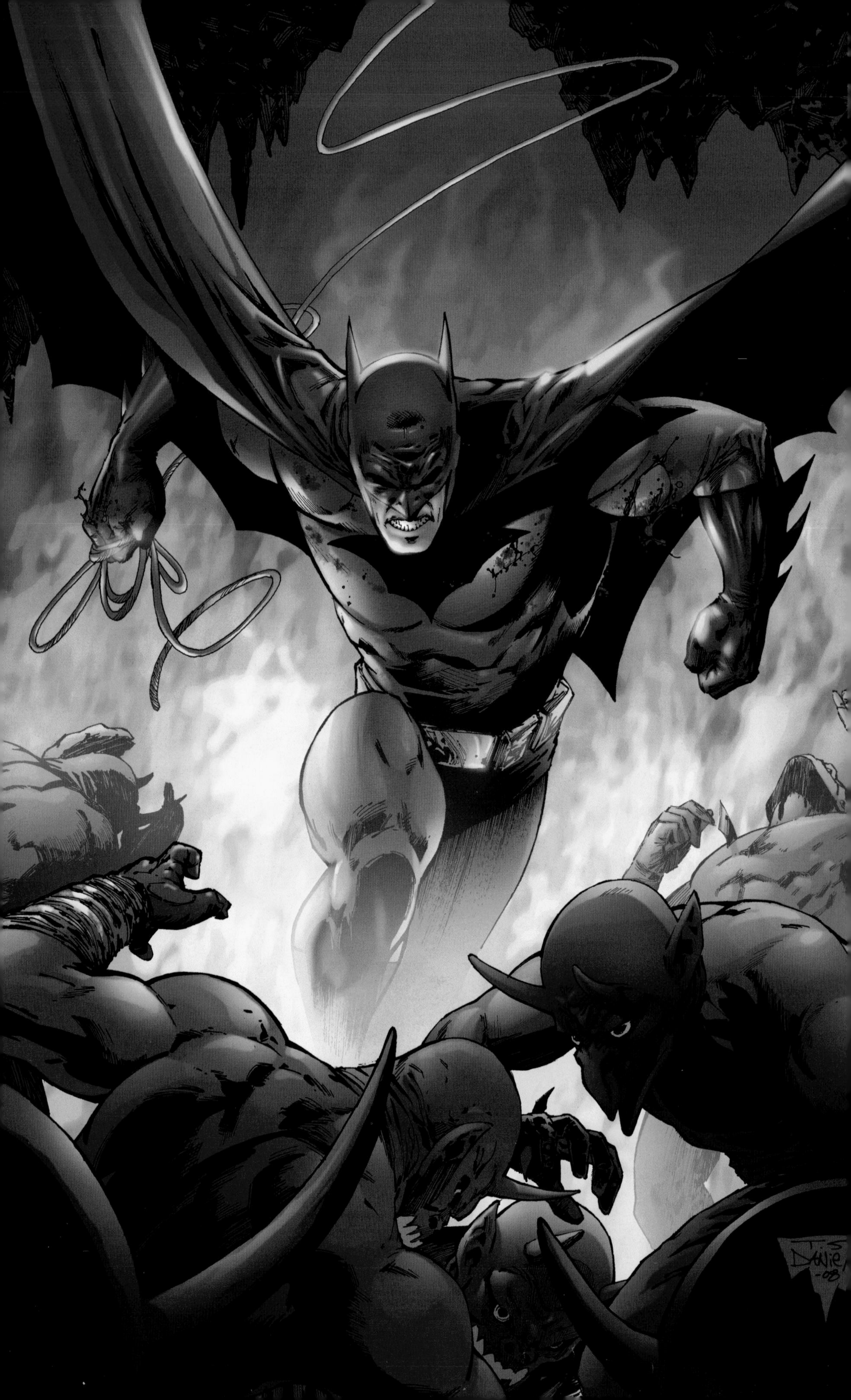

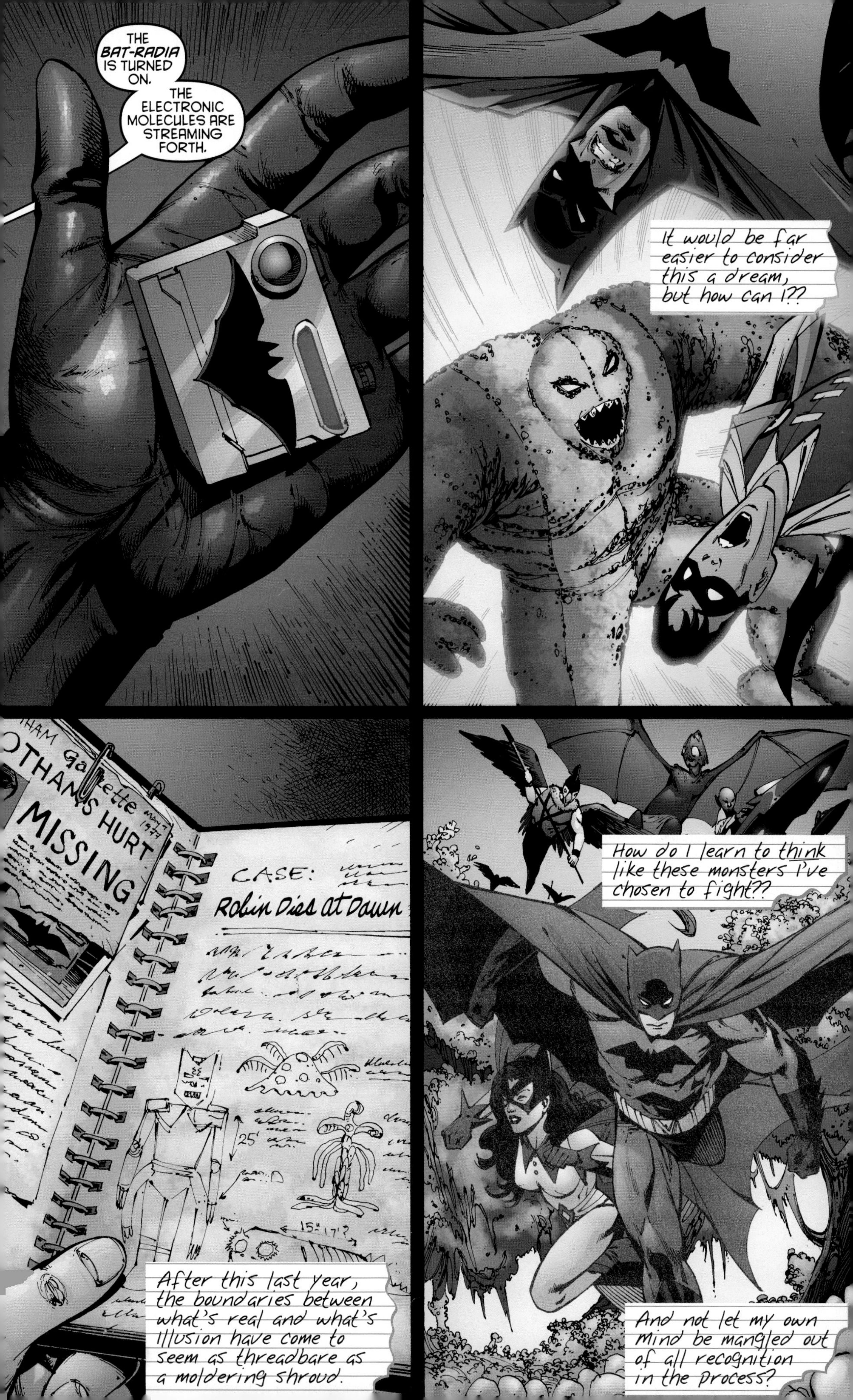
THE *BAT-RADIA* IS TURNED ON.
THE ELECTRONIC MOLECULES ARE STREAMING FORTH.
It would be far easier to consider this a dream, but how can I??
MISSING
CASE:
Robin Dies at Dawn
25'
15" 17'?
After this last year, the boundaries between what's real and what's illusion have come to seem as threadbare as a moldering shroud.
How do I learn to think like these monsters I've chosen to fight??
And not let my own mind be mangled out of all recognition in the process?

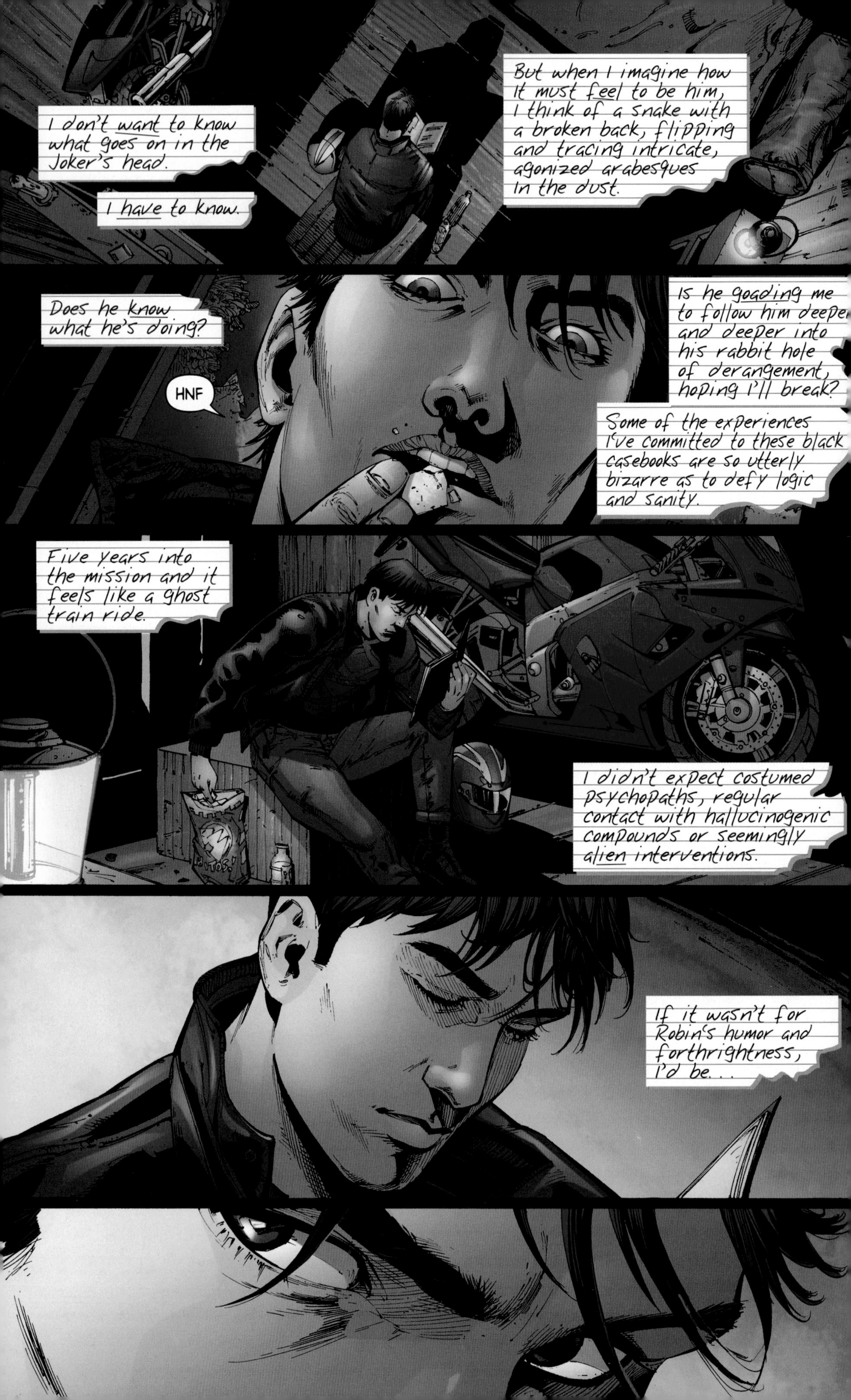
I don't want to know what goes on in the Joker's head.
I have to know.
But when I imagine how it must feel to be him, I think of a snake with a broken back, flipping and tracing intricate, agonized arabesques in the dust.
Does he know what he's doing?
HNF
Is he goading me to follow him deeper and deeper into his rabbit hole of derangement, hoping I'll break?
Some of the experiences I've committed to these black casebooks are so utterly bizarre as to defy logic and sanity.
Five years into the mission and it feels like a ghost train ride.
I didn't expect costumed psychopaths, regular contact with hallucinogenic compounds or seemingly alien interventions.
If it wasn't for Robin's humor and forthrightness, I'd be. . .

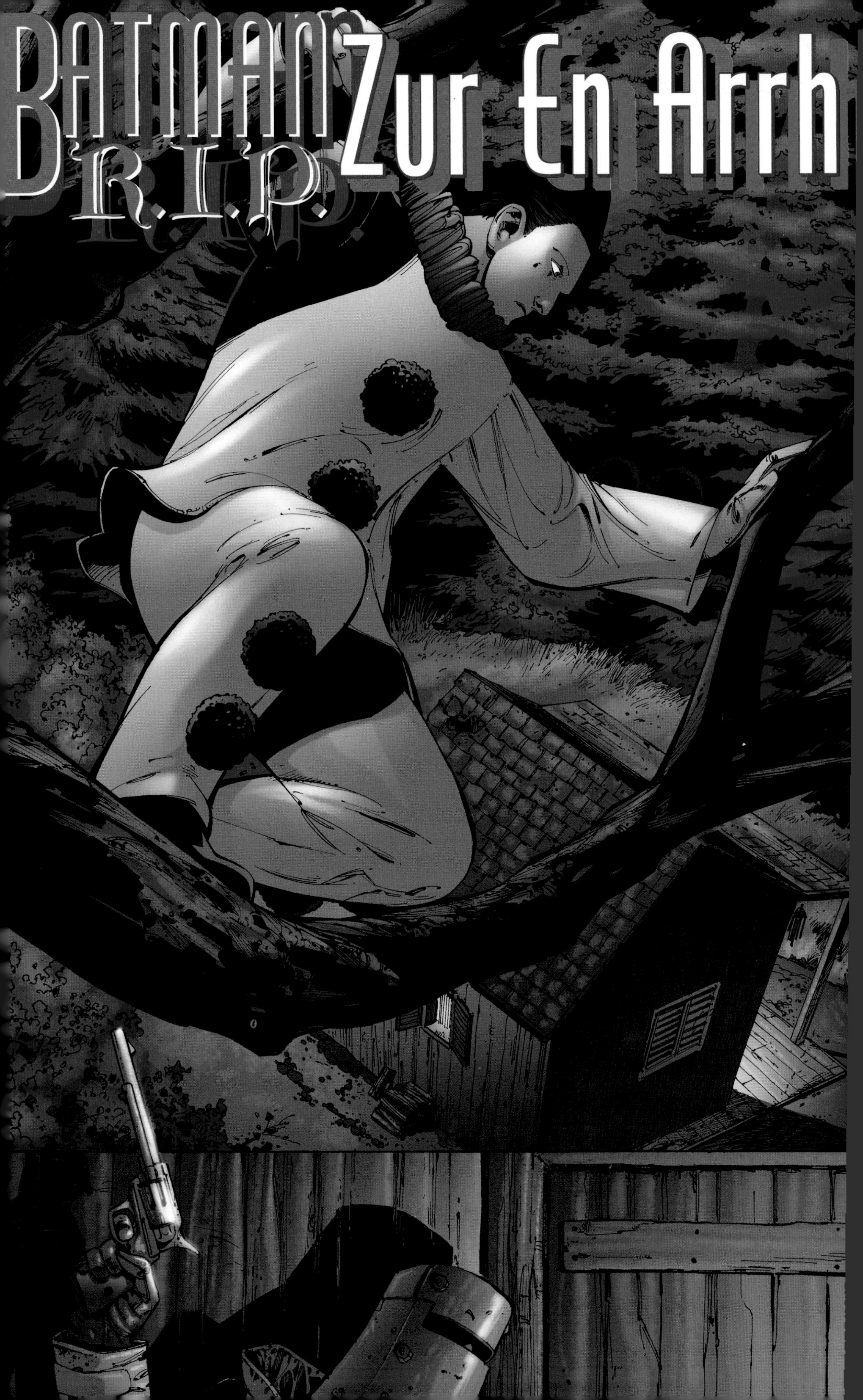
BATMAN R.I.P.
Zur En Arrh

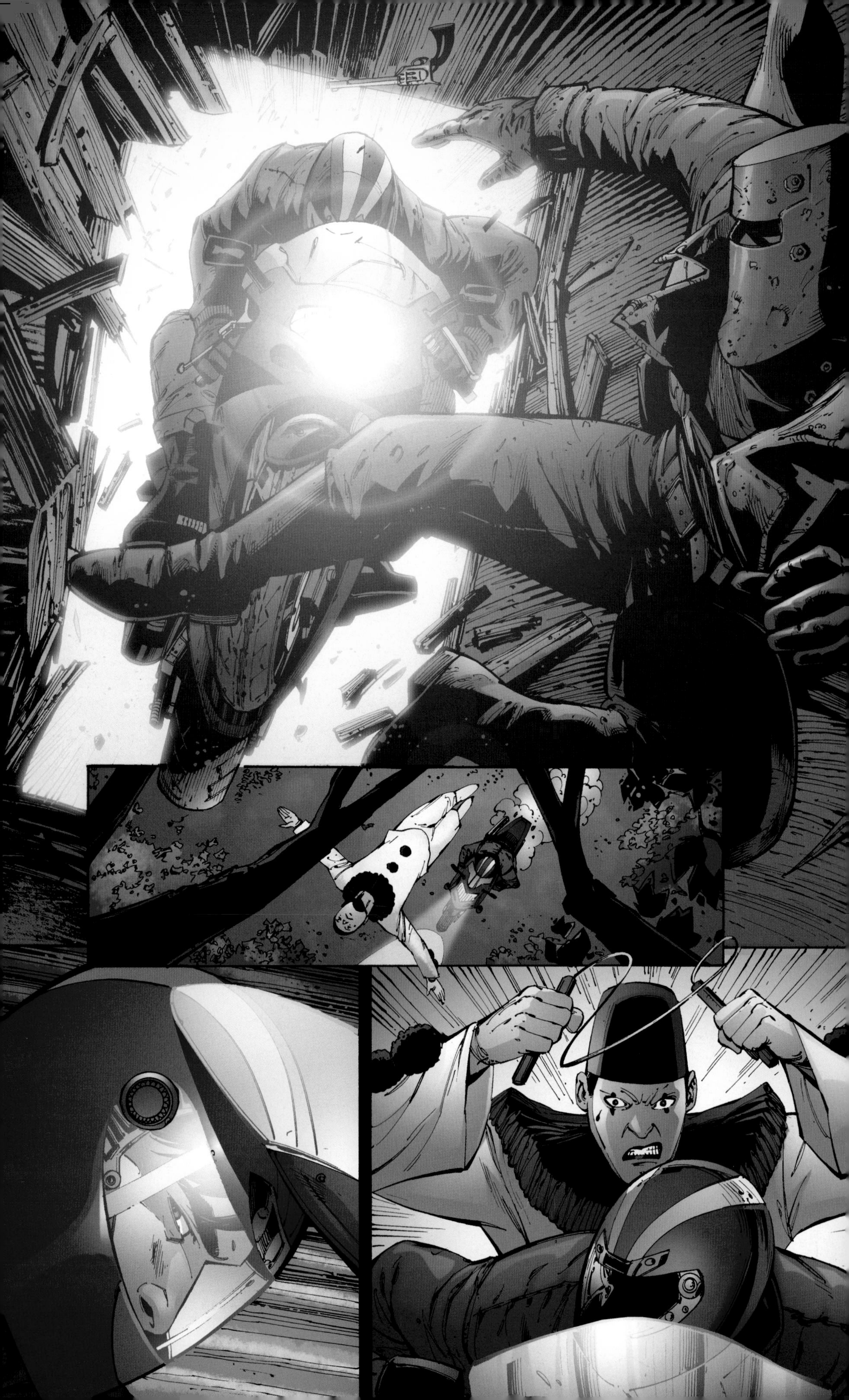

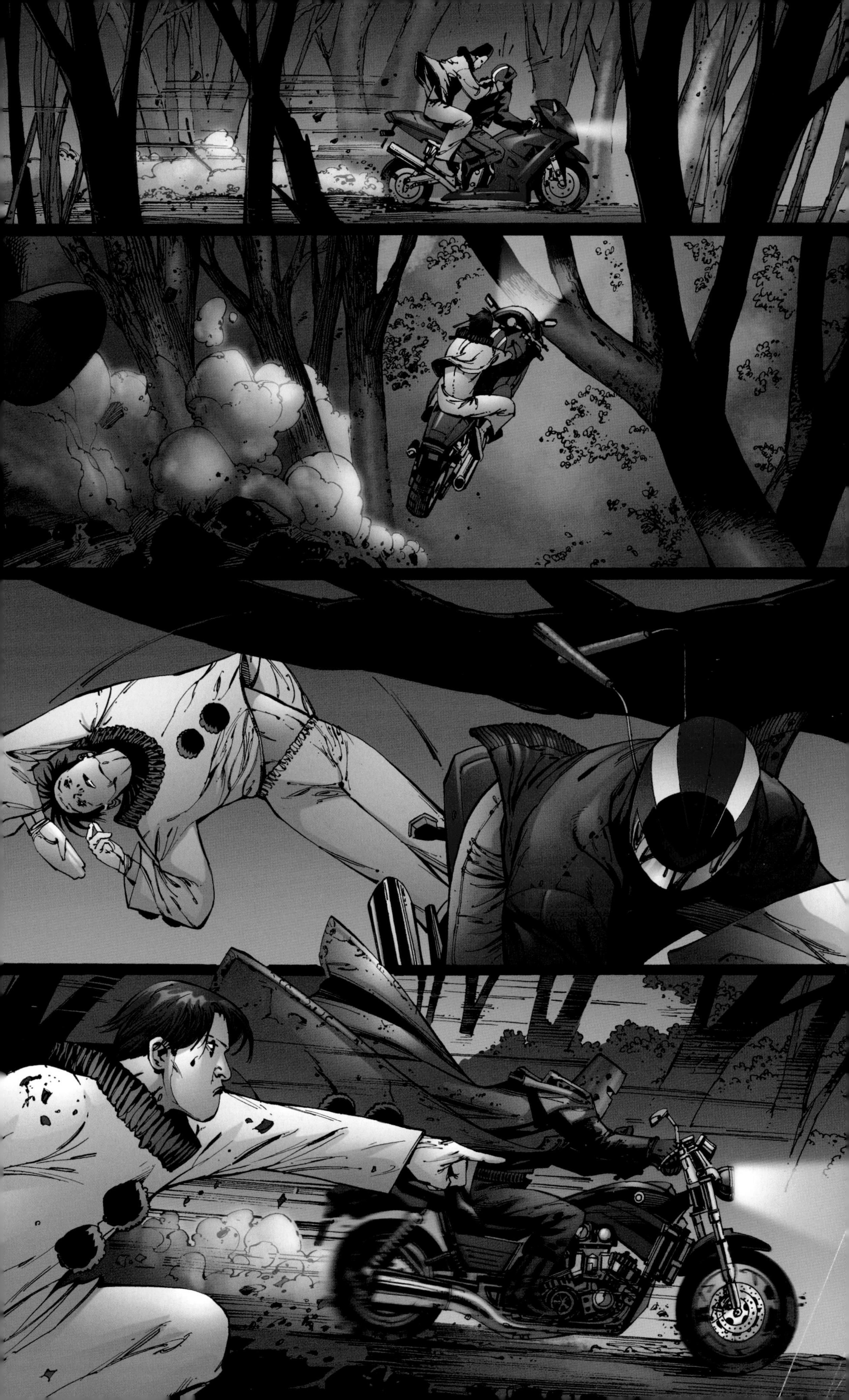

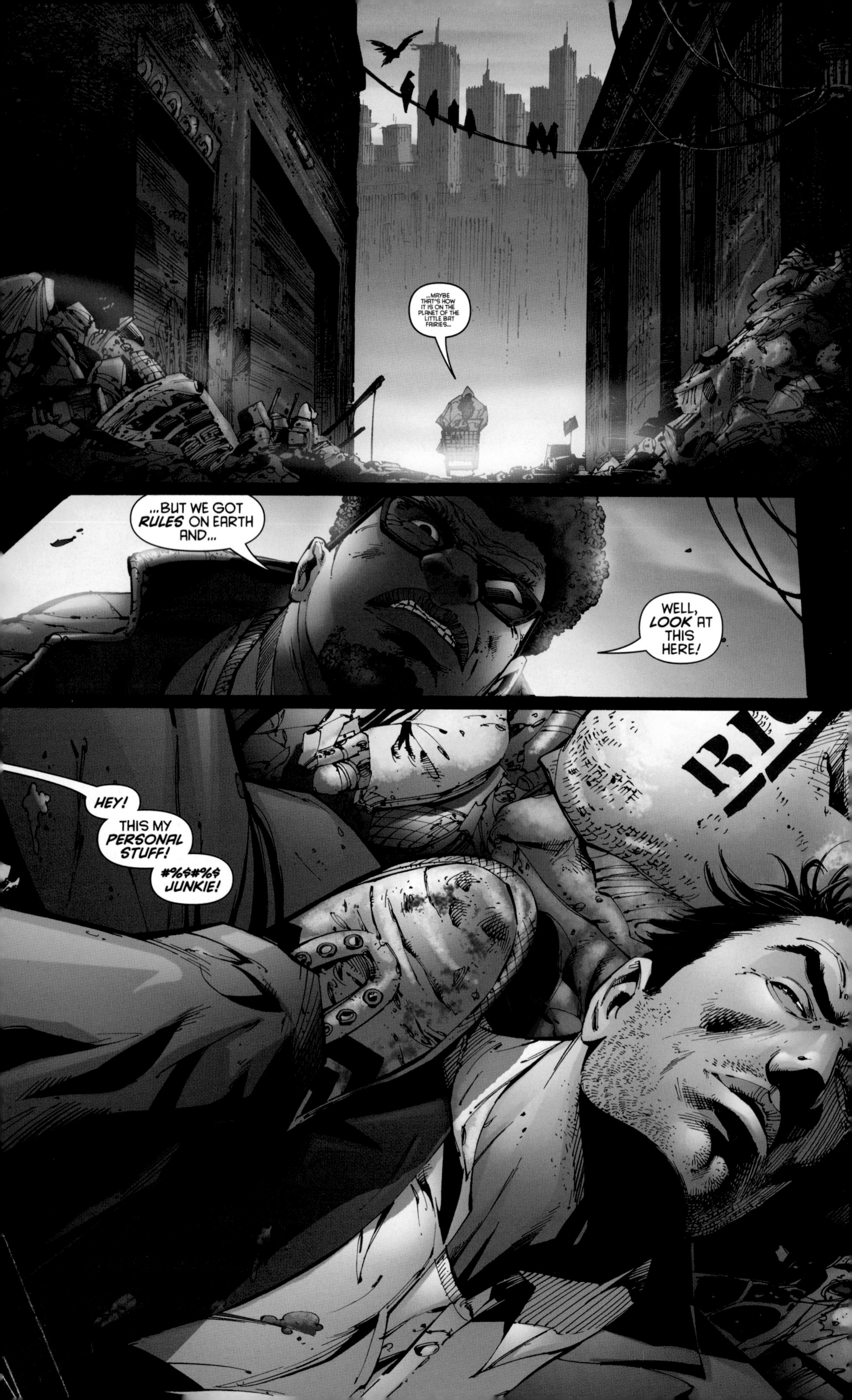
...MAYBE THAT'S HOW IT IS ON THE PLANET OF THE LITTLE BAT FAIRIES...
...BUT WE GOT RULES ON EARTH AND...
WELL, LOOK AT THIS HERE!
HEY! THIS MY PERSONAL STUFF! #%$#%$ JUNKIE!

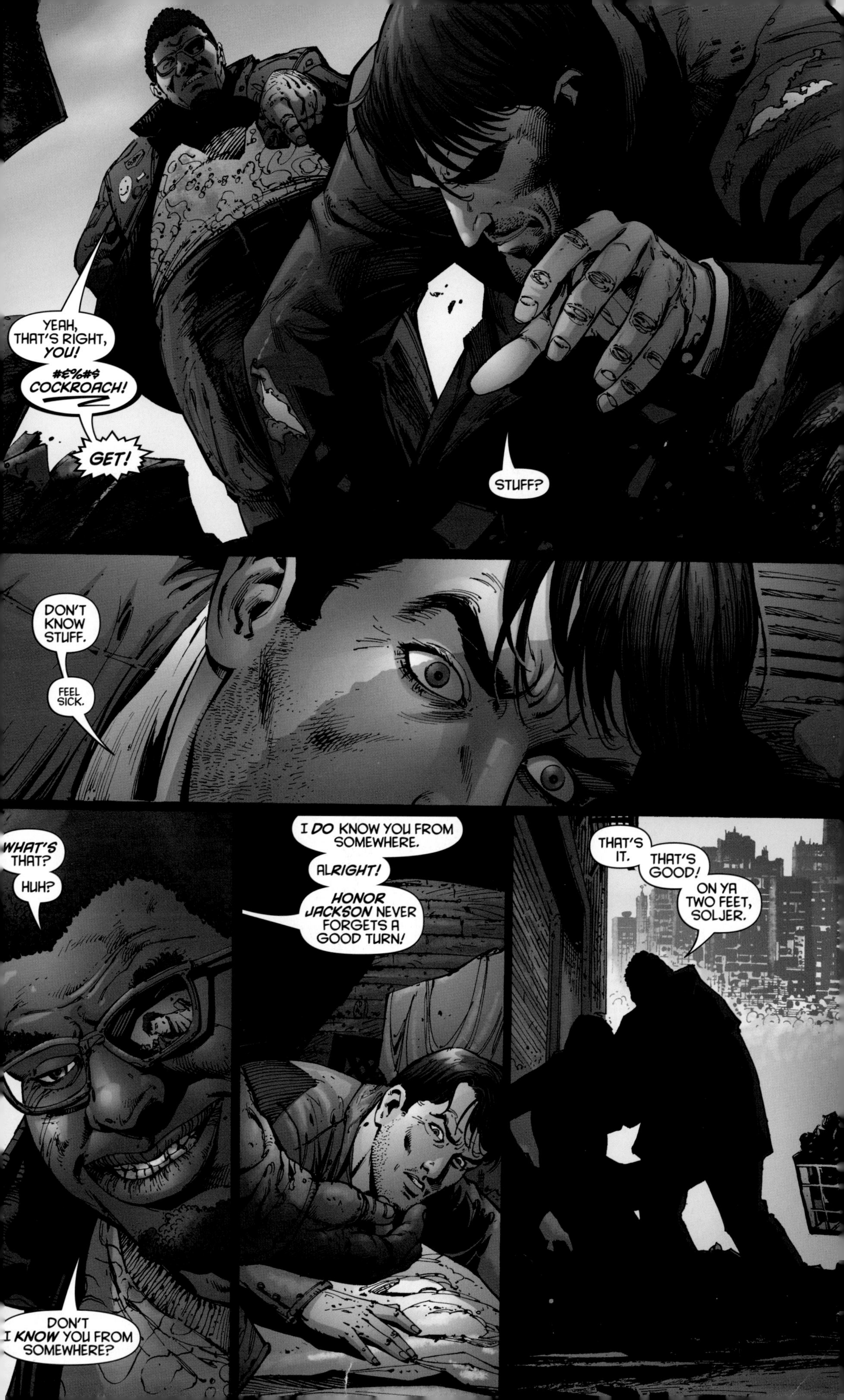
YEAH, THAT'S RIGHT, YOU!
#£%#$ COCKROACH!
GET!
STUFF?
DON'T KNOW STUFF.
FEEL SICK.
WHAT'S THAT?
HUH?
DON'T I KNOW YOU FROM SOMEWHERE?
I DO KNOW YOU FROM SOMEWHERE.
ALRIGHT!
HONOR JACKSON NEVER FORGETS A GOOD TURN!
THAT'S IT.
THAT'S GOOD!
ON YA TWO FEET, SOLJER.

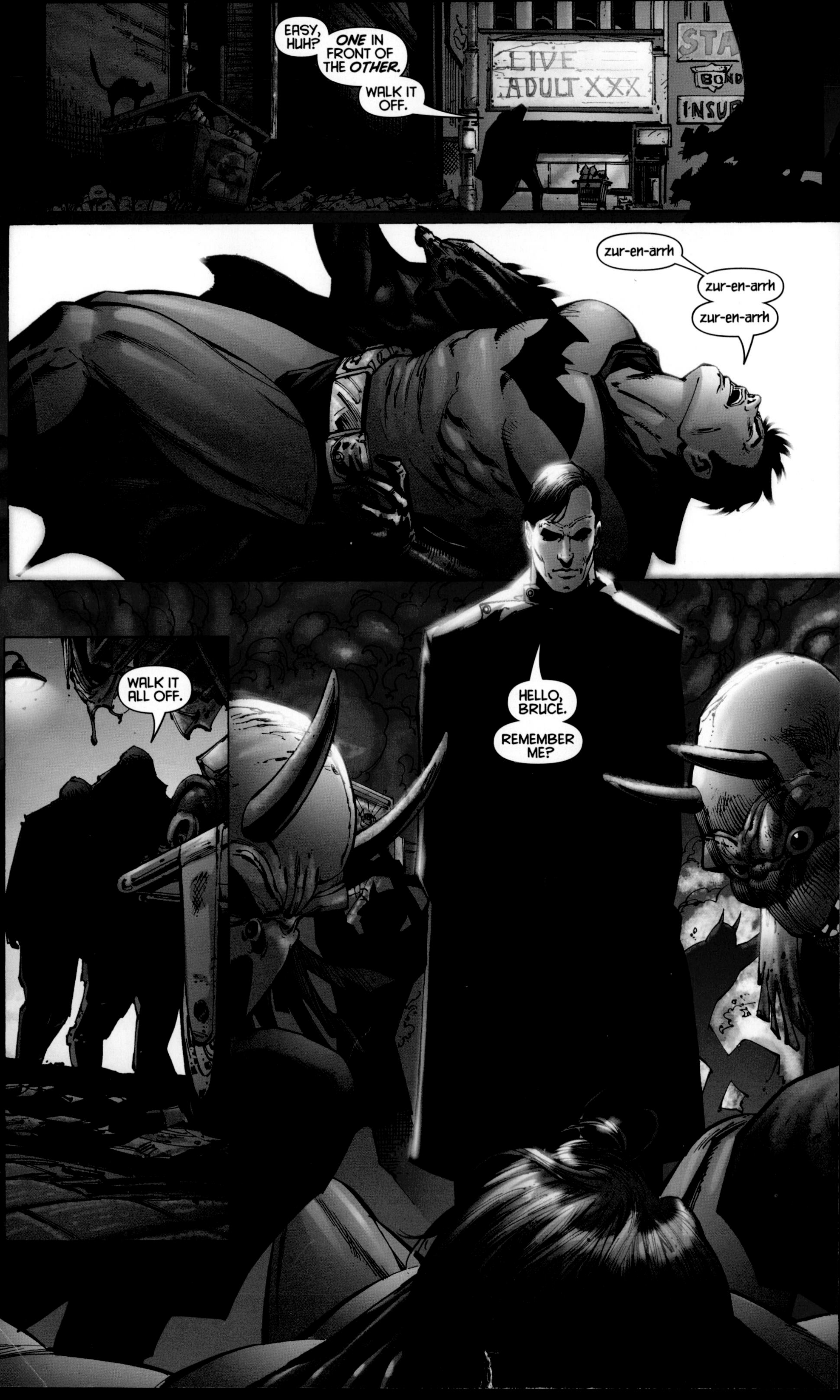

EASY, HUH? *ONE* IN FRONT OF THE *OTHER.*
WALK IT OFF.
LIVE ADULT XXX
zur-en-arrh
zur-en-arrh
zur-en-arrh
WALK IT ALL OFF.
HELLO, BRUCE.
REMEMBER ME?

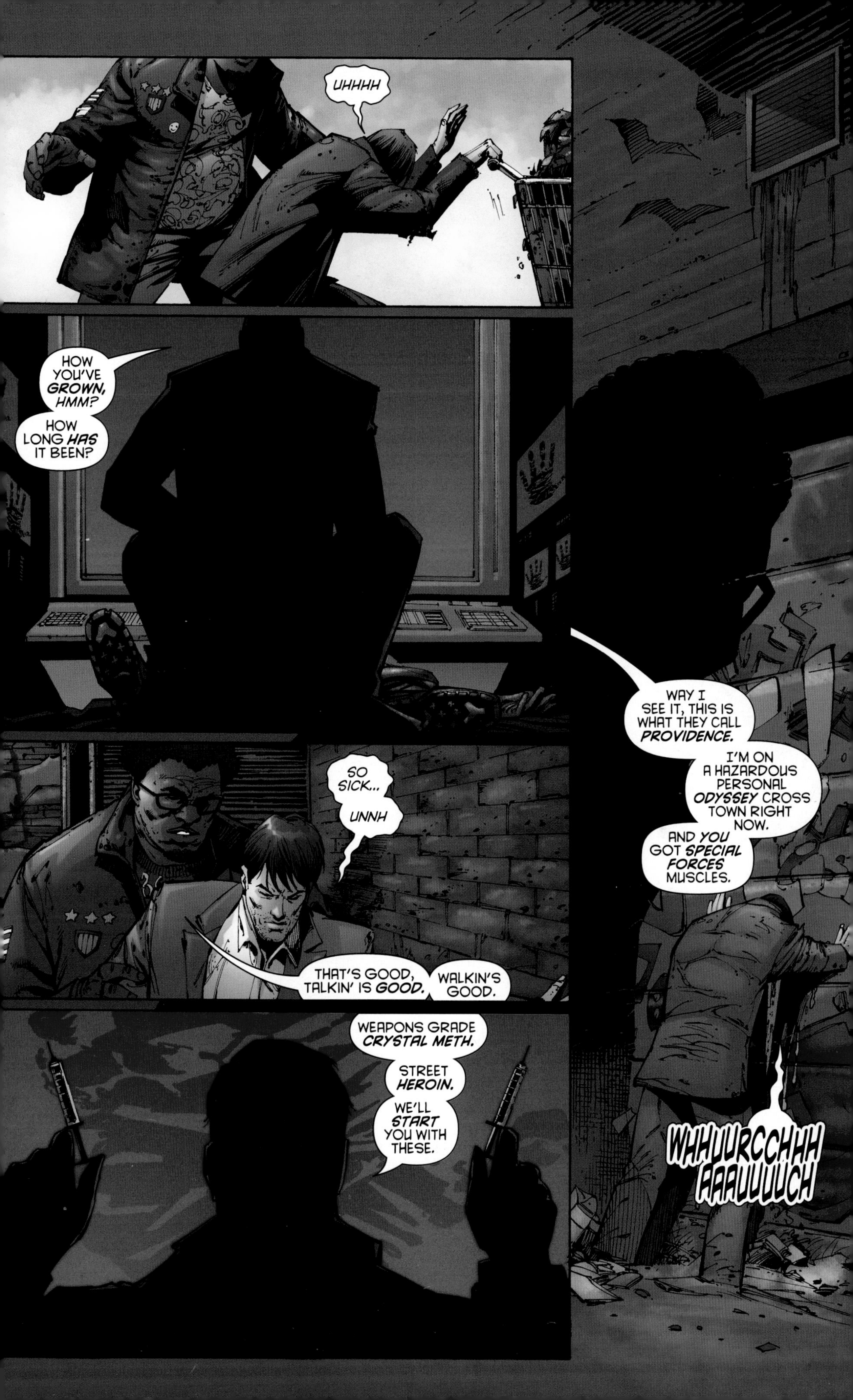
UHHHH
HOW YOU'VE GROWN, HMM?
HOW LONG HAS IT BEEN?
SO SICK...
UNNH
THAT'S GOOD, TALKIN' IS GOOD.
WALKIN'S GOOD.
WEAPONS GRADE CRYSTAL METH.
STREET HEROIN.
WE'LL START YOU WITH THESE.
WAY I SEE IT, THIS IS WHAT THEY CALL PROVIDENCE.
I'M ON A HAZARDOUS PERSONAL ODYSSEY CROSS TOWN RIGHT NOW.
AND YOU GOT SPECIAL FORCES MUSCLES.
WHHUURCCHHH AAAUUUUCH

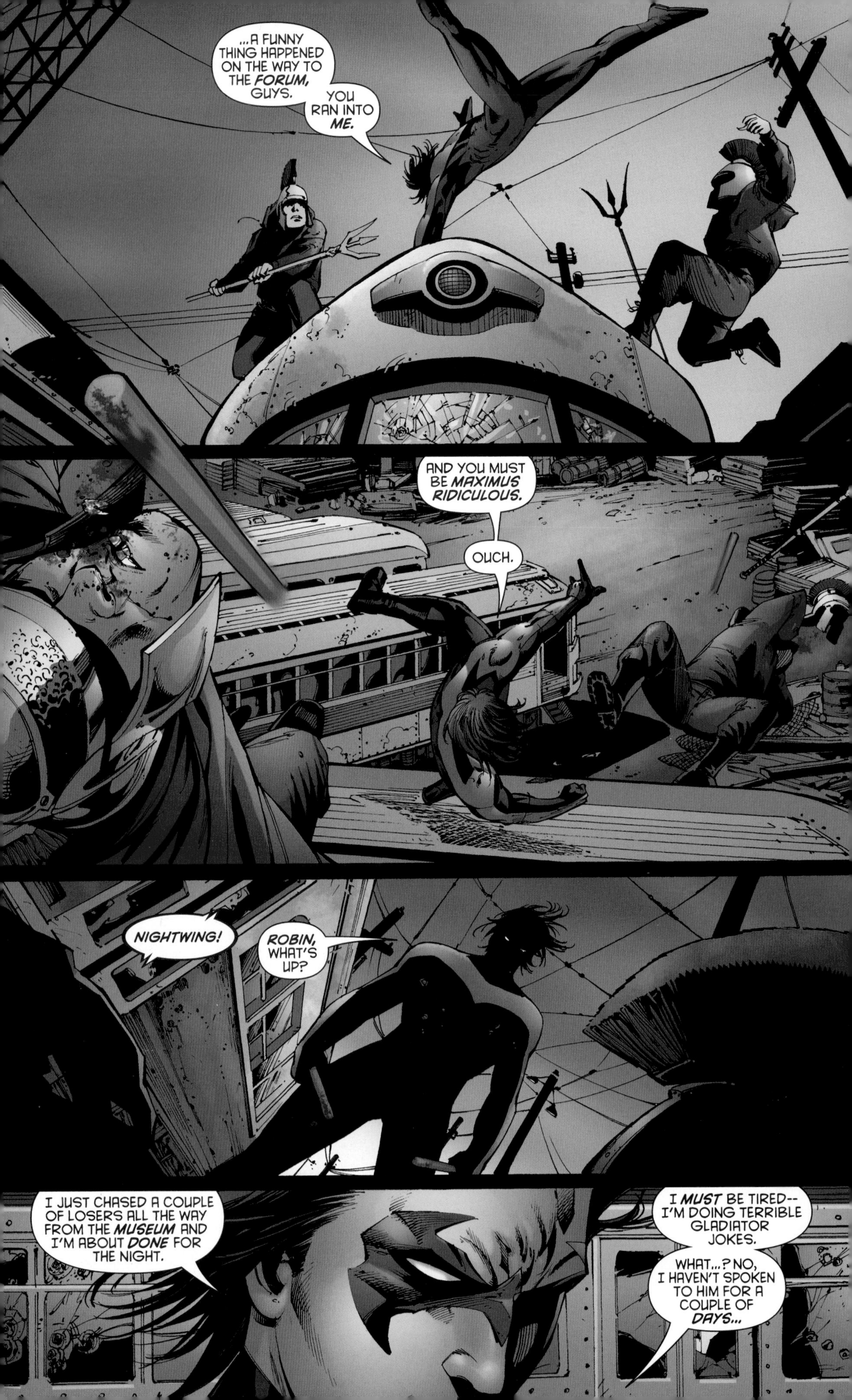
...A FUNNY THING HAPPENED ON THE WAY TO THE FORUM, GUYS.
YOU RAN INTO ME.
AND YOU MUST BE MAXIMUS RIDICULOUS.
OUCH.
NIGHTWING!
ROBIN, WHAT'S UP?
I JUST CHASED A COUPLE OF LOSERS ALL THE WAY FROM THE MUSEUM AND I'M ABOUT DONE FOR THE NIGHT.
I MUST BE TIRED-- I'M DOING TERRIBLE GLADIATOR JOKES.
WHAT...? NO, I HAVEN'T SPOKEN TO HIM FOR A COUPLE OF DAYS...

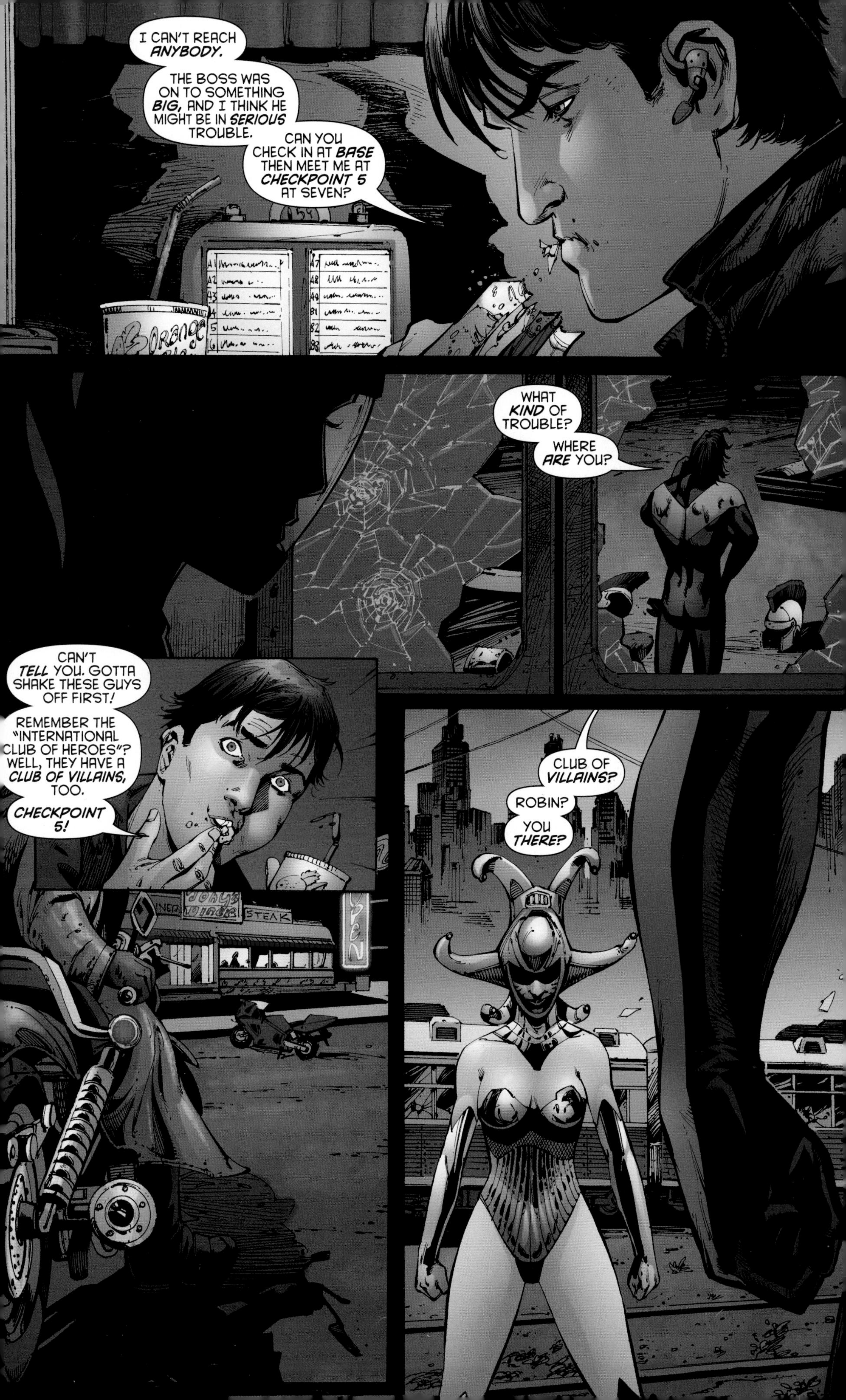
I CAN'T REACH *ANYBODY.*
THE BOSS WAS ON TO SOMETHING *BIG,* AND I THINK HE MIGHT BE IN *SERIOUS* TROUBLE.
CAN YOU CHECK IN AT *BASE* THEN MEET ME AT *CHECKPOINT 5* AT SEVEN?
WHAT *KIND* OF TROUBLE?
WHERE *ARE* YOU?
CAN'T *TELL* YOU. GOTTA SHAKE THESE GUYS OFF FIRST!
REMEMBER THE "INTERNATIONAL CLUB OF HEROES"? WELL, THEY HAVE A *CLUB OF VILLAINS,* TOO.
CHECKPOINT 5!
CLUB OF *VILLAINS?*
ROBIN?
YOU *THERE?*
STEAK
OPEN

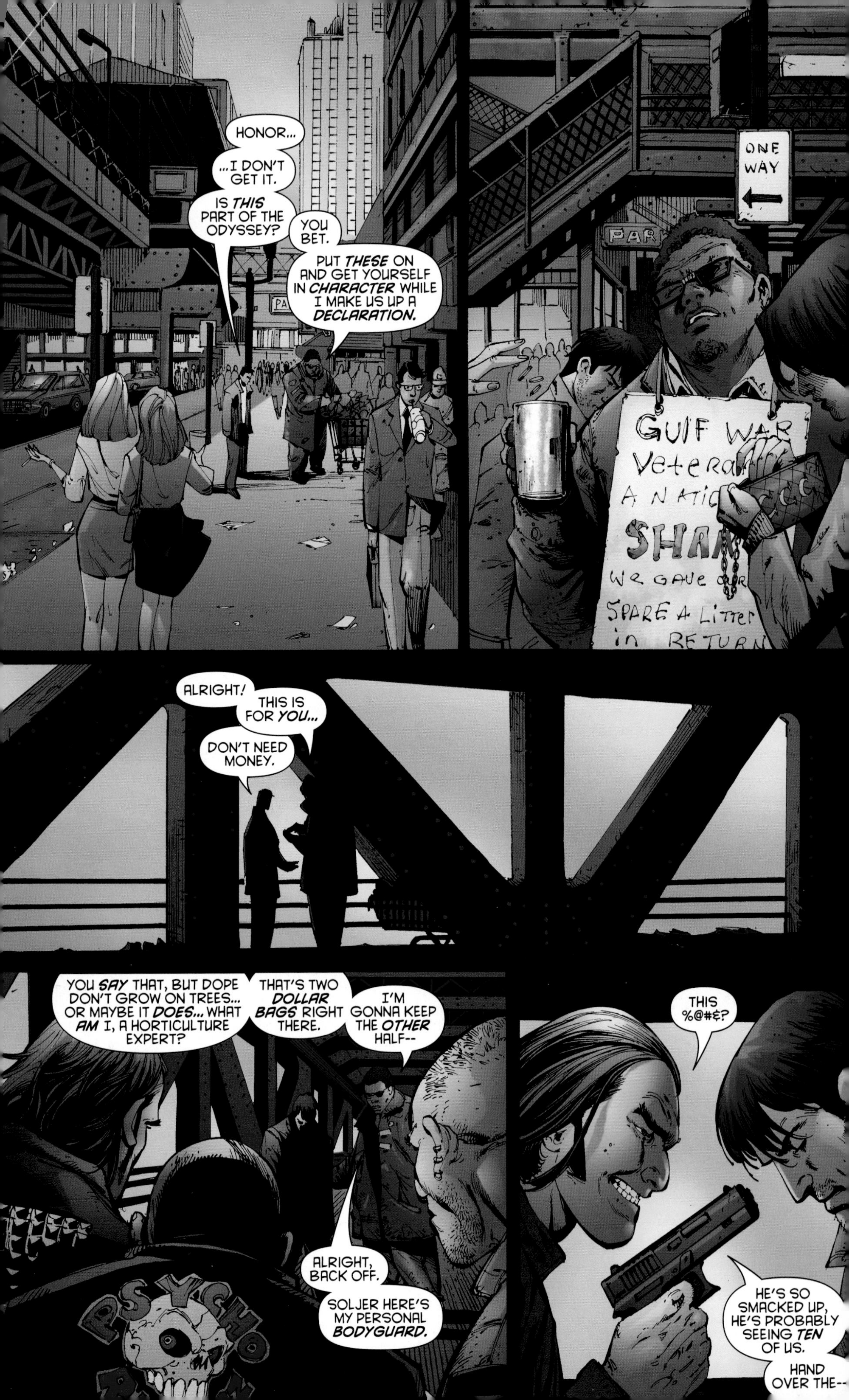
HONOR...
...I DON'T GET IT.
IS THIS PART OF THE ODYSSEY?
YOU BET.
PUT THESE ON AND GET YOURSELF IN CHARACTER WHILE I MAKE US UP A DECLARATION.
ONE WAY
GULF WAR
Veteran
SPARE A Litter
ALRIGHT!
THIS IS FOR YOU...
DON'T NEED MONEY.
YOU SAY THAT, BUT DOPE DON'T GROW ON TREES... OR MAYBE IT DOES... WHAT AM I, A HORTICULTURE EXPERT?
THAT'S TWO DOLLAR BAGS RIGHT THERE.
I'M GONNA KEEP THE OTHER HALF--
ALRIGHT, BACK OFF.
SOLJER HERE'S MY PERSONAL BODYGUARD.
PSYCHO
THIS %@#&?
HE'S SO SMACKED UP, HE'S PROBABLY SEEING TEN OF US.
HAND OVER THE--

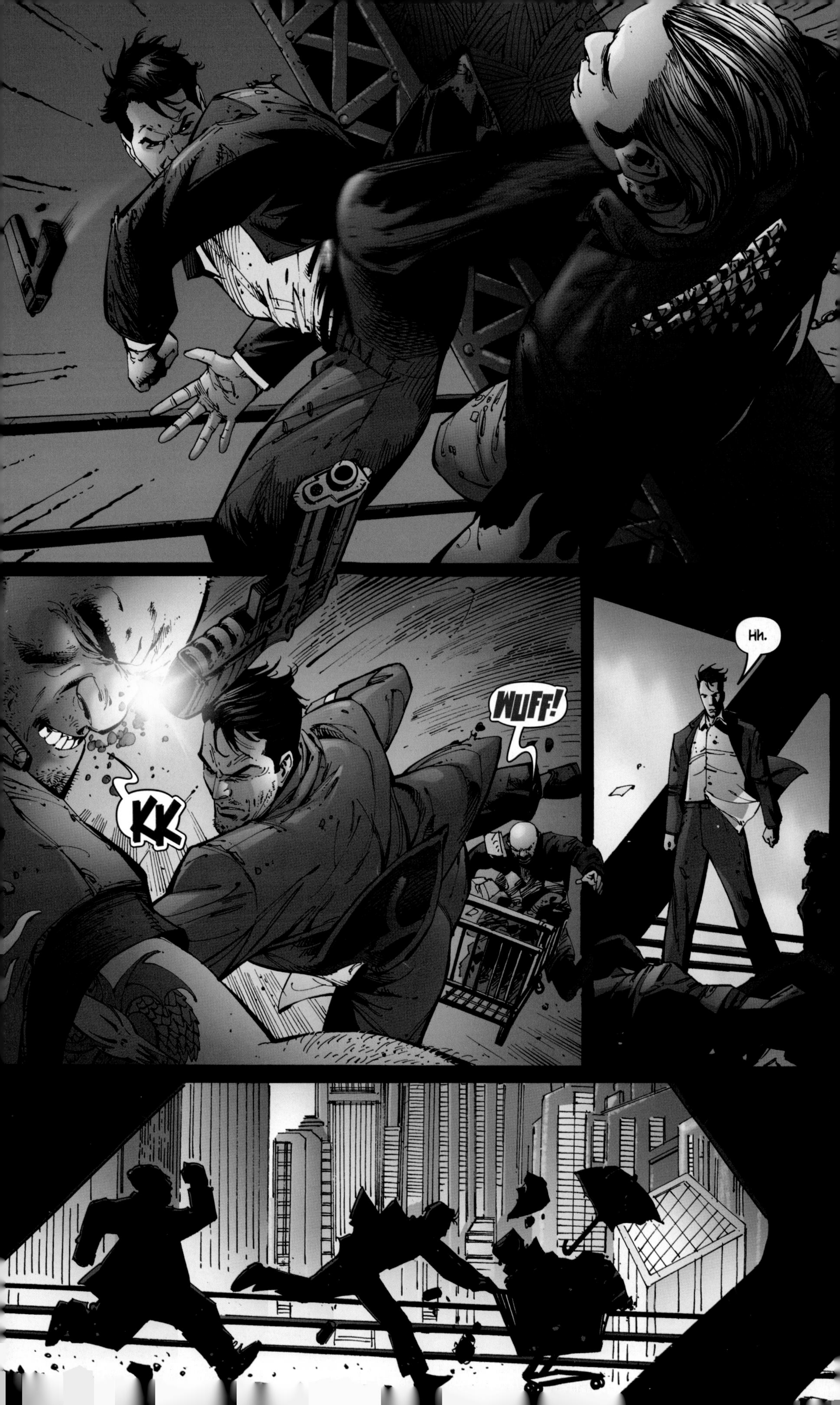

KK
WUFF!
Hh.

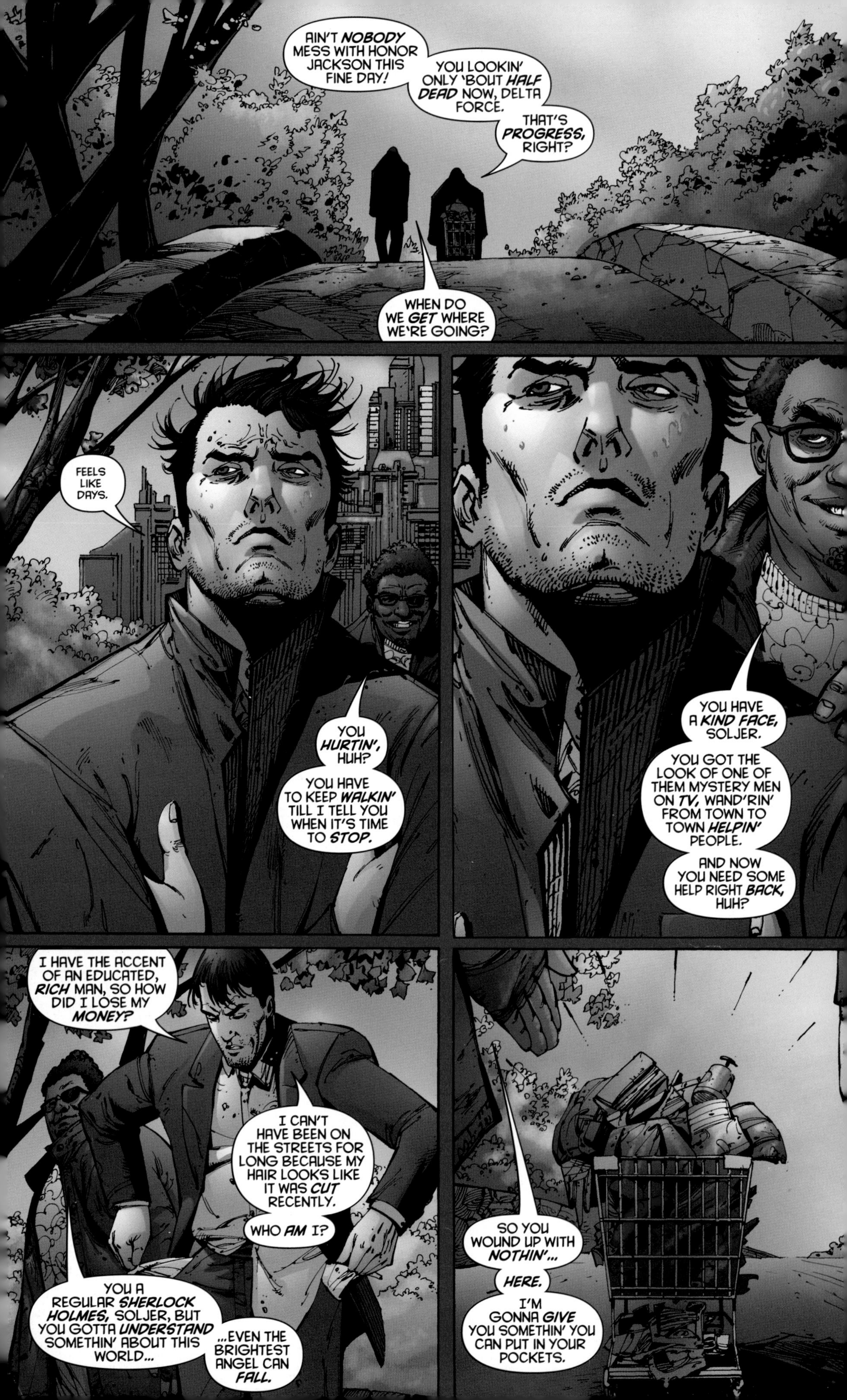
AIN'T NOBODY MESS WITH HONOR JACKSON THIS FINE DAY!
YOU LOOKIN' ONLY 'BOUT HALF DEAD NOW, DELTA FORCE.
THAT'S PROGRESS, RIGHT?
WHEN DO WE GET WHERE WE'RE GOING?
FEELS LIKE DAYS.
YOU HURTIN', HUH?
YOU HAVE TO KEEP WALKIN' TILL I TELL YOU WHEN IT'S TIME TO STOP.
YOU HAVE A KIND FACE, SOLJER.
YOU GOT THE LOOK OF ONE OF THEM MYSTERY MEN ON TV, WAND'RIN' FROM TOWN TO TOWN HELPIN' PEOPLE.
AND NOW YOU NEED SOME HELP RIGHT BACK, HUH?
I HAVE THE ACCENT OF AN EDUCATED, RICH MAN, SO HOW DID I LOSE MY MONEY?
I CAN'T HAVE BEEN ON THE STREETS FOR LONG BECAUSE MY HAIR LOOKS LIKE IT WAS CUT RECENTLY.
WHO AM I?
YOU A REGULAR SHERLOCK HOLMES, SOLJER, BUT YOU GOTTA UNDERSTAND SOMETHIN' ABOUT THIS WORLD...
...EVEN THE BRIGHTEST ANGEL CAN FALL.
SO YOU WOUND UP WITH NOTHIN'...
HERE.
I'M GONNA GIVE YOU SOMETHIN' YOU CAN PUT IN YOUR POCKETS.

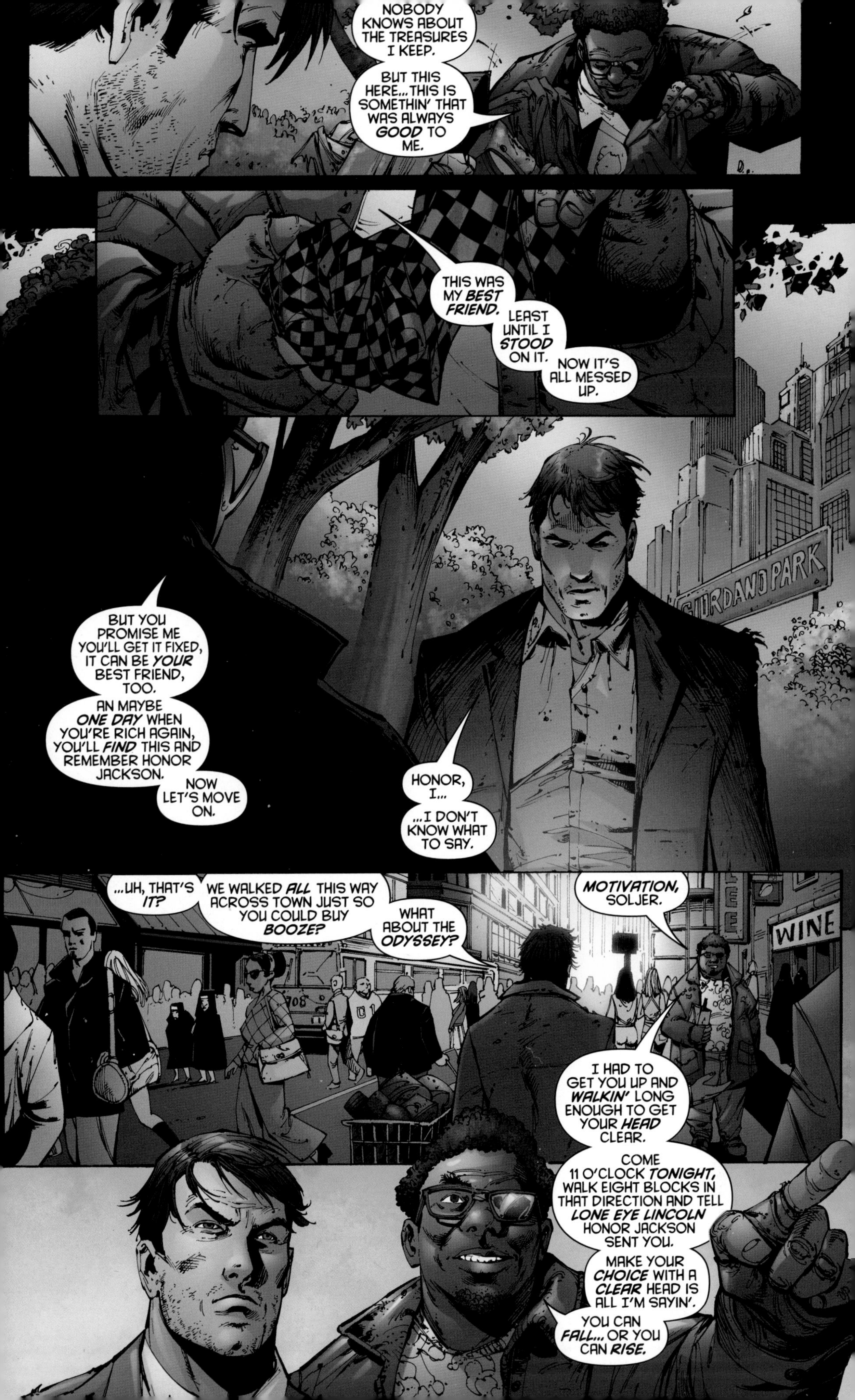
NOBODY KNOWS ABOUT THE TREASURES I KEEP.
BUT THIS HERE... THIS IS SOMETHIN' THAT WAS ALWAYS GOOD TO ME.
THIS WAS MY BEST FRIEND.
LEAST UNTIL I STOOD ON IT.
NOW IT'S ALL MESSED UP.
GIORDANO PARK
BUT YOU PROMISE ME YOU'LL GET IT FIXED, IT CAN BE YOUR BEST FRIEND, TOO.
AN MAYBE ONE DAY WHEN YOU'RE RICH AGAIN, YOU'LL FIND THIS AND REMEMBER HONOR JACKSON.
NOW LET'S MOVE ON.
HONOR, I...
...I DON'T KNOW WHAT TO SAY.
...UH, THAT'S IT?
WE WALKED ALL THIS WAY ACROSS TOWN JUST SO YOU COULD BUY BOOZE?
WHAT ABOUT THE ODYSSEY?
MOTIVATION, SOLJER.
WINE
I HAD TO GET YOU UP AND WALKIN' LONG ENOUGH TO GET YOUR HEAD CLEAR.
COME 11 O'CLOCK TONIGHT, WALK EIGHT BLOCKS IN THAT DIRECTION AND TELL LONE EYE LINCOLN HONOR JACKSON SENT YOU.
MAKE YOUR CHOICE WITH A CLEAR HEAD IS ALL I'M SAYIN'.
YOU CAN FALL... OR YOU CAN RISE.

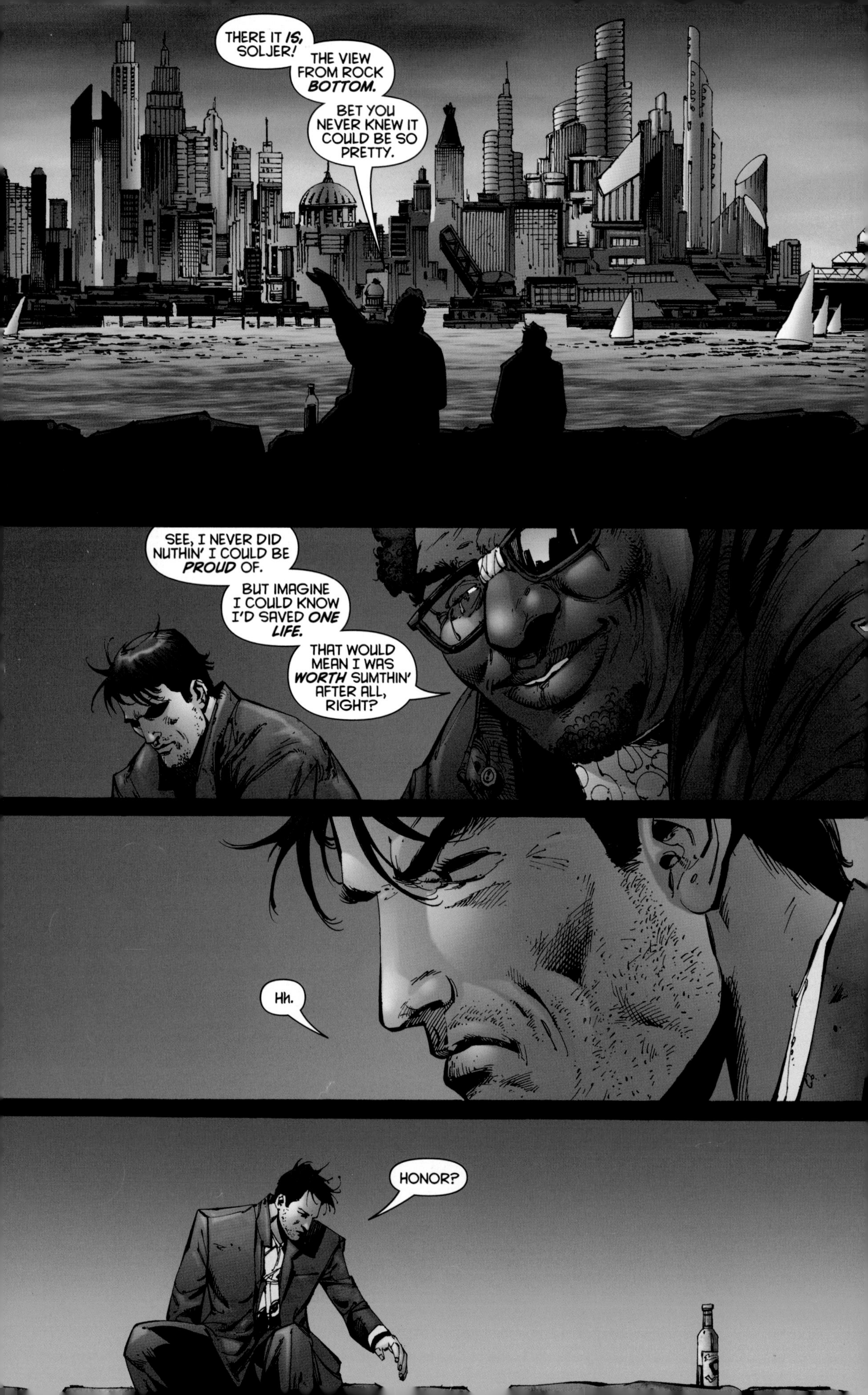
THERE IT *IS*, SOLJER!
THE VIEW FROM ROCK **BOTTOM.**
BET YOU NEVER KNEW IT COULD BE SO PRETTY.
SEE, I NEVER DID NUTHIN' I COULD BE **PROUD** OF.
BUT IMAGINE I COULD KNOW I'D SAVED **ONE LIFE.**
THAT WOULD MEAN I WAS **WORTH** SUMTHIN' AFTER ALL, RIGHT?
Hh.
HONOR?

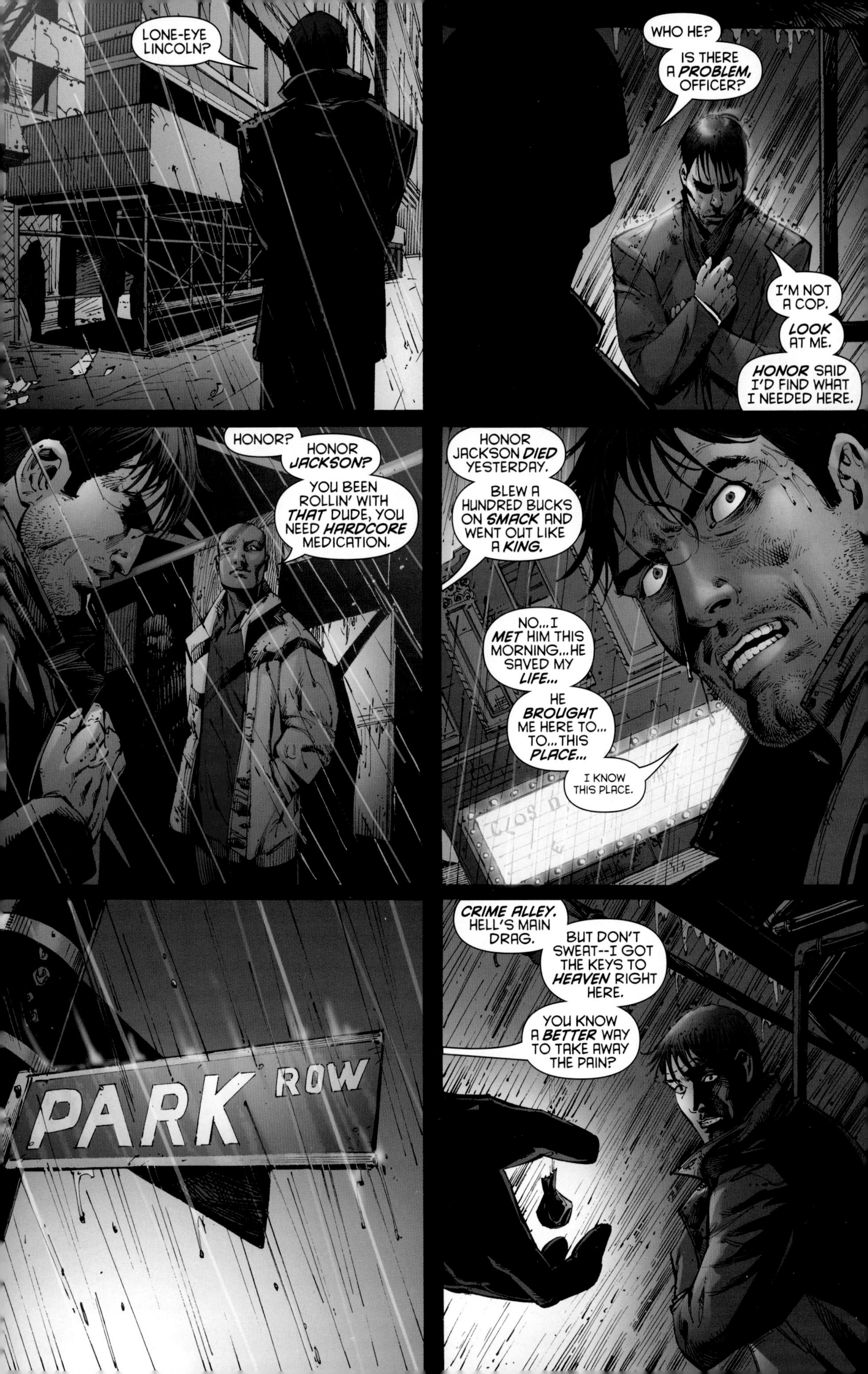
LONE-EYE LINCOLN?
WHO HE?
IS THERE A PROBLEM, OFFICER?
I'M NOT A COP.
LOOK AT ME.
HONOR SAID I'D FIND WHAT I NEEDED HERE.
HONOR?
HONOR JACKSON?
YOU BEEN ROLLIN' WITH THAT DUDE, YOU NEED HARDCORE MEDICATION.
HONOR JACKSON DIED YESTERDAY.
BLEW A HUNDRED BUCKS ON SMACK AND WENT OUT LIKE A KING.
NO...I MET HIM THIS MORNING...HE SAVED MY LIFE...
HE BROUGHT ME HERE TO... TO...THIS PLACE...
I KNOW THIS PLACE.
PARK ROW
CRIME ALLEY. HELL'S MAIN DRAG.
BUT DON'T SWEAT--I GOT THE KEYS TO HEAVEN RIGHT HERE.
YOU KNOW A BETTER WAY TO TAKE AWAY THE PAIN?

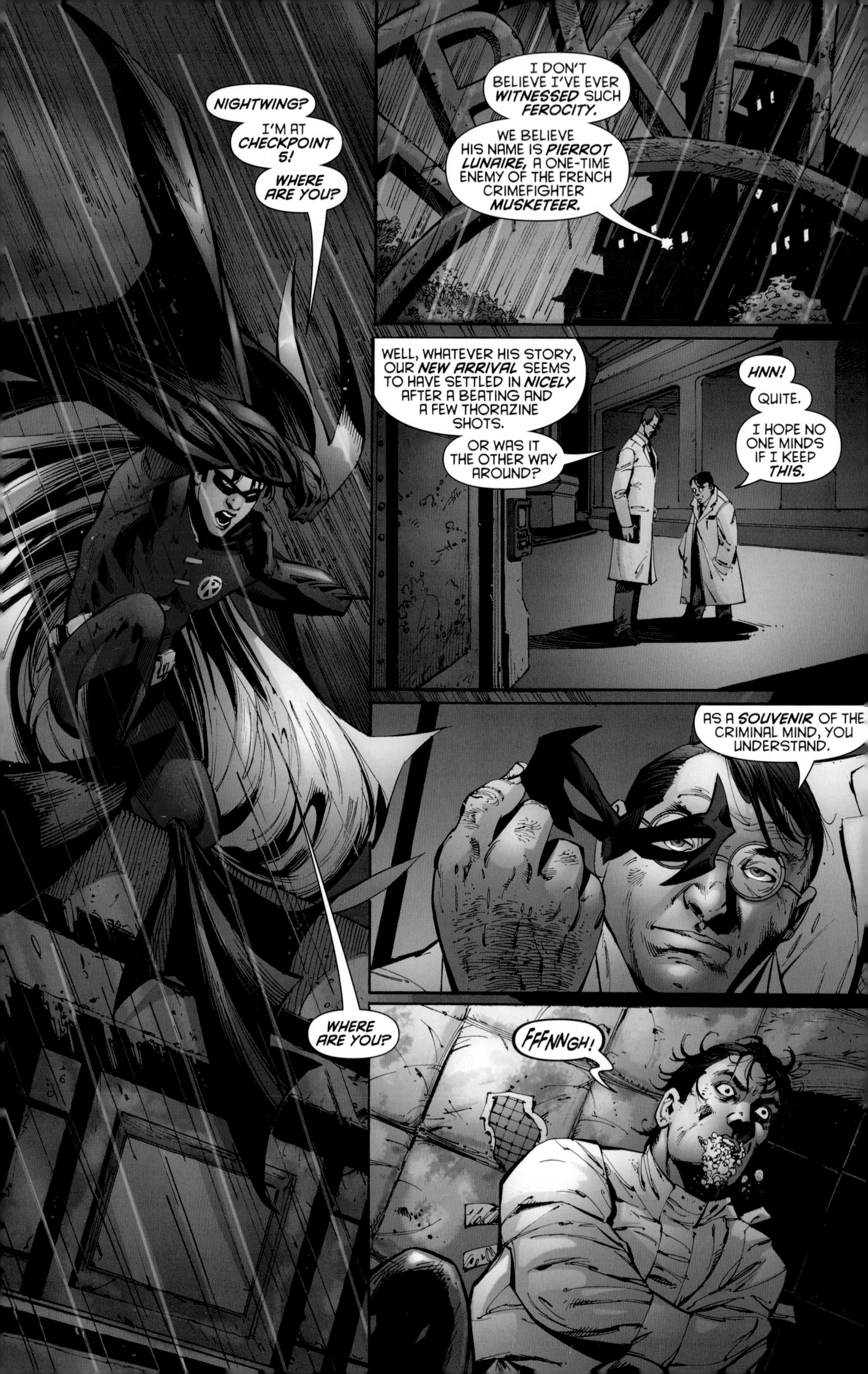
NIGHTWING?
I'M AT CHECKPOINT 5!
WHERE ARE YOU?
I DON'T BELIEVE I'VE EVER WITNESSED SUCH FEROCITY.
WE BELIEVE HIS NAME IS PIERROT LUNAIRE, A ONE-TIME ENEMY OF THE FRENCH CRIMEFIGHTER MUSKETEER.
WELL, WHATEVER HIS STORY, OUR NEW ARRIVAL SEEMS TO HAVE SETTLED IN NICELY AFTER A BEATING AND A FEW THORAZINE SHOTS.
OR WAS IT THE OTHER WAY AROUND?
HNN!
QUITE.
I HOPE NO ONE MINDS IF I KEEP THIS.
AS A SOUVENIR OF THE CRIMINAL MIND, YOU UNDERSTAND.
WHERE ARE YOU?
FFFNNGH!

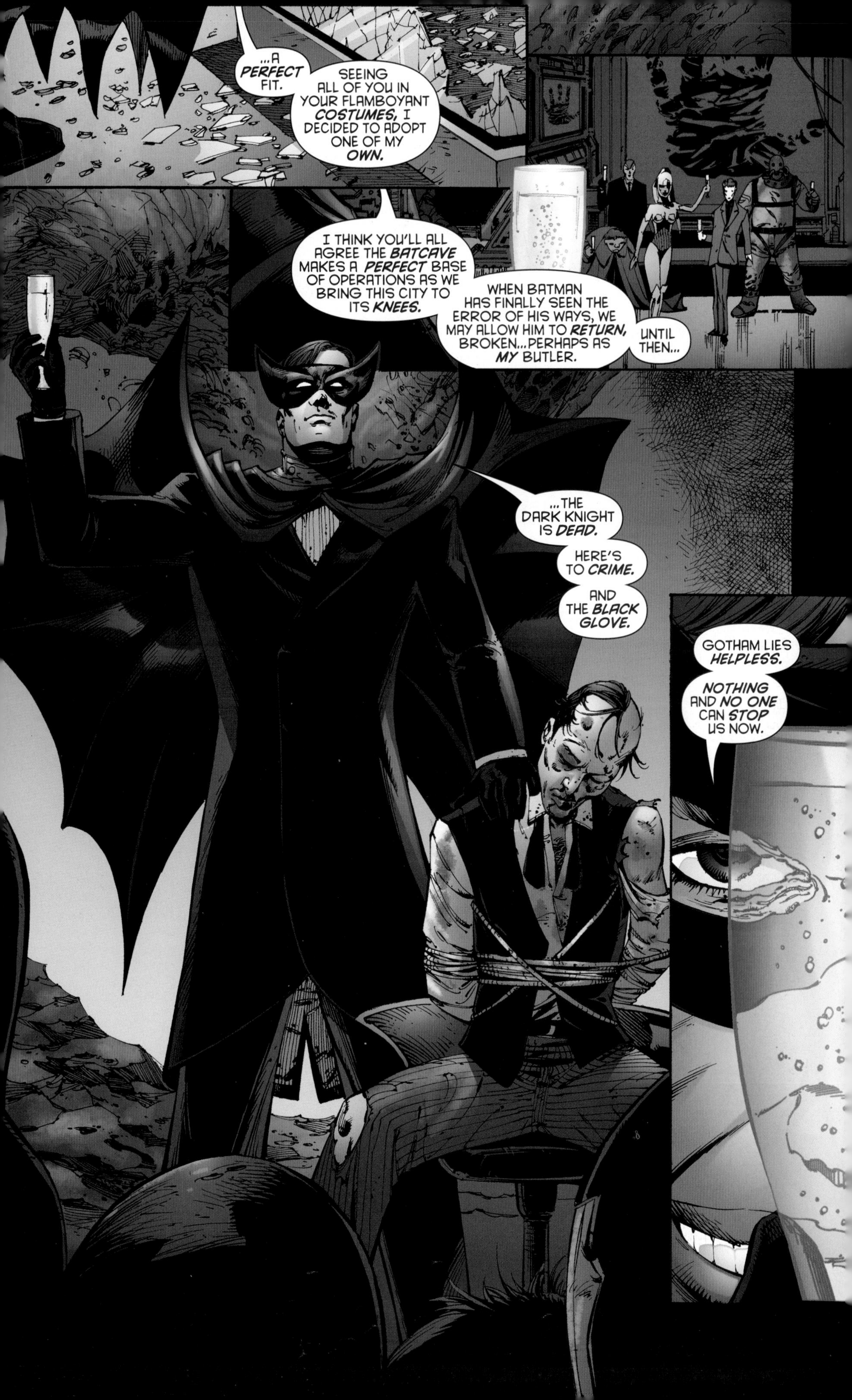
...A PERFECT FIT.
SEEING ALL OF YOU IN YOUR FLAMBOYANT COSTUMES, I DECIDED TO ADOPT ONE OF MY OWN.
I THINK YOU'LL ALL AGREE THE BATCAVE MAKES A PERFECT BASE OF OPERATIONS AS WE BRING THIS CITY TO ITS KNEES.
WHEN BATMAN HAS FINALLY SEEN THE ERROR OF HIS WAYS, WE MAY ALLOW HIM TO RETURN, BROKEN...PERHAPS AS MY BUTLER.
UNTIL THEN...
...THE DARK KNIGHT IS DEAD.
HERE'S TO CRIME.
AND THE BLACK GLOVE.
GOTHAM LIES HELPLESS.
NOTHING AND NO ONE CAN STOP US NOW.

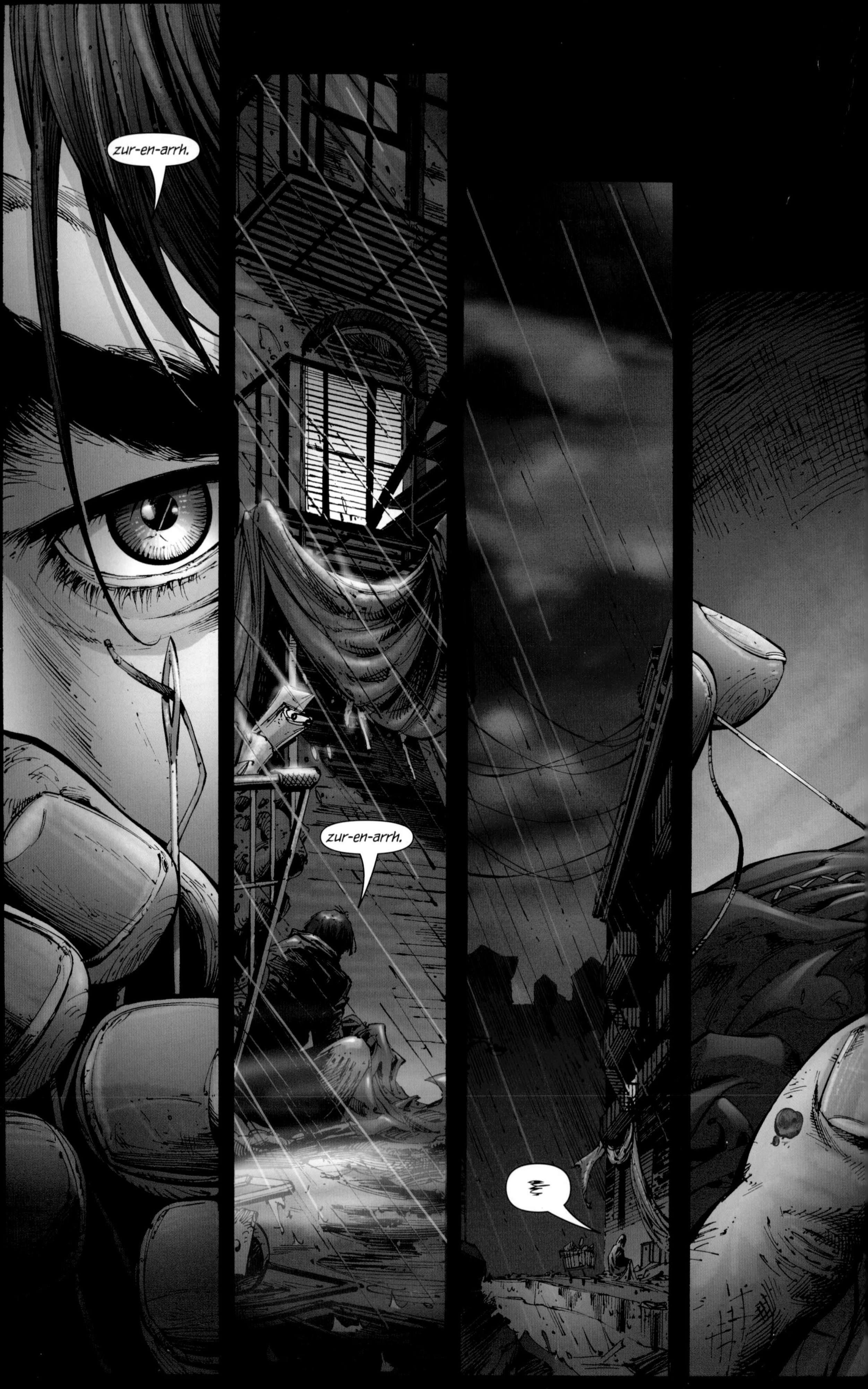
zur-en-arrh.
zur-en-arrh.

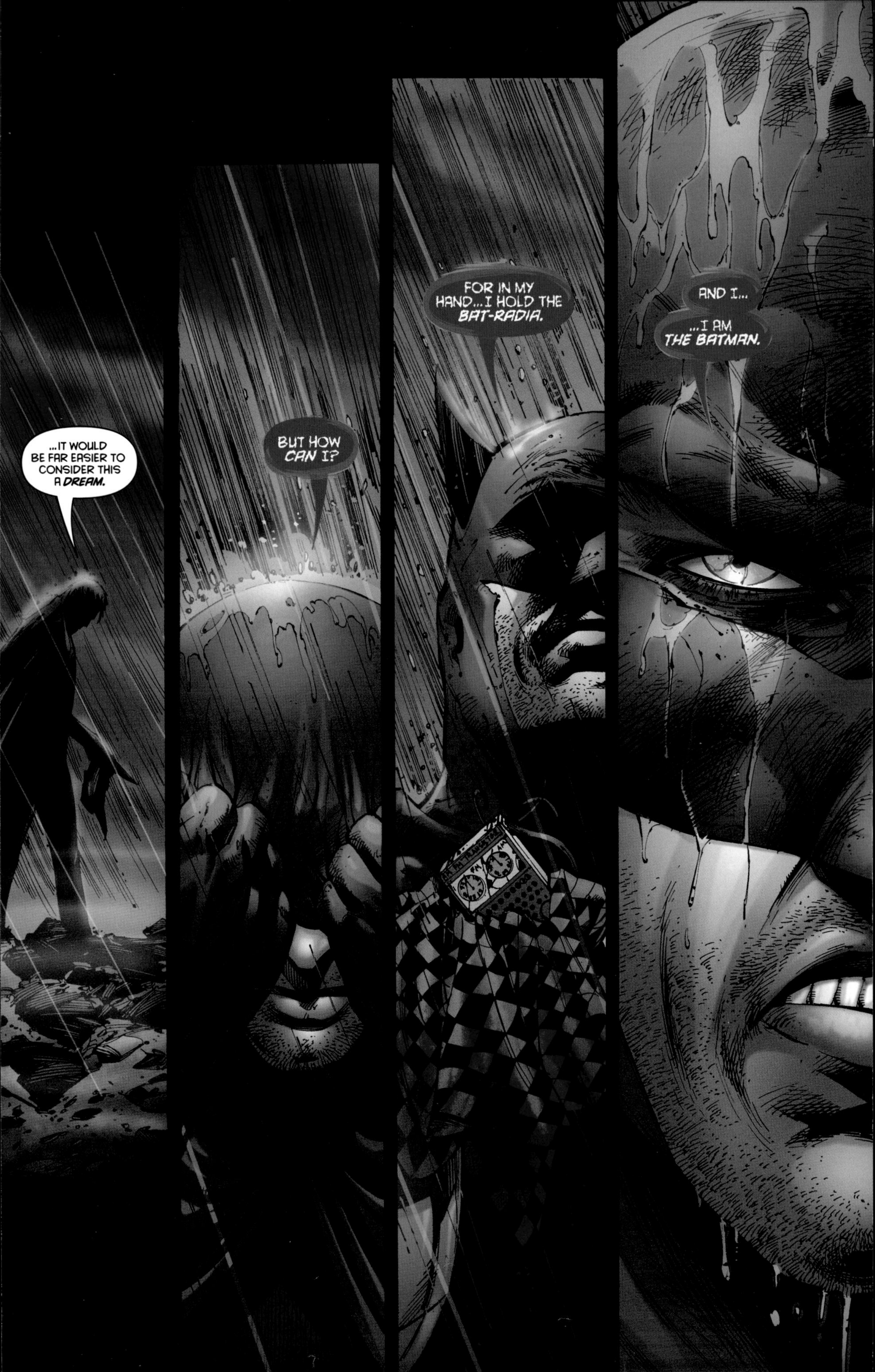
...IT WOULD BE FAR EASIER TO CONSIDER THIS A *DREAM.*
BUT HOW *CAN* I?
FOR IN MY HAND...I HOLD THE *BAT-RADIA.*
AND I...
...I AM *THE BATMAN.*

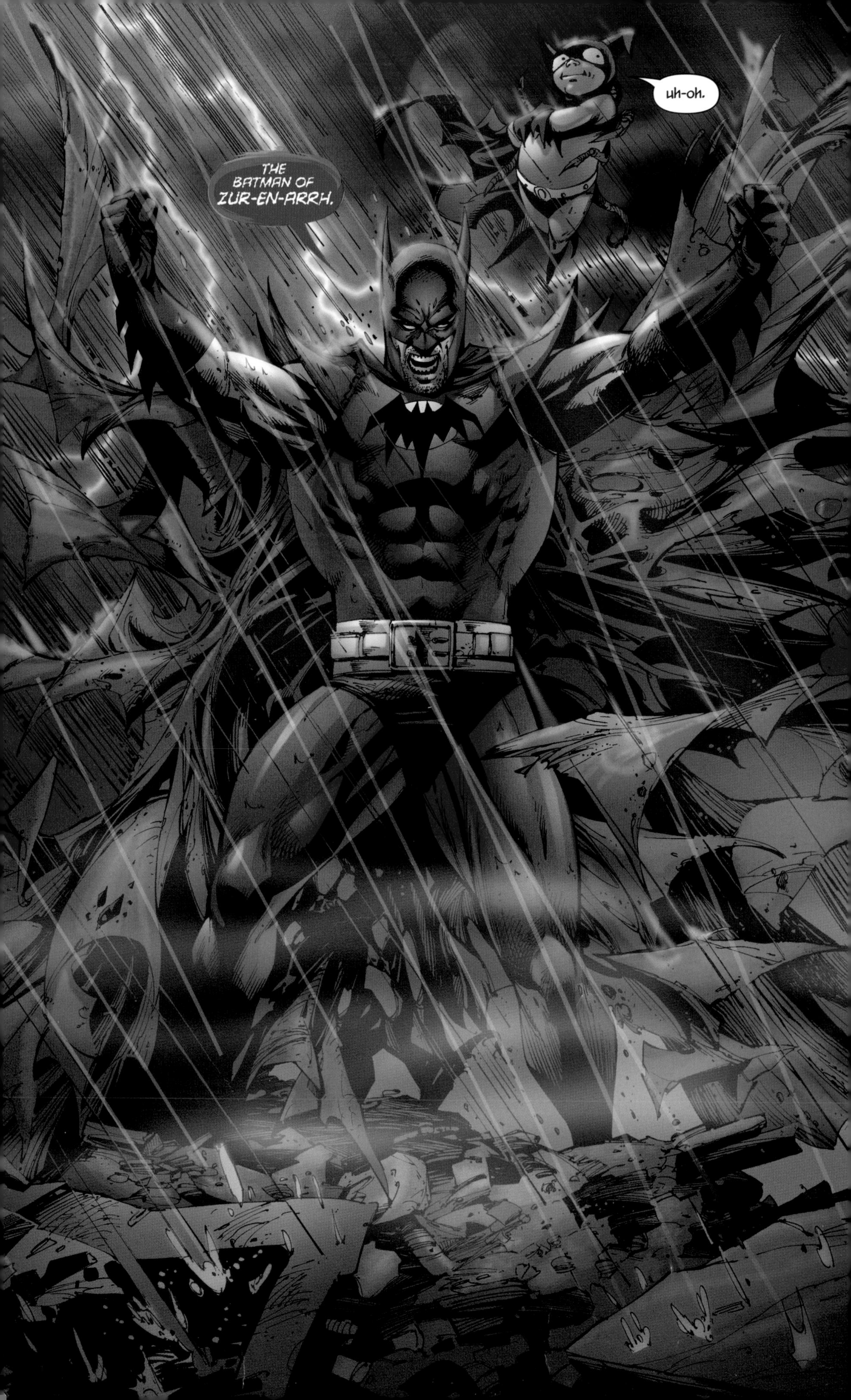
uh-oh.
THE BATMAN OF ZUR-EN-ARRH.

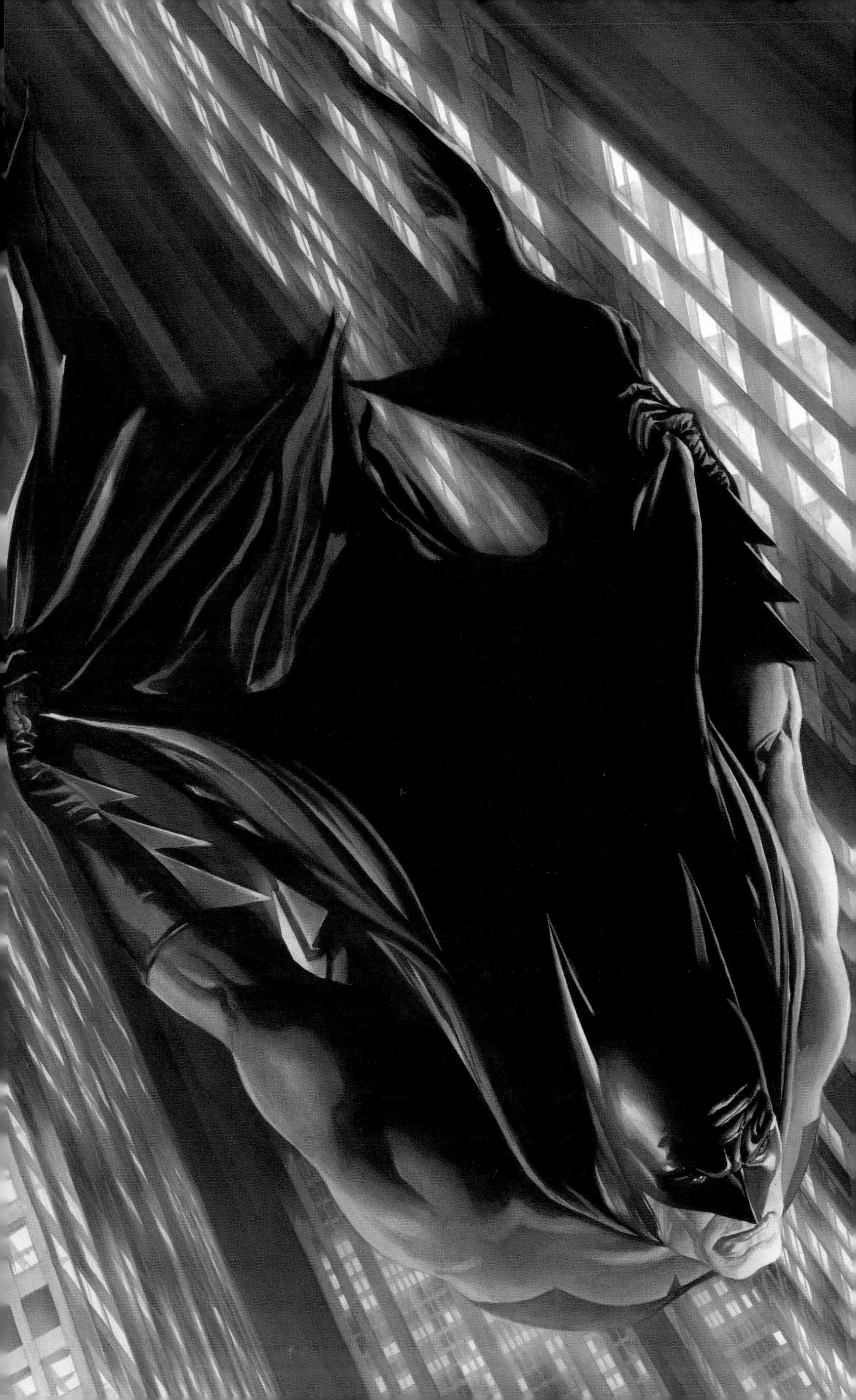

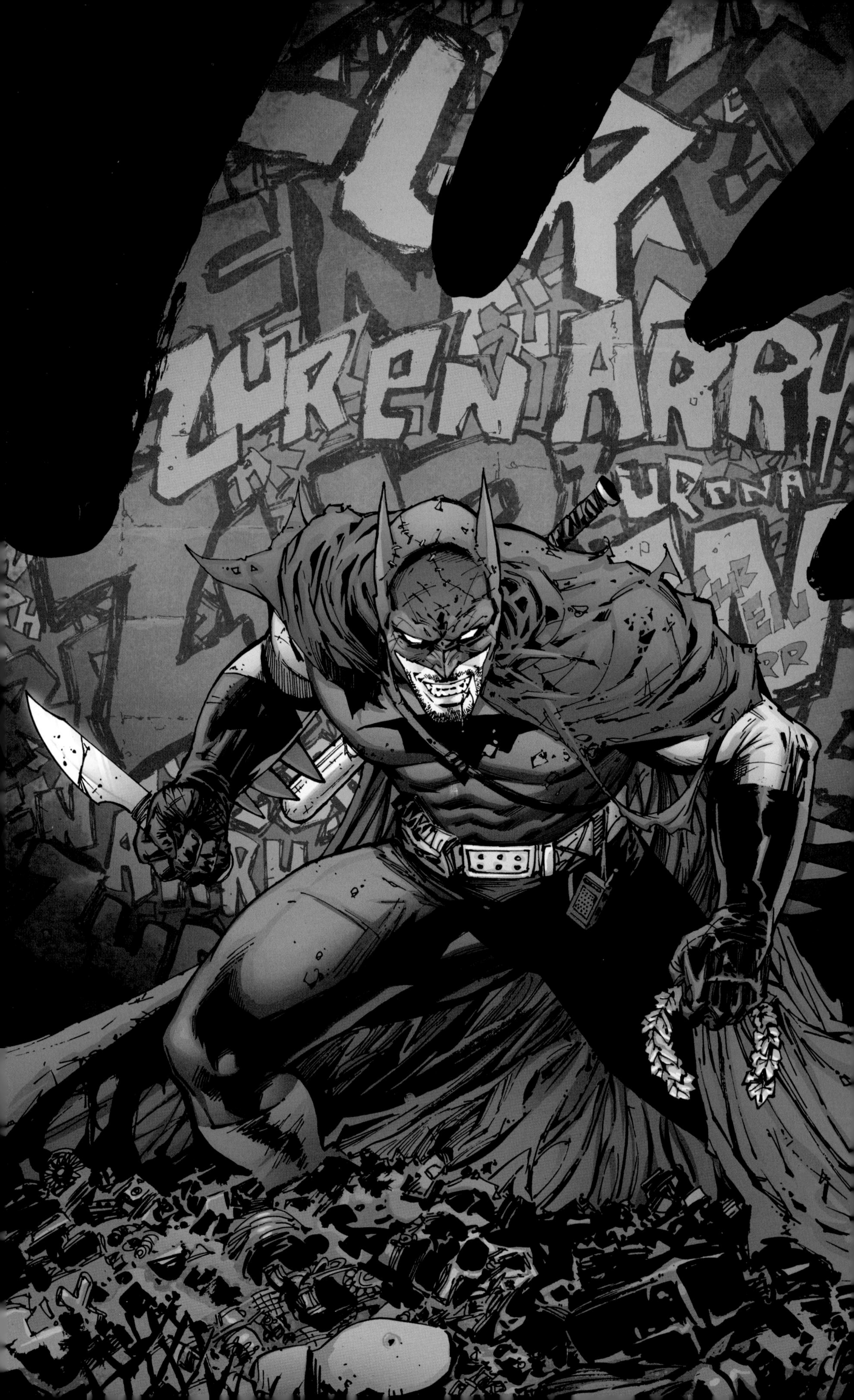

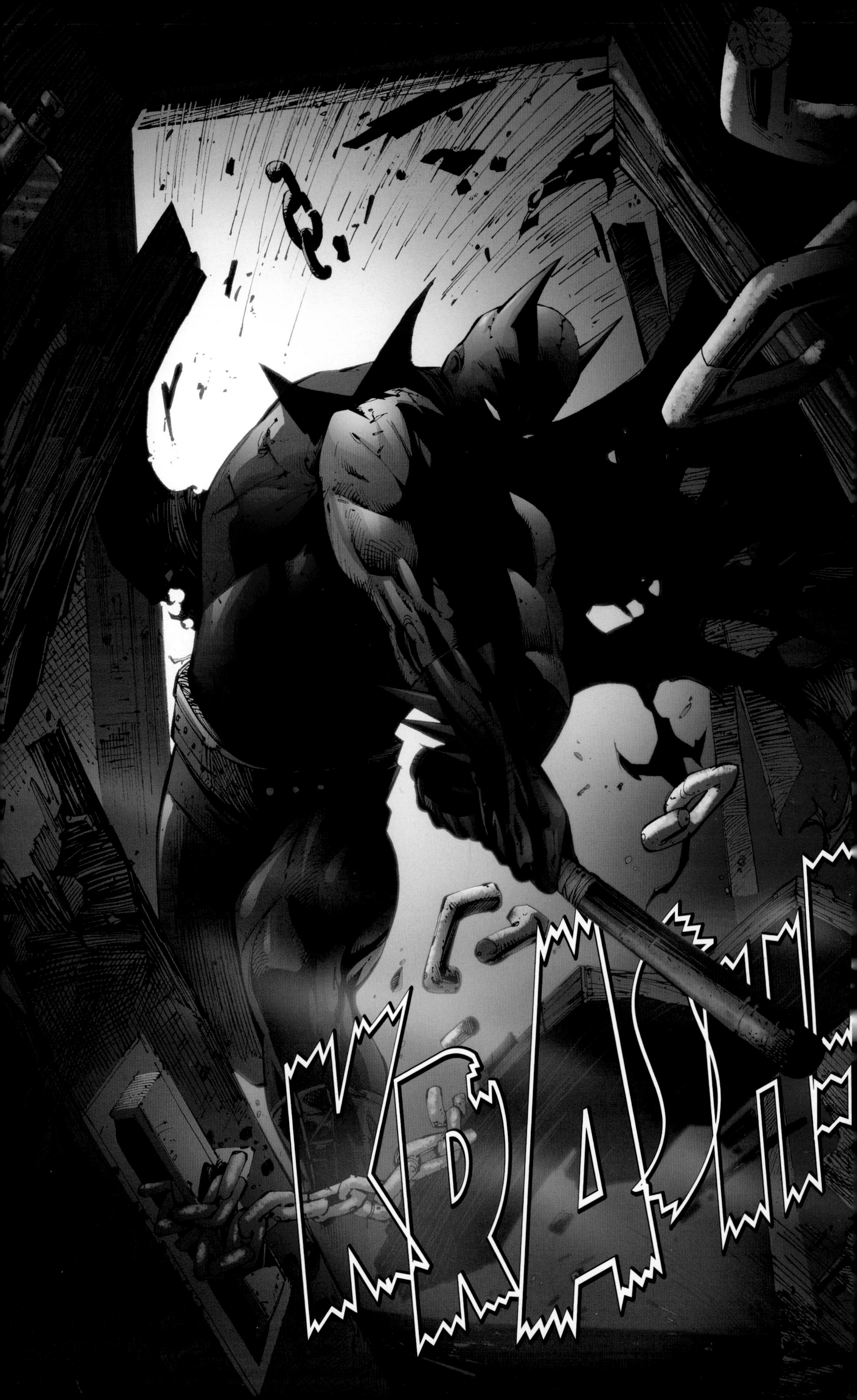
KRASH

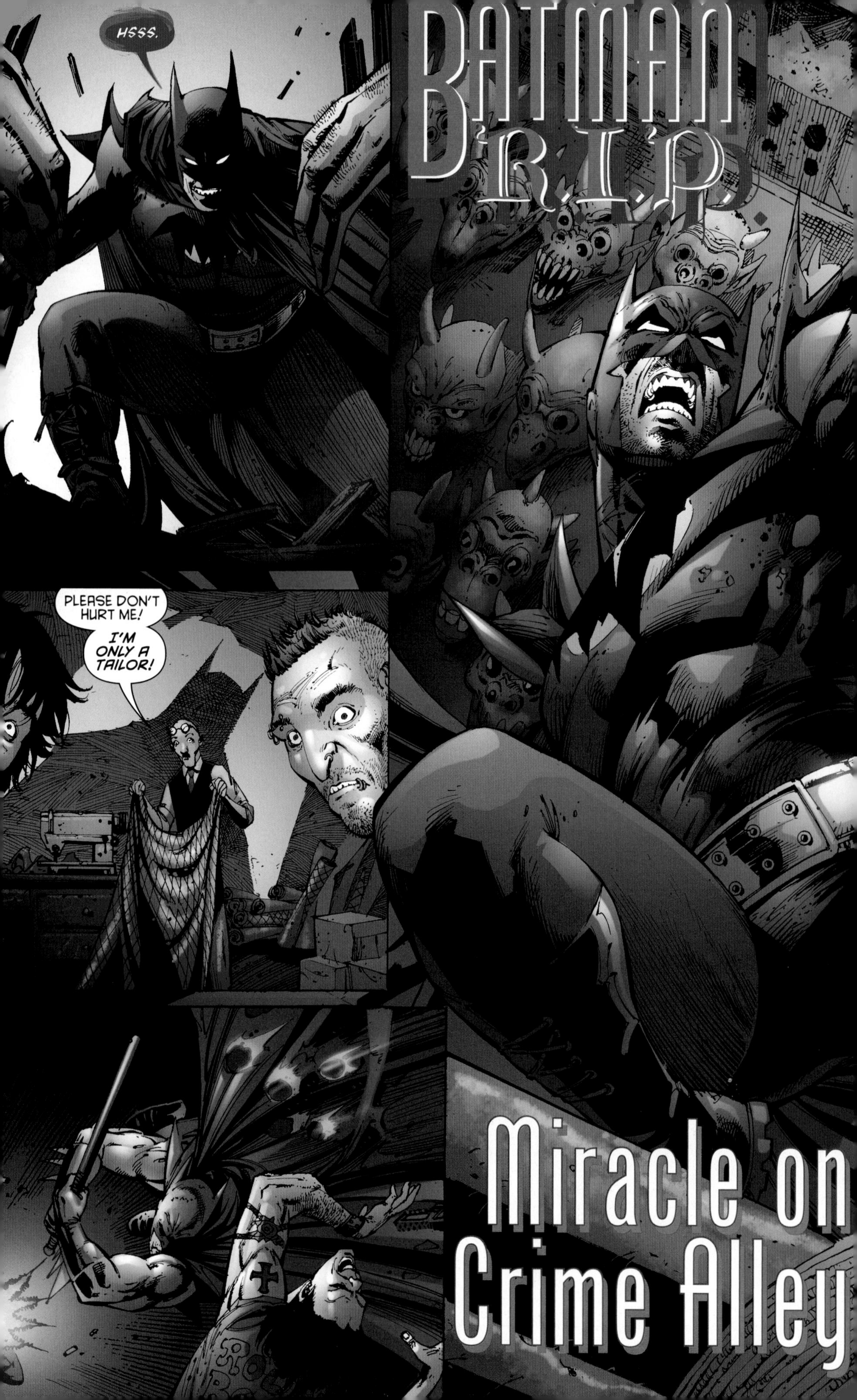

HSSS.
BATMAN R.I.P.
PLEASE DON'T HURT ME! I'M ONLY A TAILOR!
Miracle on Crime Alley

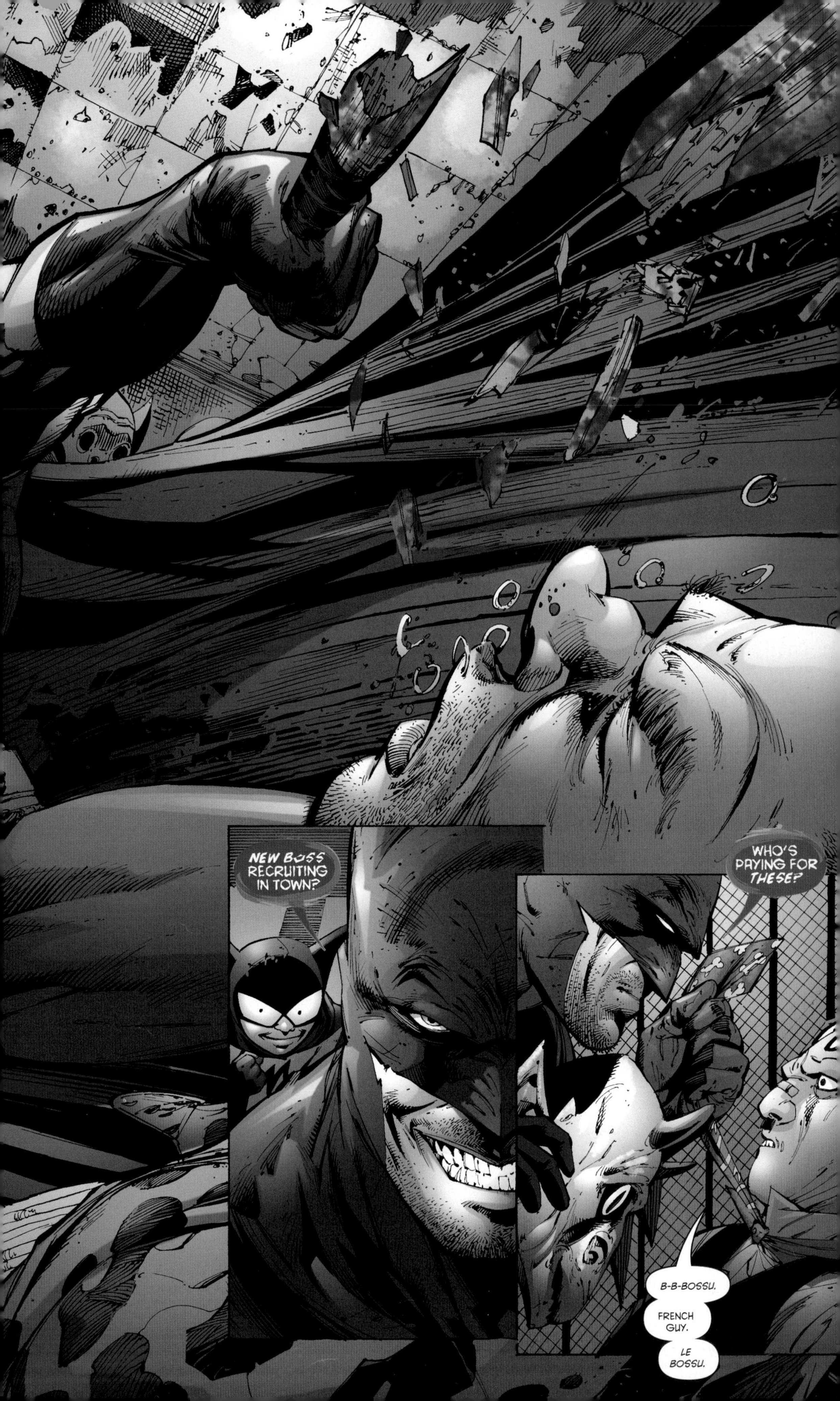
NEW BOSS RECRUITING IN TOWN?
WHO'S PAYING FOR THESE?
B-B-BOSSU.
FRENCH GUY.
LE BOSSU.

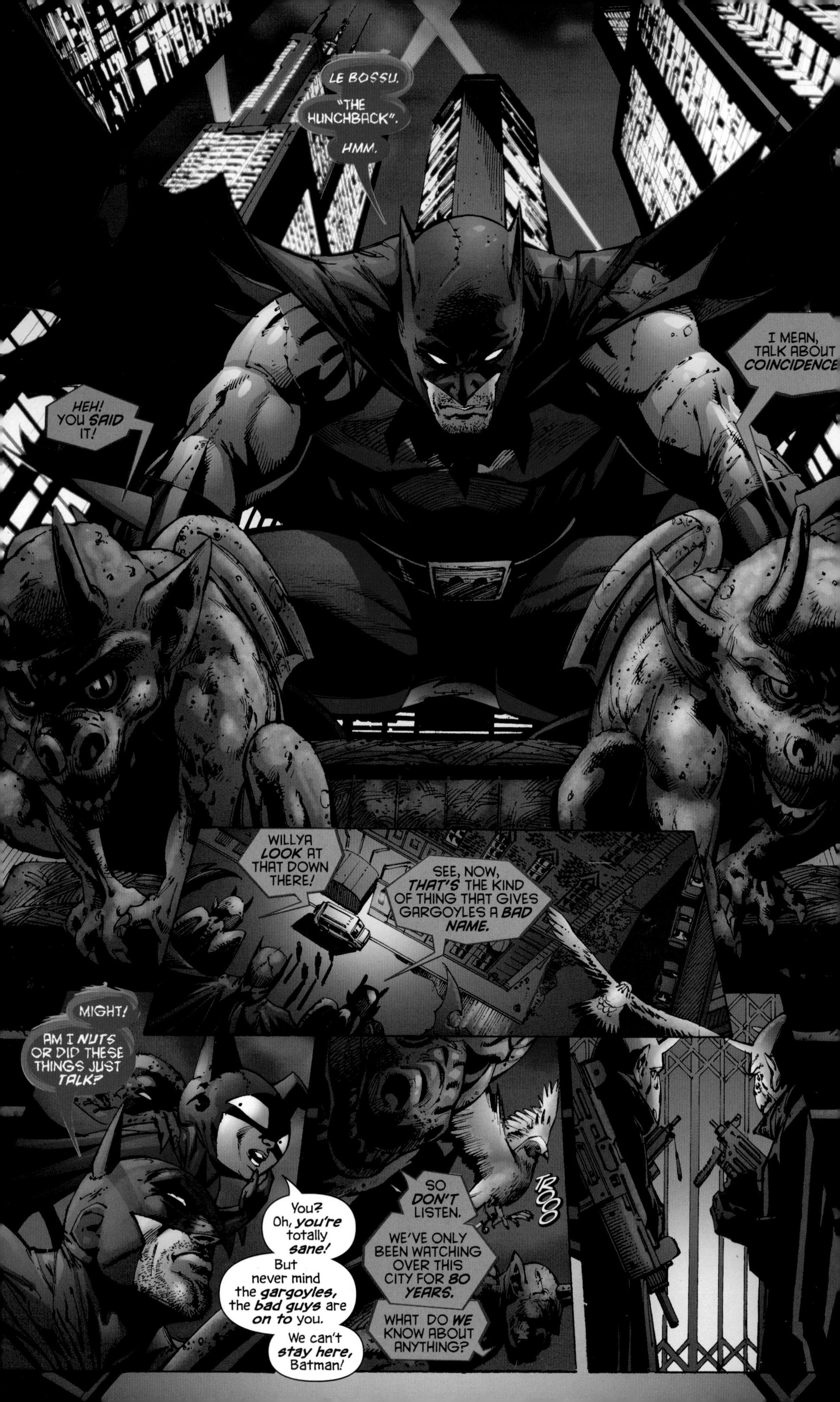

LE BOSSU.
"THE HUNCHBACK".
HMM.
HEH! YOU SAID IT!
I MEAN, TALK ABOUT COINCIDENCE
WILLYA LOOK AT THAT DOWN THERE!
SEE, NOW, THAT'S THE KIND OF THING THAT GIVES GARGOYLES A BAD NAME.
MIGHT!
AM I NUTS OR DID THESE THINGS JUST TALK?
You? Oh, you're totally sane!
But never mind the gargoyles, the bad guys are on to you.
We can't stay here, Batman!
SO DON'T LISTEN.
WE'VE ONLY BEEN WATCHING OVER THIS CITY FOR 80 YEARS.
WHAT DO WE KNOW ABOUT ANYTHING?
TROOO

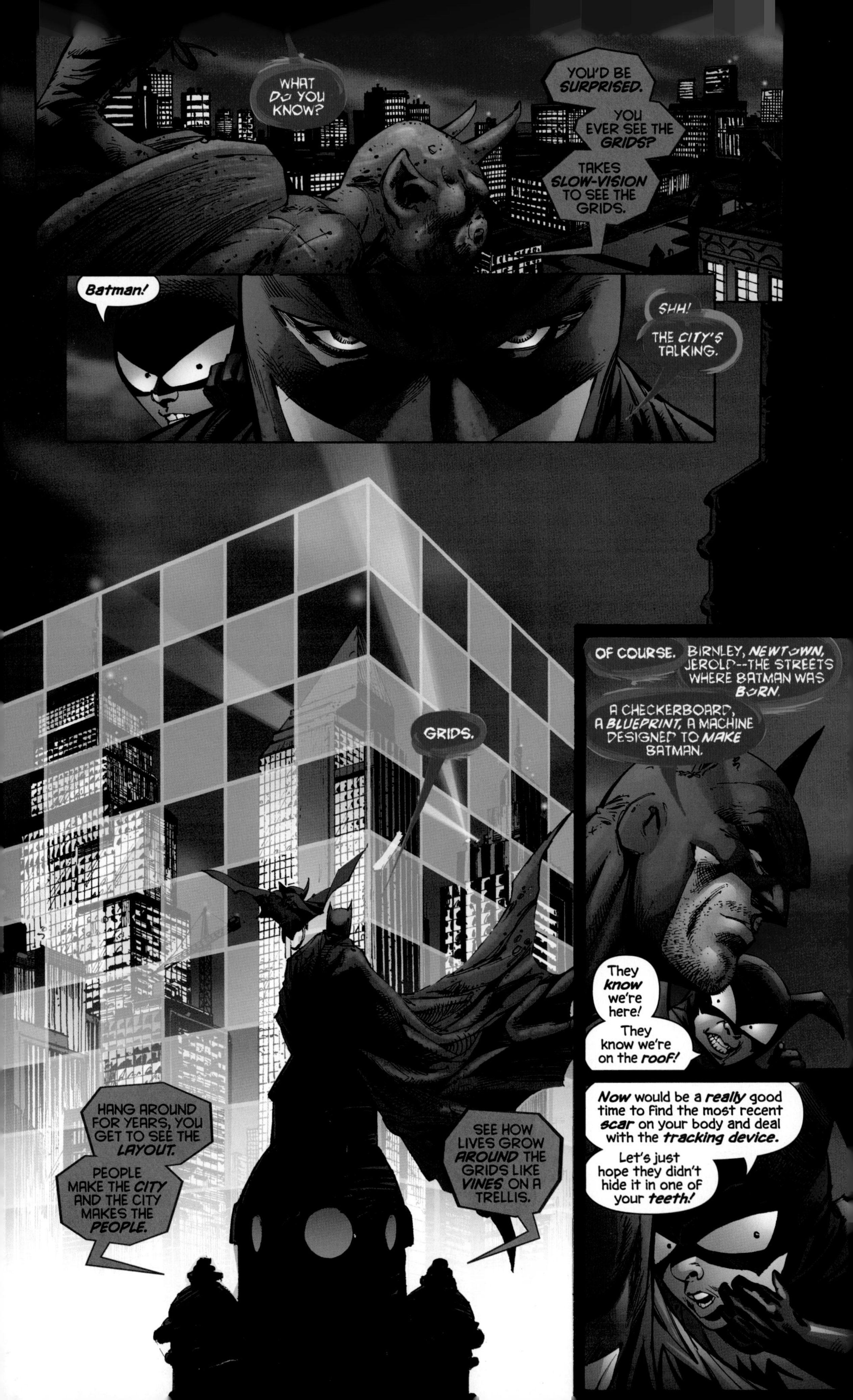
WHAT DO YOU KNOW?
YOU'D BE SURPRISED.
YOU EVER SEE THE GRIDS?
TAKES SLOW-VISION TO SEE THE GRIDS.
Batman!
SHH!
THE CITY'S TALKING.
GRIDS.
HANG AROUND FOR YEARS, YOU GET TO SEE THE LAYOUT.
PEOPLE MAKE THE CITY AND THE CITY MAKES THE PEOPLE.
SEE HOW LIVES GROW AROUND THE GRIDS LIKE VINES ON A TRELLIS.
OF COURSE.
BIRNLEY, NEWTOWN, JEROLD--THE STREETS WHERE BATMAN WAS BORN.
A CHECKERBOARD, A BLUEPRINT, A MACHINE DESIGNED TO MAKE BATMAN.
They know we're here!
They know we're on the roof!
Now would be a really good time to find the most recent scar on your body and deal with the tracking device.
Let's just hope they didn't hide it in one of your teeth!

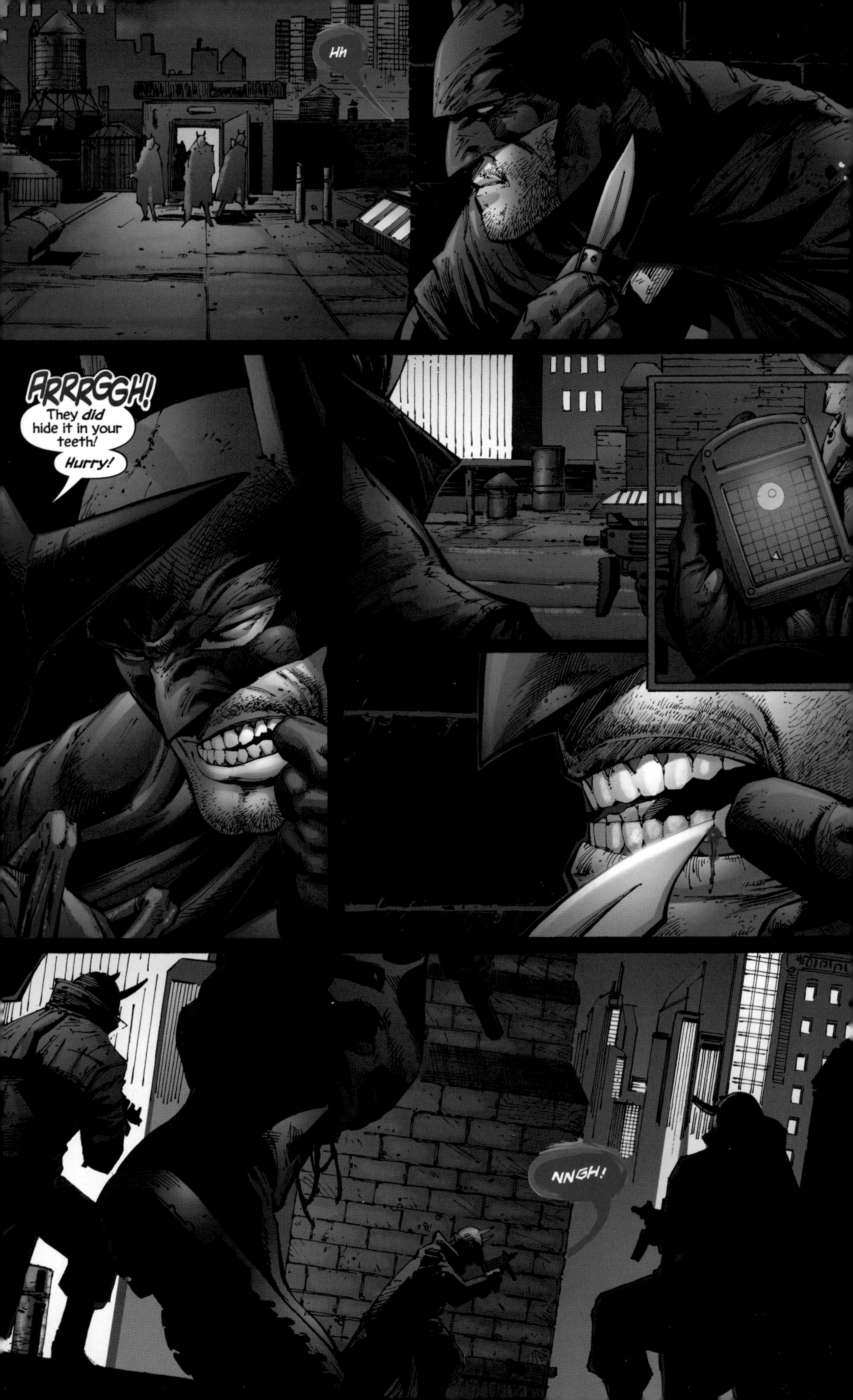
Hh
ARRRGGH!
They did hide it in your teeth!
Hurry!
NNGH!

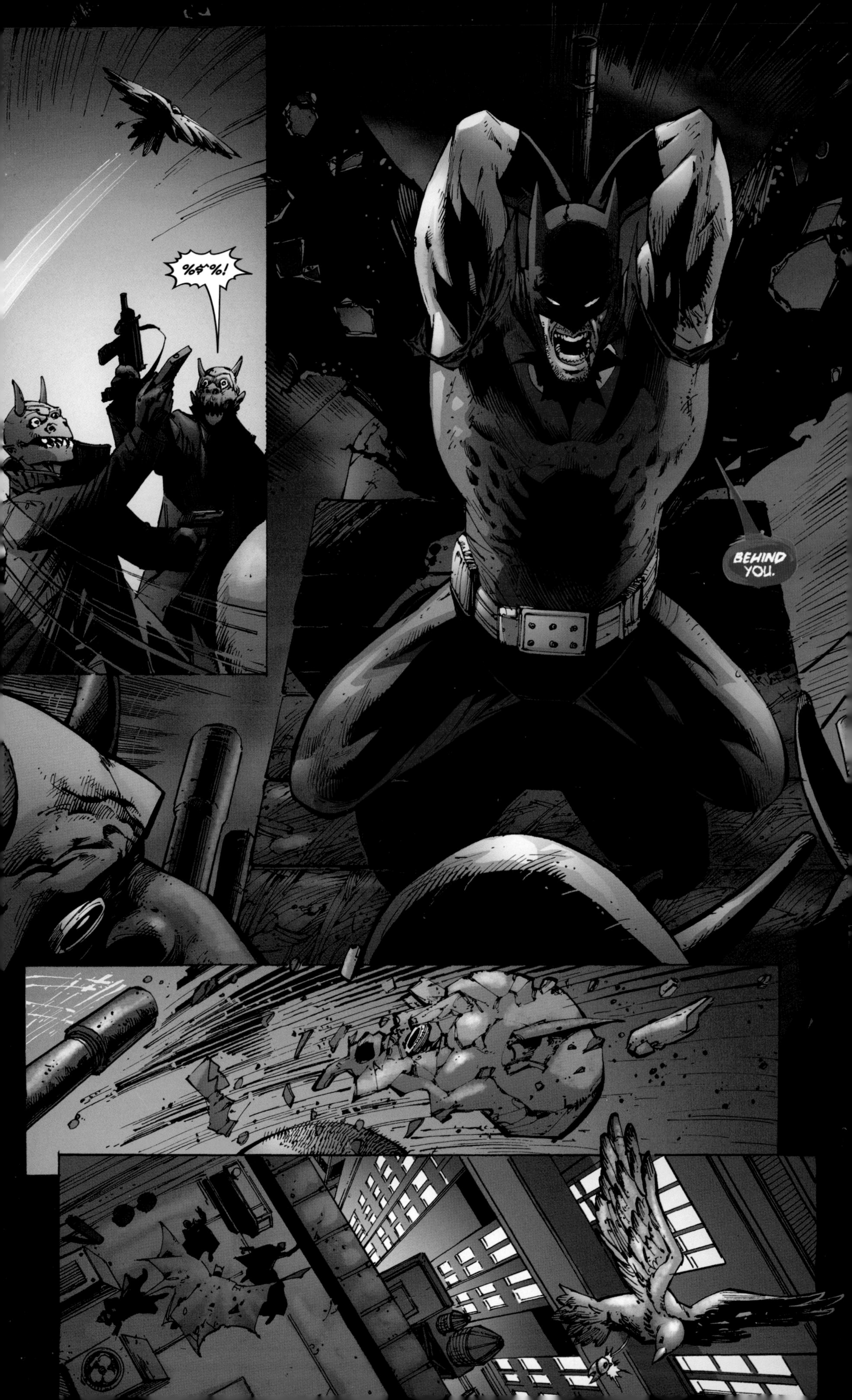
%$*%!
BEHIND YOU.

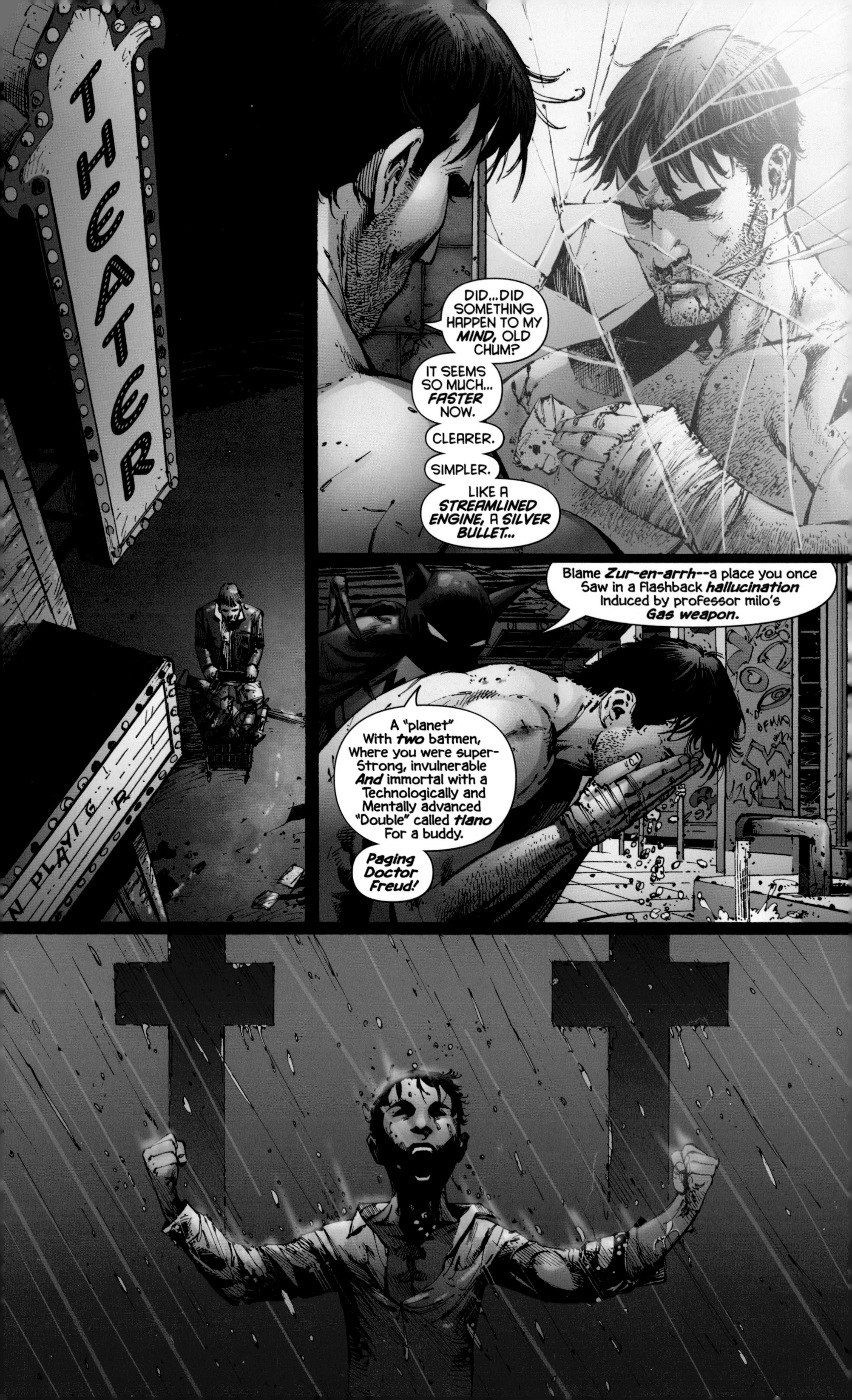
THEATER
N PLAYI G R
DID...DID SOMETHING HAPPEN TO MY MIND, OLD CHUM?
IT SEEMS SO MUCH... FASTER NOW.
CLEARER.
SIMPLER.
LIKE A STREAMLINED ENGINE, A SILVER BULLET...
Blame Zur-en-arrh--a place you once Saw in a flashback hallucination Induced by professor milo's Gas weapon.
A "planet" With two batmen, Where you were super-Strong, invulnerable And immortal with a Technologically and Mentally advanced "Double" called tlano For a buddy.
Paging Doctor Freud!

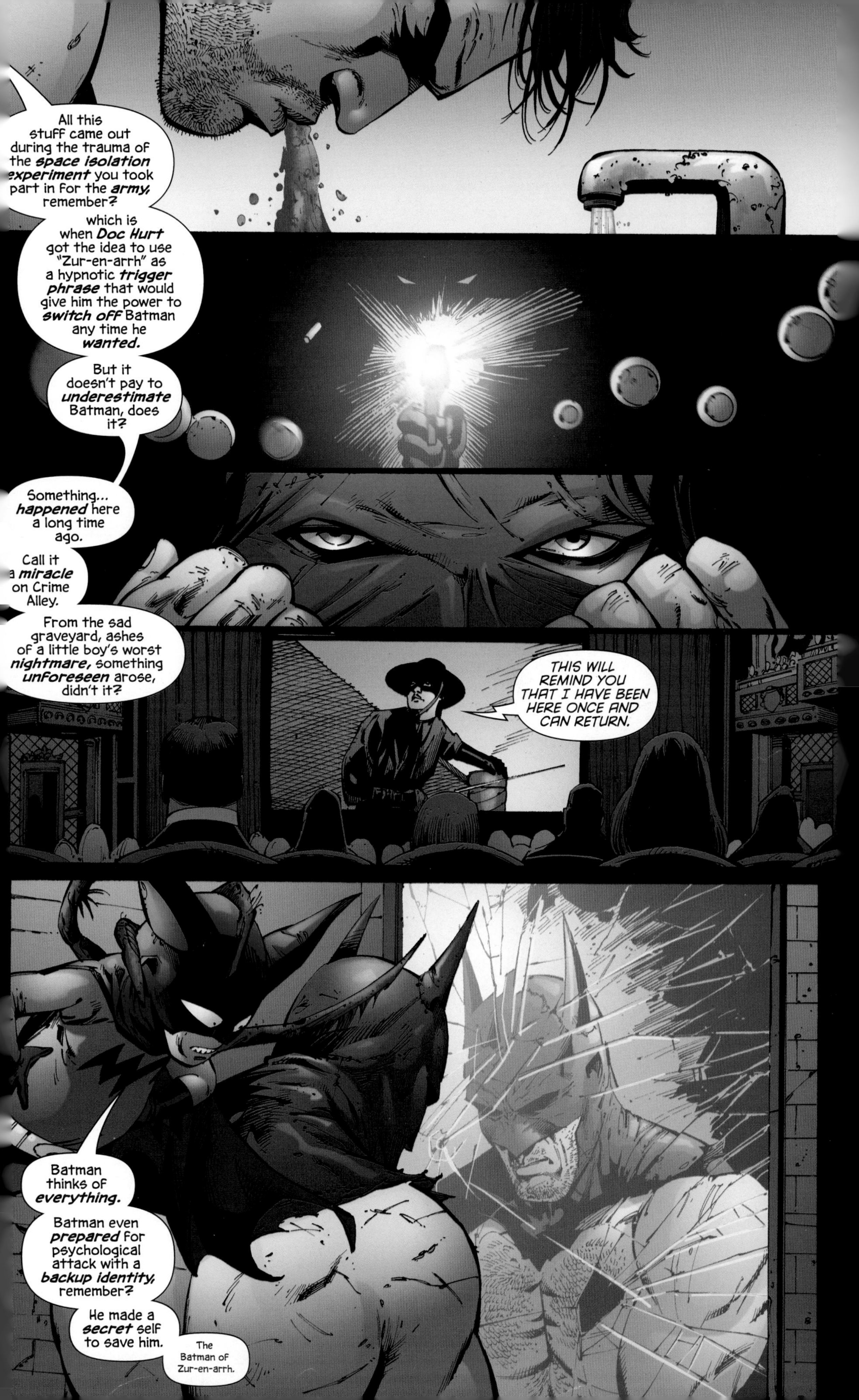

All this stuff came out during the trauma of the space isolation experiment you took part in for the army, remember?
which is when Doc Hurt got the idea to use "Zur-en-arrh" as a hypnotic trigger phrase that would give him the power to switch off Batman any time he wanted.
But it doesn't pay to underestimate Batman, does it?
Something... happened here a long time ago.
Call it a miracle on Crime Alley.
From the sad graveyard, ashes of a little boy's worst nightmare, something unforeseen arose, didn't it?
THIS WILL REMIND YOU THAT I HAVE BEEN HERE ONCE AND CAN RETURN.
Batman thinks of everything.
Batman even prepared for psychological attack with a backup identity, remember?
He made a secret self to save him.
The Batman of Zur-en-arrh.

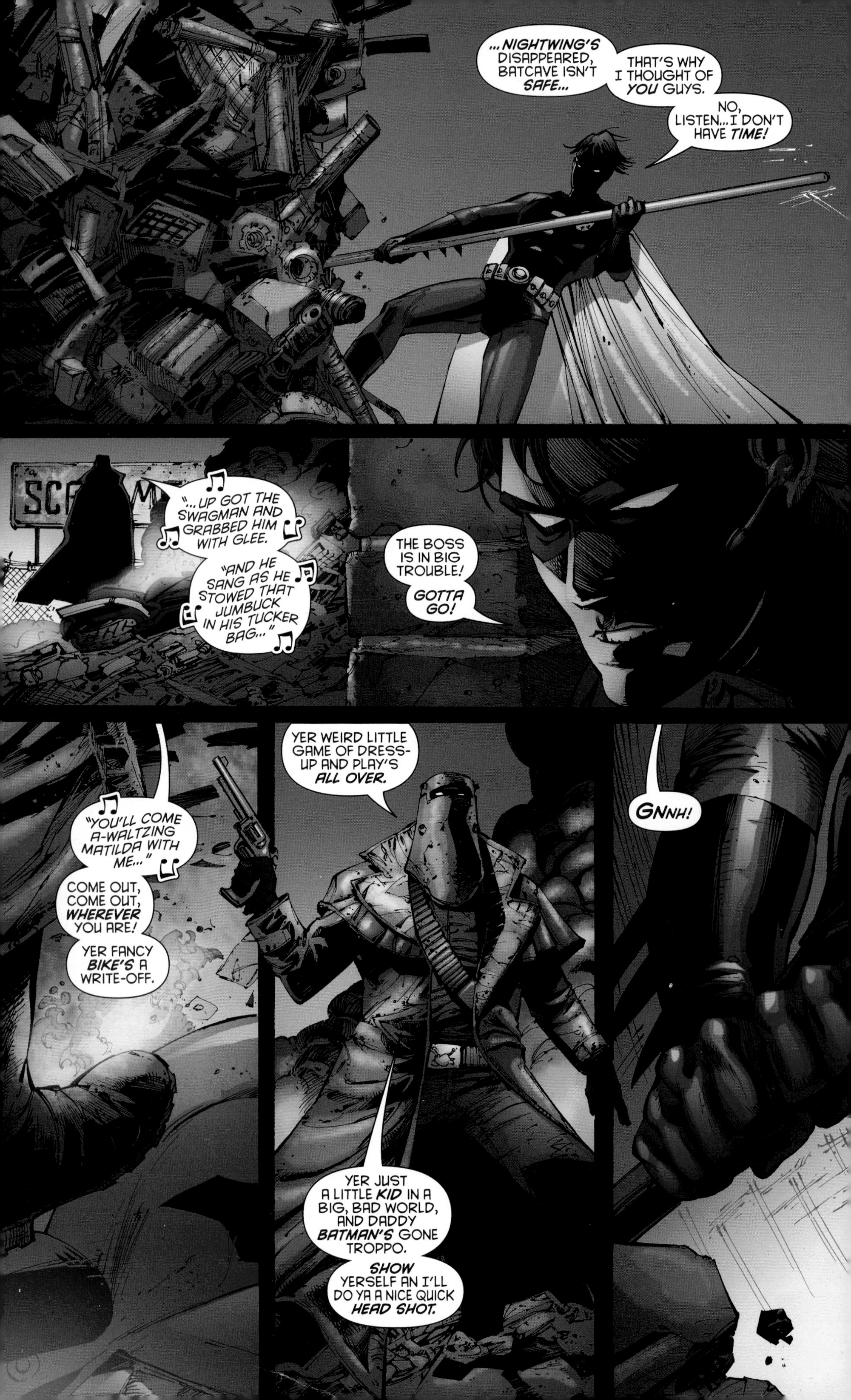

...NIGHTWING'S DISAPPEARED, BATCAVE ISN'T SAFE...
THAT'S WHY I THOUGHT OF YOU GUYS.
NO, LISTEN...I DON'T HAVE TIME!
"...UP GOT THE SWAGMAN AND GRABBED HIM WITH GLEE.
"AND HE SANG AS HE STOWED THAT JUMBUCK IN HIS TUCKER BAG..."
THE BOSS IS IN BIG TROUBLE!
GOTTA GO!
"YOU'LL COME A-WALTZING MATILDA WITH ME..."
COME OUT, COME OUT, WHEREVER YOU ARE!
YER FANCY BIKE'S A WRITE-OFF.
YER WEIRD LITTLE GAME OF DRESS-UP AND PLAY'S ALL OVER.
YER JUST A LITTLE KID IN A BIG, BAD WORLD, AND DADDY BATMAN'S GONE TROPPO.
SHOW YERSELF AN I'LL DO YA A NICE QUICK HEAD SHOT.
GNNH!

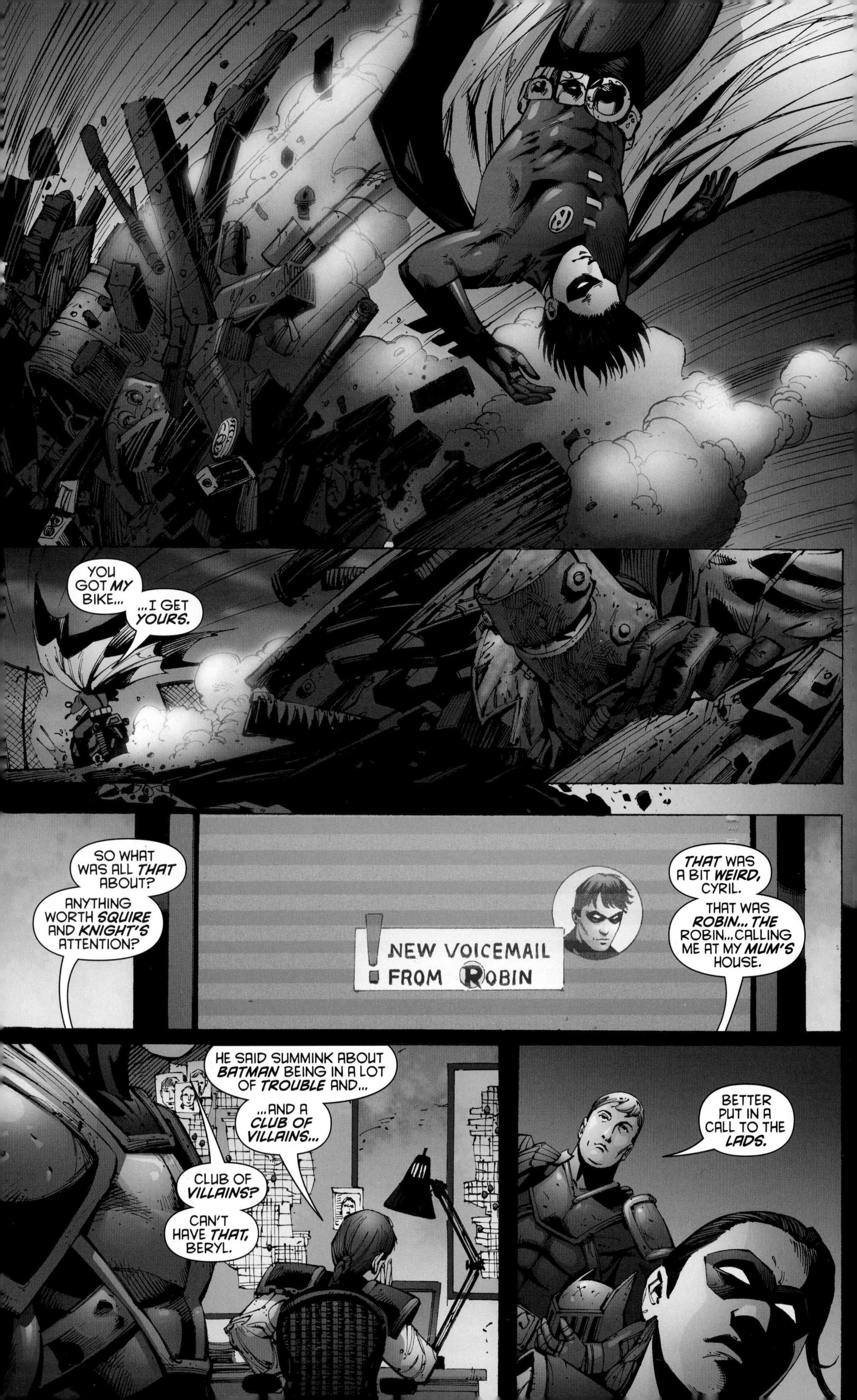
YOU GOT MY BIKE...
...I GET YOURS.
SO WHAT WAS ALL THAT ABOUT?
ANYTHING WORTH SQUIRE AND KNIGHT'S ATTENTION?
NEW VOICEMAIL FROM ROBIN
THAT WAS A BIT WEIRD, CYRIL.
THAT WAS ROBIN... THE ROBIN...CALLING ME AT MY MUM'S HOUSE.
HE SAID SUMMINK ABOUT BATMAN BEING IN A LOT OF TROUBLE AND...
...AND A CLUB OF VILLAINS...
CLUB OF VILLAINS?
CAN'T HAVE THAT, BERYL.
BETTER PUT IN A CALL TO THE LADS.

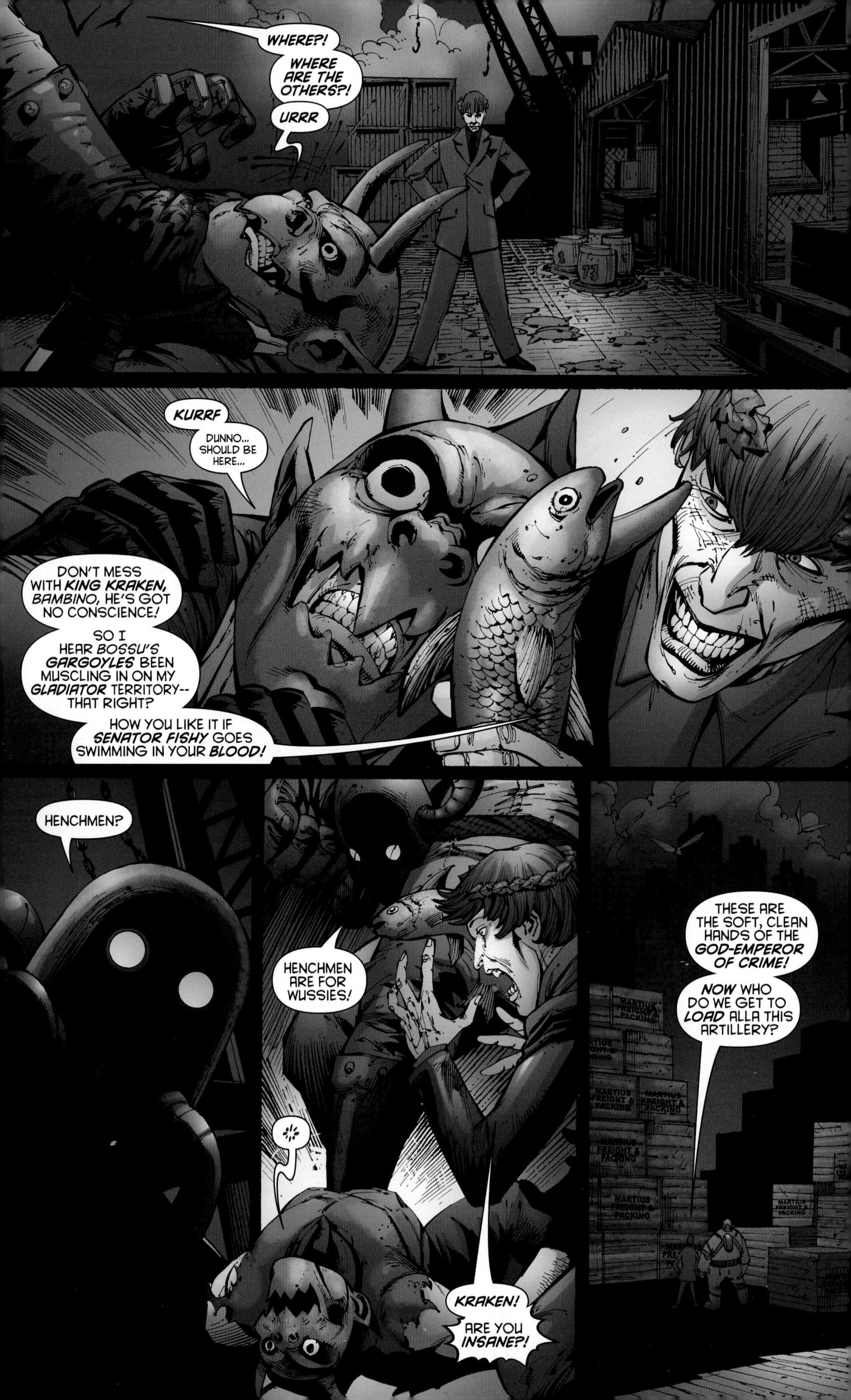
WHERE?!
WHERE ARE THE OTHERS?!
URRR
KURRF
DUNNO... SHOULD BE HERE...
DON'T MESS WITH KING KRAKEN, BAMBINO, HE'S GOT NO CONSCIENCE!
SO I HEAR BOSSU'S GARGOYLES BEEN MUSCLING IN ON MY GLADIATOR TERRITORY-- THAT RIGHT?
HOW YOU LIKE IT IF SENATOR FISHY GOES SWIMMING IN YOUR BLOOD!
HENCHMEN?
HENCHMEN ARE FOR WUSSIES!
KRAKEN!
ARE YOU INSANE?!
THESE ARE THE SOFT, CLEAN HANDS OF THE GOD-EMPEROR OF CRIME!
NOW WHO DO WE GET TO LOAD ALLA THIS ARTILLERY?
MARTIUS FREIGHT & PACKING

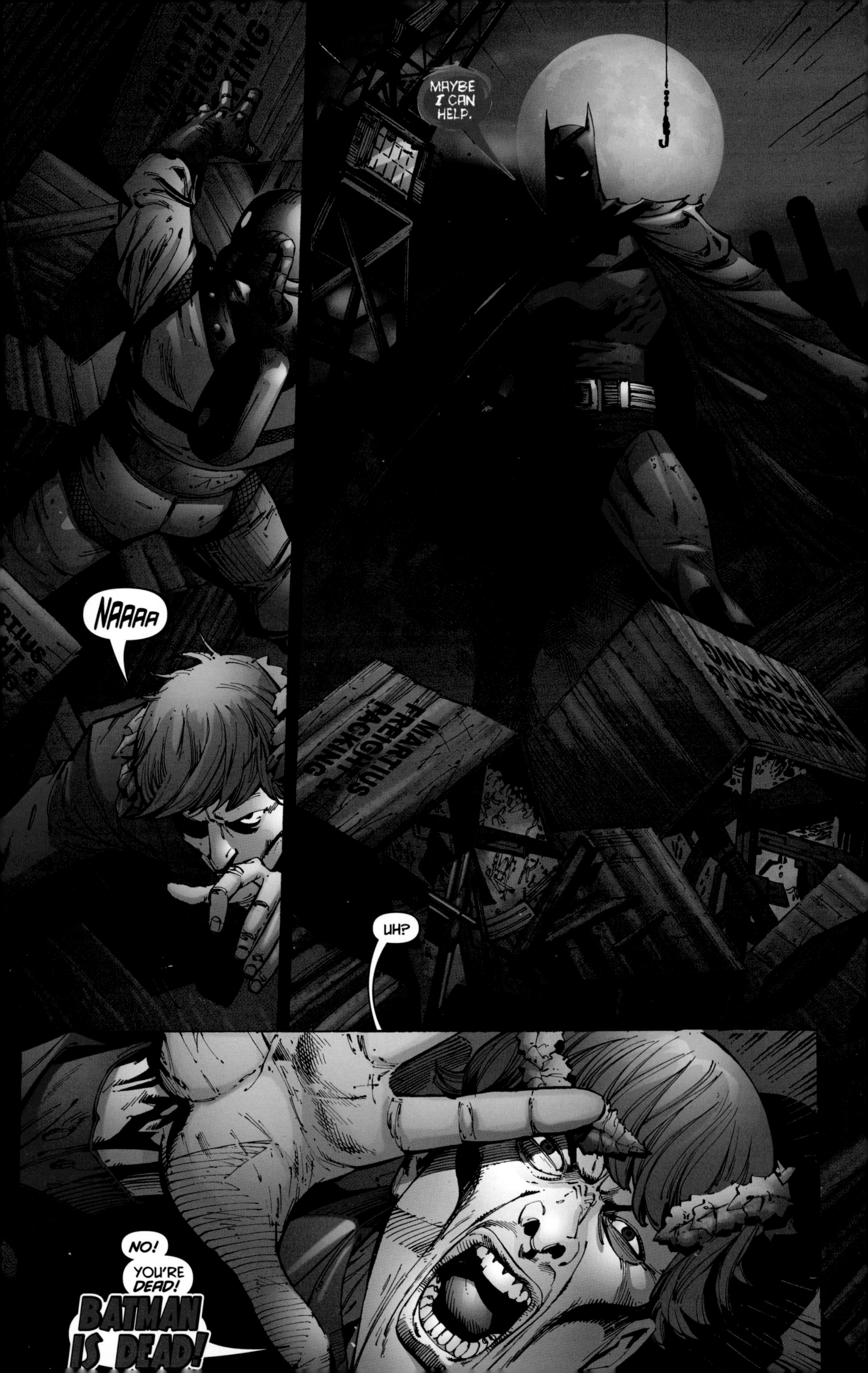
NAAAA
MAYBE I CAN HELP.
MARTIUS FREIGHT & PACKING
UH?
NO!
YOU'RE DEAD!
BATMAN IS DEAD!

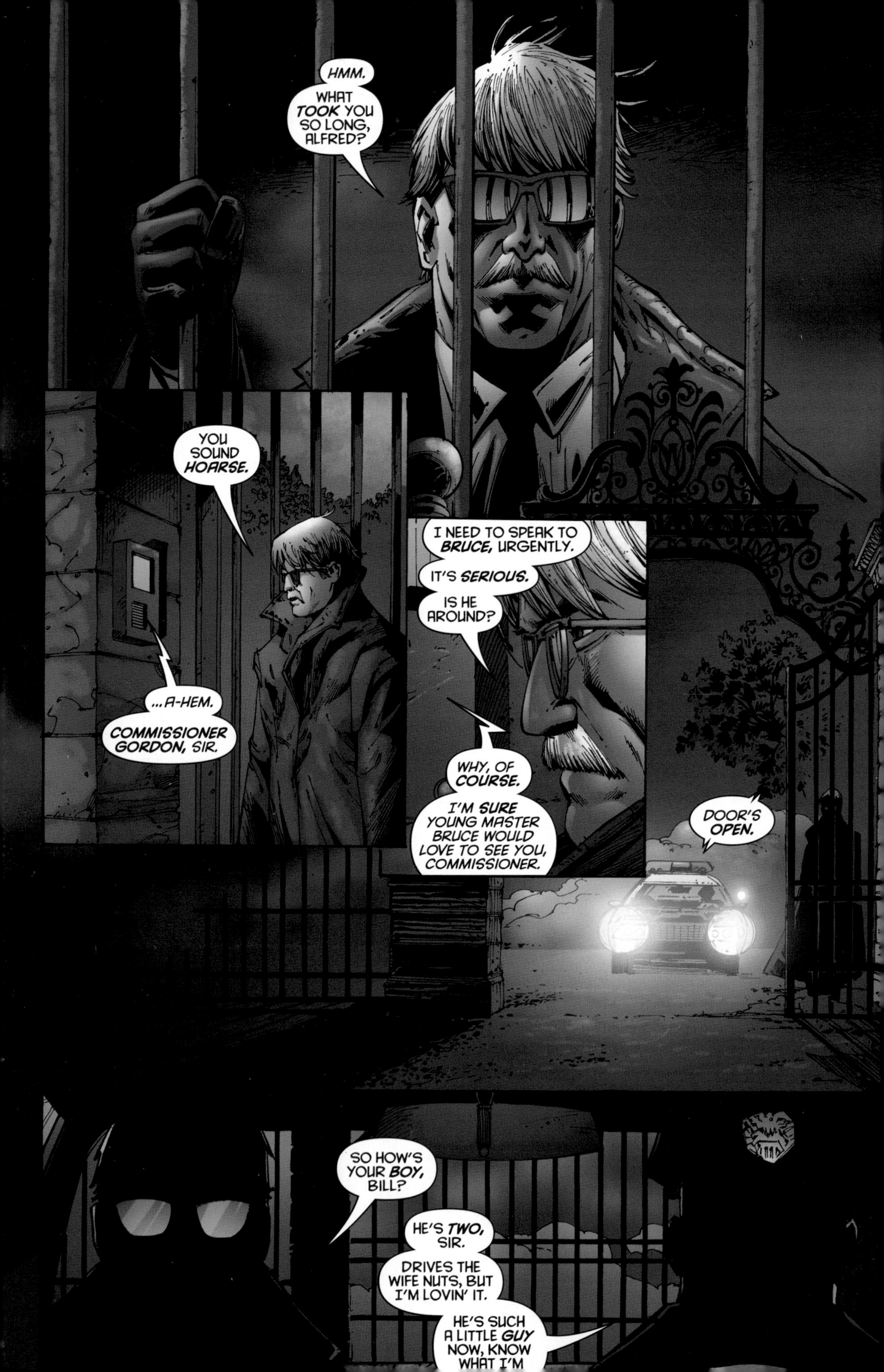
HMM.
WHAT TOOK YOU SO LONG, ALFRED?
YOU SOUND HOARSE.
...A-HEM.
COMMISSIONER GORDON, SIR.
I NEED TO SPEAK TO BRUCE, URGENTLY.
IT'S SERIOUS.
IS HE AROUND?
WHY, OF COURSE.
I'M SURE YOUNG MASTER BRUCE WOULD LOVE TO SEE YOU, COMMISSIONER.
DOOR'S OPEN.
SO HOW'S YOUR BOY, BILL?
HE'S TWO, SIR.
DRIVES THE WIFE NUTS, BUT I'M LOVIN' IT.
HE'S SUCH A LITTLE GUY NOW, KNOW WHAT I'M

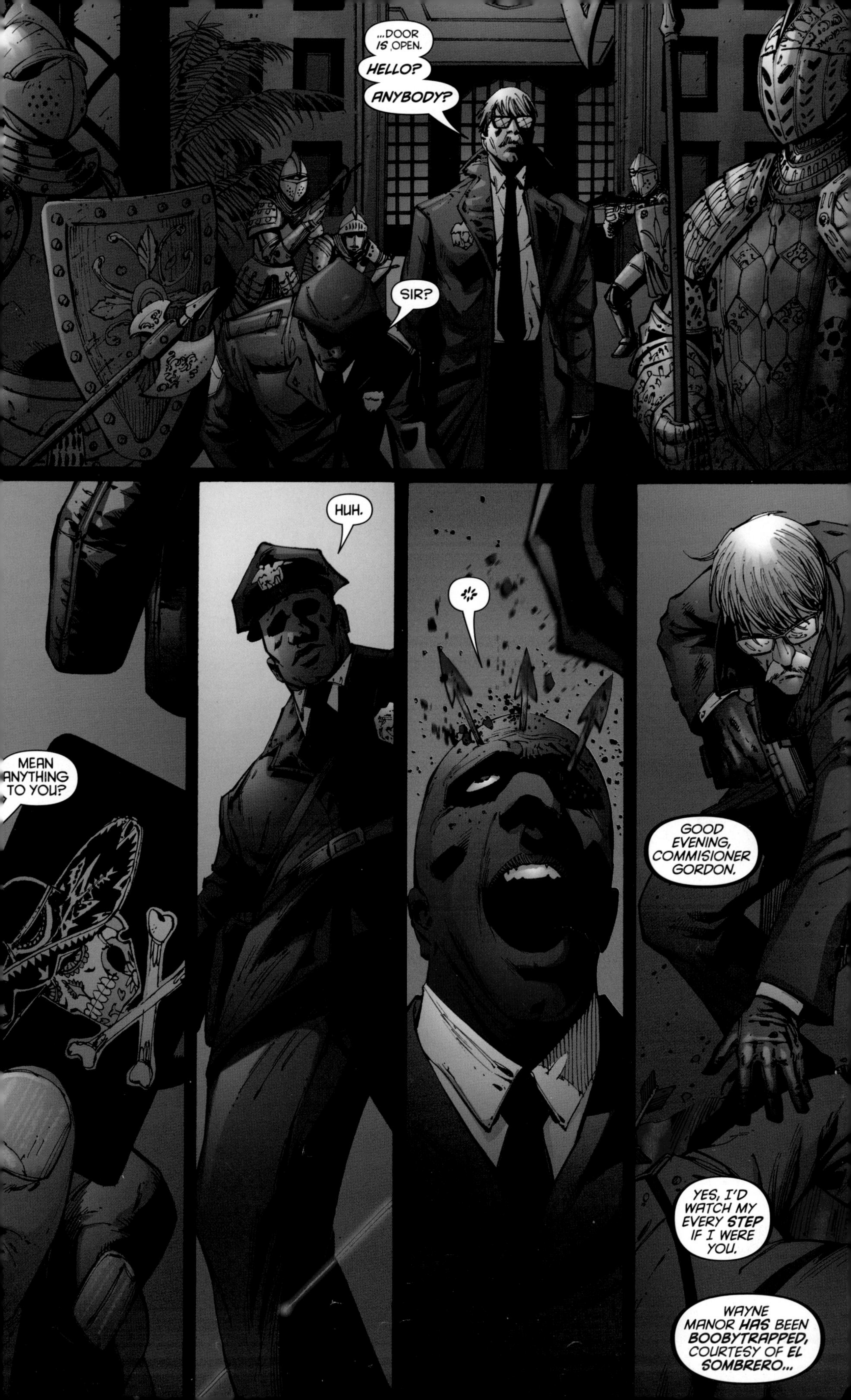
...DOOR IS OPEN.
HELLO?
ANYBODY?
SIR?
MEAN ANYTHING TO YOU?
HUH.
GOOD EVENING, COMMISIONER GORDON.
YES, I'D WATCH MY EVERY STEP IF I WERE YOU.
WAYNE MANOR HAS BEEN BOOBYTRAPPED, COURTESY OF EL SOMBRERO...

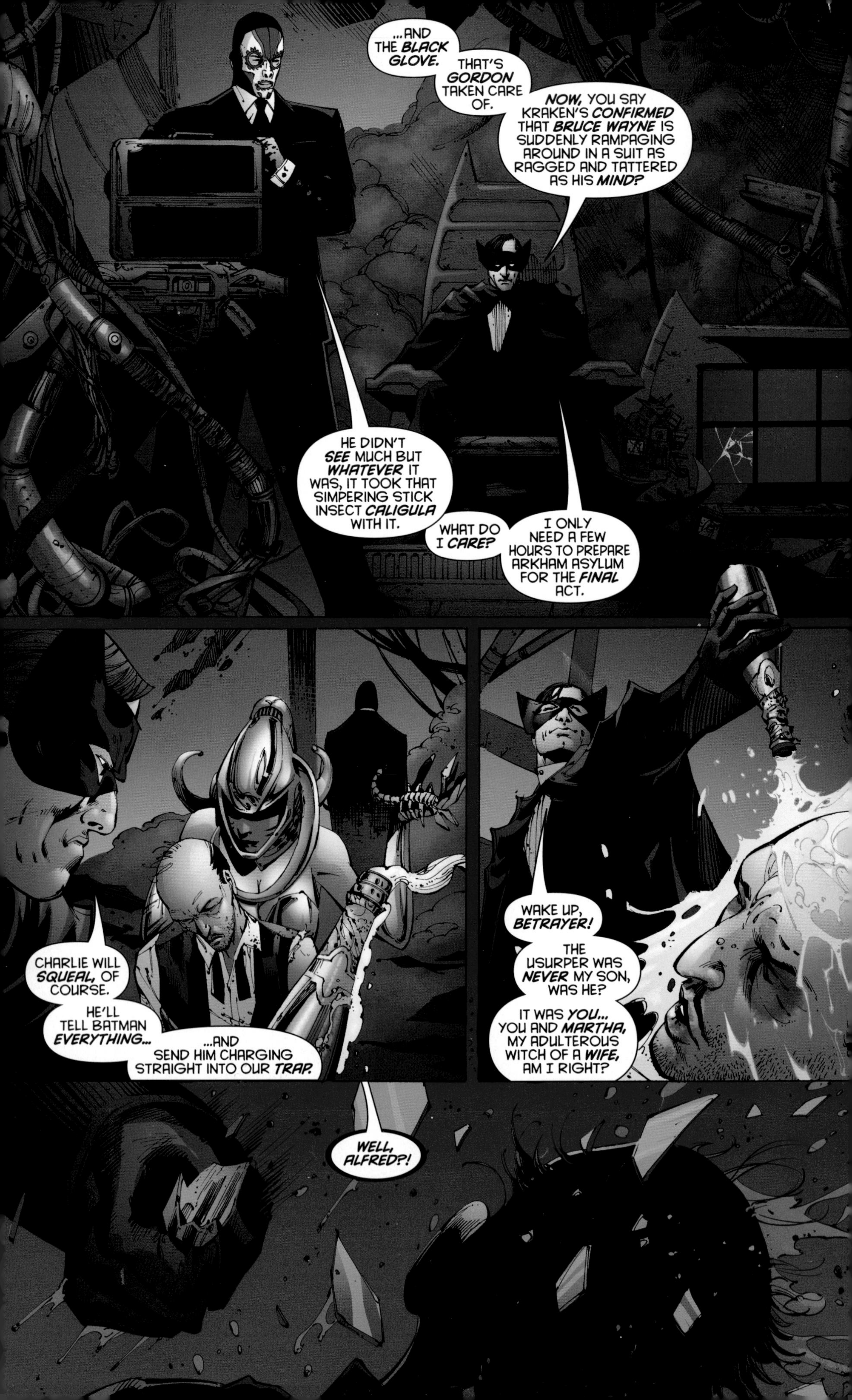
...AND THE BLACK GLOVE.
THAT'S GORDON TAKEN CARE OF.
NOW, YOU SAY KRAKEN'S CONFIRMED THAT BRUCE WAYNE IS SUDDENLY RAMPAGING AROUND IN A SUIT AS RAGGED AND TATTERED AS HIS MIND?
HE DIDN'T SEE MUCH BUT WHATEVER IT WAS, IT TOOK THAT SIMPERING STICK INSECT CALIGULA WITH IT.
WHAT DO I CARE?
I ONLY NEED A FEW HOURS TO PREPARE ARKHAM ASYLUM FOR THE FINAL ACT.
CHARLIE WILL SQUEAL, OF COURSE.
HE'LL TELL BATMAN EVERYTHING...
...AND SEND HIM CHARGING STRAIGHT INTO OUR TRAP.
WAKE UP, BETRAYER!
THE USURPER WAS NEVER MY SON, WAS HE?
IT WAS YOU... YOU AND MARTHA, MY ADULTEROUS WITCH OF A WIFE, AM I RIGHT?
WELL, ALFRED?!

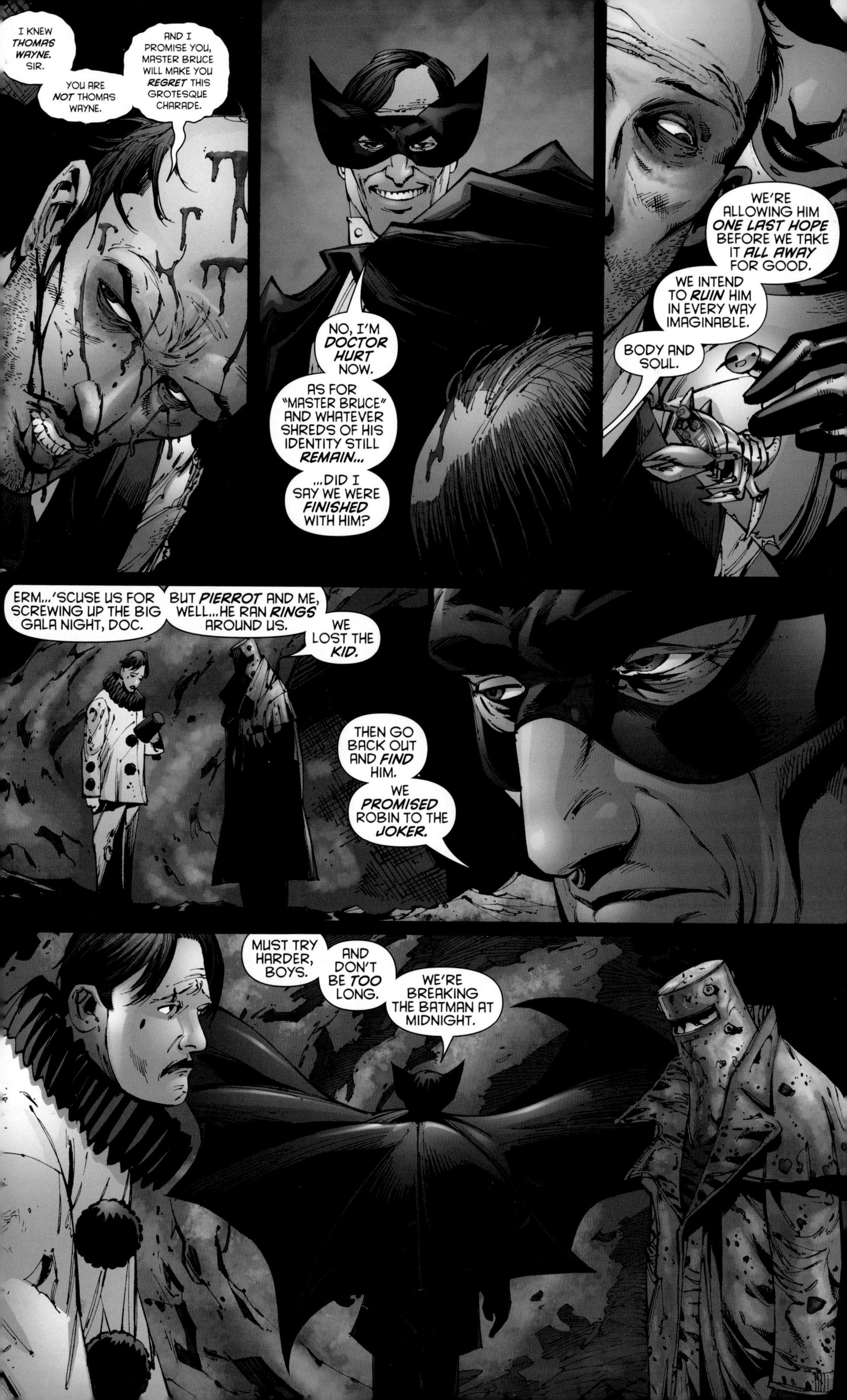
I KNEW *THOMAS WAYNE.* SIR.
YOU ARE *NOT* THOMAS WAYNE.
AND I PROMISE YOU, MASTER BRUCE WILL MAKE YOU *REGRET* THIS GROTESQUE CHARADE.
NO, I'M *DOCTOR HURT* NOW.
AS FOR "MASTER BRUCE" AND WHATEVER SHREDS OF HIS IDENTITY STILL *REMAIN...*
...DID I SAY WE WERE *FINISHED* WITH HIM?
WE'RE ALLOWING HIM *ONE LAST HOPE* BEFORE WE TAKE IT *ALL AWAY* FOR GOOD.
WE INTEND TO *RUIN* HIM IN EVERY WAY IMAGINABLE.
BODY AND SOUL.
ERM...'SCUSE US FOR SCREWING UP THE BIG GALA NIGHT, DOC.
BUT *PIERROT* AND ME, WELL...HE RAN *RINGS* AROUND US.
WE LOST THE *KID.*
THEN GO BACK OUT AND *FIND* HIM.
WE *PROMISED* ROBIN TO THE *JOKER.*
MUST TRY HARDER, BOYS.
AND DON'T BE *TOO* LONG.
WE'RE BREAKING THE BATMAN AT MIDNIGHT.

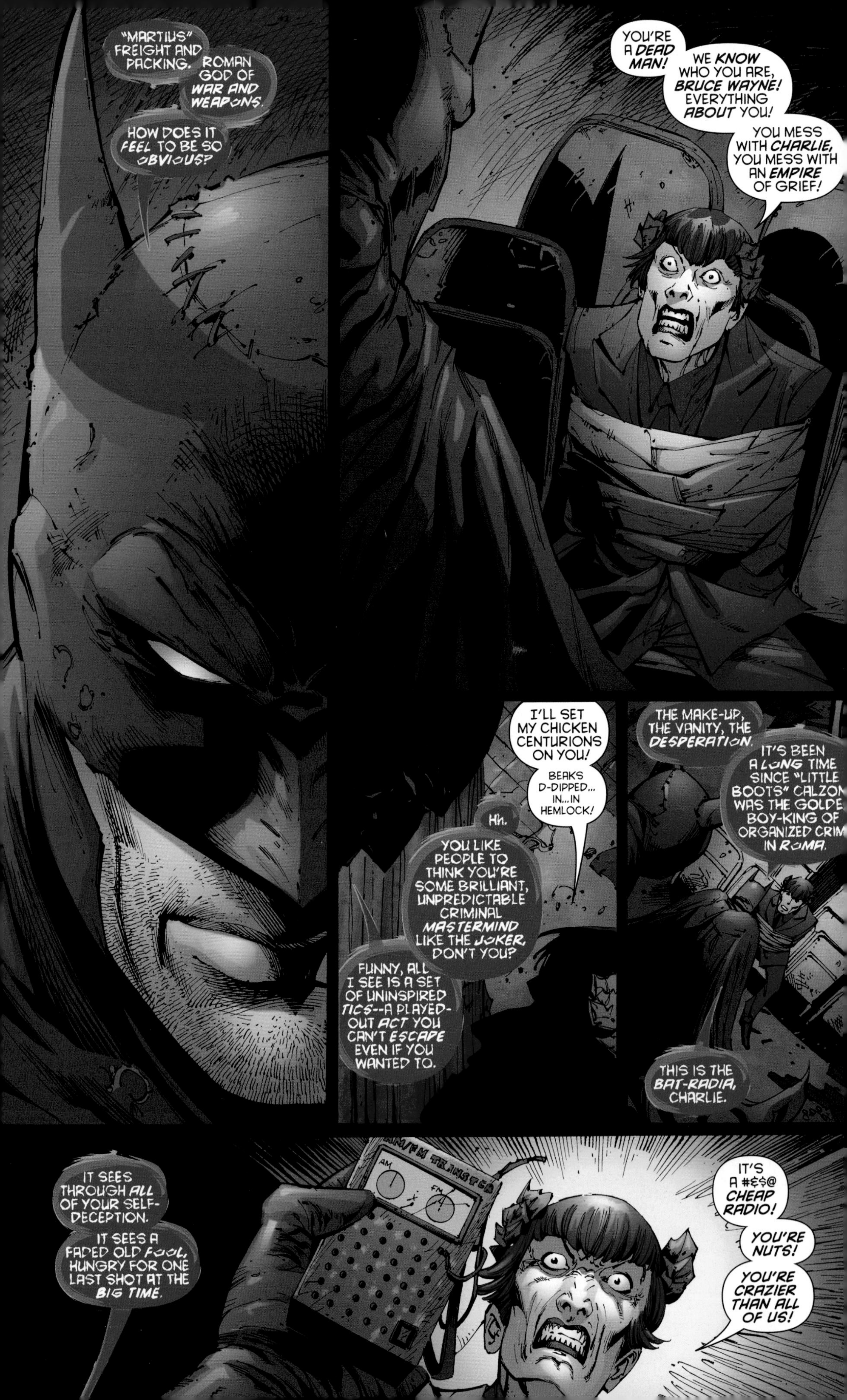

"MARTIUS" FREIGHT AND PACKING.
ROMAN GOD OF WAR AND WEAPONS.
HOW DOES IT FEEL TO BE SO OBVIOUS?
YOU'RE A DEAD MAN!
WE KNOW WHO YOU ARE, BRUCE WAYNE! EVERYTHING ABOUT YOU!
YOU MESS WITH CHARLIE, YOU MESS WITH AN EMPIRE OF GRIEF!
I'LL SET MY CHICKEN CENTURIONS ON YOU!
BEAKS D-DIPPED... IN...IN HEMLOCK!
Hh.
YOU LIKE PEOPLE TO THINK YOU'RE SOME BRILLIANT, UNPREDICTABLE CRIMINAL MASTERMIND LIKE THE JOKER, DON'T YOU?
FUNNY, ALL I SEE IS A SET OF UNINSPIRED TICS--A PLAYED-OUT ACT YOU CAN'T ESCAPE EVEN IF YOU WANTED TO.
THE MAKE-UP, THE VANITY, THE DESPERATION.
IT'S BEEN A LONG TIME SINCE "LITTLE BOOTS" CALZON WAS THE GOLDE BOY-KING OF ORGANIZED CRIM IN ROMA.
THIS IS THE BAT-RADIA, CHARLIE.
IT SEES THROUGH ALL OF YOUR SELF-DECEPTION.
IT SEES A FADED OLD FOOL, HUNGRY FOR ONE LAST SHOT AT THE BIG TIME.
IT'S A #€$@ CHEAP RADIO!
YOU'RE NUTS!
YOU'RE CRAZIER THAN ALL OF US!

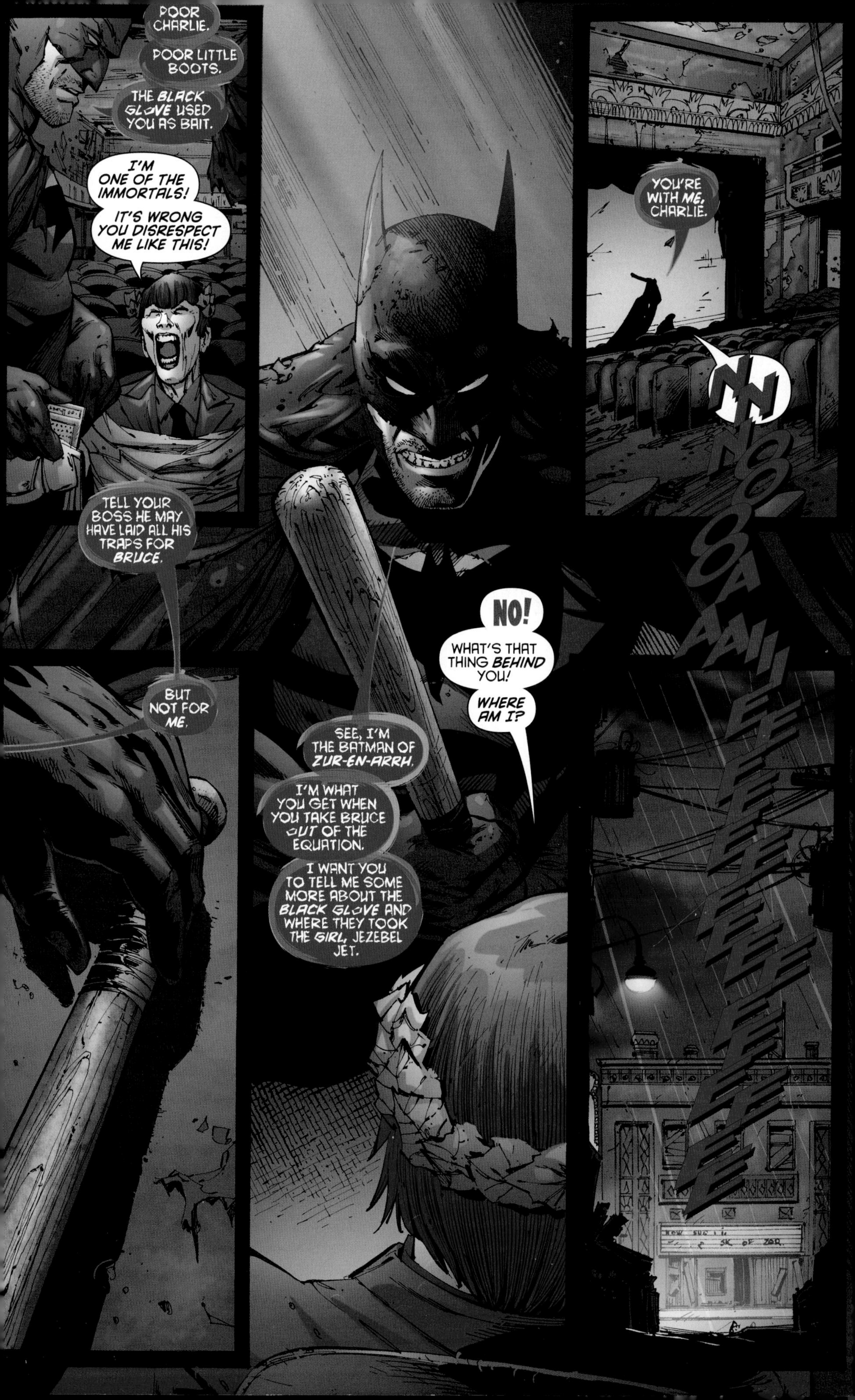

POOR CHARLIE.
POOR LITTLE BOOTS.
THE *BLACK GLOVE* USED YOU AS BAIT.
I'M ONE OF THE IMMORTALS!
IT'S WRONG YOU DISRESPECT ME LIKE THIS!
YOU'RE WITH *ME*, CHARLIE.
NNNOOOOAAAIIIEEEEEEEEEEE
TELL YOUR BOSS HE MAY HAVE LAID ALL HIS TRAPS FOR *BRUCE*.
BUT NOT FOR *ME*.
NO!
WHAT'S THAT THING *BEHIND* YOU!
WHERE AM I?
SEE, I'M THE BATMAN OF *ZUR-EN-ARRH*.
I'M WHAT YOU GET WHEN YOU TAKE BRUCE *OUT* OF THE EQUATION.
I WANT YOU TO TELL ME SOME MORE ABOUT THE *BLACK GLOVE* AND WHERE THEY TOOK THE *GIRL*, JEZEBEL JET.

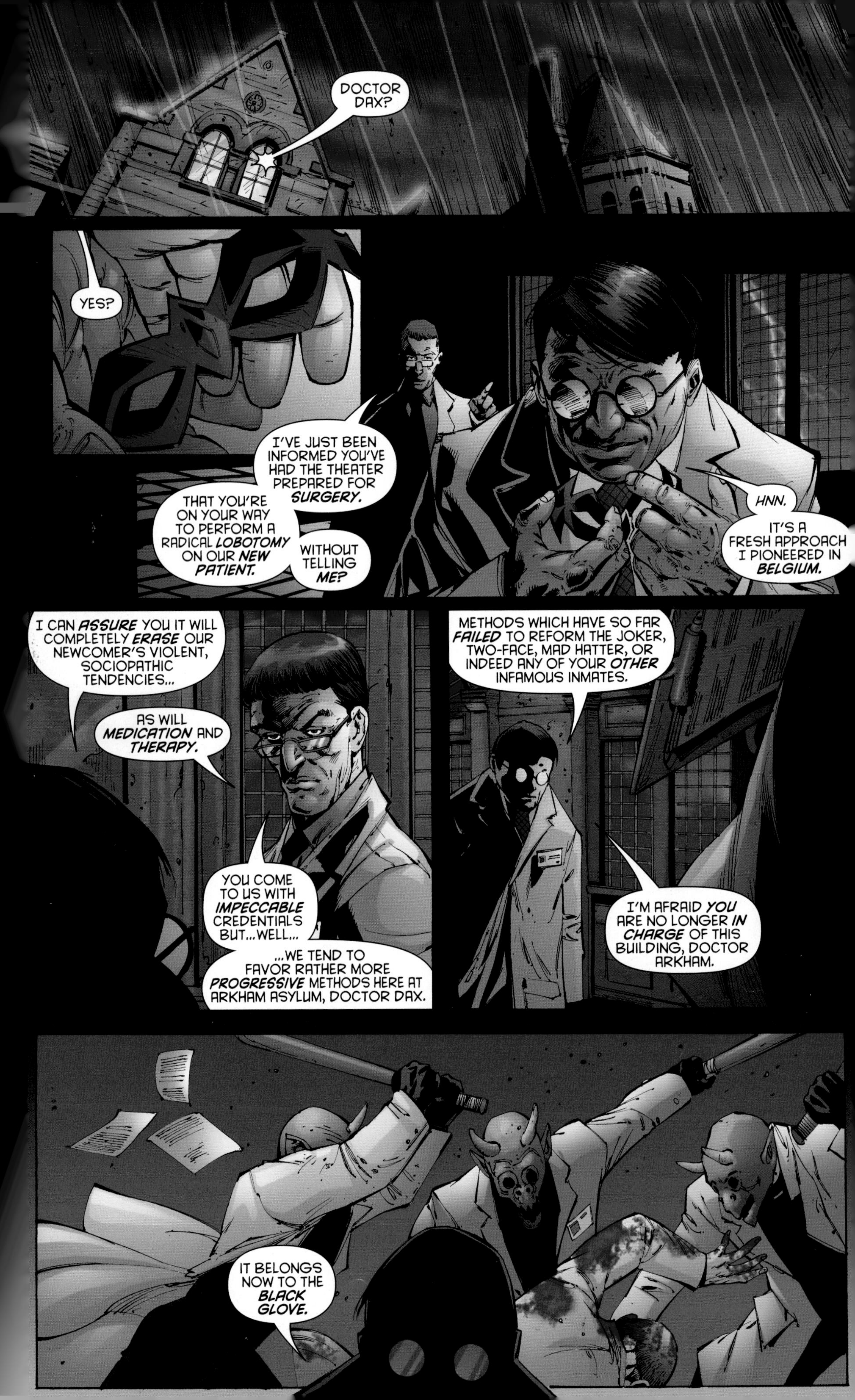
DOCTOR DAX?
YES?
I'VE JUST BEEN INFORMED YOU'VE HAD THE THEATER PREPARED FOR *SURGERY.*
THAT YOU'RE ON YOUR WAY TO PERFORM A RADICAL *LOBOTOMY* ON OUR *NEW PATIENT.*
WITHOUT TELLING *ME?*
HNN.
IT'S A FRESH APPROACH I PIONEERED IN *BELGIUM.*
I CAN *ASSURE* YOU IT WILL COMPLETELY *ERASE* OUR NEWCOMER'S VIOLENT, SOCIOPATHIC TENDENCIES...
AS WILL *MEDICATION* AND *THERAPY.*
YOU COME TO US WITH *IMPECCABLE* CREDENTIALS BUT...WELL...
...WE TEND TO FAVOR RATHER MORE *PROGRESSIVE* METHODS HERE AT ARKHAM ASYLUM, DOCTOR DAX.
METHODS WHICH HAVE SO FAR *FAILED* TO REFORM THE JOKER, TWO-FACE, MAD HATTER, OR INDEED ANY OF YOUR *OTHER* INFAMOUS INMATES.
I'M AFRAID *YOU* ARE NO LONGER *IN CHARGE* OF THIS BUILDING, DOCTOR ARKHAM.
IT BELONGS NOW TO THE *BLACK GLOVE.*

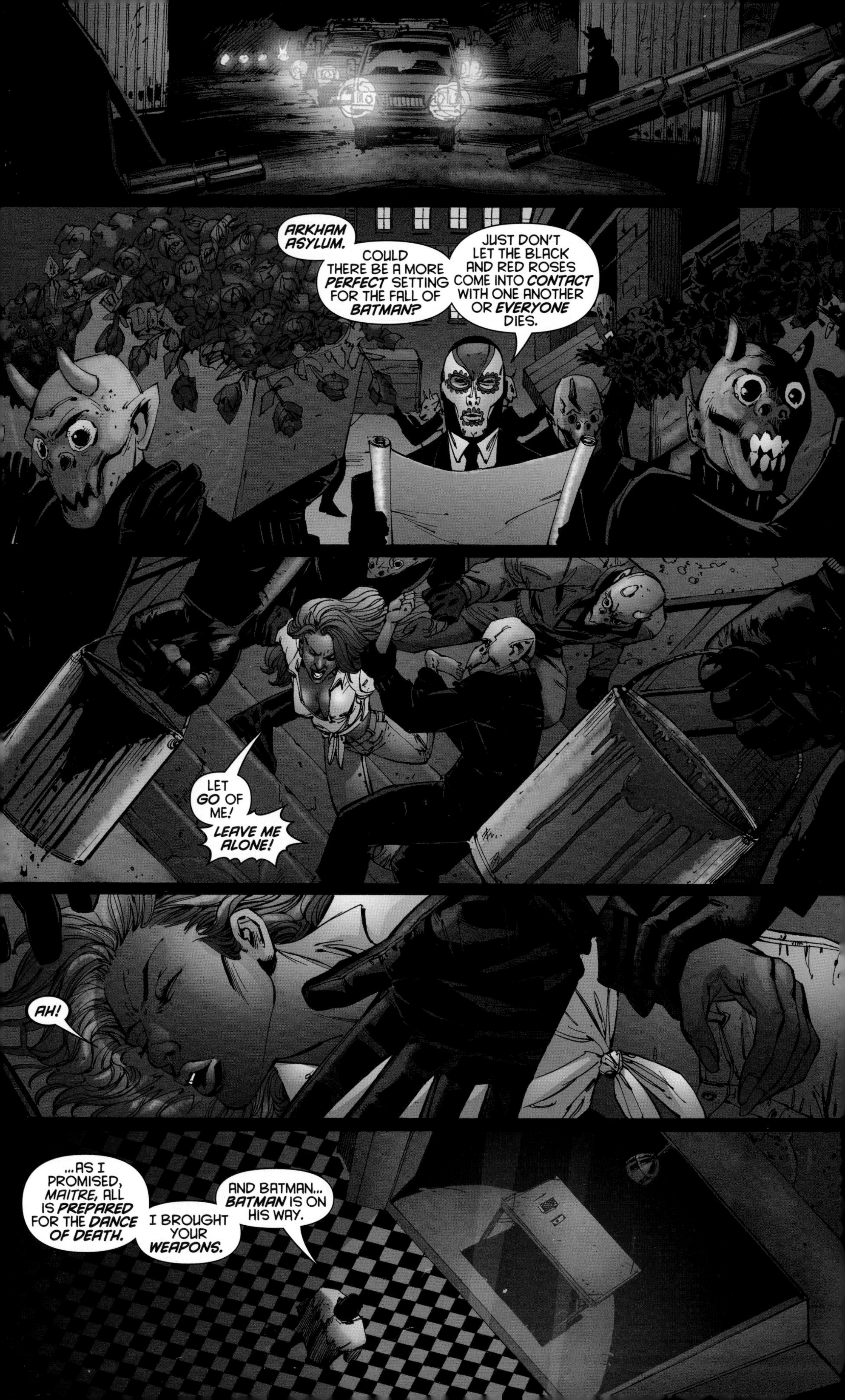
ARKHAM ASYLUM.
COULD THERE BE A MORE PERFECT SETTING FOR THE FALL OF BATMAN?
JUST DON'T LET THE BLACK AND RED ROSES COME INTO CONTACT WITH ONE ANOTHER OR EVERYONE DIES.
LET GO OF ME! LEAVE ME ALONE!
AH!
...AS I PROMISED, MAITRE, ALL IS PREPARED FOR THE DANCE OF DEATH.
I BROUGHT YOUR WEAPONS.
AND BATMAN... BATMAN IS ON HIS WAY.

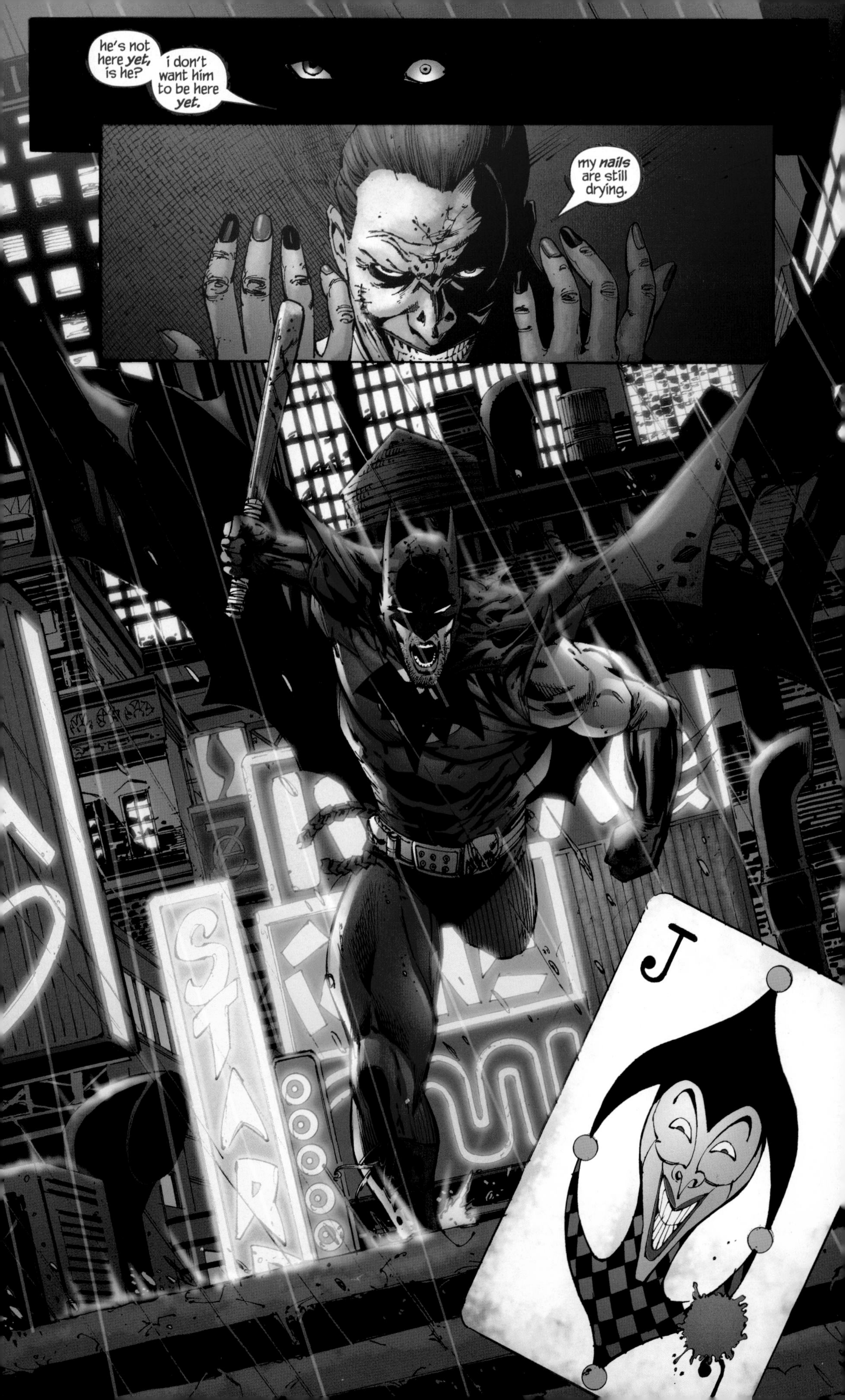
he's not here *yet*, is he?
i don't want him to be here *yet*.
my *nails* are still drying.
J

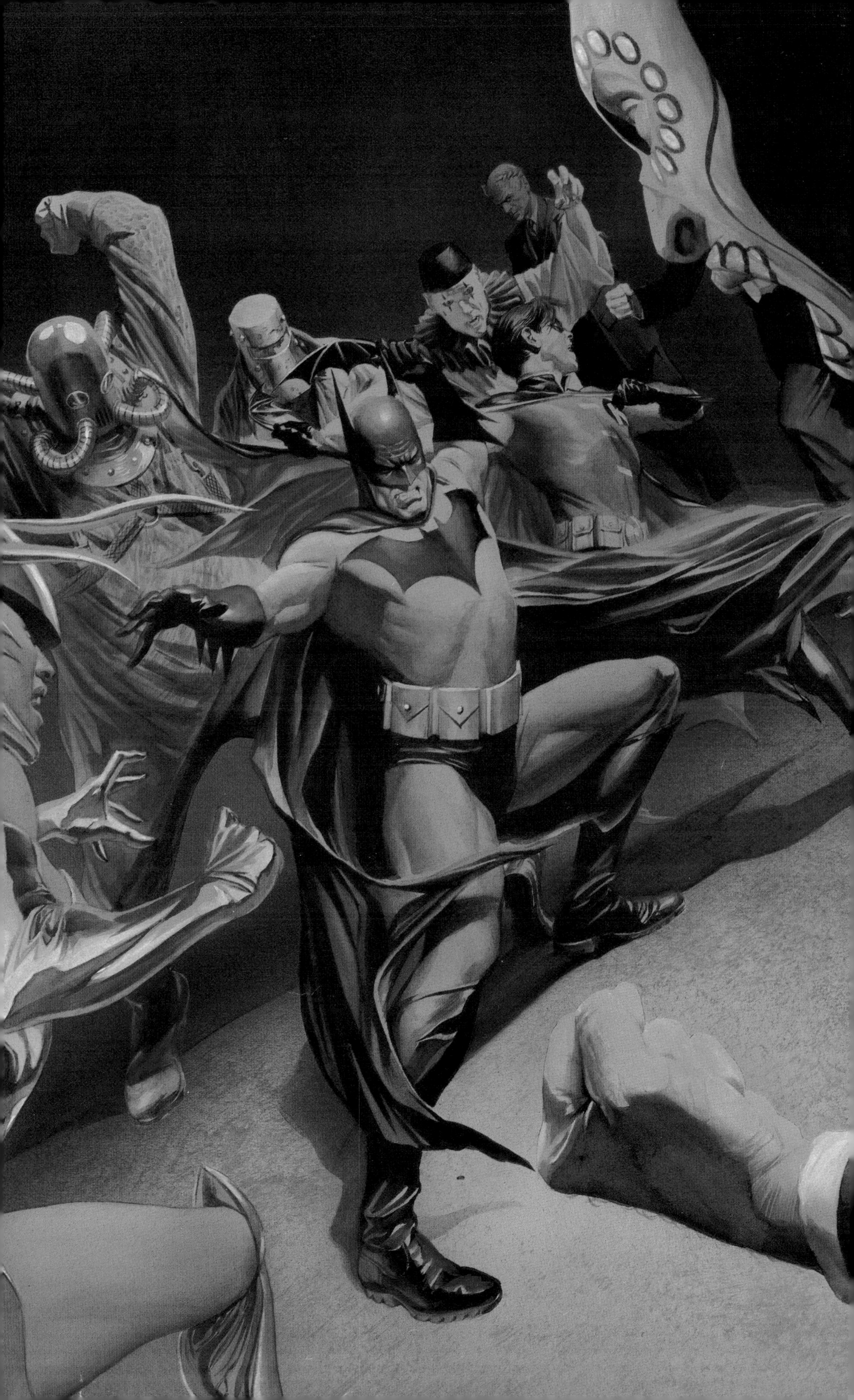

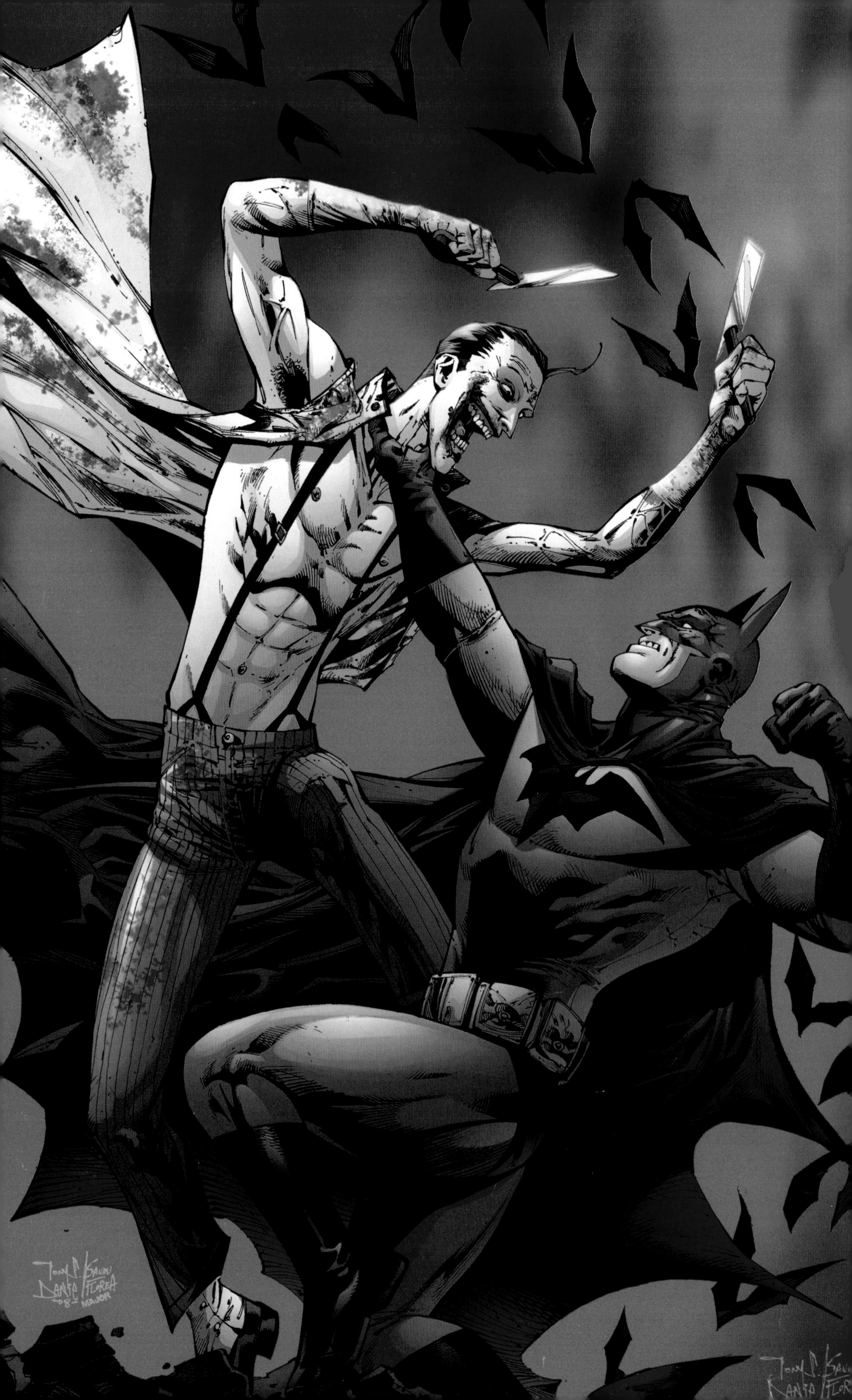

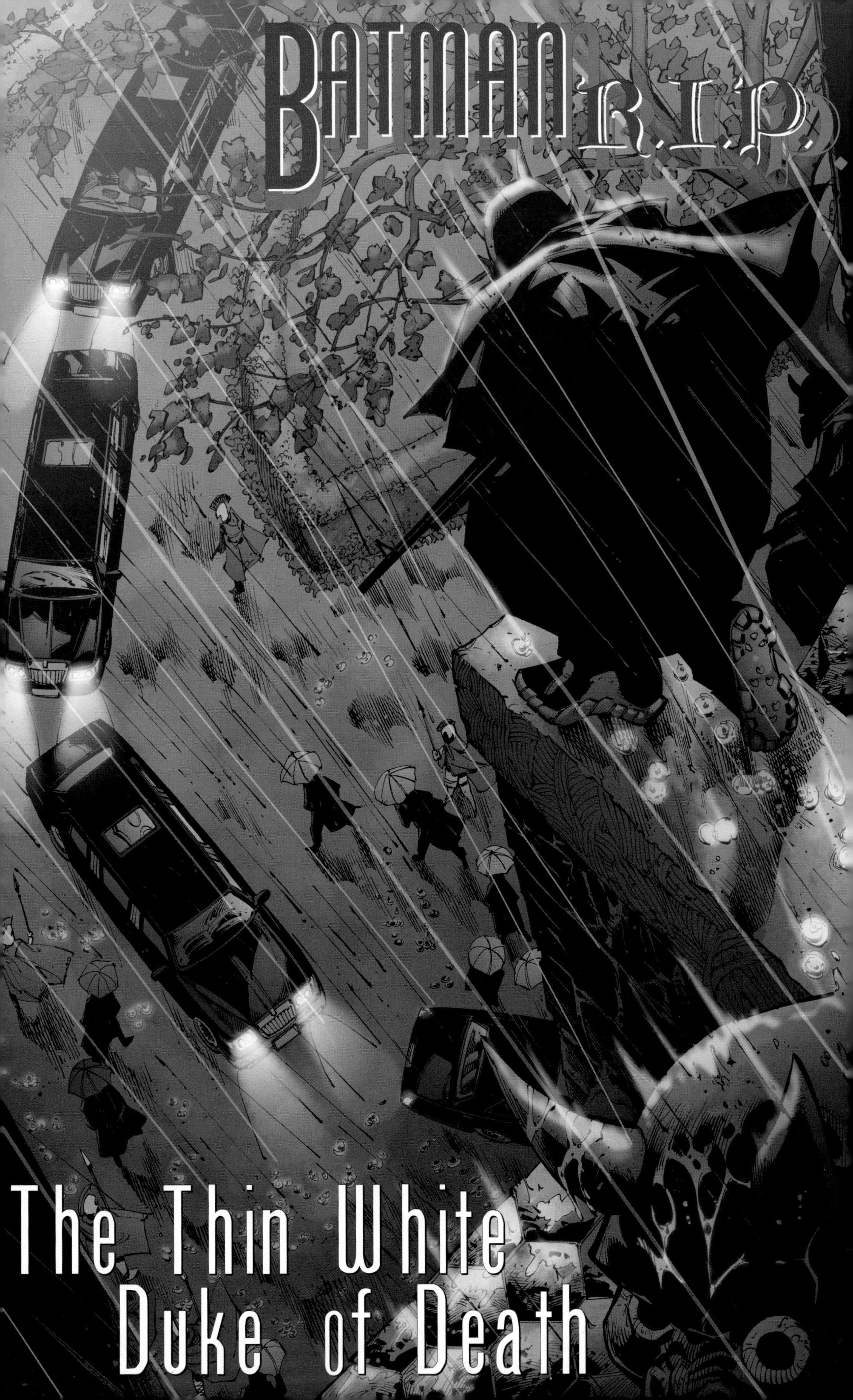
BATMAN R.I.P.
The Thin White
Duke of Death

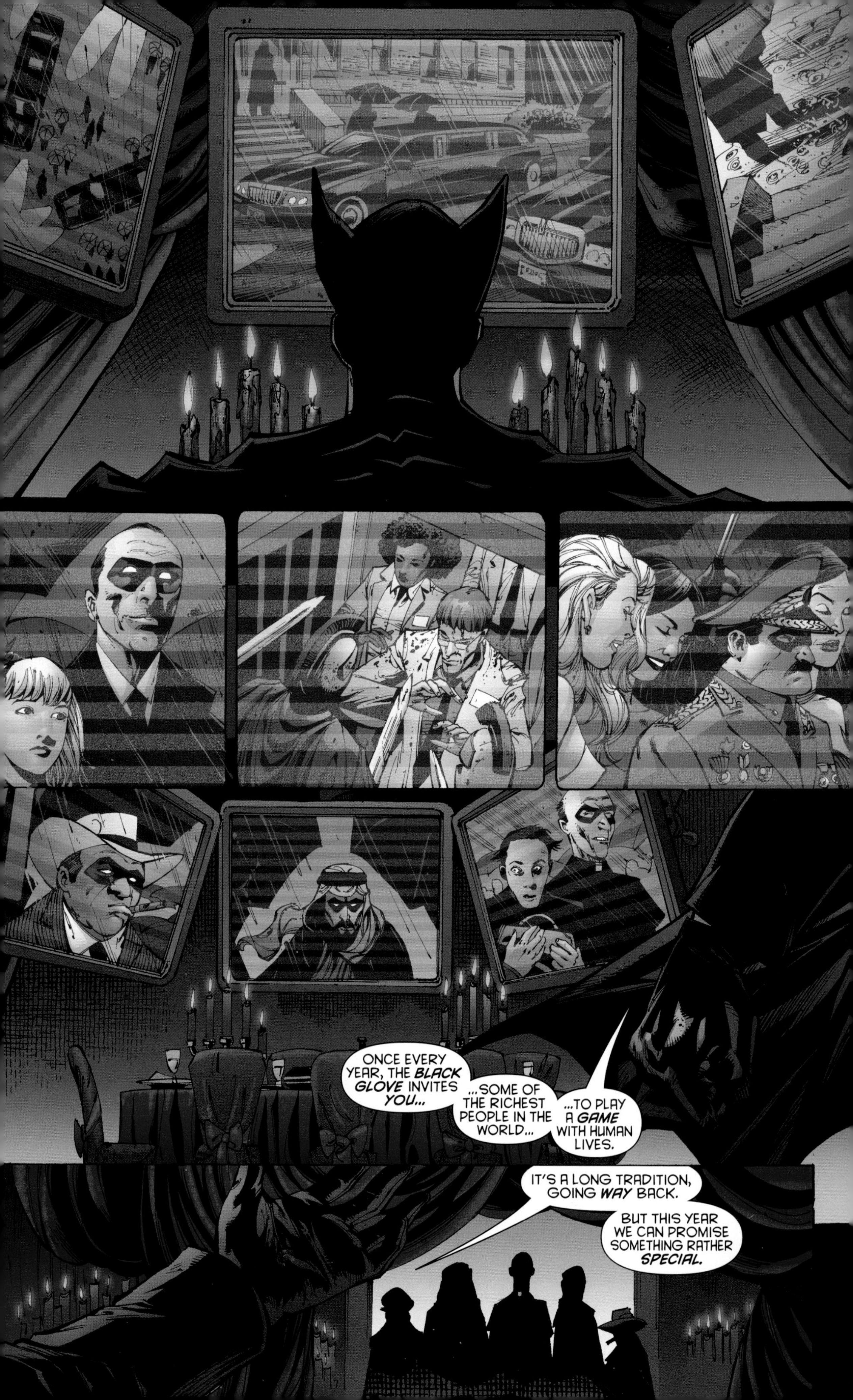
ONCE EVERY YEAR, THE BLACK GLOVE INVITES YOU...
...SOME OF THE RICHEST PEOPLE IN THE WORLD...
...TO PLAY A GAME WITH HUMAN LIVES.
IT'S A LONG TRADITION, GOING WAY BACK.
BUT THIS YEAR WE CAN PROMISE SOMETHING RATHER SPECIAL.

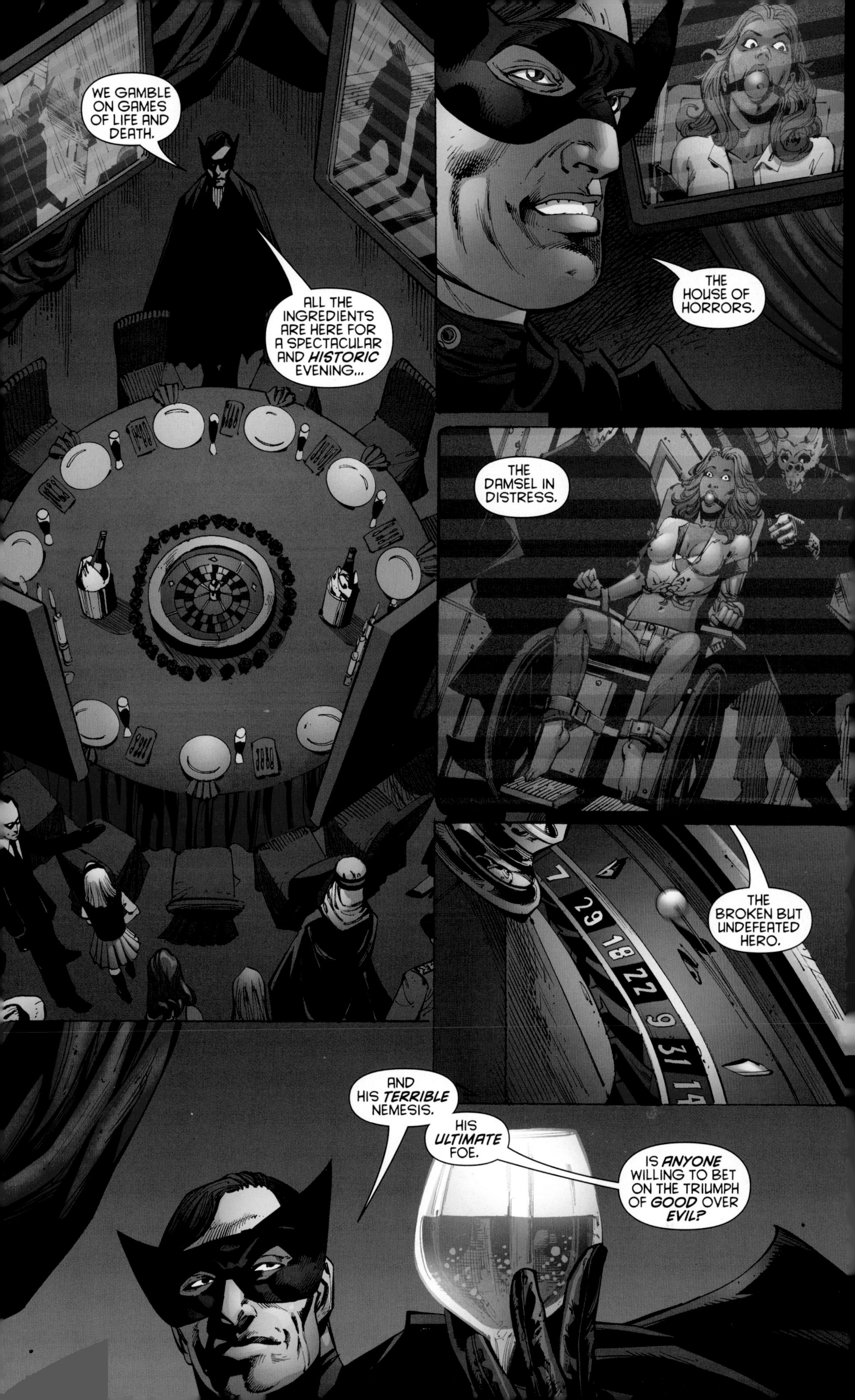
WE GAMBLE ON GAMES OF LIFE AND DEATH.
ALL THE INGREDIENTS ARE HERE FOR A SPECTACULAR AND *HISTORIC* EVENING...
THE HOUSE OF HORRORS.
THE DAMSEL IN DISTRESS.
THE BROKEN BUT UNDEFEATED HERO.
AND HIS *TERRIBLE* NEMESIS.
HIS *ULTIMATE* FOE.
IS *ANYONE* WILLING TO BET ON THE TRIUMPH OF *GOOD* OVER *EVIL?*

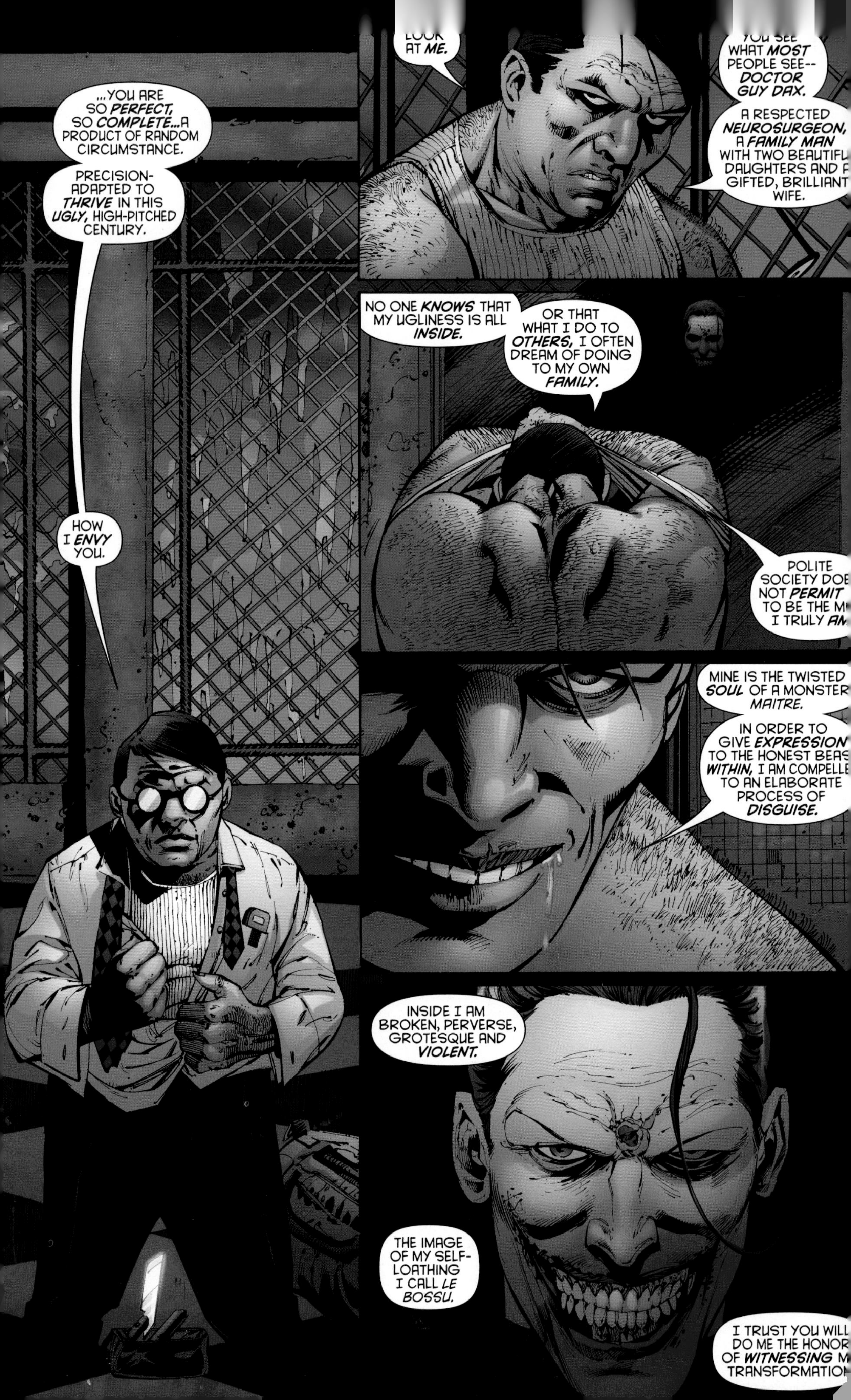
...YOU ARE SO PERFECT, SO COMPLETE...A PRODUCT OF RANDOM CIRCUMSTANCE.
PRECISION-ADAPTED TO THRIVE IN THIS UGLY, HIGH-PITCHED CENTURY.
HOW I ENVY YOU.
LOOK AT ME.
YOU SEE WHAT MOST PEOPLE SEE-- DOCTOR GUY DAX.
A RESPECTED NEUROSURGEON, A FAMILY MAN WITH TWO BEAUTIFL DAUGHTERS AND A GIFTED, BRILLIANT WIFE.
NO ONE KNOWS THAT MY UGLINESS IS ALL INSIDE.
OR THAT WHAT I DO TO OTHERS, I OFTEN DREAM OF DOING TO MY OWN FAMILY.
POLITE SOCIETY DOE NOT PERMIT TO BE THE M I TRULY AM.
MINE IS THE TWISTED SOUL OF A MONSTER MAITRE.
IN ORDER TO GIVE EXPRESSION TO THE HONEST BEAS WITHIN, I AM COMPELLE TO AN ELABORATE PROCESS OF DISGUISE.
INSIDE I AM BROKEN, PERVERSE, GROTESQUE AND VIOLENT.
THE IMAGE OF MY SELF-LOATHING I CALL LE BOSSU.
I TRUST YOU WILL DO ME THE HONOR OF WITNESSING M TRANSFORMATIO

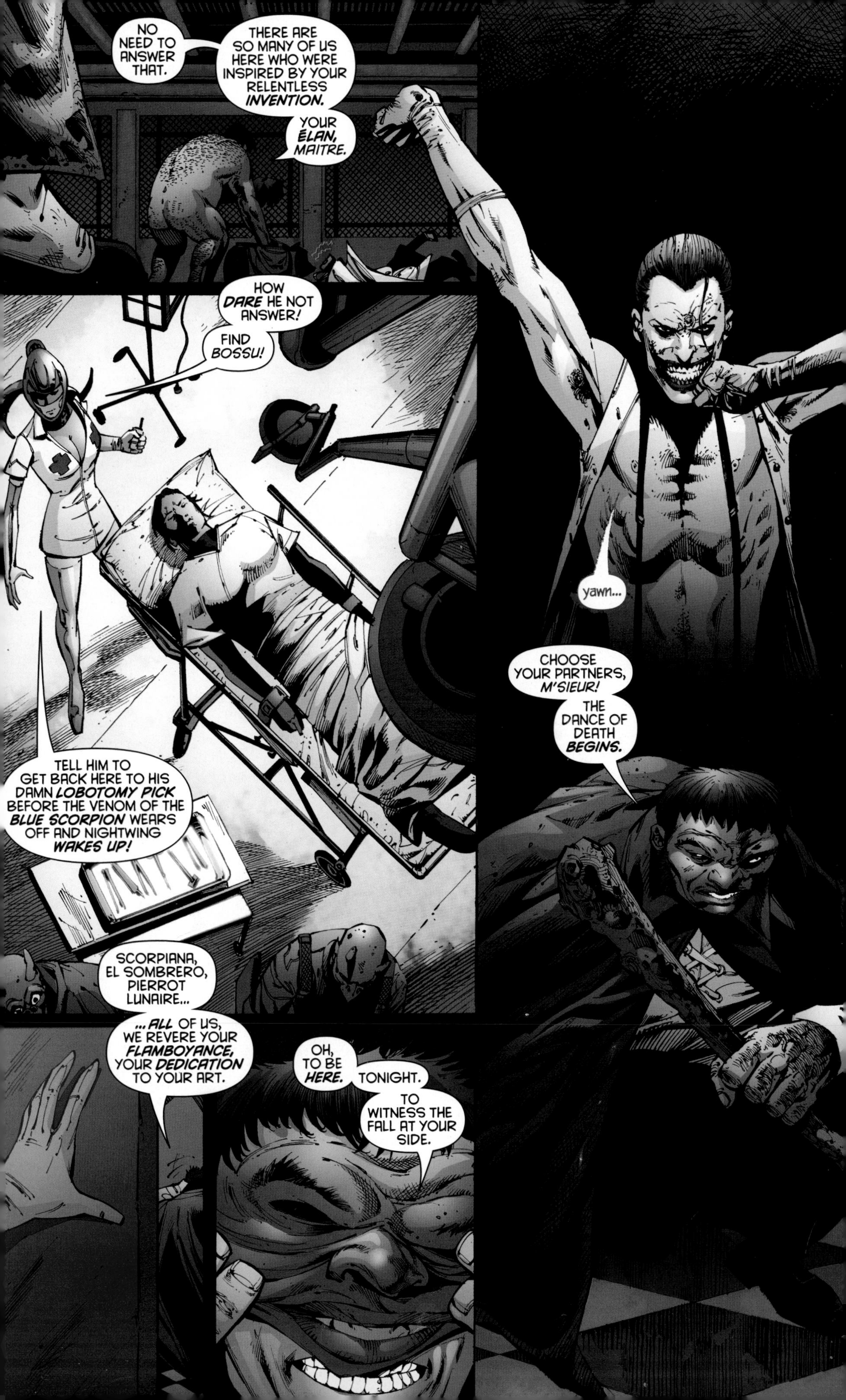
NO NEED TO ANSWER THAT.
THERE ARE SO MANY OF US HERE WHO WERE INSPIRED BY YOUR RELENTLESS INVENTION.
YOUR ÉLAN, MAITRE.
HOW DARE HE NOT ANSWER!
FIND BOSSU!
TELL HIM TO GET BACK HERE TO HIS DAMN LOBOTOMY PICK BEFORE THE VENOM OF THE BLUE SCORPION WEARS OFF AND NIGHTWING WAKES UP!
SCORPIANA, EL SOMBRERO, PIERROT LUNAIRE...
...ALL OF US, WE REVERE YOUR FLAMBOYANCE, YOUR DEDICATION TO YOUR ART.
OH, TO BE HERE.
TONIGHT.
TO WITNESS THE FALL AT YOUR SIDE.
yawn...
CHOOSE YOUR PARTNERS, M'SIEUR!
THE DANCE OF DEATH BEGINS.

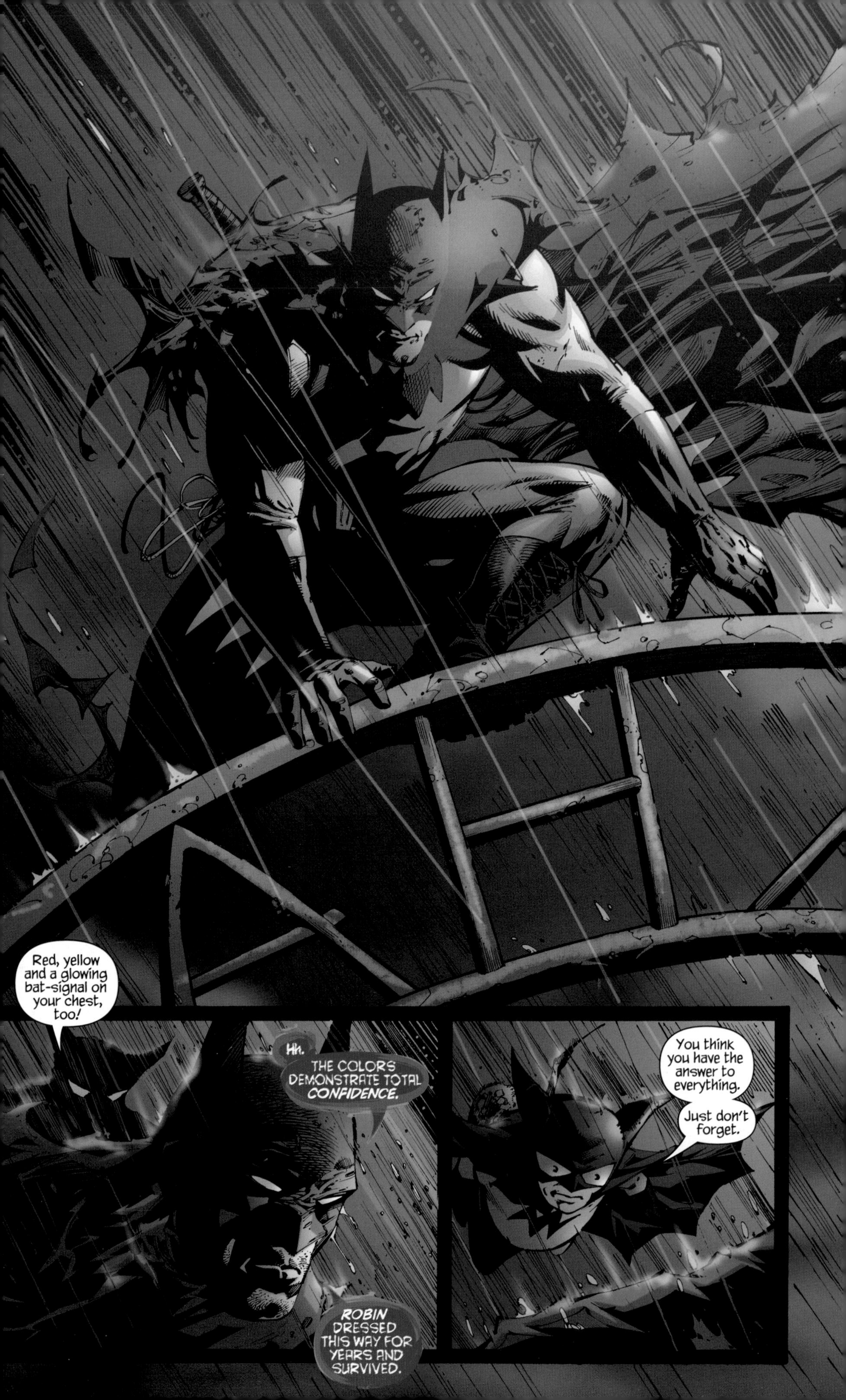
Red, yellow and a glowing bat-signal on your chest, too!
Hh.
THE COLORS DEMONSTRATE TOTAL CONFIDENCE.
ROBIN DRESSED THIS WAY FOR YEARS AND SURVIVED.
You think you have the answer to everything.
Just don't forget.

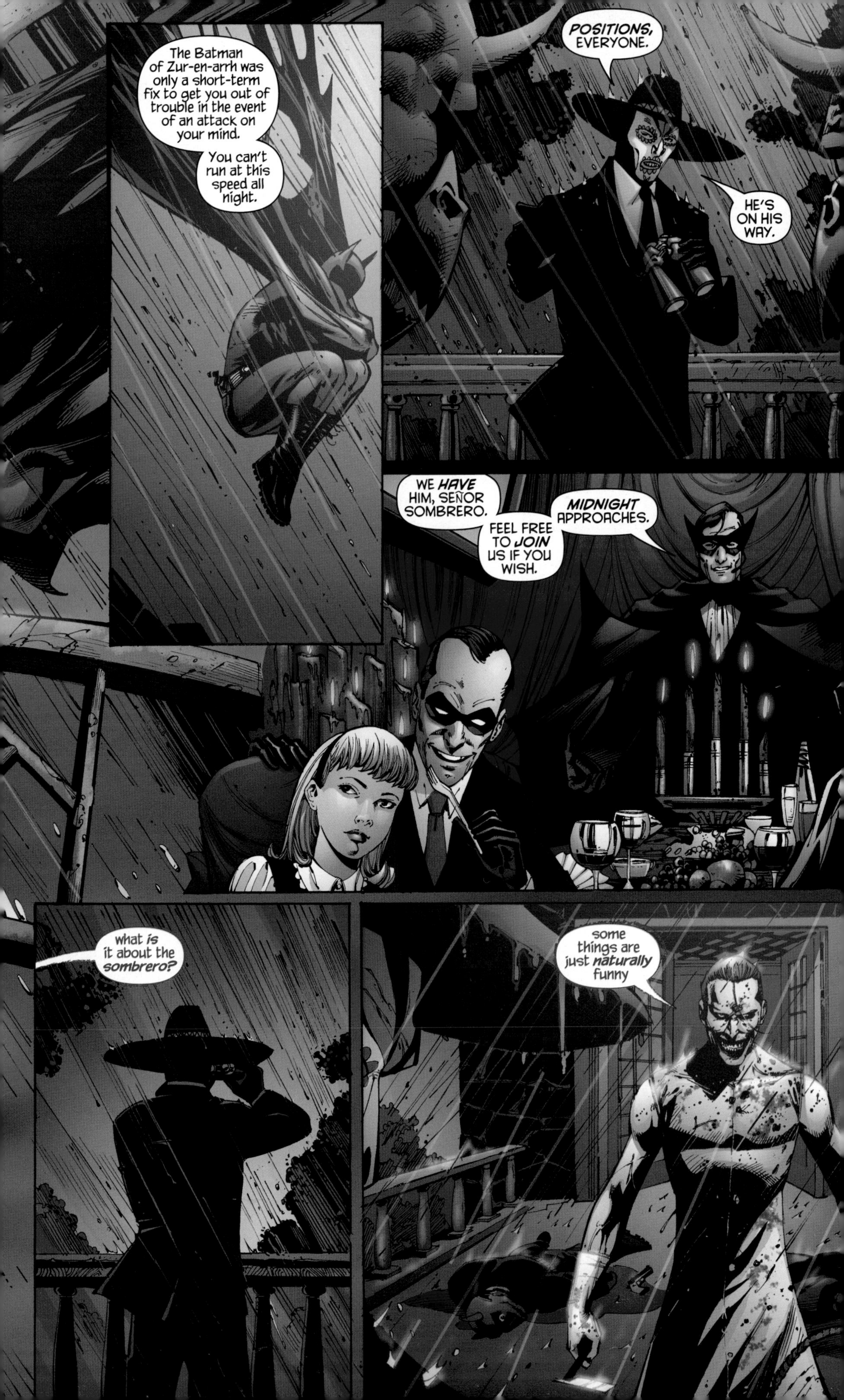
The Batman of Zur-en-arrh was only a short-term fix to get you out of trouble in the event of an attack on your mind.
You can't run at this speed all night.
POSITIONS, EVERYONE.
HE'S ON HIS WAY.
WE HAVE HIM, SEÑOR SOMBRERO.
FEEL FREE TO JOIN US IF YOU WISH.
MIDNIGHT APPROACHES.
what is it about the sombrero?
some things are just naturally funny

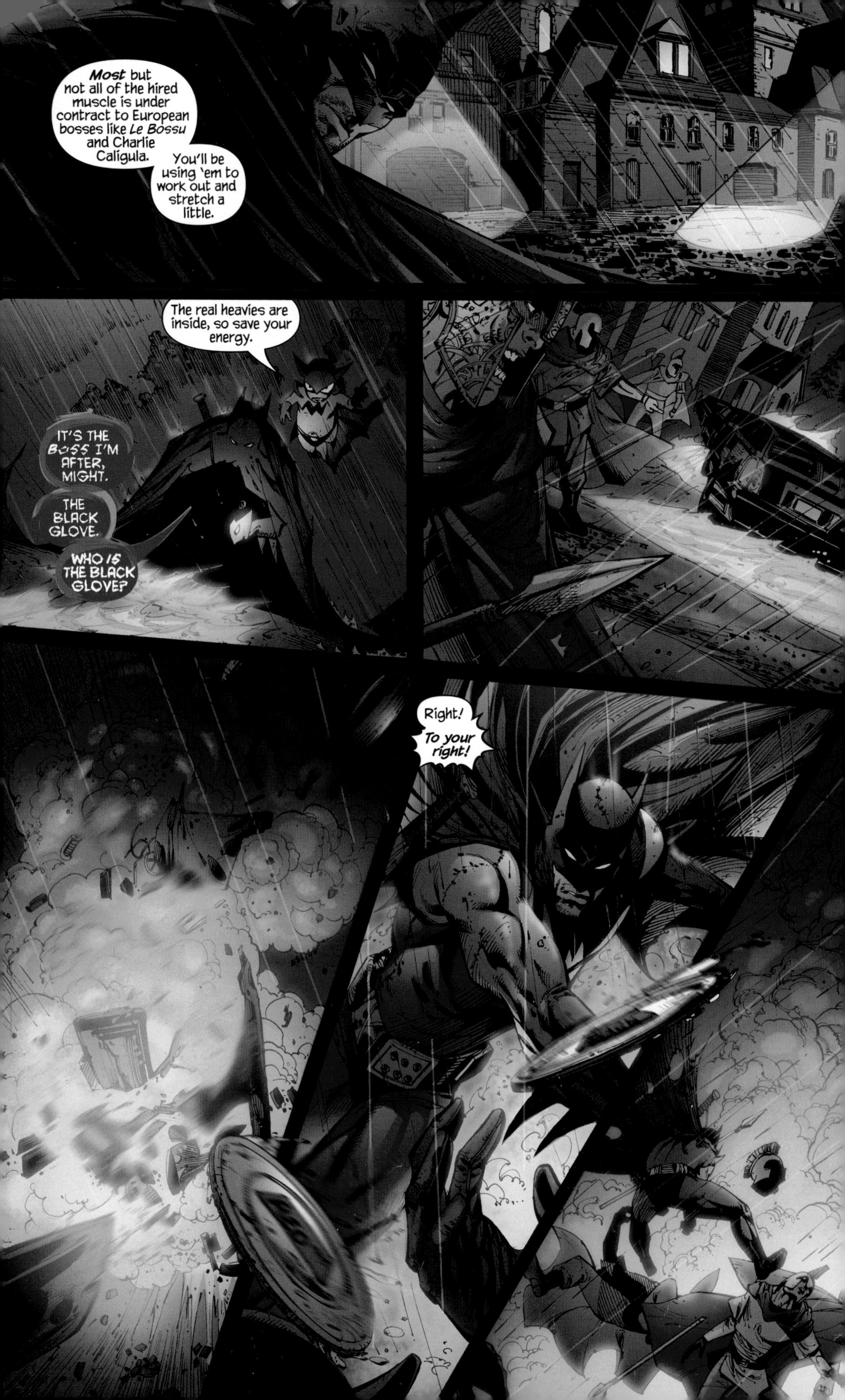
Most but not all of the hired muscle is under contract to European bosses like *Le Bossu* and Charlie Caligula.
You'll be using 'em to work out and stretch a little.
The real heavies are inside, so save your energy.
IT'S THE *BOSS* I'M AFTER, MIGHT.
THE BLACK GLOVE.
WHO *IS* THE BLACK GLOVE?
Right!
To your right!

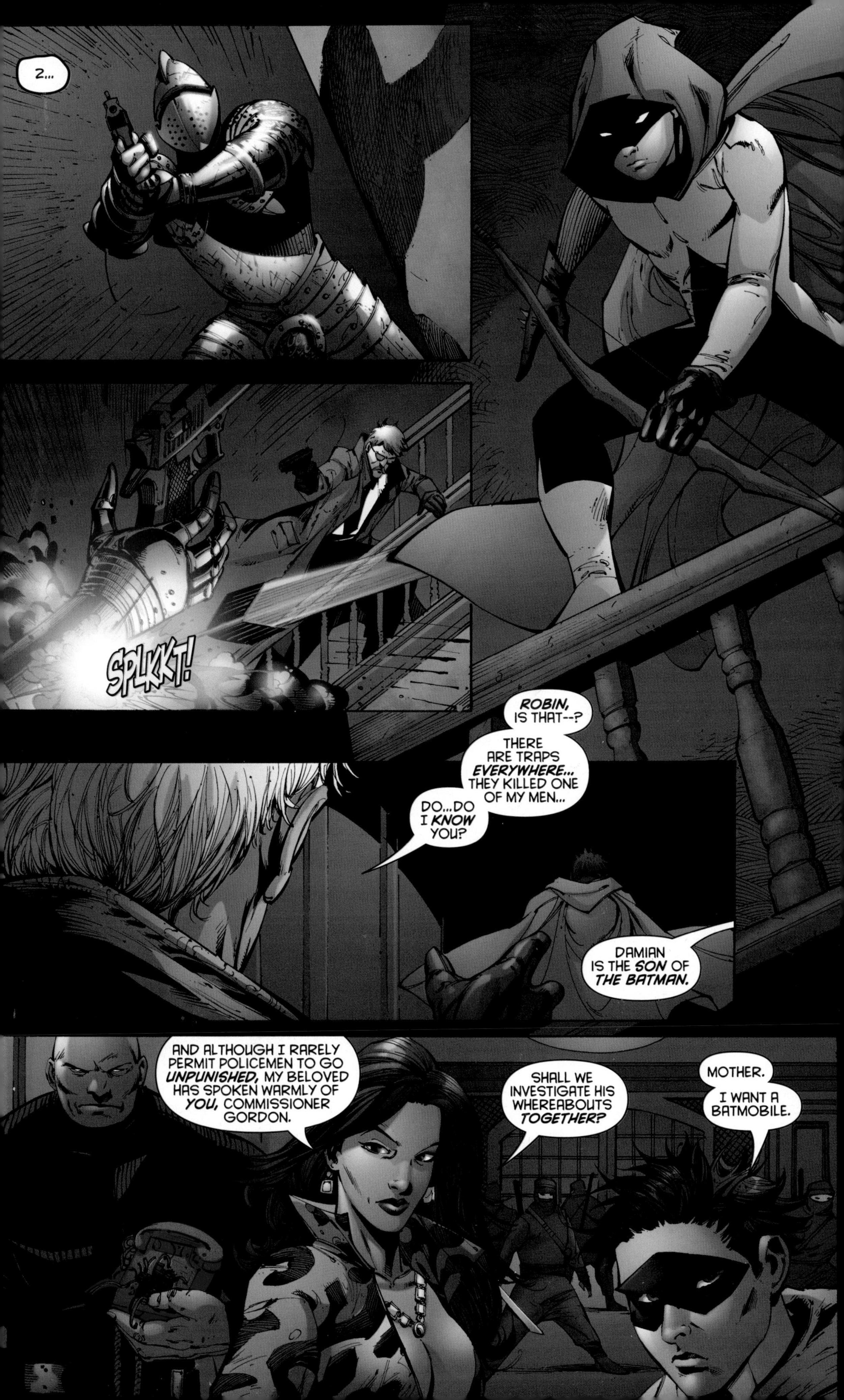
2...
SPLKKT!
ROBIN, IS THAT--?
THERE ARE TRAPS EVERYWHERE... THEY KILLED ONE OF MY MEN...
DO...DO I KNOW YOU?
DAMIAN IS THE SON OF THE BATMAN.
AND ALTHOUGH I RARELY PERMIT POLICEMEN TO GO UNPUNISHED, MY BELOVED HAS SPOKEN WARMLY OF YOU, COMMISSIONER GORDON.
SHALL WE INVESTIGATE HIS WHEREABOUTS TOGETHER?
MOTHER.
I WANT A BATMOBILE.

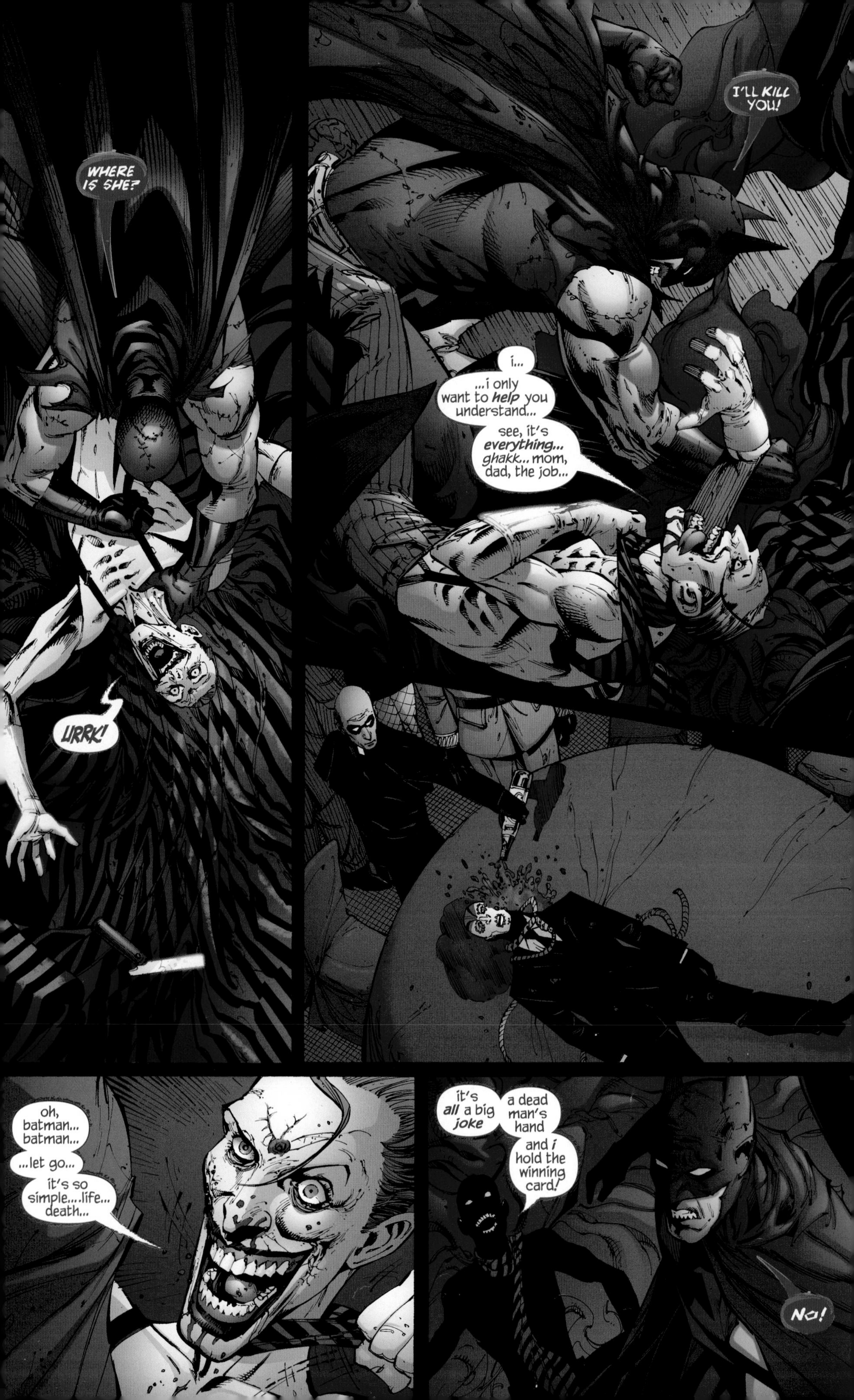
WHERE IS SHE?
URRK!
I'LL KILL YOU!
i...
...i only want to *help* you understand...
see, it's *everything...* *ghakk...* mom, dad, the job...
oh, batman... batman...
...let go...
it's so simple....life... death...
it's *all* a big *joke*
a dead man's hand
and *i* hold the winning card!
No!

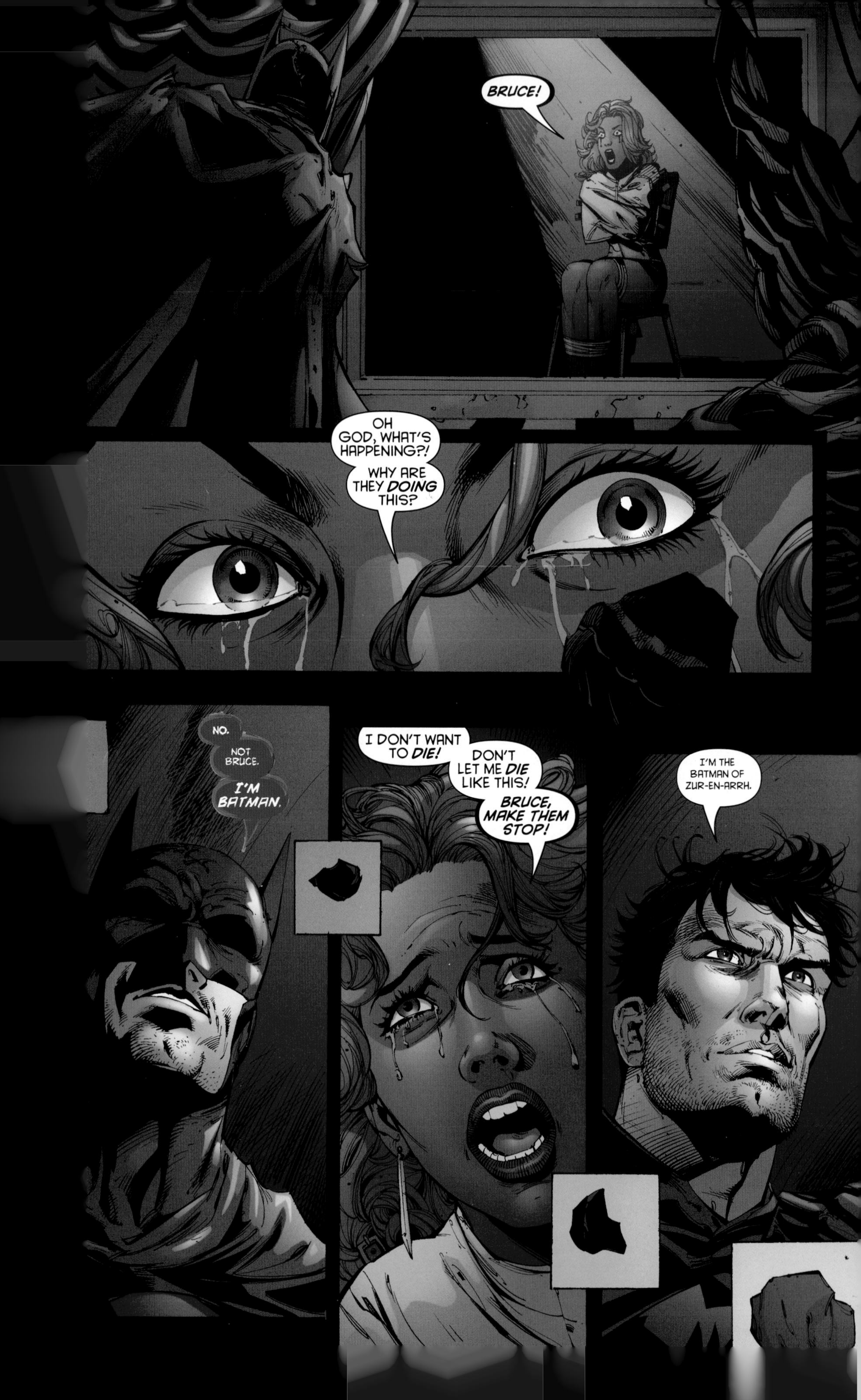
BRUCE!
OH GOD, WHAT'S HAPPENING?!
WHY ARE THEY DOING THIS?
NO.
NOT BRUCE.
I'M BATMAN.
I DON'T WANT TO DIE!
DON'T LET ME DIE LIKE THIS!
BRUCE, MAKE THEM STOP!
I'M THE BATMAN OF ZUR-EN-ARRH.

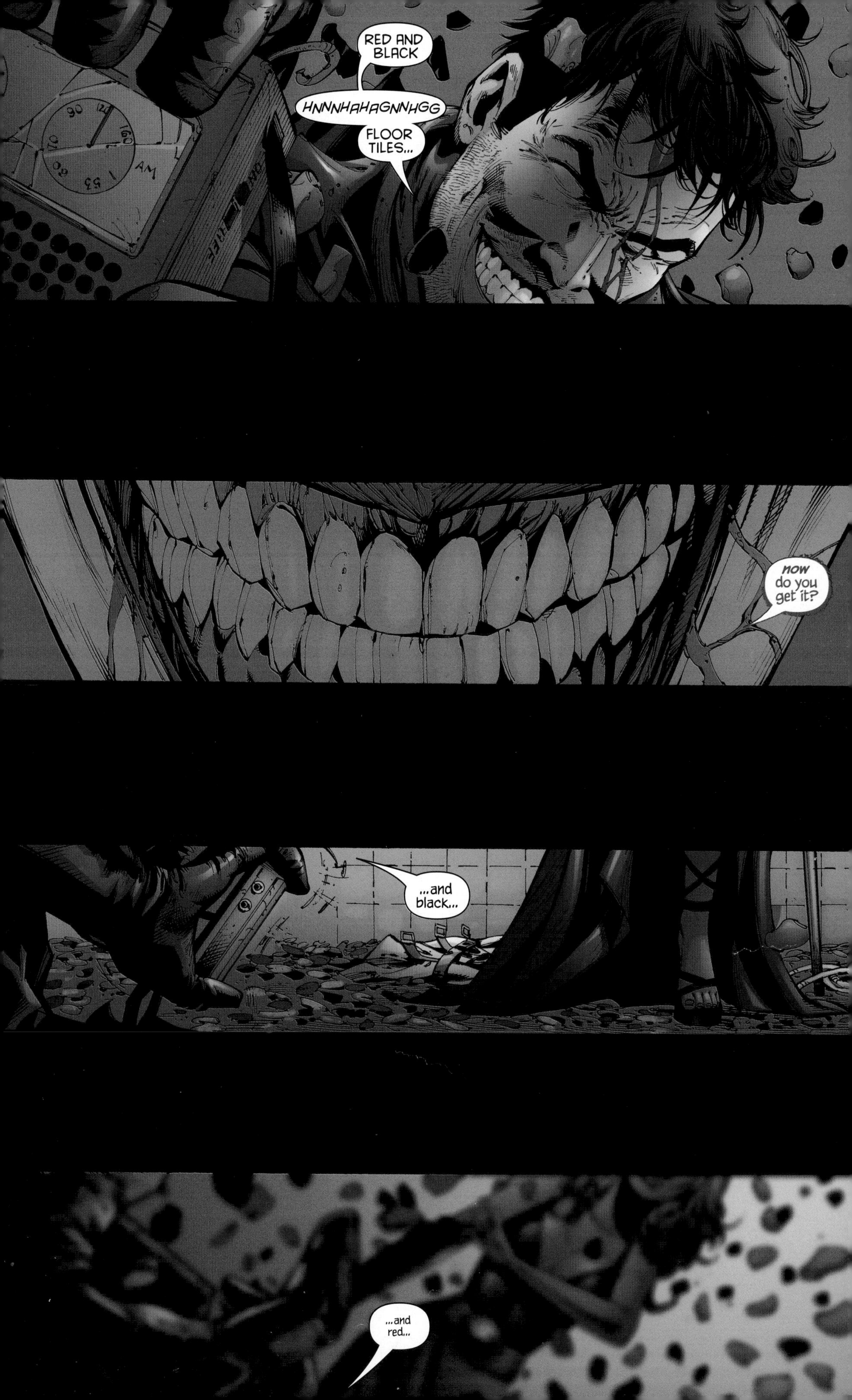
RED AND BLACK
HNNNHAHAGNNHGG
FLOOR TILES...
now do you get it?
...and black...
...and red...

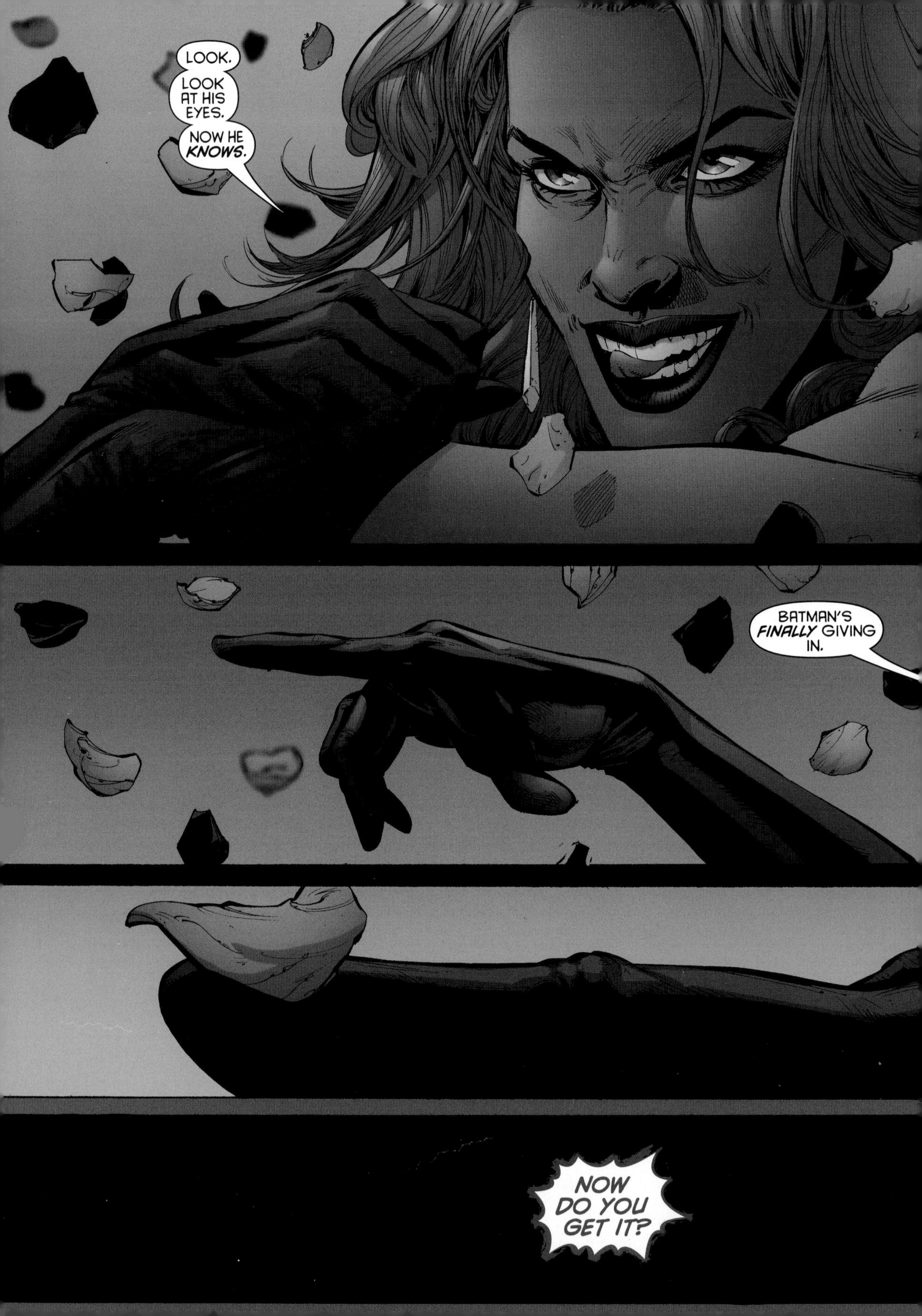
LOOK.
LOOK AT HIS EYES.
NOW HE *KNOWS*.
BATMAN'S *FINALLY* GIVING IN.
NOW DO YOU GET IT?

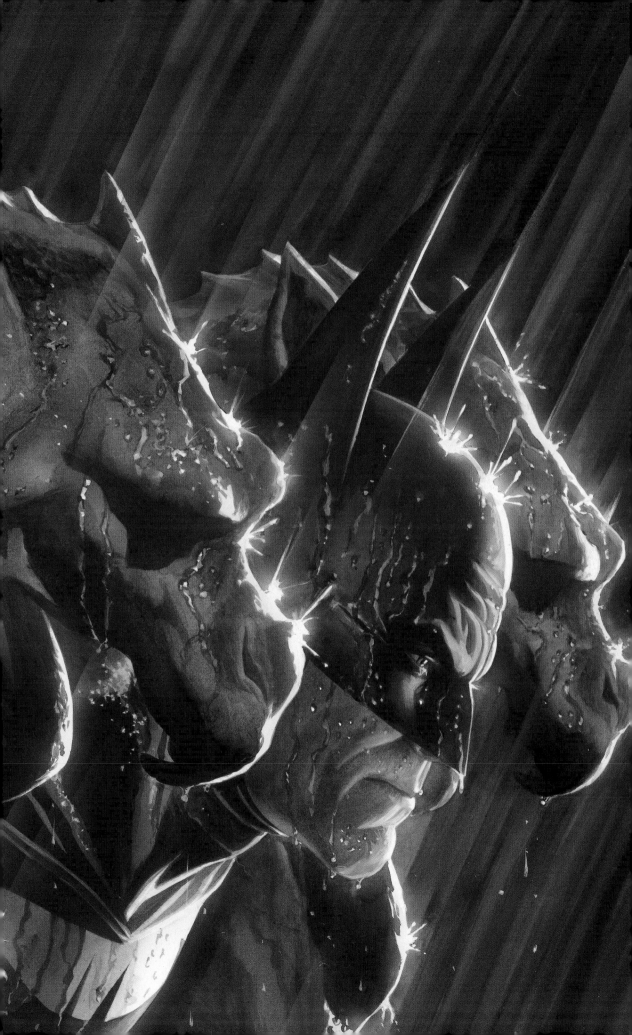

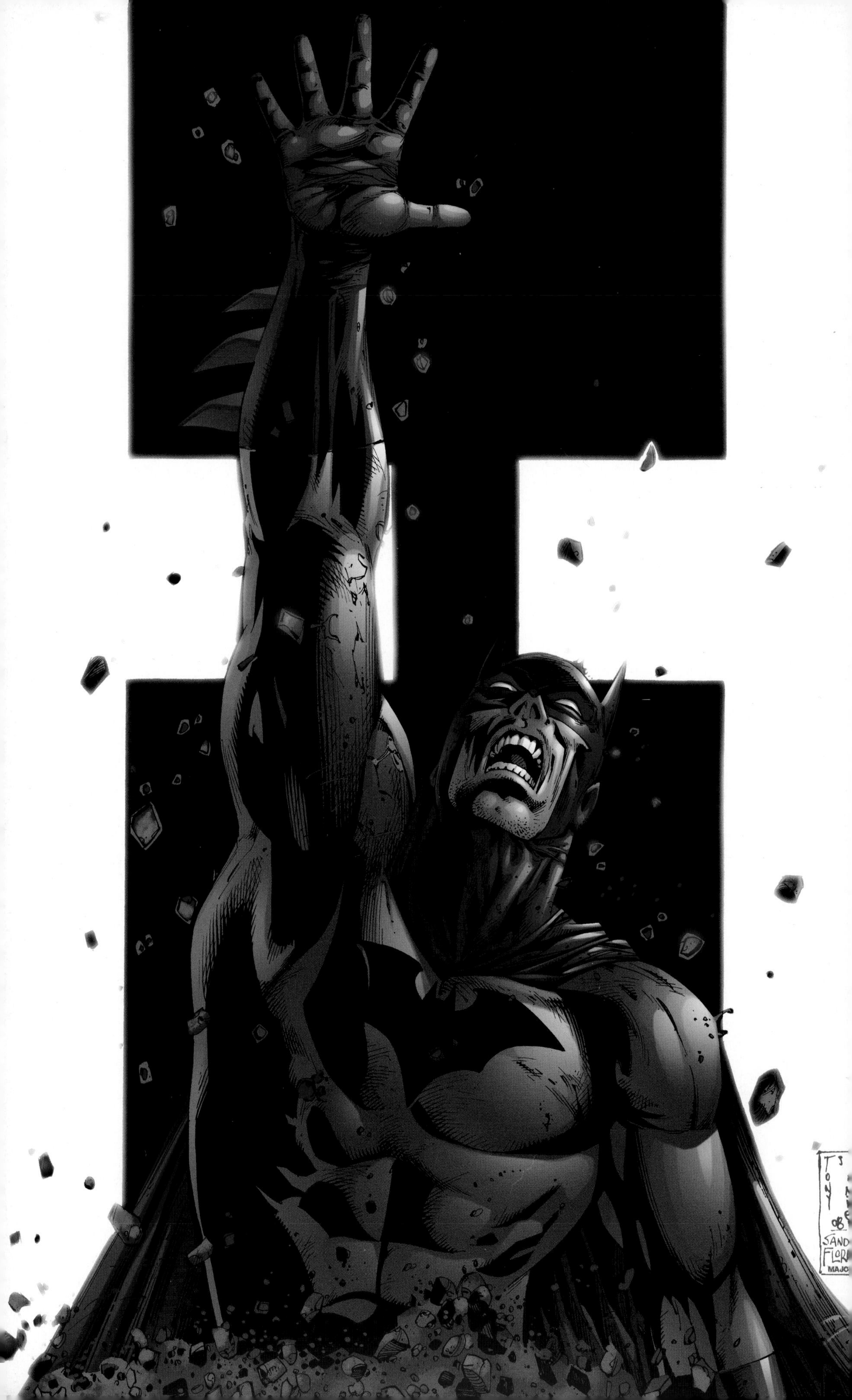

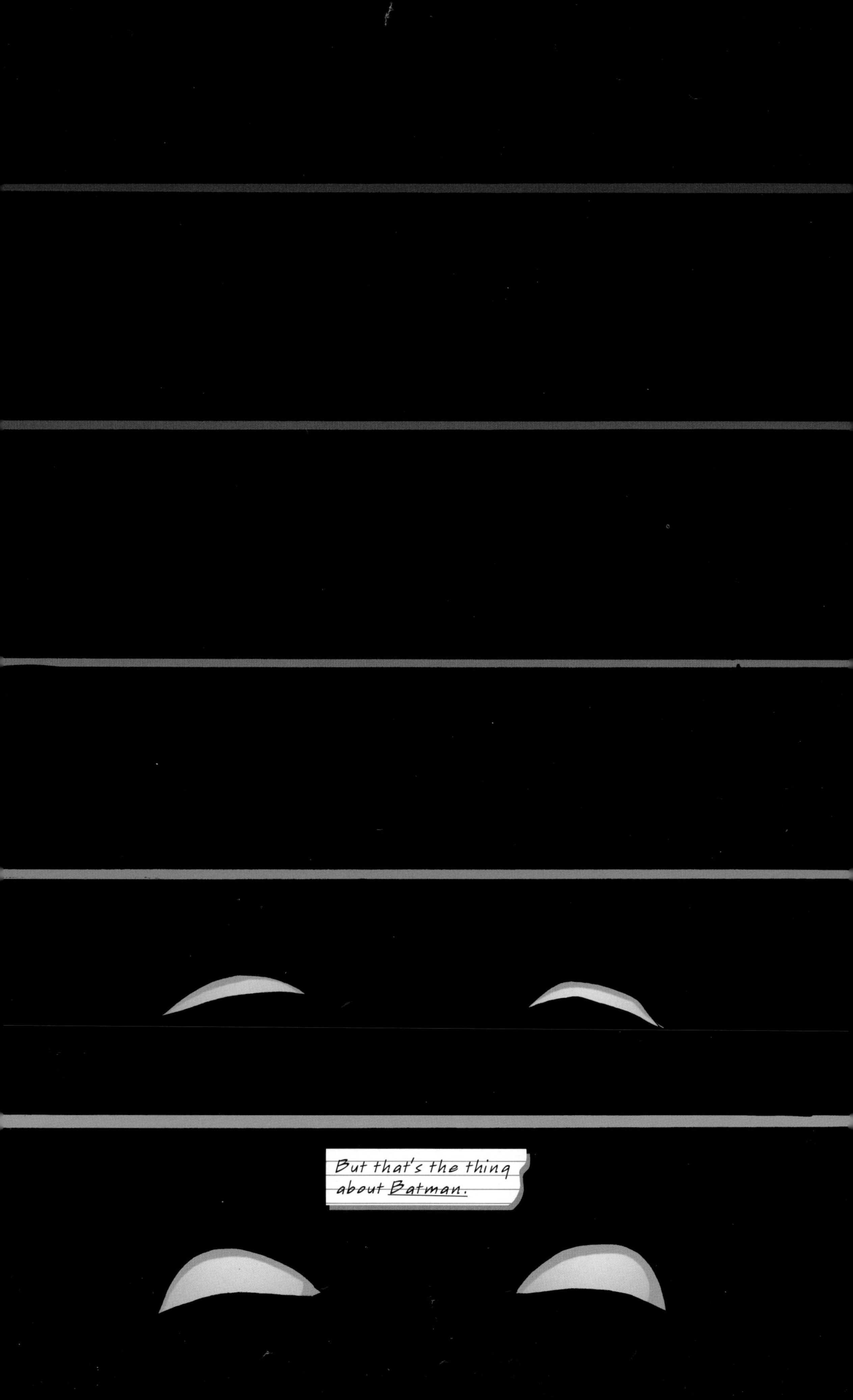
But that's the thing about Batman.

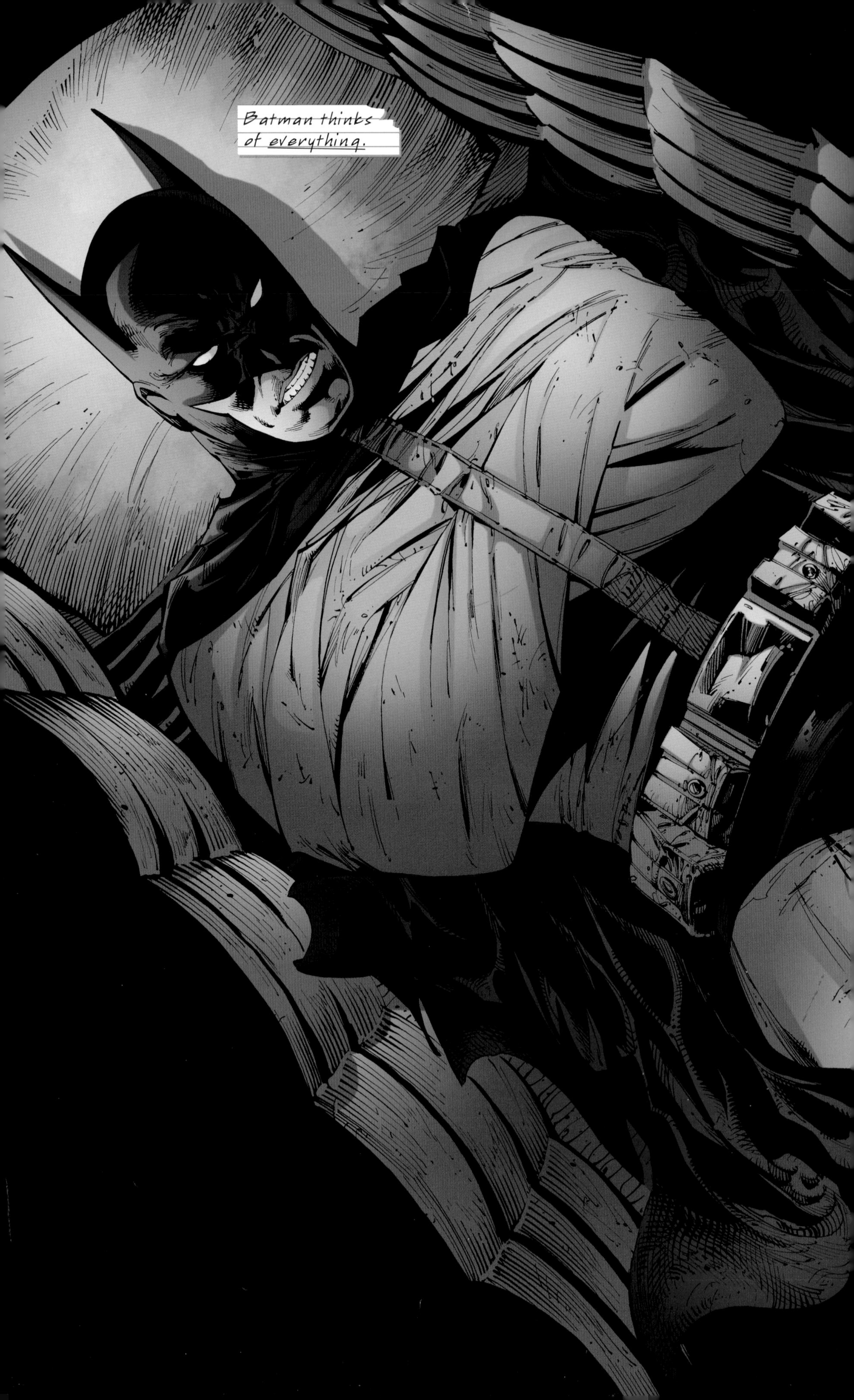
Batman thinks of everything.

BATMAN R.I.P. the conclusion
HEARTS in DARKNESS

"The superior man thinks
of evil that will come and
guards against it."
--The Book of Changes

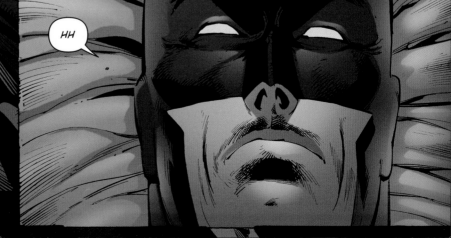

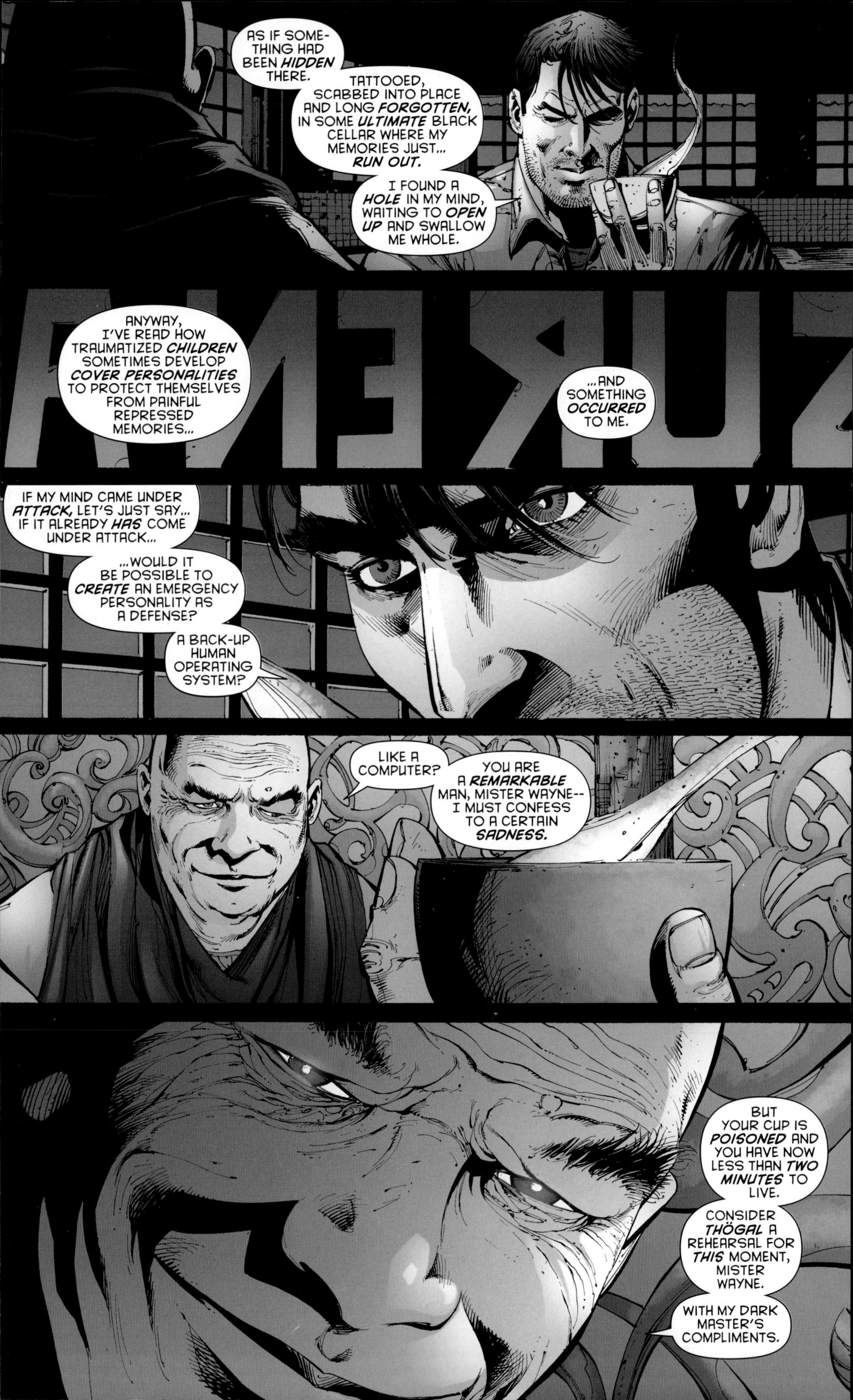
AS IF SOME-THING HAD BEEN *HIDDEN* THERE.
TATTOOED, SCABBED INTO PLACE AND LONG *FORGOTTEN,* IN SOME *ULTIMATE* BLACK CELLAR WHERE MY MEMORIES JUST... *RUN OUT.*
I FOUND A *HOLE* IN MY MIND, WAITING TO *OPEN UP* AND SWALLOW ME WHOLE.
ANYWAY, I'VE READ HOW TRAUMATIZED *CHILDREN* SOMETIMES DEVELOP *COVER PERSONALITIES* TO PROTECT THEMSELVES FROM PAINFUL REPRESSED MEMORIES...
...AND SOMETHING *OCCURRED* TO ME.
IF MY MIND CAME UNDER *ATTACK,* LET'S JUST SAY... IF IT ALREADY *HAS* COME UNDER ATTACK...
...WOULD IT BE POSSIBLE TO *CREATE* AN EMERGENCY PERSONALITY AS A DEFENSE?
A BACK-UP HUMAN OPERATING SYSTEM?
LIKE A COMPUTER?
YOU ARE A *REMARKABLE* MAN, MISTER WAYNE-- I MUST CONFESS TO A CERTAIN *SADNESS.*
BUT YOUR CUP IS *POISONED* AND YOU HAVE NOW LESS THAN *TWO MINUTES* TO LIVE.
CONSIDER *THÖGAL* A REHEARSAL FOR *THIS* MOMENT, MISTER WAYNE.
WITH MY DARK MASTER'S COMPLIMENTS.

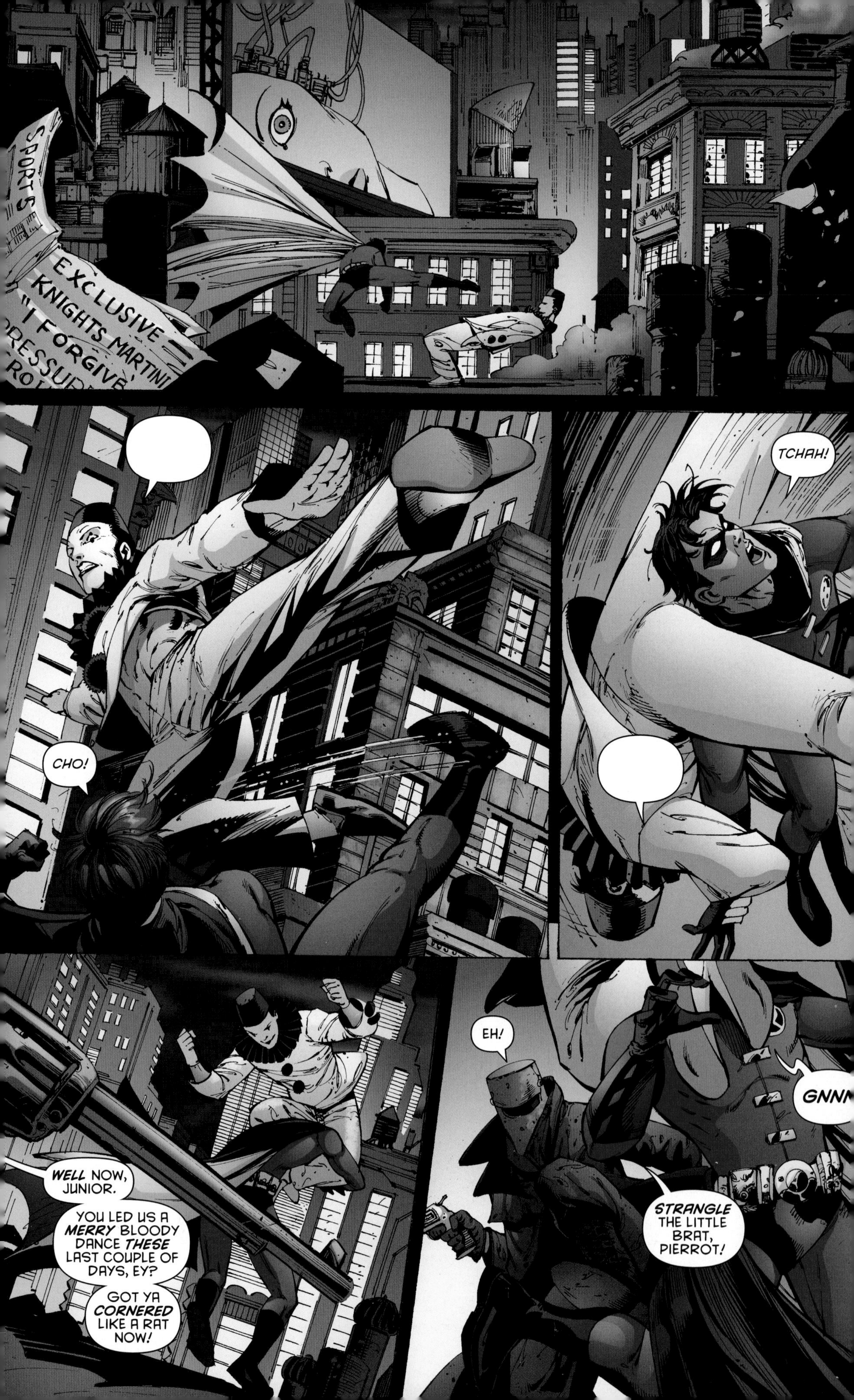

SPORTS
EXCLUSIVE
KNIGHTS MARTINI
"I FORGIVE"
PRESSURE
TCHAH!
CHO!
WELL NOW, JUNIOR.
YOU LED US A MERRY BLOODY DANCE THESE LAST COUPLE OF DAYS, EY?
GOT YA CORNERED LIKE A RAT NOW!
EH!
GNNN
STRANGLE THE LITTLE BRAT, PIERROT!

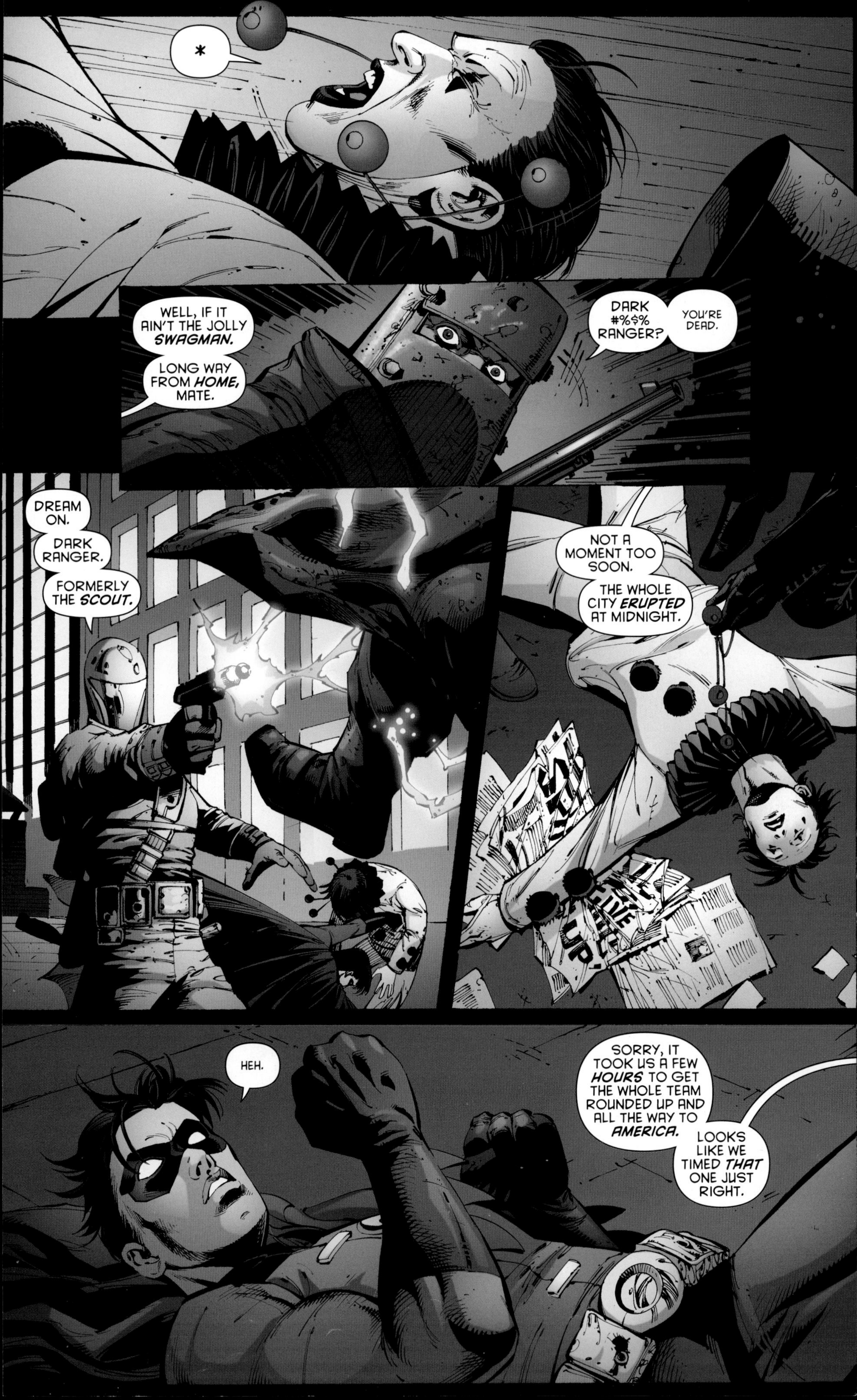
*
WELL, IF IT AIN'T THE JOLLY SWAGMAN.
LONG WAY FROM HOME, MATE.
DARK #%$% RANGER?
YOU'RE DEAD.
DREAM ON.
DARK RANGER.
FORMERLY THE SCOUT.
NOT A MOMENT TOO SOON.
THE WHOLE CITY ERUPTED AT MIDNIGHT.
HEH.
SORRY, IT TOOK US A FEW HOURS TO GET THE WHOLE TEAM ROUNDED UP AND ALL THE WAY TO AMERICA.
LOOKS LIKE WE TIMED THAT ONE JUST RIGHT.

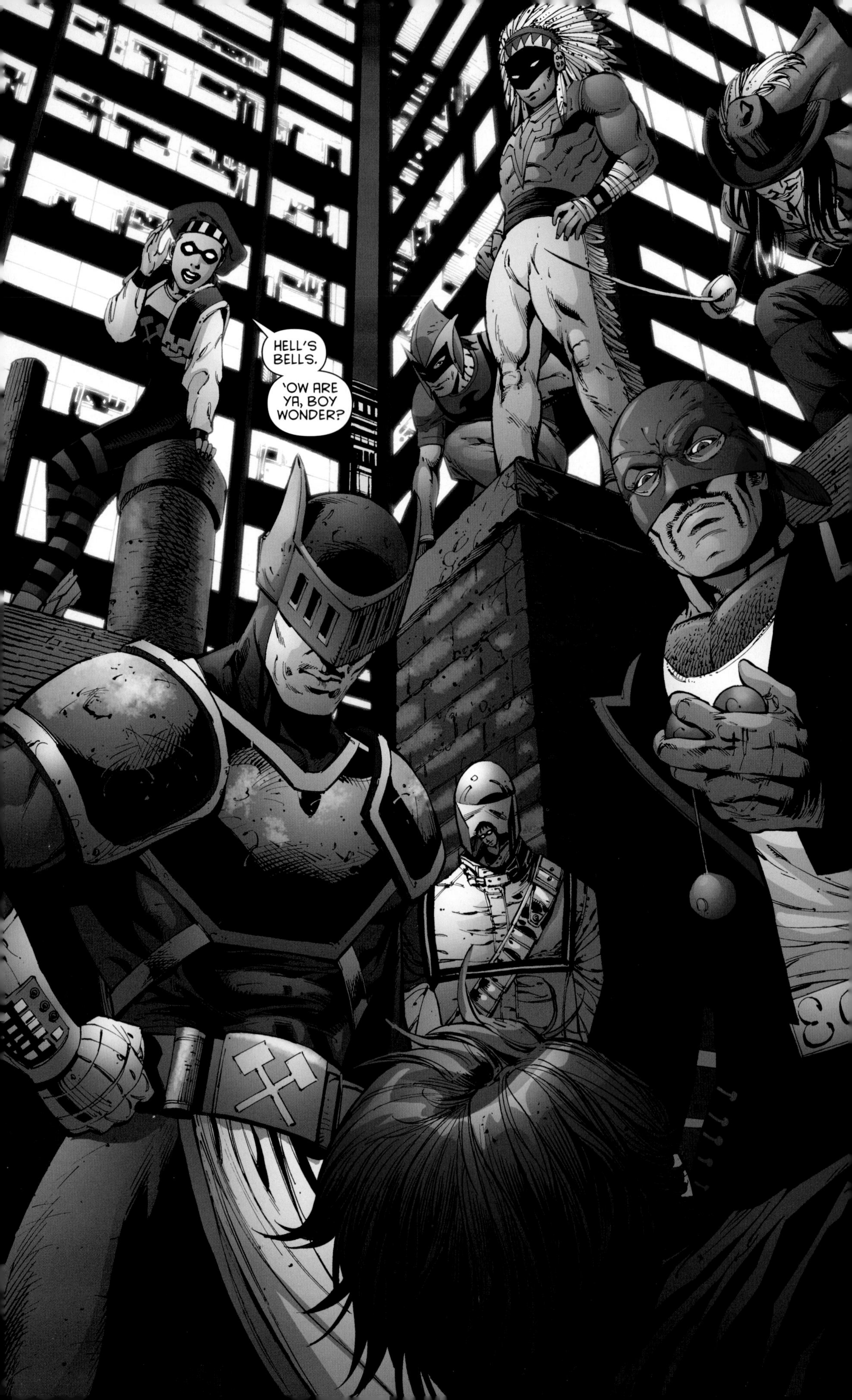
HELL'S BELLS.
'OW ARE YA, BOY WONDER?

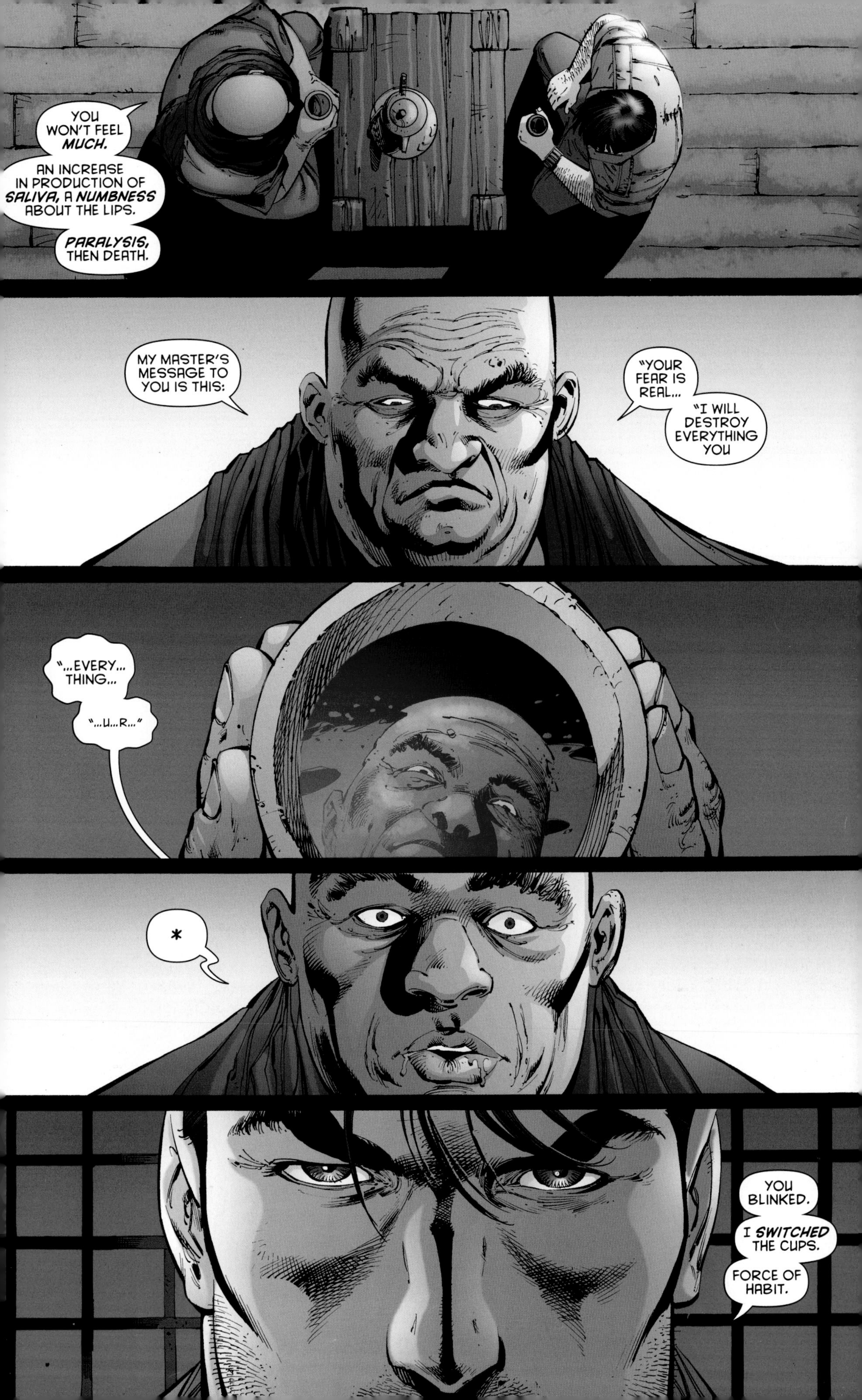
YOU WON'T FEEL *MUCH.*
AN INCREASE IN PRODUCTION OF *SALIVA,* A *NUMBNESS* ABOUT THE LIPS.
PARALYSIS, THEN DEATH.
MY MASTER'S MESSAGE TO YOU IS THIS:
"YOUR FEAR IS REAL...
"I WILL DESTROY EVERYTHING YOU
"...EVERY... THING...
"...U...R..."
*
YOU BLINKED.
I *SWITCHED* THE CUPS.
FORCE OF HABIT.

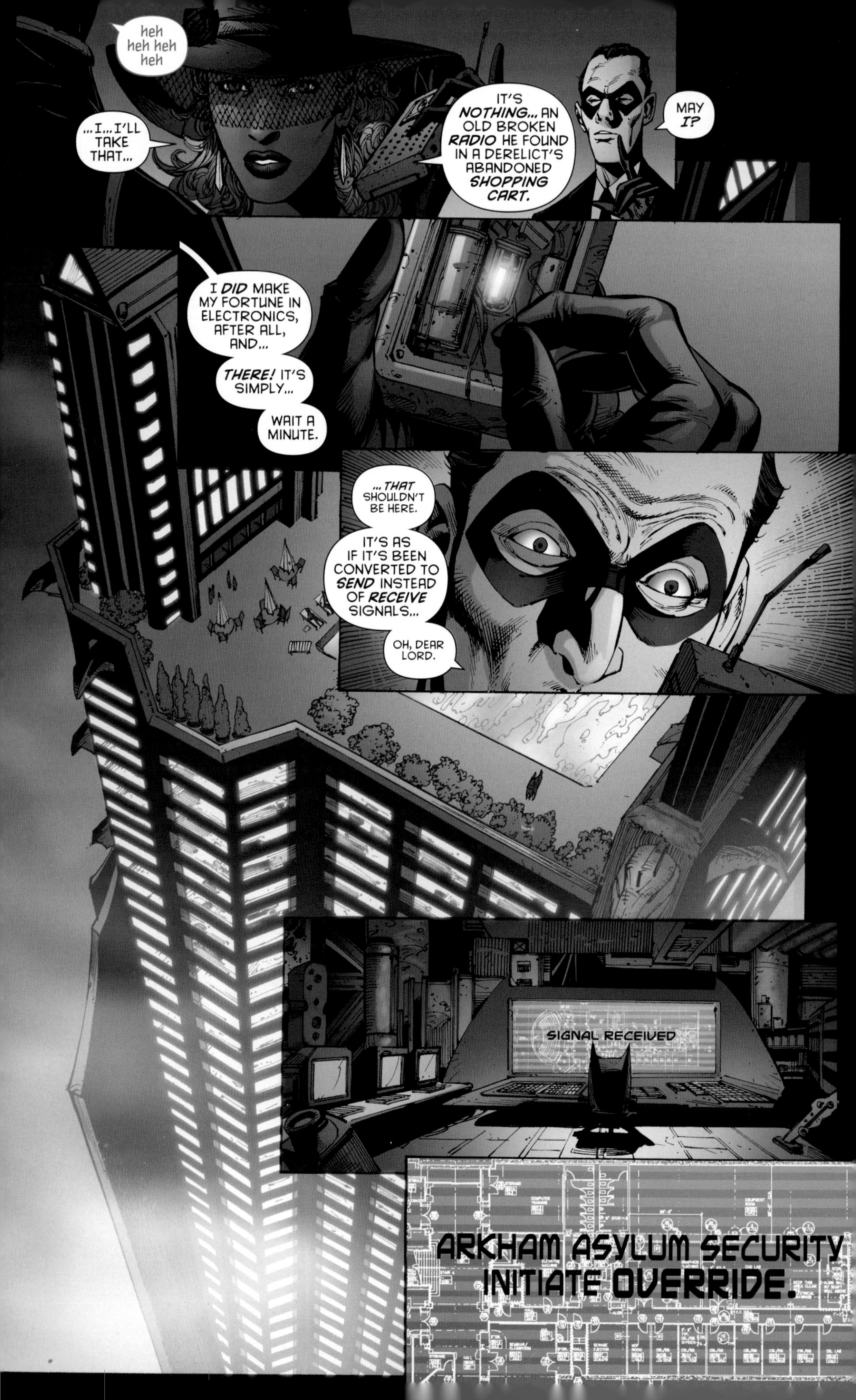
heh heh heh heh
...I...I'LL TAKE THAT...
IT'S NOTHING... AN OLD BROKEN RADIO HE FOUND IN A DERELICT'S ABANDONED SHOPPING CART.
MAY I?
I DID MAKE MY FORTUNE IN ELECTRONICS, AFTER ALL, AND...
THERE! IT'S SIMPLY...
WAIT A MINUTE.
...THAT SHOULDN'T BE HERE.
IT'S AS IF IT'S BEEN CONVERTED TO SEND INSTEAD OF RECEIVE SIGNALS...
OH, DEAR LORD.
SIGNAL RECEIVED
ARKHAM ASYLUM SECURITY
INITIATE OVERRIDE.

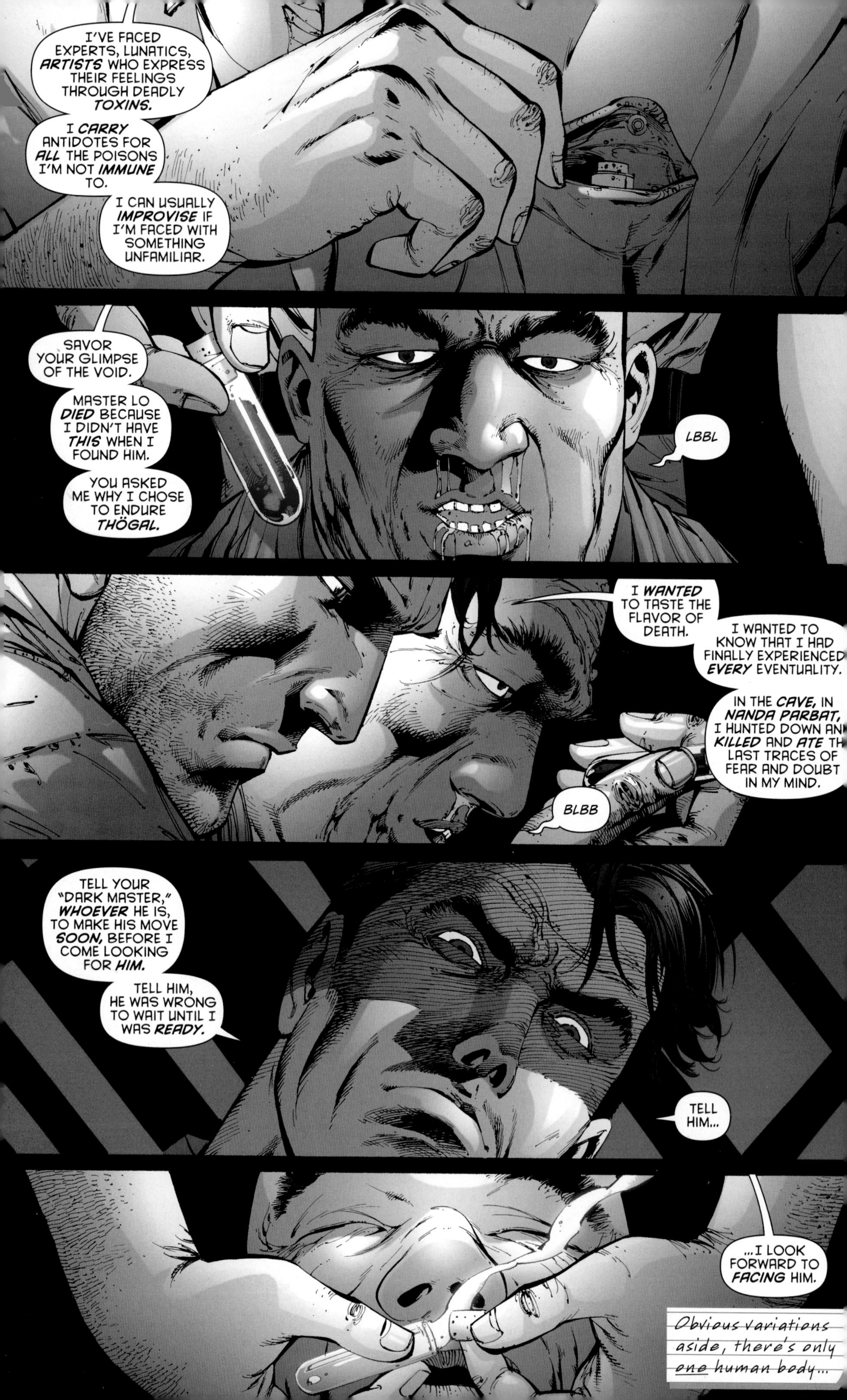
I'VE FACED EXPERTS, LUNATICS, ARTISTS WHO EXPRESS THEIR FEELINGS THROUGH DEADLY TOXINS.
I CARRY ANTIDOTES FOR ALL THE POISONS I'M NOT IMMUNE TO.
I CAN USUALLY IMPROVISE IF I'M FACED WITH SOMETHING UNFAMILIAR.
SAVOR YOUR GLIMPSE OF THE VOID.
MASTER LO DIED BECAUSE I DIDN'T HAVE THIS WHEN I FOUND HIM.
YOU ASKED ME WHY I CHOSE TO ENDURE THÖGAL.
LBBL
I WANTED TO TASTE THE FLAVOR OF DEATH.
I WANTED TO KNOW THAT I HAD FINALLY EXPERIENCED EVERY EVENTUALITY.
IN THE CAVE, IN NANDA PARBAT, I HUNTED DOWN AND KILLED AND ATE THE LAST TRACES OF FEAR AND DOUBT IN MY MIND.
BLBB
TELL YOUR "DARK MASTER," WHOEVER HE IS, TO MAKE HIS MOVE SOON, BEFORE I COME LOOKING FOR HIM.
TELL HIM, HE WAS WRONG TO WAIT UNTIL I WAS READY.
TELL HIM...
...I LOOK FORWARD TO FACING HIM.
Obvious variations aside, there's only one human body...

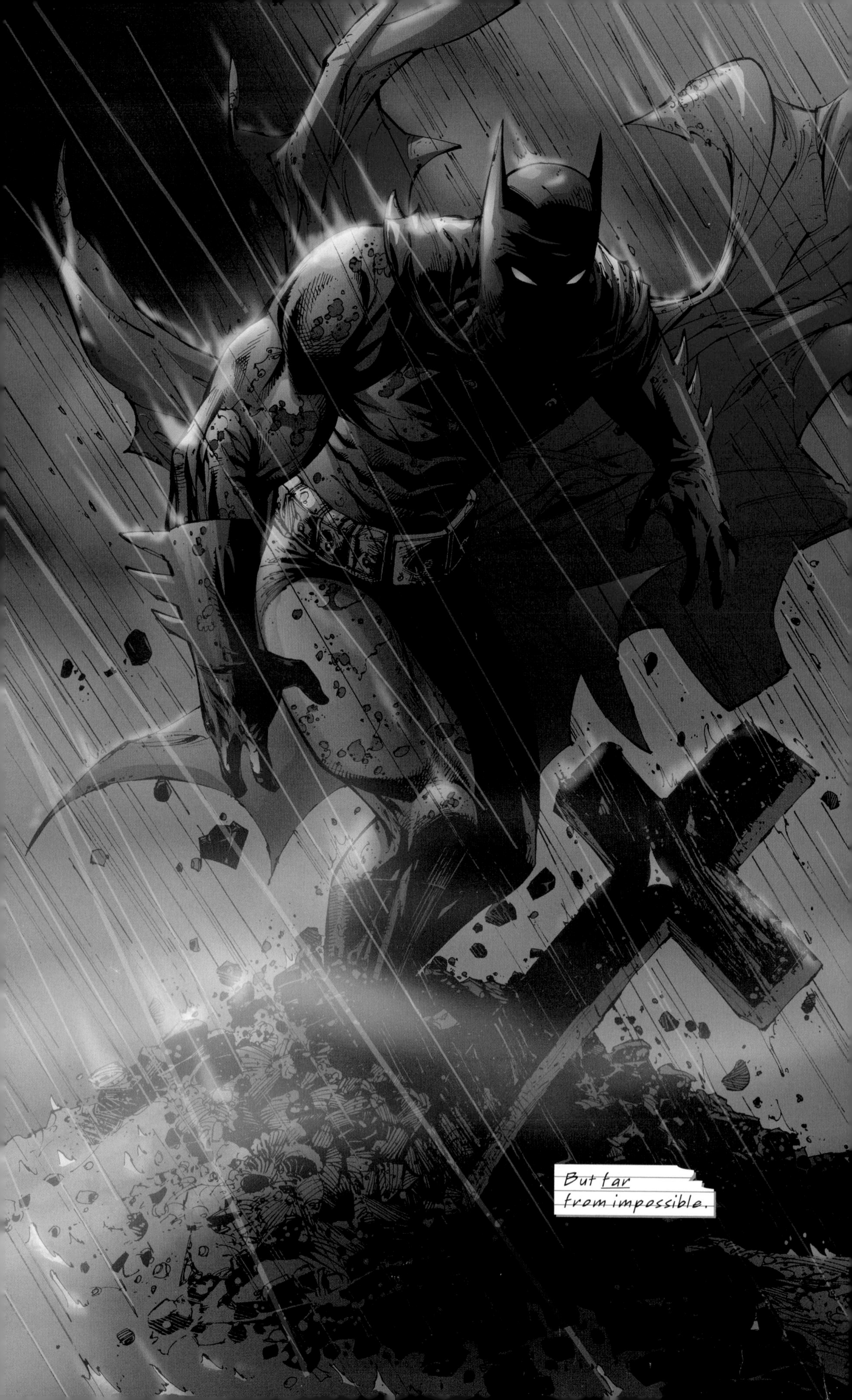

But far from impossible.

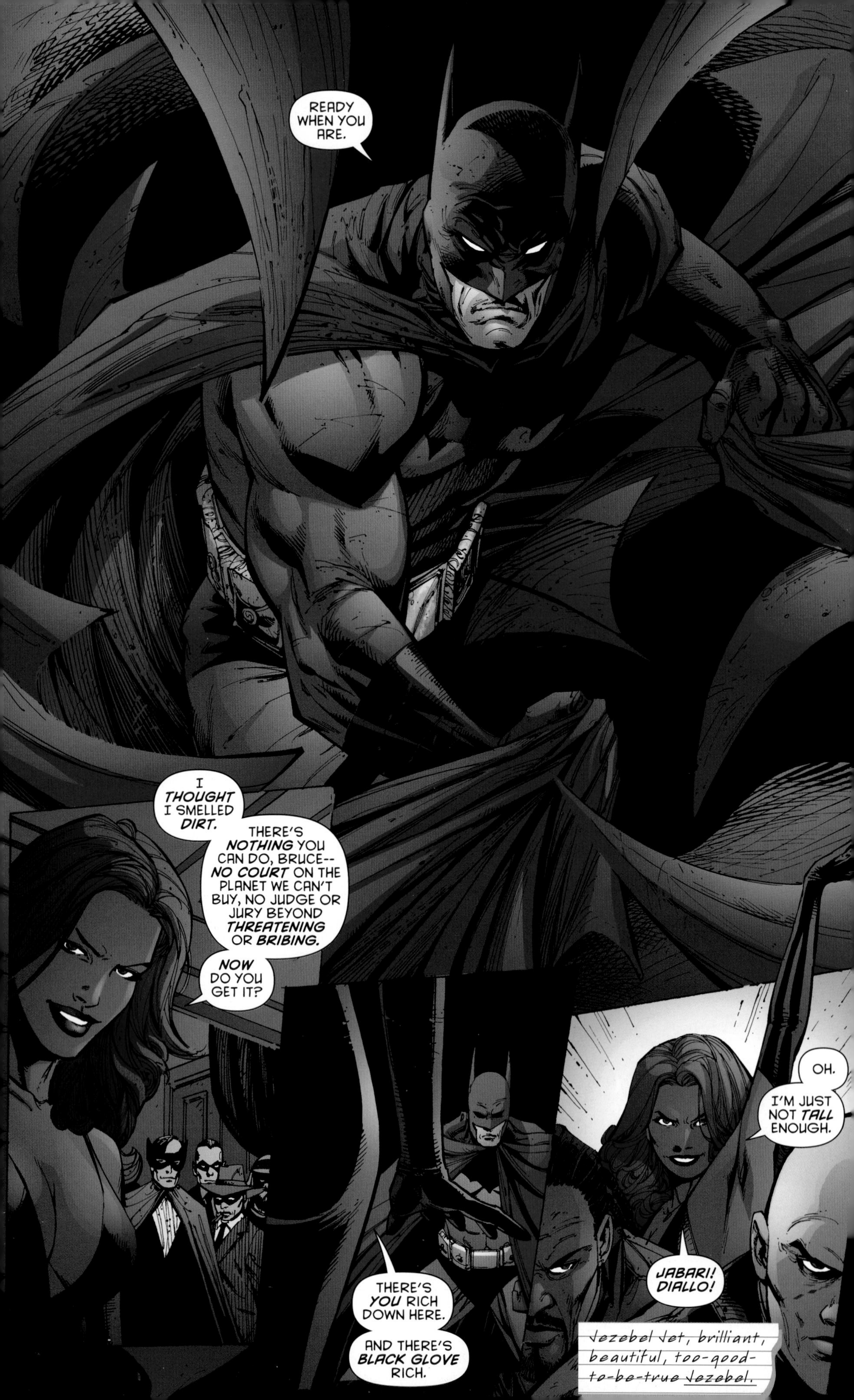
READY WHEN YOU ARE.
I *THOUGHT* I SMELLED *DIRT.*
THERE'S *NOTHING* YOU CAN DO, BRUCE-- *NO COURT* ON THE PLANET WE CAN'T BUY, NO JUDGE OR JURY BEYOND *THREATENING* OR *BRIBING.*
NOW DO YOU GET IT?
THERE'S *YOU* RICH DOWN HERE.
AND THERE'S *BLACK GLOVE* RICH.
OH.
I'M JUST NOT *TALL* ENOUGH.
JABARI! DIALLO!
Jezebel Jet, brilliant, beautiful, too-good-to-be-true Jezebel.

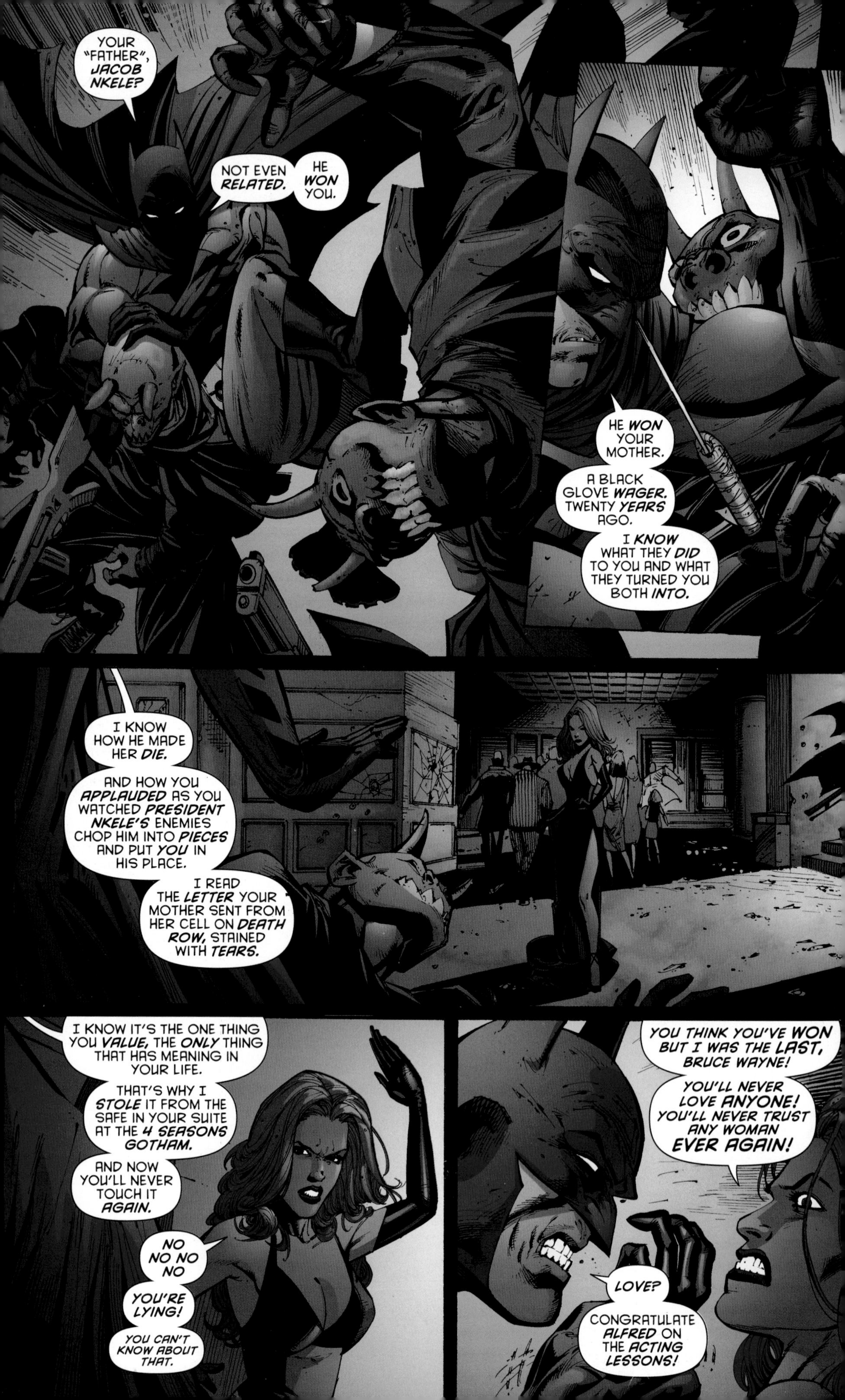
YOUR "FATHER", JACOB NKELE?
NOT EVEN RELATED.
HE WON YOU.
HE WON YOUR MOTHER.
A BLACK GLOVE WAGER. TWENTY YEARS AGO.
I KNOW WHAT THEY DID TO YOU AND WHAT THEY TURNED YOU BOTH INTO.
I KNOW HOW HE MADE HER DIE.
AND HOW YOU APPLAUDED AS YOU WATCHED PRESIDENT NKELE'S ENEMIES CHOP HIM INTO PIECES AND PUT YOU IN HIS PLACE.
I READ THE LETTER YOUR MOTHER SENT FROM HER CELL ON DEATH ROW, STAINED WITH TEARS.
I KNOW IT'S THE ONE THING YOU VALUE, THE ONLY THING THAT HAS MEANING IN YOUR LIFE.
THAT'S WHY I STOLE IT FROM THE SAFE IN YOUR SUITE AT THE 4 SEASONS GOTHAM.
AND NOW YOU'LL NEVER TOUCH IT AGAIN.
NO NO NO NO
YOU'RE LYING!
YOU CAN'T KNOW ABOUT THAT.
YOU THINK YOU'VE WON BUT I WAS THE LAST, BRUCE WAYNE!
YOU'LL NEVER LOVE ANYONE! YOU'LL NEVER TRUST ANY WOMAN EVER AGAIN!
LOVE?
CONGRATULATE ALFRED ON THE ACTING LESSONS!

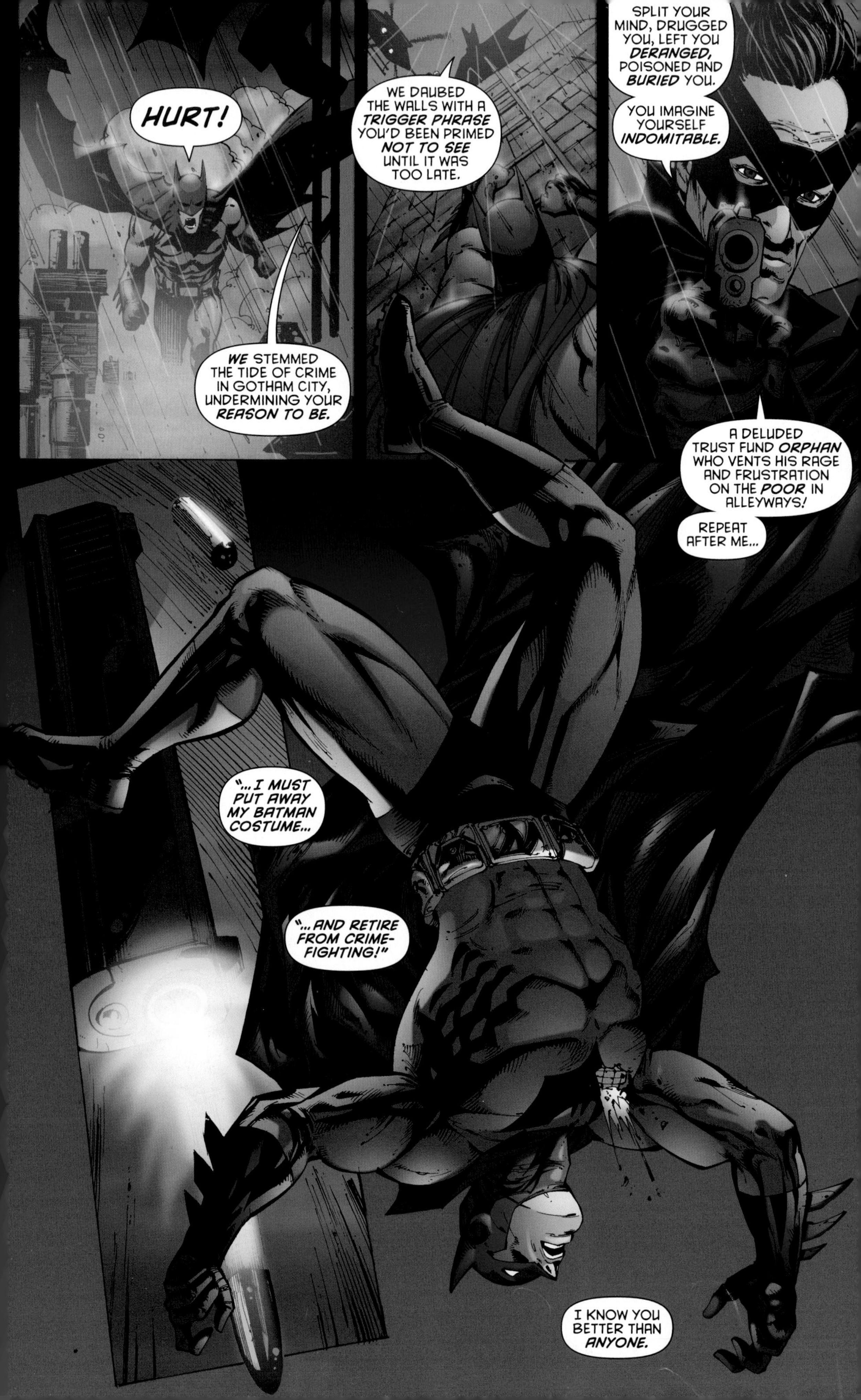

HURT!
WE STEMMED THE TIDE OF CRIME IN GOTHAM CITY, UNDERMINING YOUR REASON TO BE.
WE DAUBED THE WALLS WITH A TRIGGER PHRASE YOU'D BEEN PRIMED NOT TO SEE UNTIL IT WAS TOO LATE.
SPLIT YOUR MIND, DRUGGED YOU, LEFT YOU DERANGED, POISONED AND BURIED YOU.
YOU IMAGINE YOURSELF INDOMITABLE.
A DELUDED TRUST FUND ORPHAN WHO VENTS HIS RAGE AND FRUSTRATION ON THE POOR IN ALLEYWAYS!
REPEAT AFTER ME...
"...I MUST PUT AWAY MY BATMAN COSTUME...
"...AND RETIRE FROM CRIME-FIGHTING!"
I KNOW YOU BETTER THAN ANYONE.

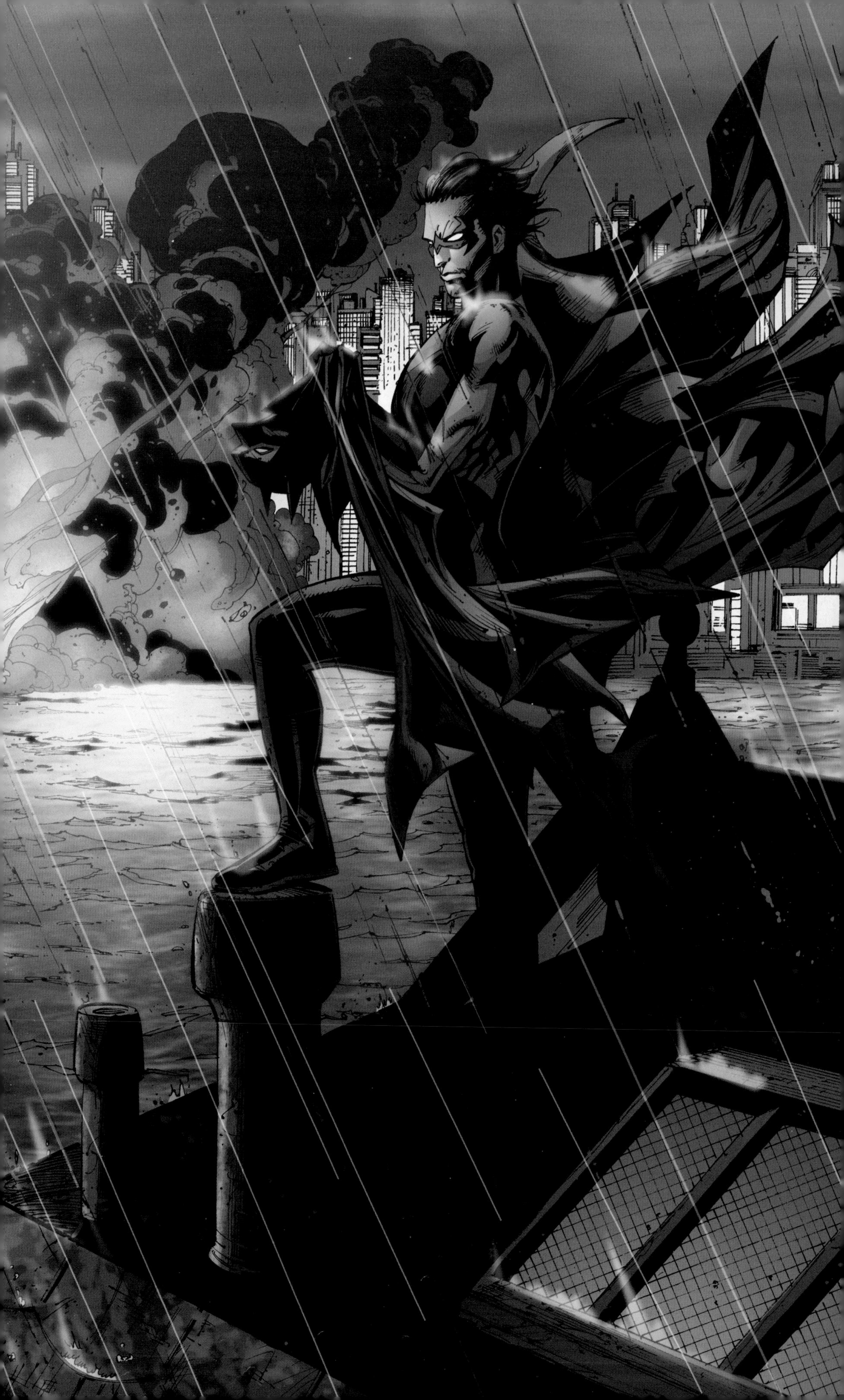

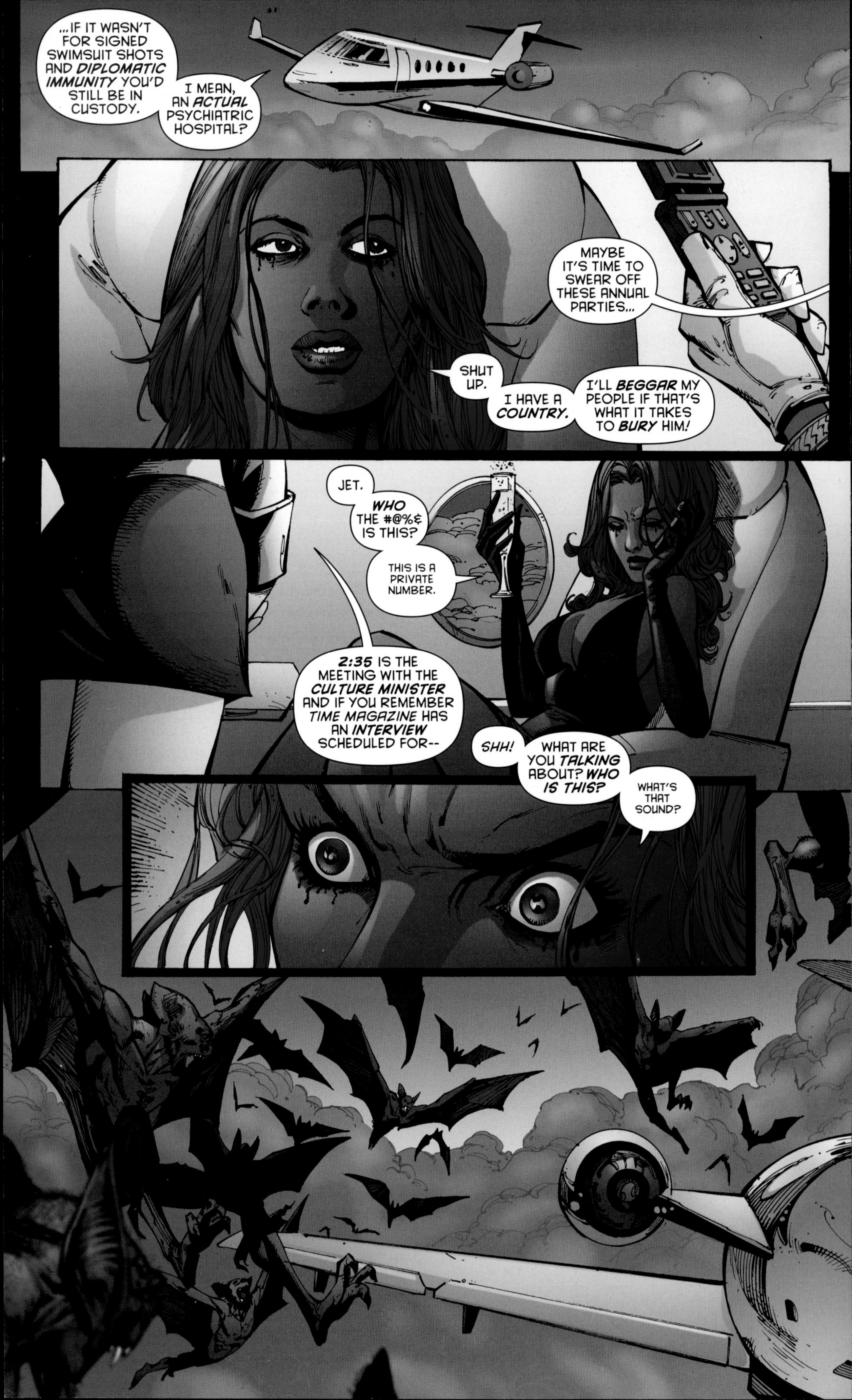
...IF IT WASN'T FOR SIGNED SWIMSUIT SHOTS AND DIPLOMATIC IMMUNITY YOU'D STILL BE IN CUSTODY.
I MEAN, AN ACTUAL PSYCHIATRIC HOSPITAL?
MAYBE IT'S TIME TO SWEAR OFF THESE ANNUAL PARTIES...
SHUT UP.
I HAVE A COUNTRY.
I'LL BEGGAR MY PEOPLE IF THAT'S WHAT IT TAKES TO BURY HIM!
JET.
WHO THE #@%& IS THIS?
THIS IS A PRIVATE NUMBER.
2:35 IS THE MEETING WITH THE CULTURE MINISTER AND IF YOU REMEMBER TIME MAGAZINE HAS AN INTERVIEW SCHEDULED FOR--
SHH!
WHAT ARE YOU TALKING ABOUT? WHO IS THIS?
WHAT'S THAT SOUND?

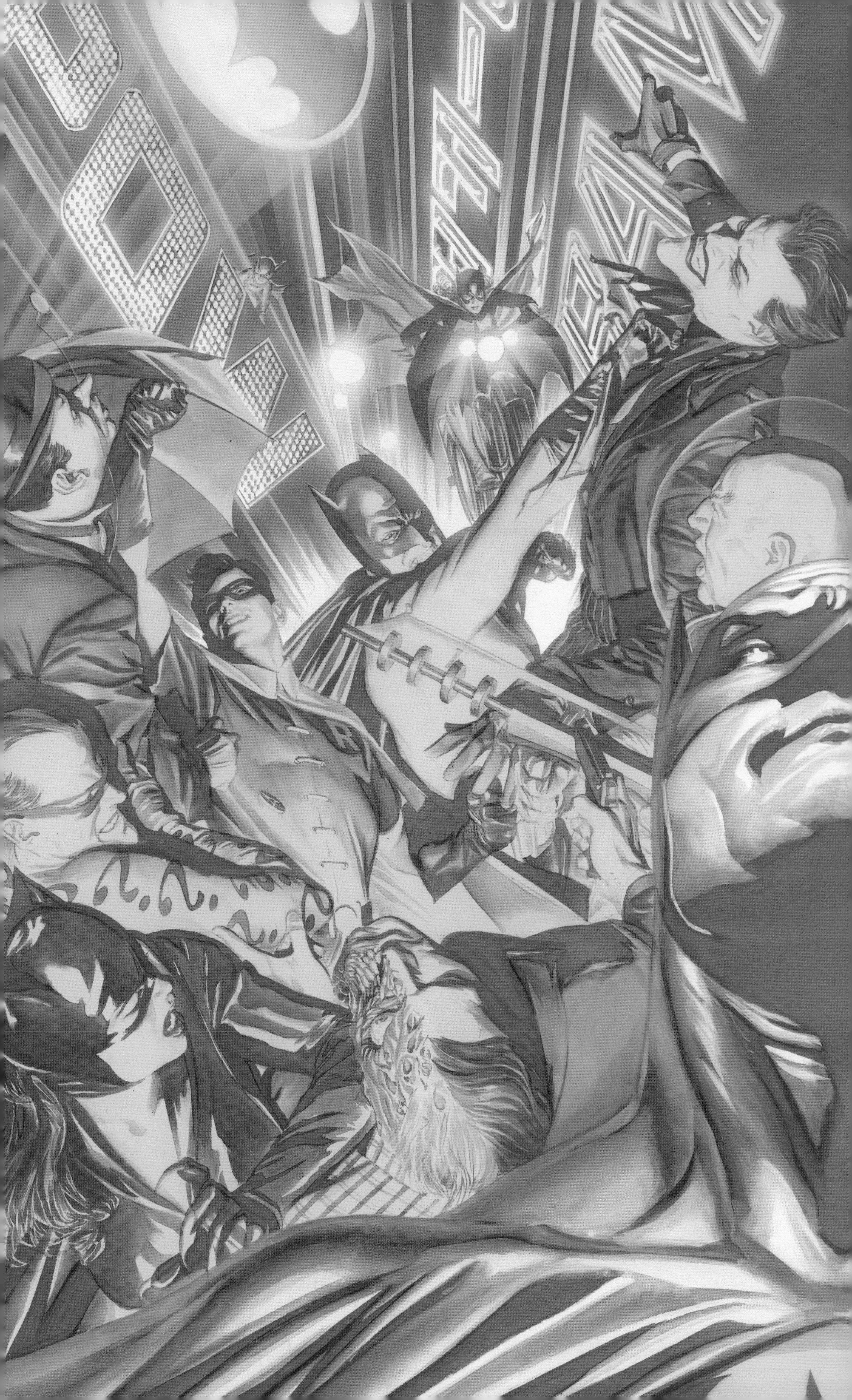

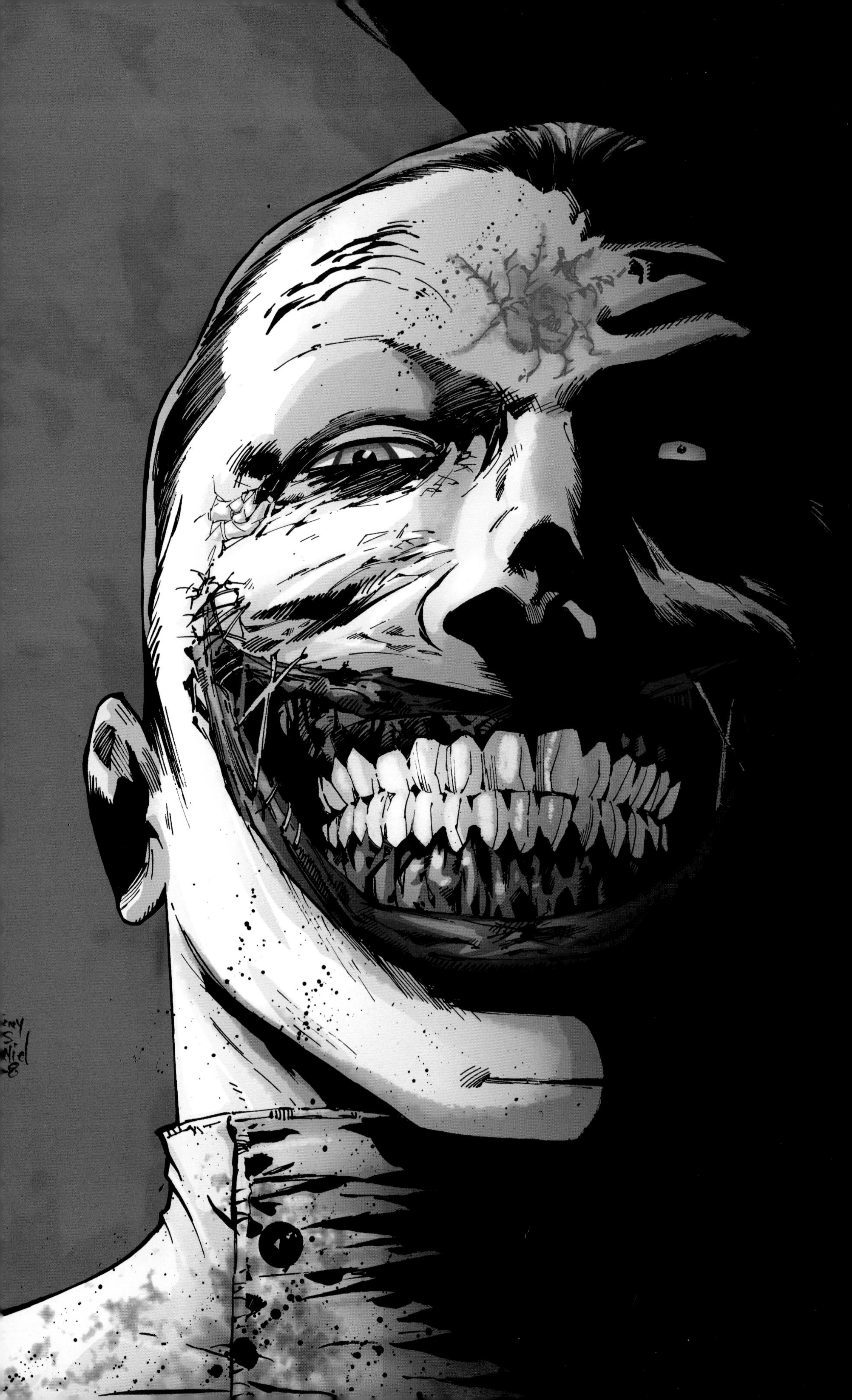

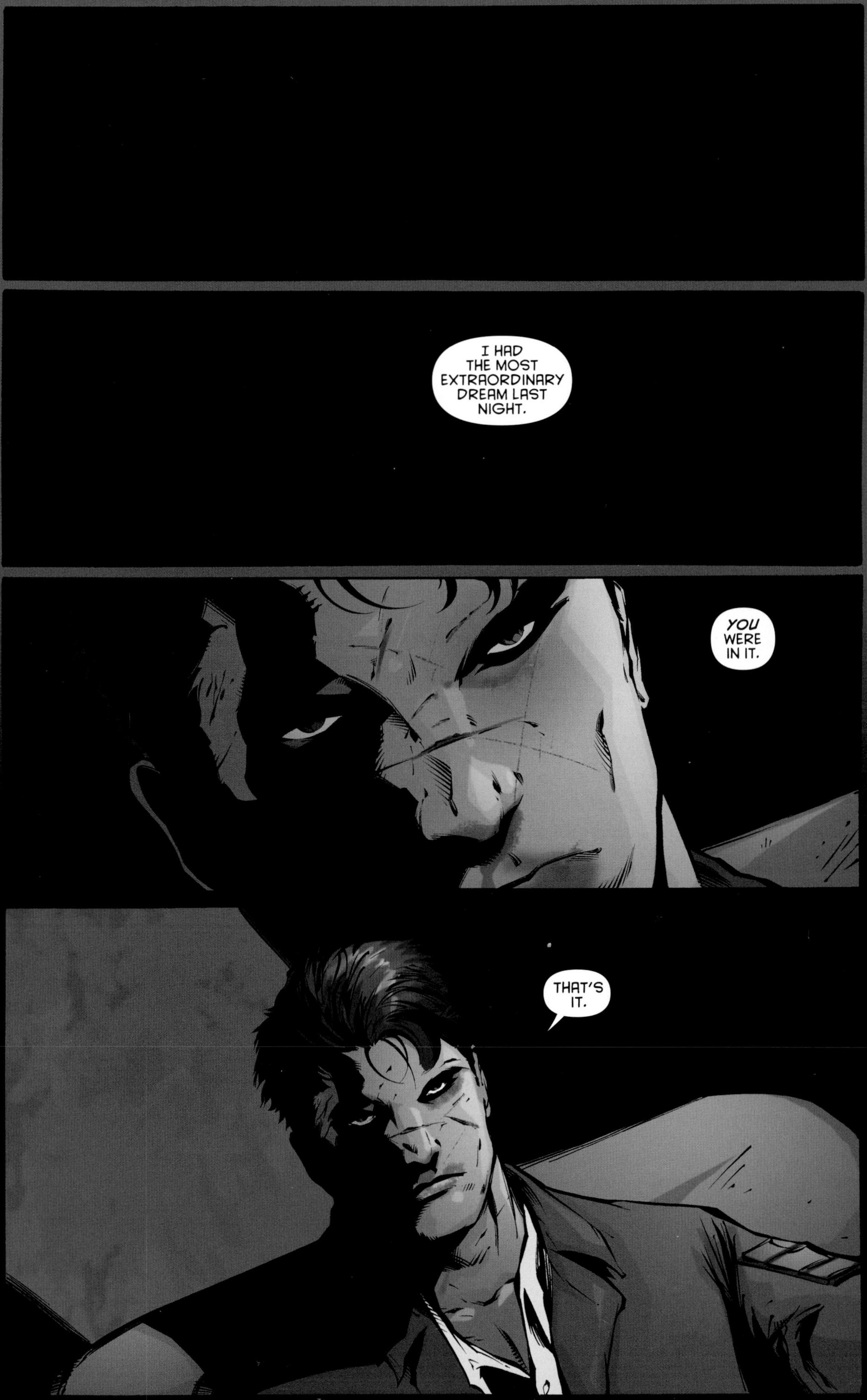
I HAD THE MOST EXTRAORDINARY DREAM LAST NIGHT.
YOU WERE IN IT.
THAT'S IT.

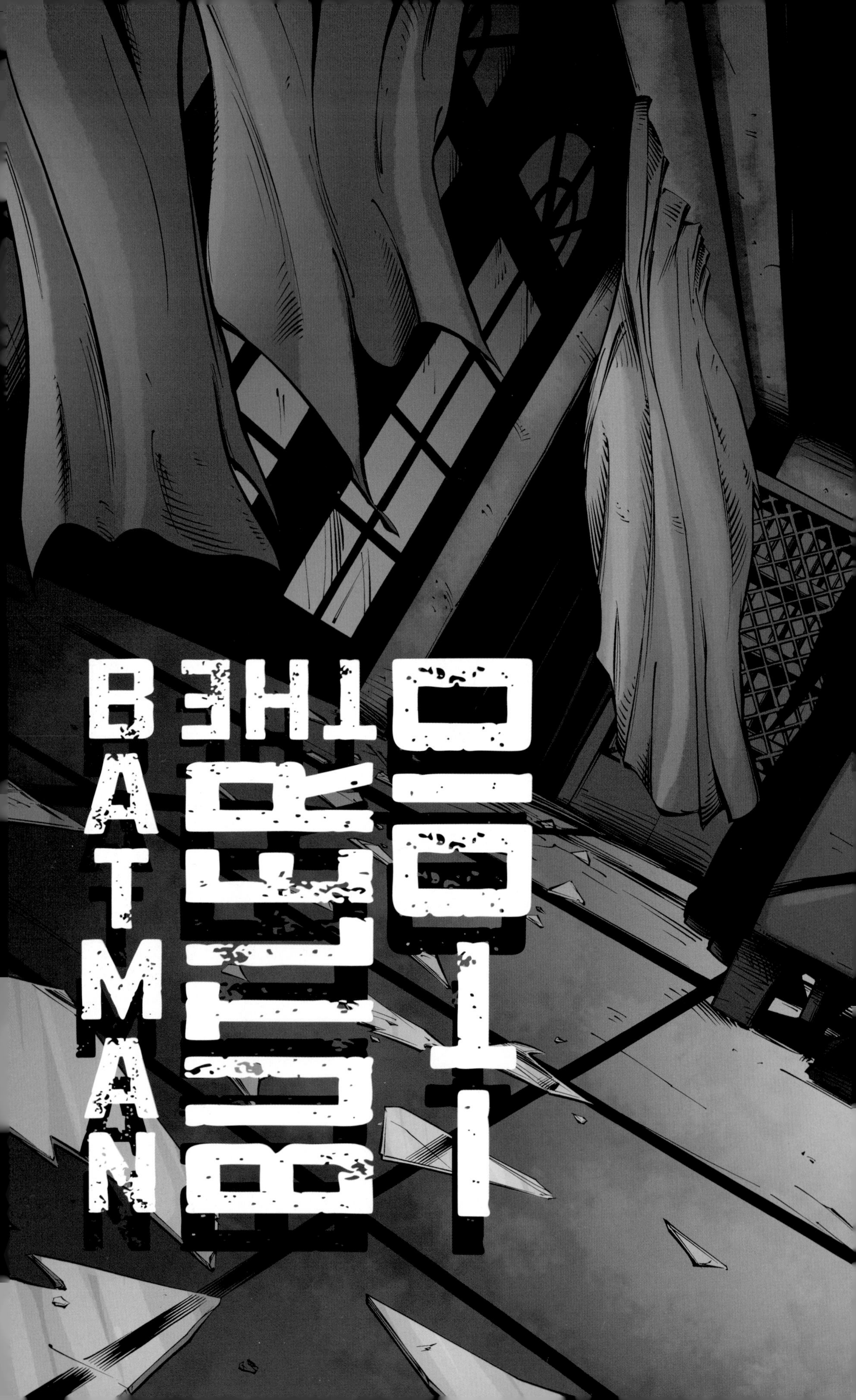
BATMAN
THE BUTLER DID IT

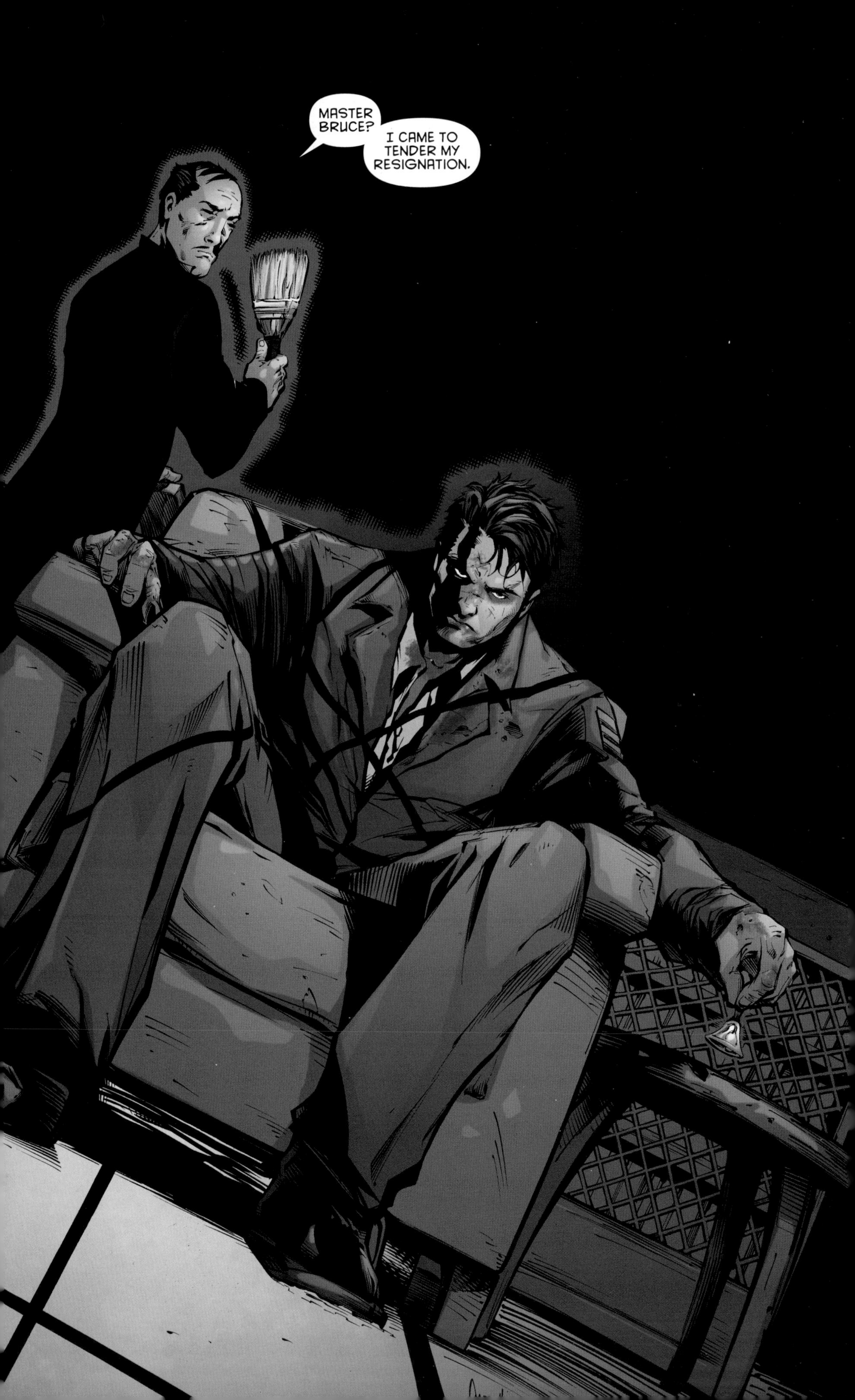
MASTER BRUCE?
I CAME TO TENDER MY RESIGNATION.

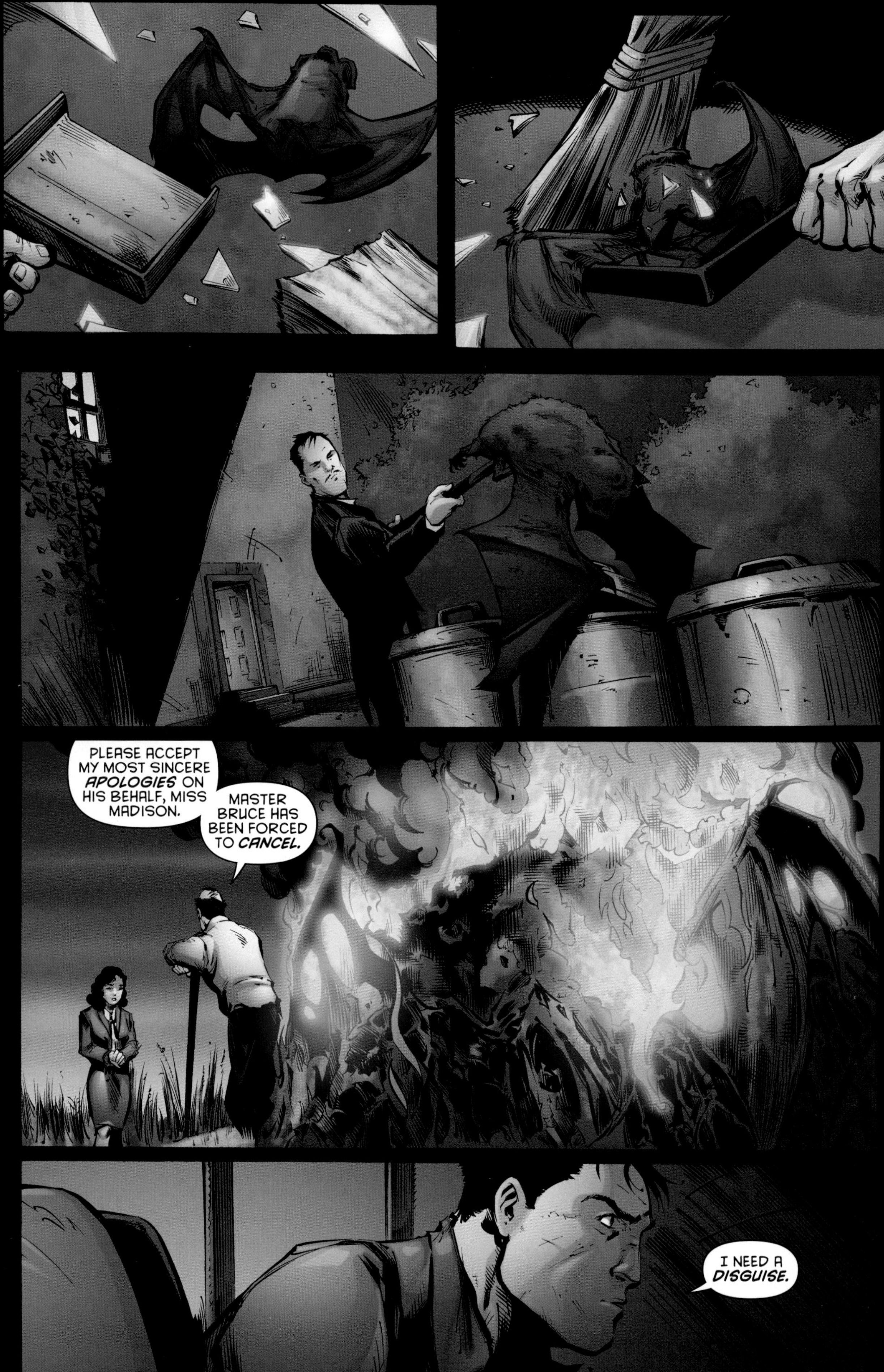
PLEASE ACCEPT MY MOST SINCERE *APOLOGIES* ON HIS BEHALF, MISS MADISON.
MASTER BRUCE HAS BEEN FORCED TO *CANCEL.*
I NEED A *DISGUISE.*

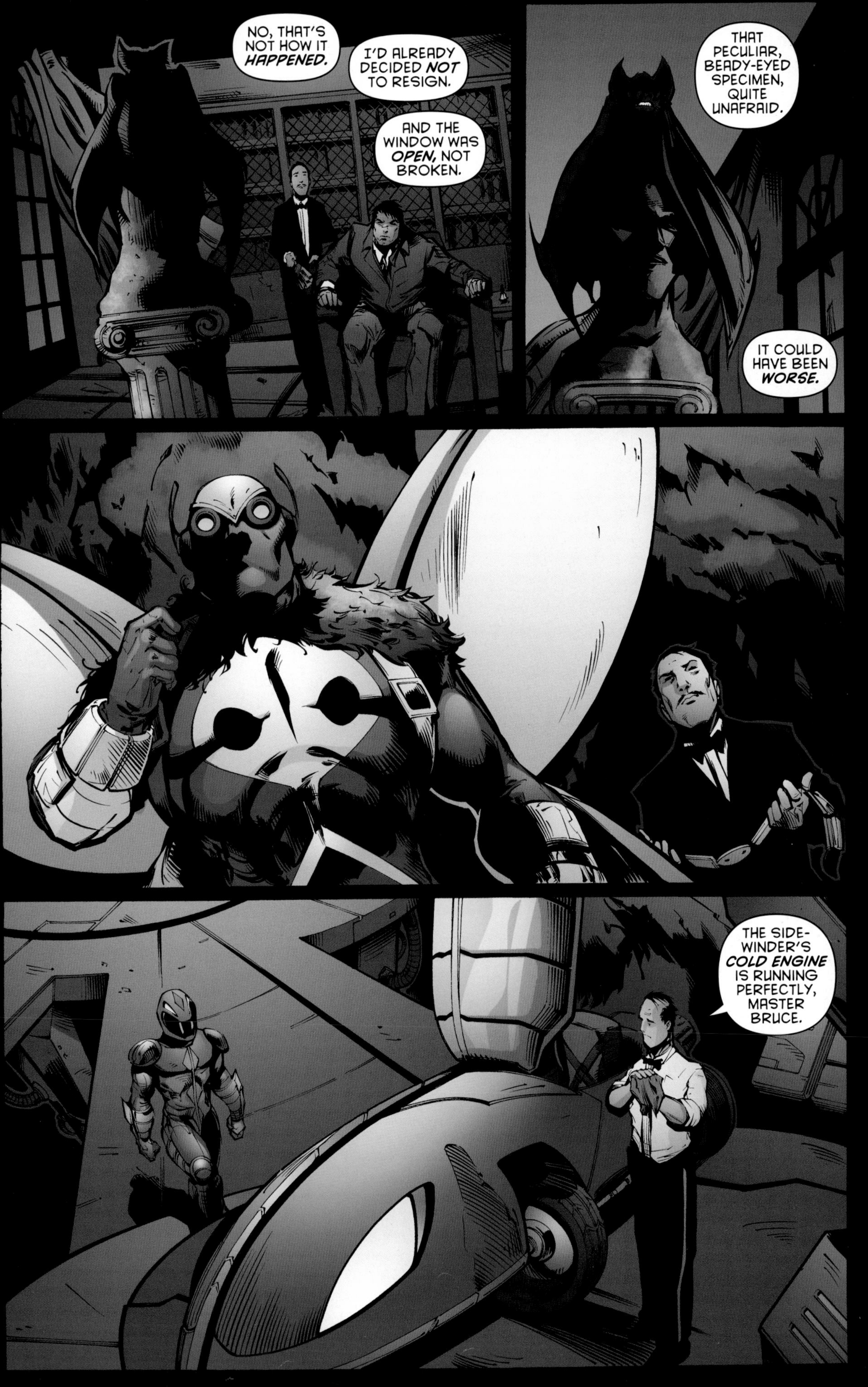
NO, THAT'S NOT HOW IT *HAPPENED.*
I'D ALREADY DECIDED *NOT* TO RESIGN.
AND THE WINDOW WAS *OPEN,* NOT BROKEN.
THAT PECULIAR, BEADY-EYED SPECIMEN, QUITE UNAFRAID.
IT COULD HAVE BEEN *WORSE.*
THE SIDE-WINDER'S *COLD ENGINE* IS RUNNING PERFECTLY, MASTER BRUCE.

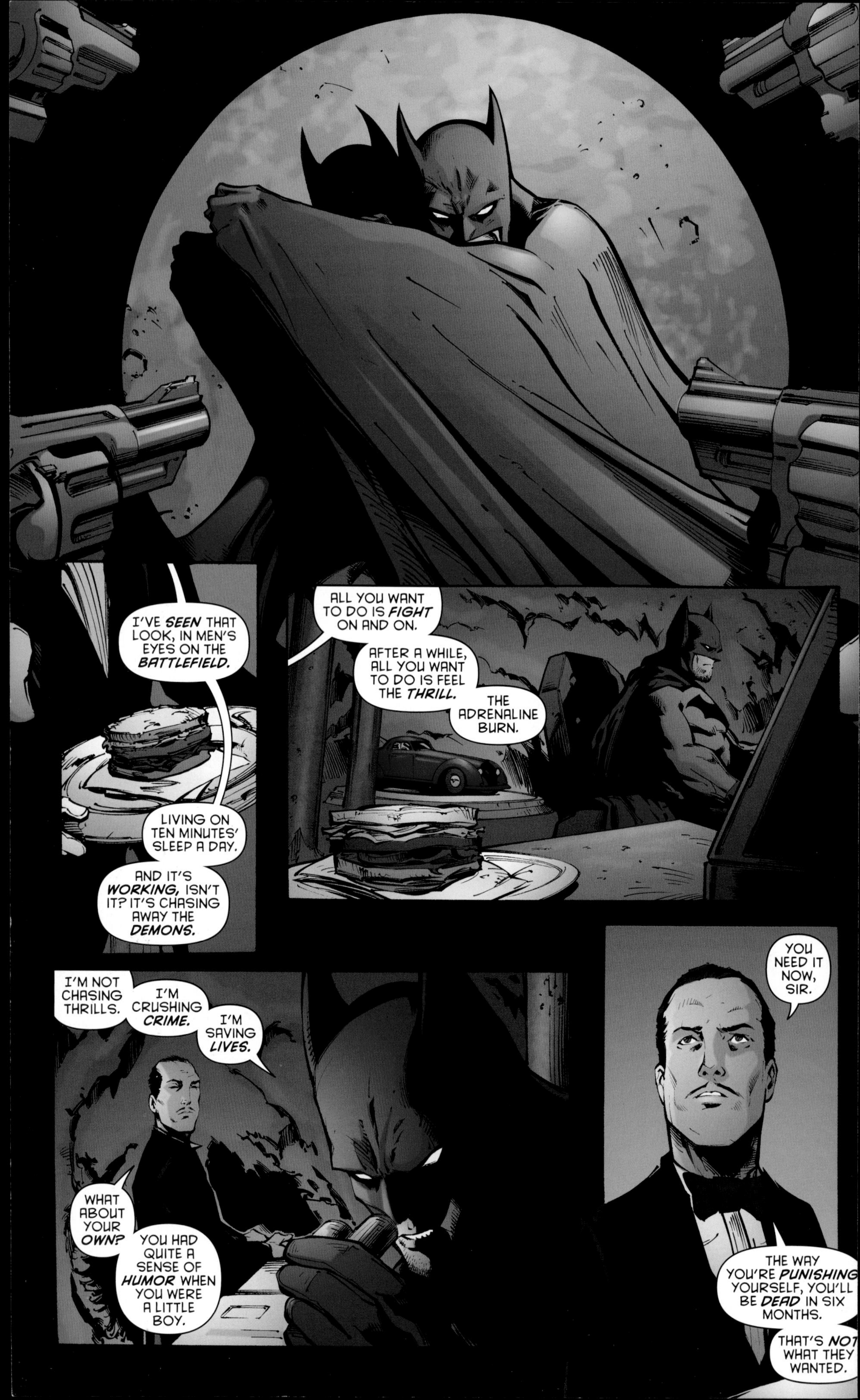
I'VE SEEN THAT LOOK, IN MEN'S EYES ON THE BATTLEFIELD.
LIVING ON TEN MINUTES' SLEEP A DAY.
AND IT'S WORKING, ISN'T IT? IT'S CHASING AWAY THE DEMONS.
ALL YOU WANT TO DO IS FIGHT ON AND ON.
AFTER A WHILE, ALL YOU WANT TO DO IS FEEL THE THRILL.
THE ADRENALINE BURN.
I'M NOT CHASING THRILLS.
I'M CRUSHING CRIME.
I'M SAVING LIVES.
WHAT ABOUT YOUR OWN?
YOU HAD QUITE A SENSE OF HUMOR WHEN YOU WERE A LITTLE BOY.
YOU NEED IT NOW, SIR.
THE WAY YOU'RE PUNISHING YOURSELF, YOU'LL BE DEAD IN SIX MONTHS.
THAT'S NOT WHAT THEY WANTED.

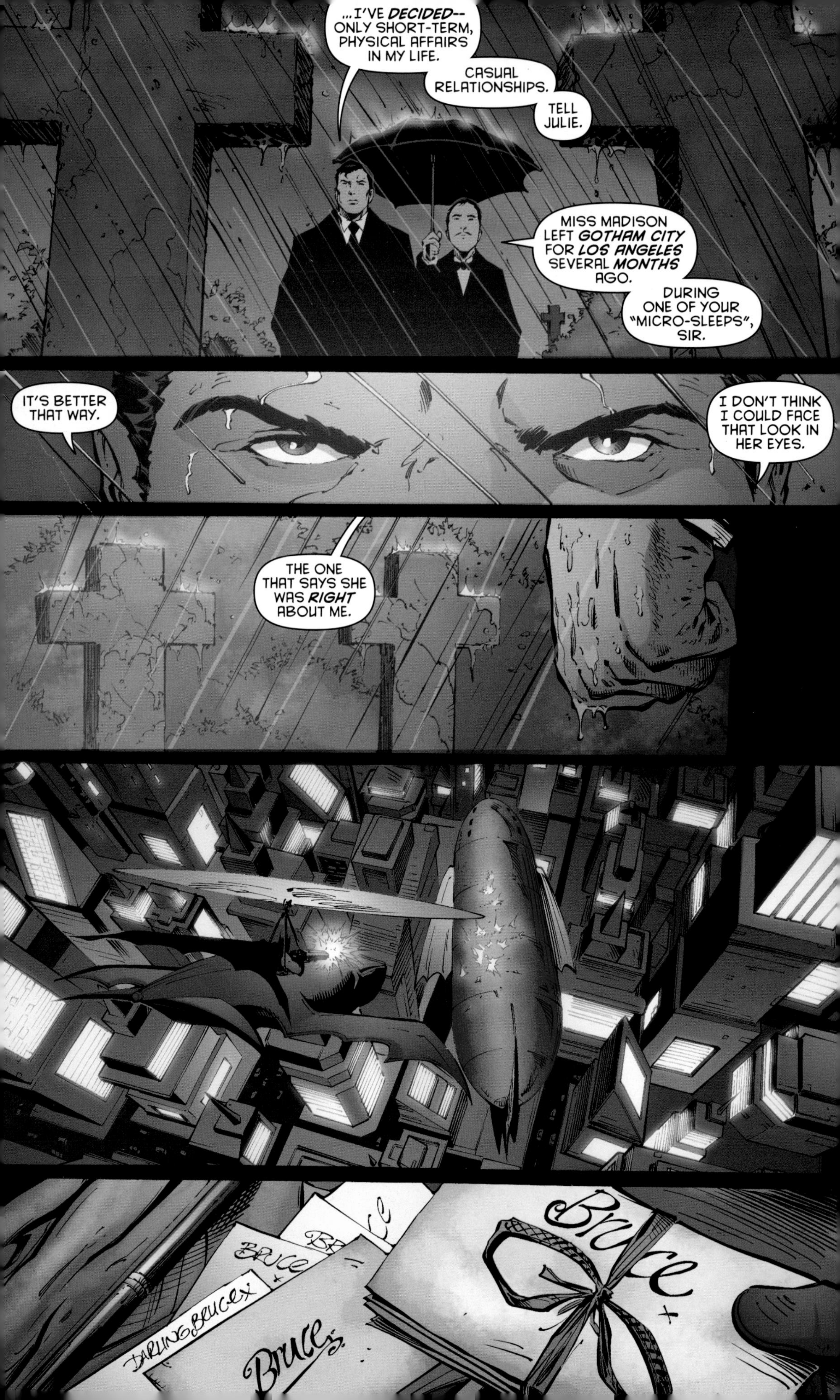

...I'VE DECIDED-- ONLY SHORT-TERM, PHYSICAL AFFAIRS IN MY LIFE.
CASUAL RELATIONSHIPS.
TELL JULIE.
MISS MADISON LEFT GOTHAM CITY FOR LOS ANGELES SEVERAL MONTHS AGO.
DURING ONE OF YOUR "MICRO-SLEEPS", SIR.
IT'S BETTER THAT WAY.
I DON'T THINK I COULD FACE THAT LOOK IN HER EYES.
THE ONE THAT SAYS SHE WAS RIGHT ABOUT ME.
BRUCE
DARLING BRUCE X
BRUCE

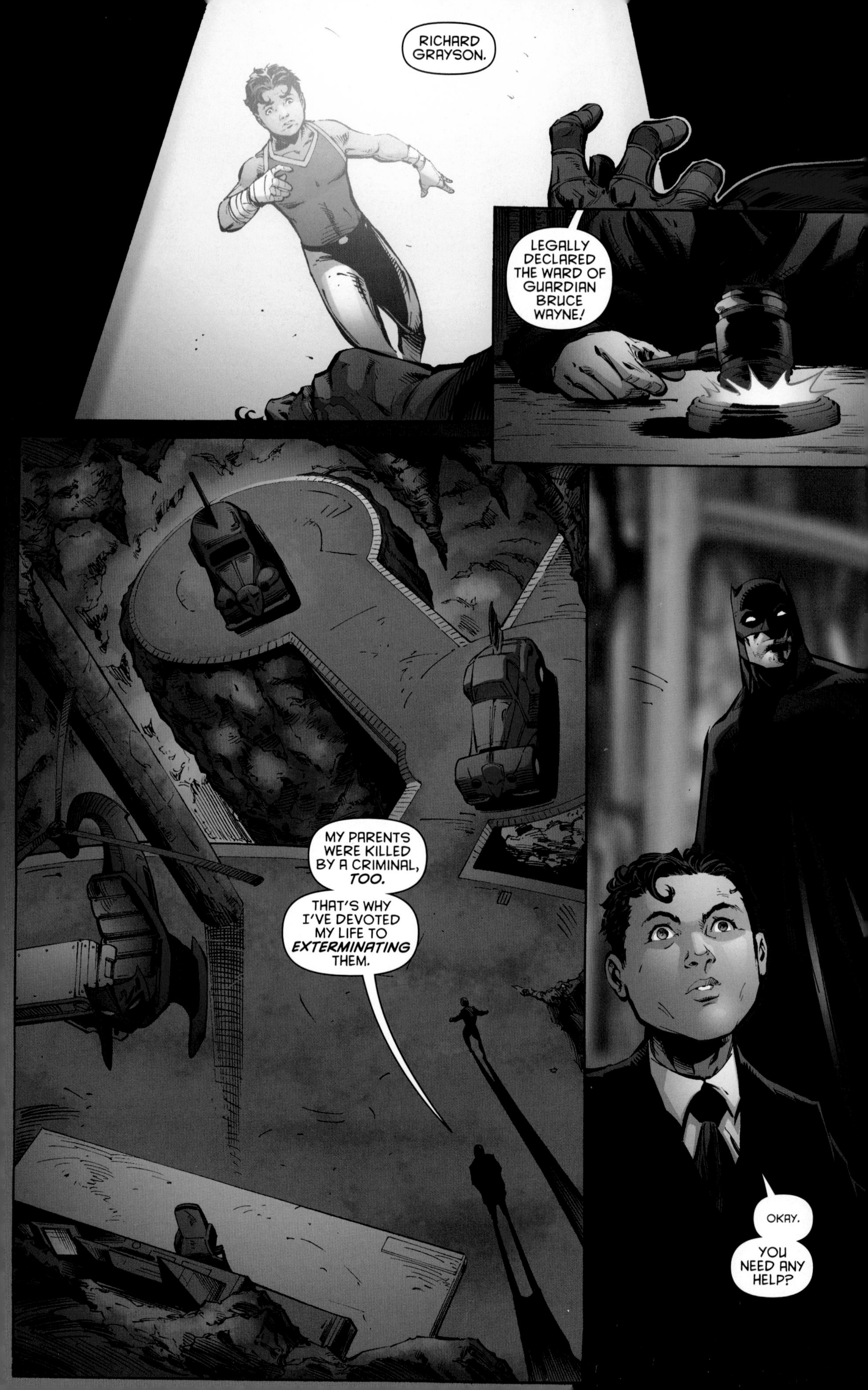
RICHARD GRAYSON.
LEGALLY DECLARED THE WARD OF GUARDIAN BRUCE WAYNE!
MY PARENTS WERE KILLED BY A CRIMINAL, *TOO.*
THAT'S WHY I'VE DEVOTED MY LIFE TO *EXTERMINATING* THEM.
OKAY.
YOU NEED ANY HELP?

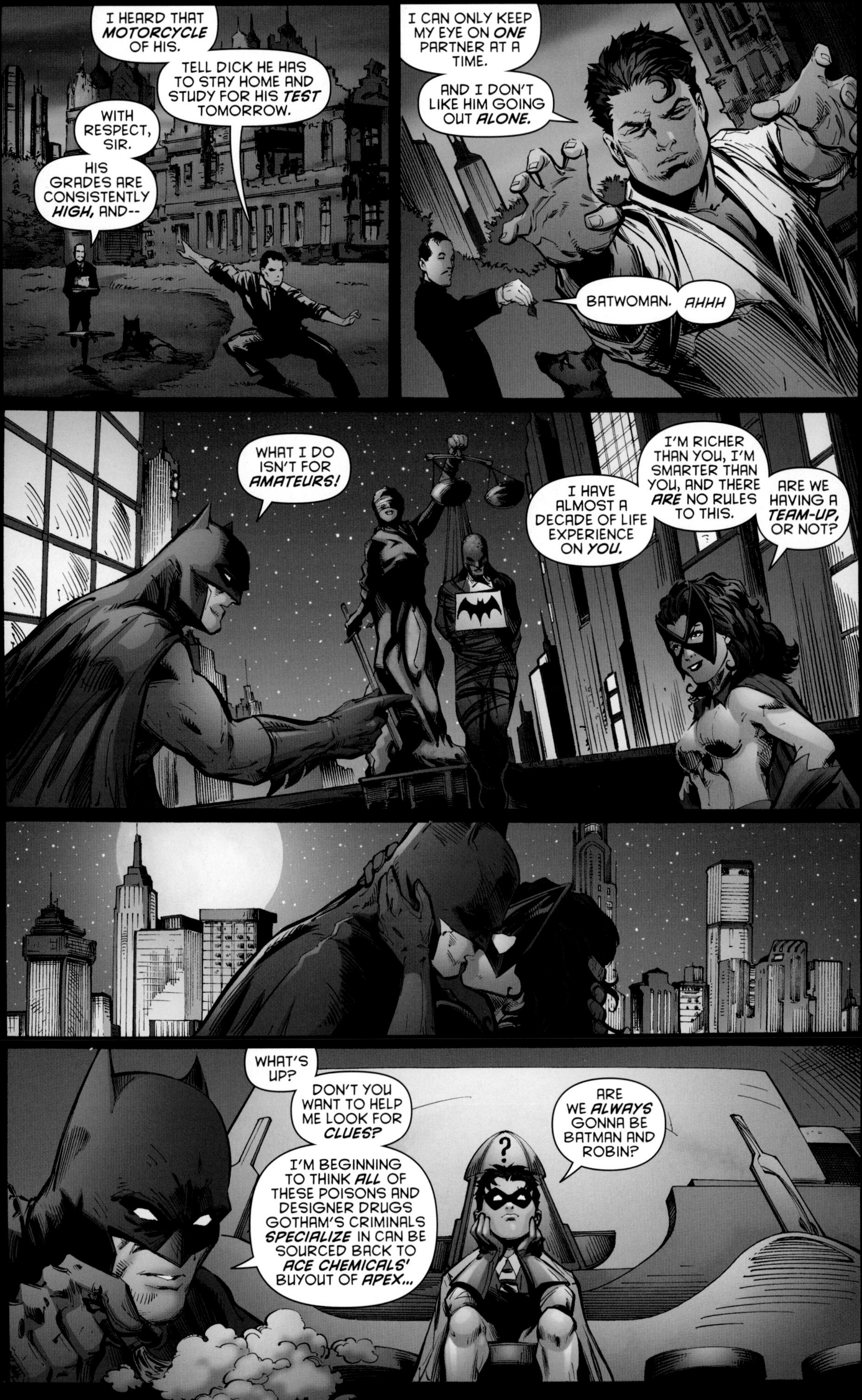
I HEARD THAT *MOTORCYCLE* OF HIS.
TELL DICK HE HAS TO STAY HOME AND STUDY FOR HIS *TEST* TOMORROW.
WITH RESPECT, SIR.
HIS GRADES ARE CONSISTENTLY *HIGH,* AND--
I CAN ONLY KEEP MY EYE ON *ONE* PARTNER AT A TIME.
AND I DON'T LIKE HIM GOING OUT *ALONE.*
BATWOMAN. *AHHH*
WHAT I DO ISN'T FOR *AMATEURS!*
I HAVE ALMOST A DECADE OF LIFE EXPERIENCE ON *YOU.*
I'M RICHER THAN YOU, I'M SMARTER THAN YOU, AND THERE *ARE* NO RULES TO THIS.
ARE WE HAVING A *TEAM-UP,* OR NOT?
WHAT'S UP?
DON'T YOU WANT TO HELP ME LOOK FOR *CLUES?*
I'M BEGINNING TO THINK *ALL* OF THESE POISONS AND DESIGNER DRUGS GOTHAM'S CRIMINALS *SPECIALIZE* IN CAN BE SOURCED BACK TO *ACE CHEMICALS'* BUYOUT OF *APEX...*
ARE WE *ALWAYS* GONNA BE BATMAN AND ROBIN?

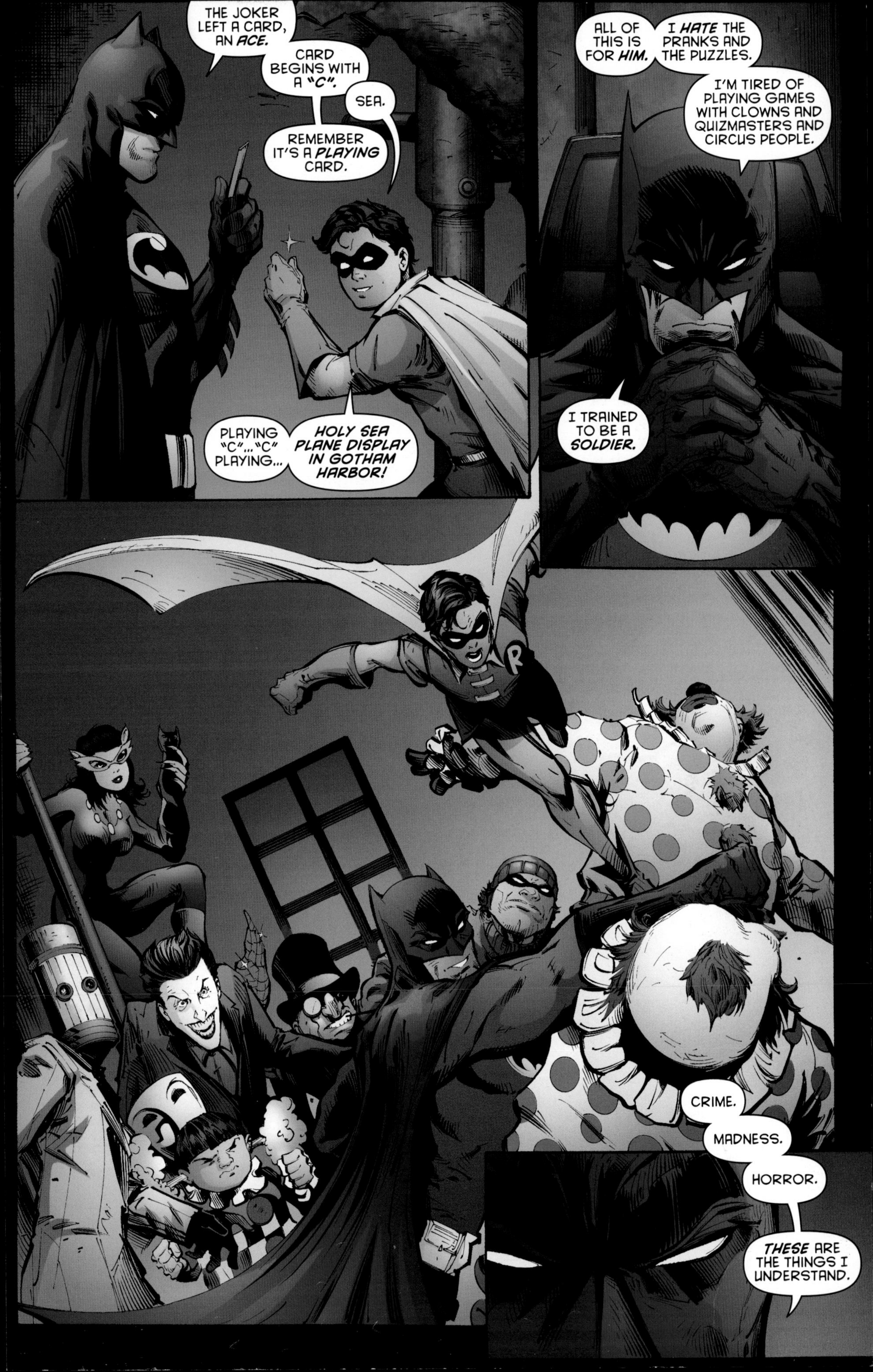
THE JOKER LEFT A CARD, AN *ACE.*
CARD BEGINS WITH A *"C".*
SEA.
REMEMBER IT'S A *PLAYING* CARD.
PLAYING "C"..."C" PLAYING...
HOLY SEA PLANE DISPLAY IN GOTHAM HARBOR!
ALL OF THIS IS FOR *HIM.*
I *HATE* THE PRANKS AND THE PUZZLES.
I'M TIRED OF PLAYING GAMES WITH CLOWNS AND QUIZMASTERS AND CIRCUS PEOPLE.
I TRAINED TO BE A *SOLDIER.*
CRIME.
MADNESS.
HORROR.
THESE ARE THE THINGS I UNDERSTAND.

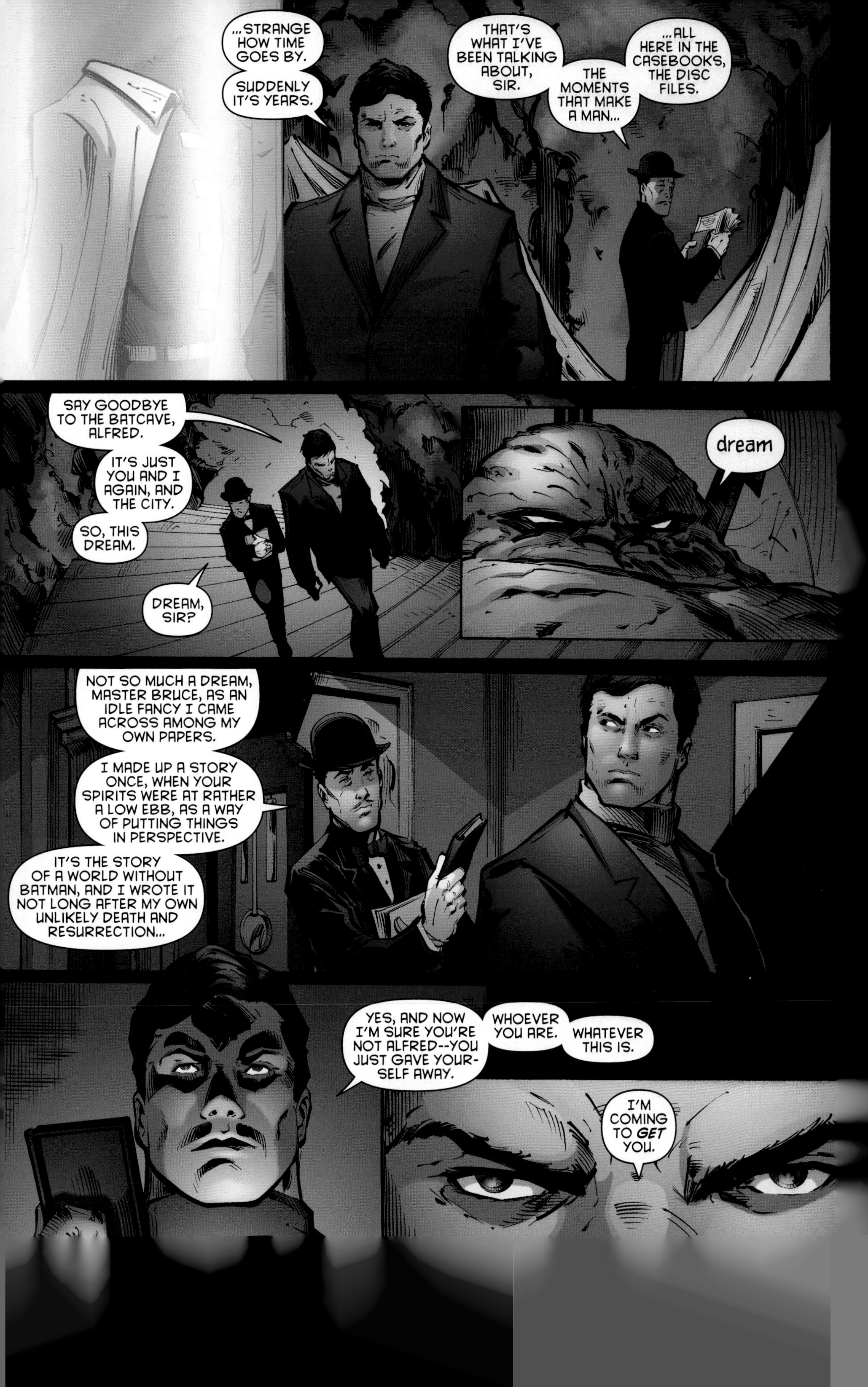
...STRANGE HOW TIME GOES BY.
SUDDENLY IT'S YEARS.
THAT'S WHAT I'VE BEEN TALKING ABOUT, SIR.
THE MOMENTS THAT MAKE A MAN...
...ALL HERE IN THE CASEBOOKS, THE DISC FILES.
SAY GOODBYE TO THE BATCAVE, ALFRED.
IT'S JUST YOU AND I AGAIN, AND THE CITY.
SO, THIS DREAM.
DREAM, SIR?
dream
NOT SO MUCH A DREAM, MASTER BRUCE, AS AN IDLE FANCY I CAME ACROSS AMONG MY OWN PAPERS.
I MADE UP A STORY ONCE, WHEN YOUR SPIRITS WERE AT RATHER A LOW EBB, AS A WAY OF PUTTING THINGS IN PERSPECTIVE.
IT'S THE STORY OF A WORLD WITHOUT BATMAN, AND I WROTE IT NOT LONG AFTER MY OWN UNLIKELY DEATH AND RESURRECTION...
YES, AND NOW I'M SURE YOU'RE NOT ALFRED--YOU JUST GAVE YOURSELF AWAY.
WHOEVER YOU ARE.
WHATEVER THIS IS.
I'M COMING TO *GET* YOU.

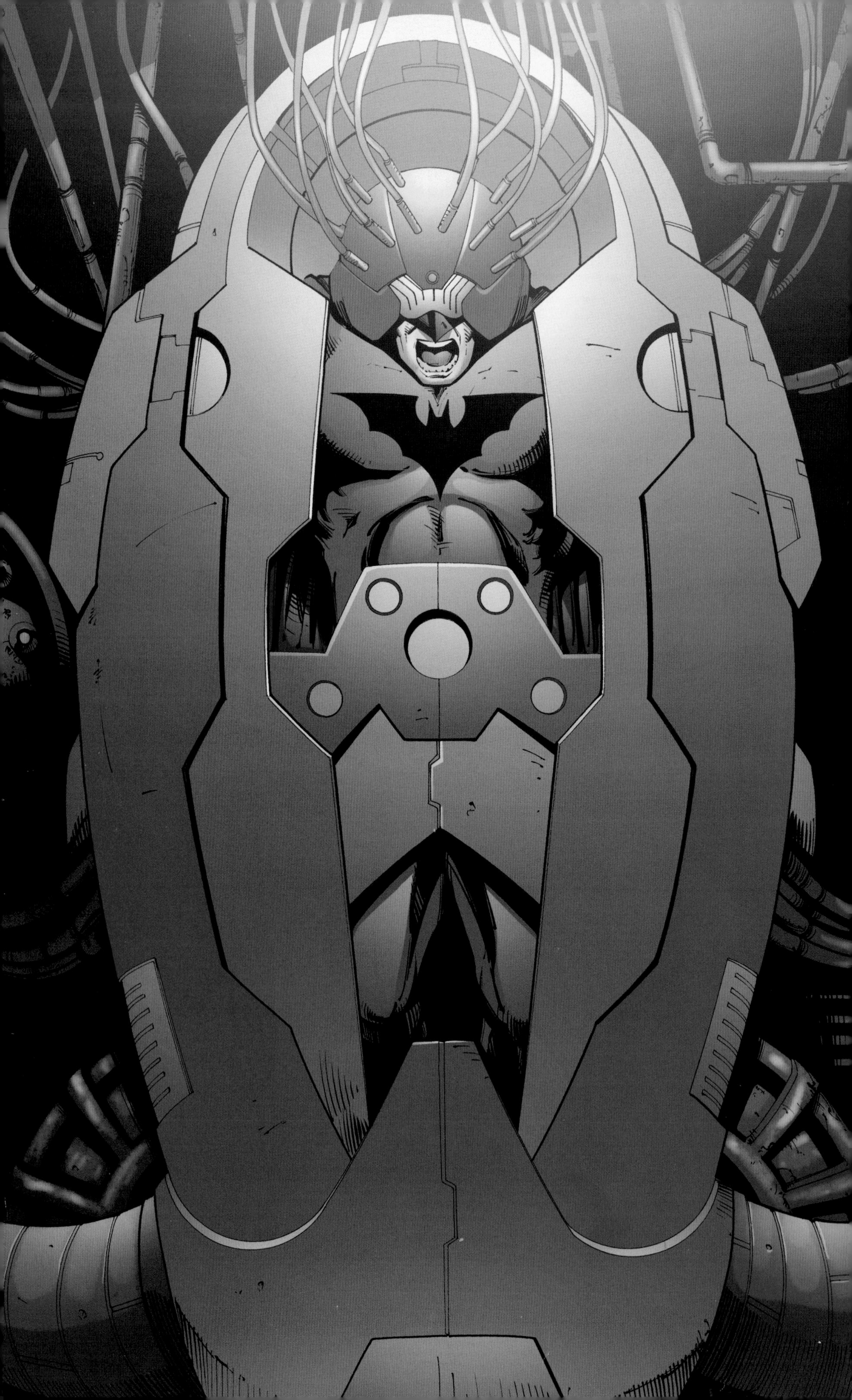

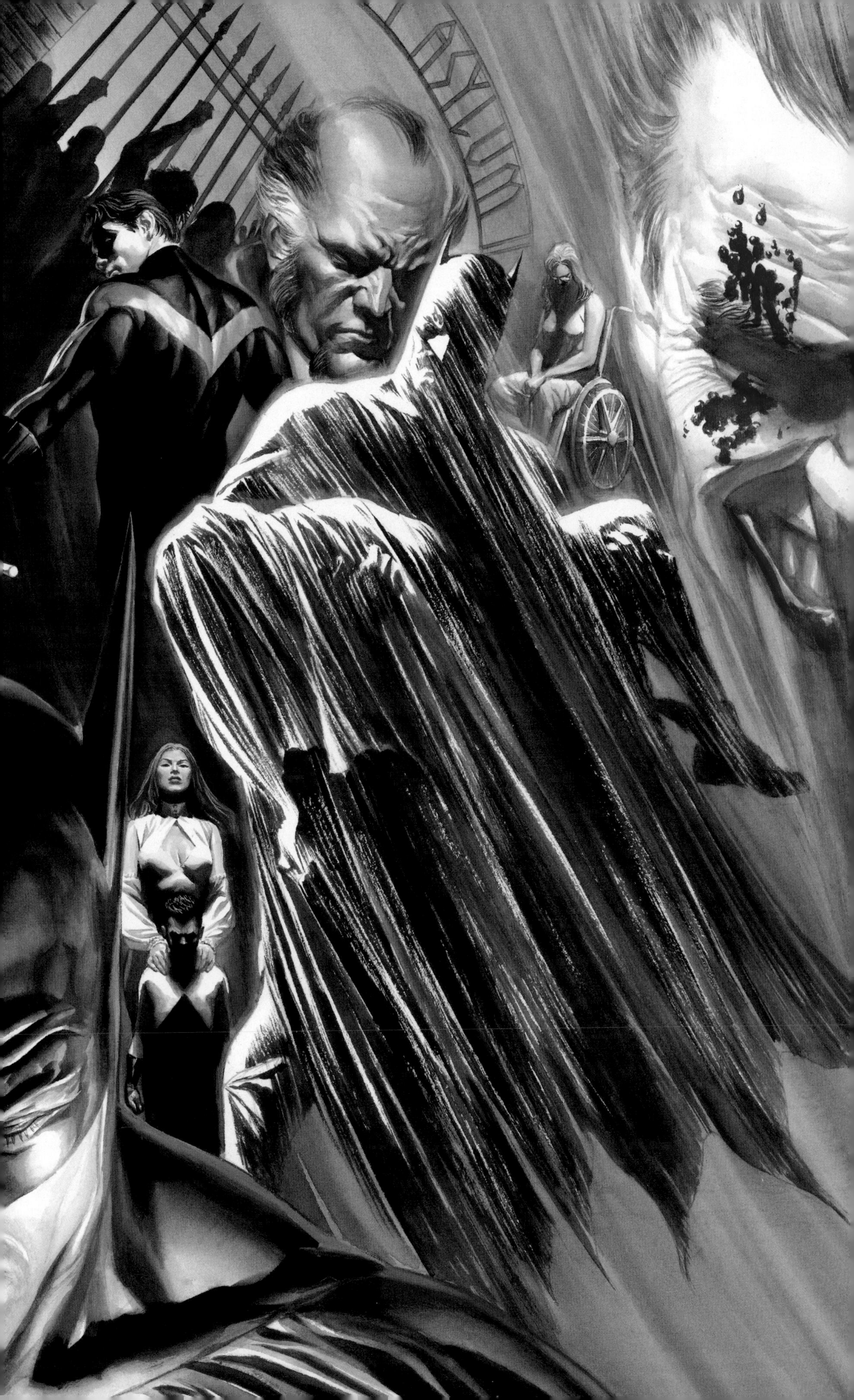
ASYLUM

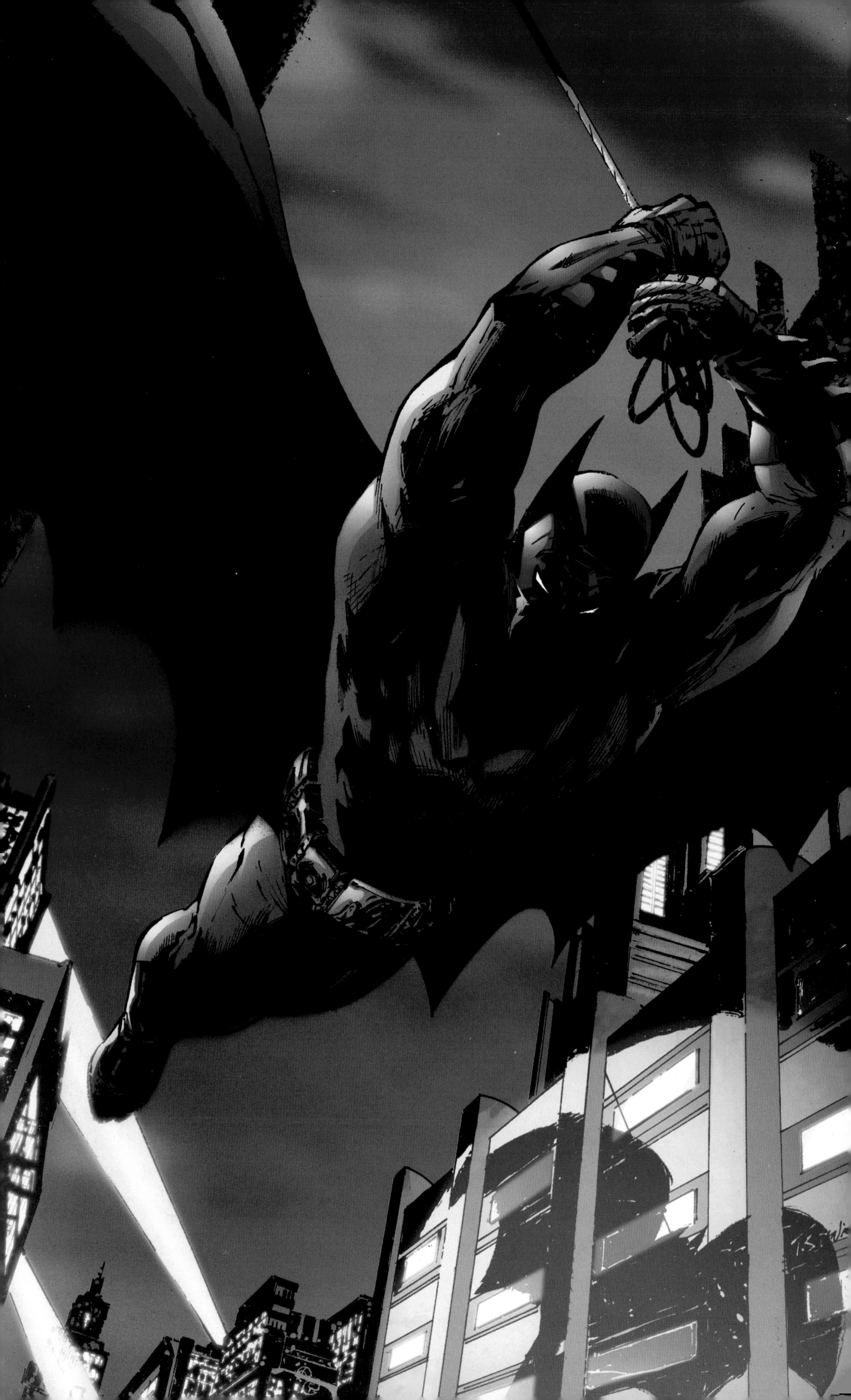

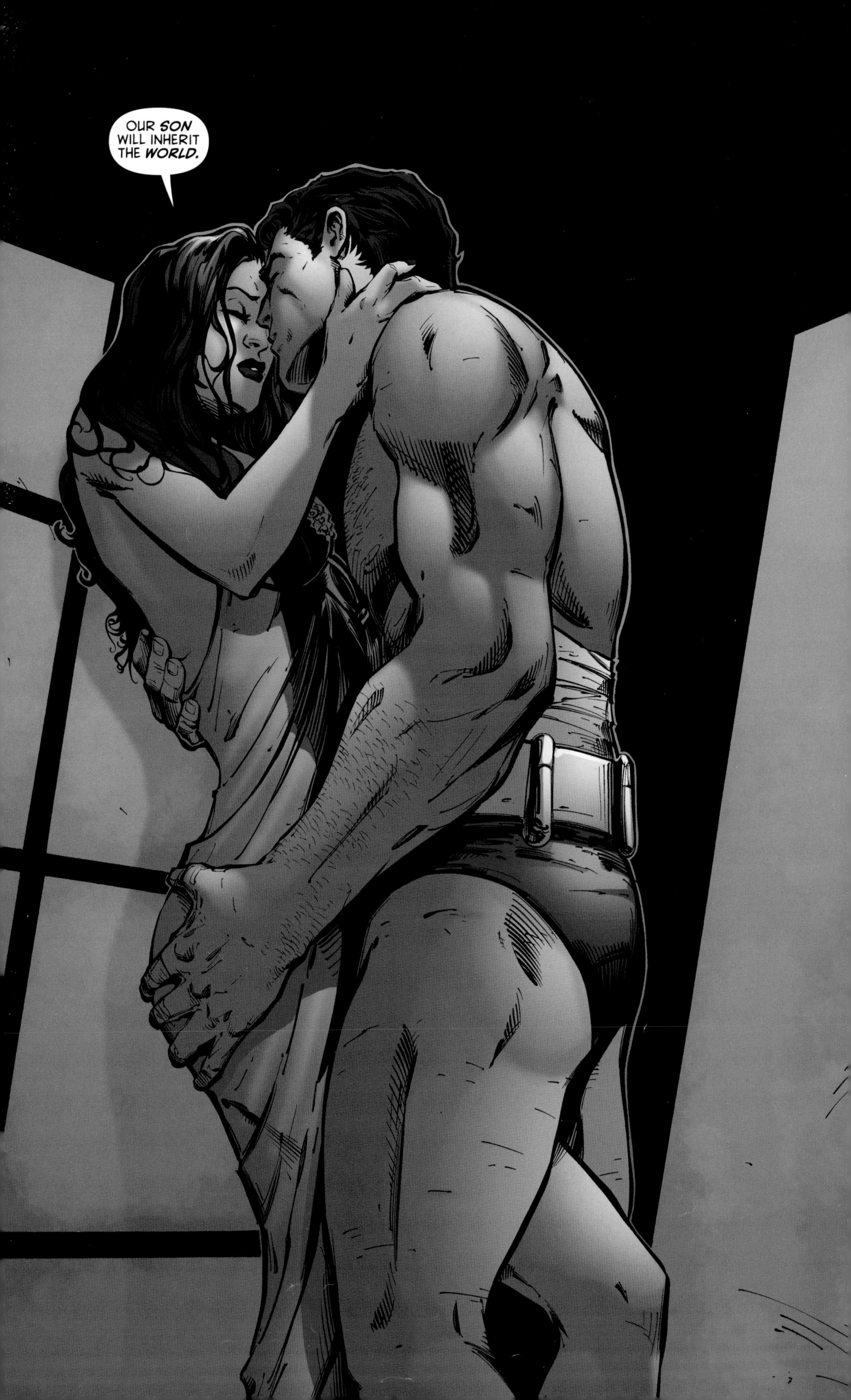
OUR *SON* WILL INHERIT THE *WORLD.*

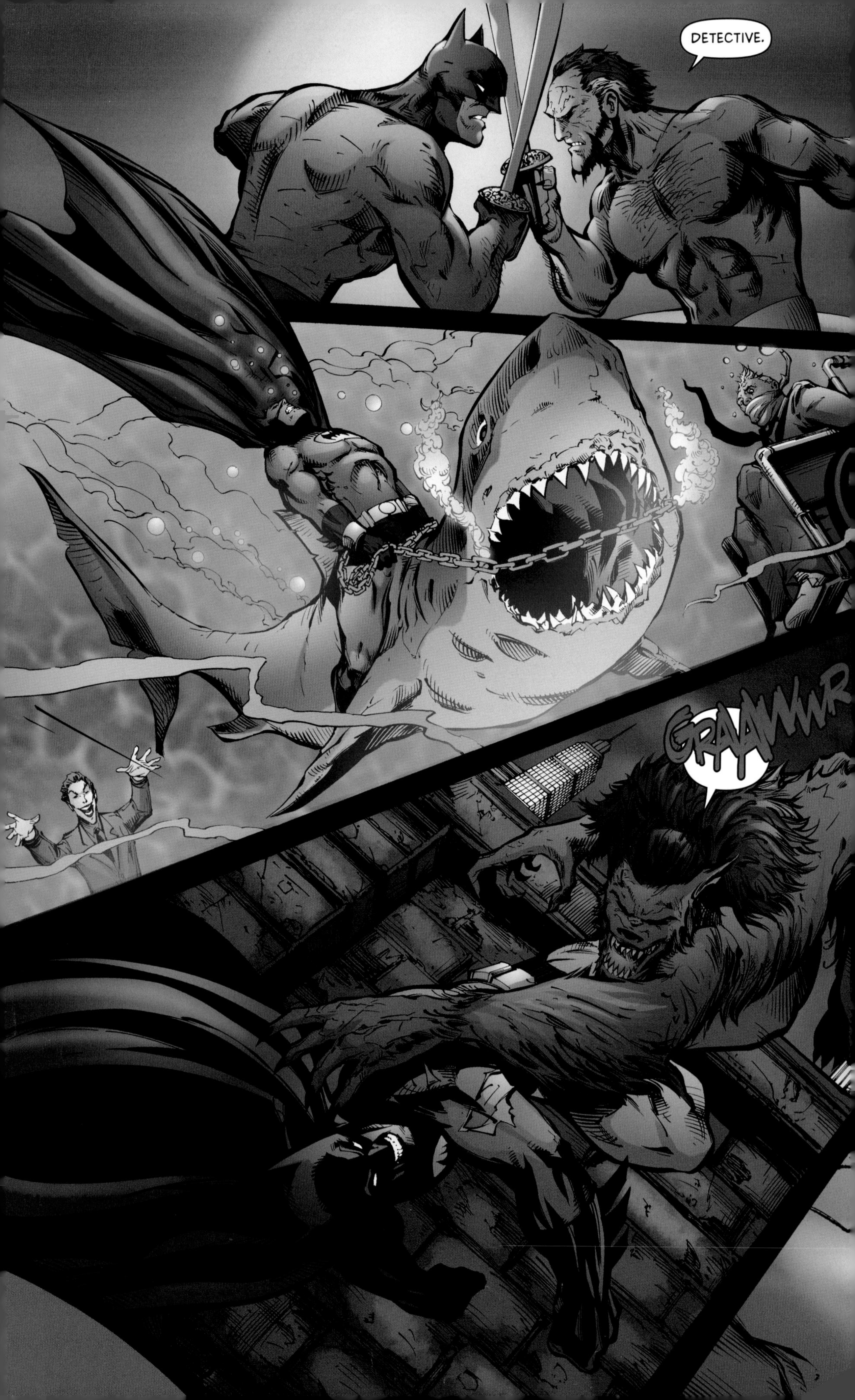
DETECTIVE.
GRAAWWR

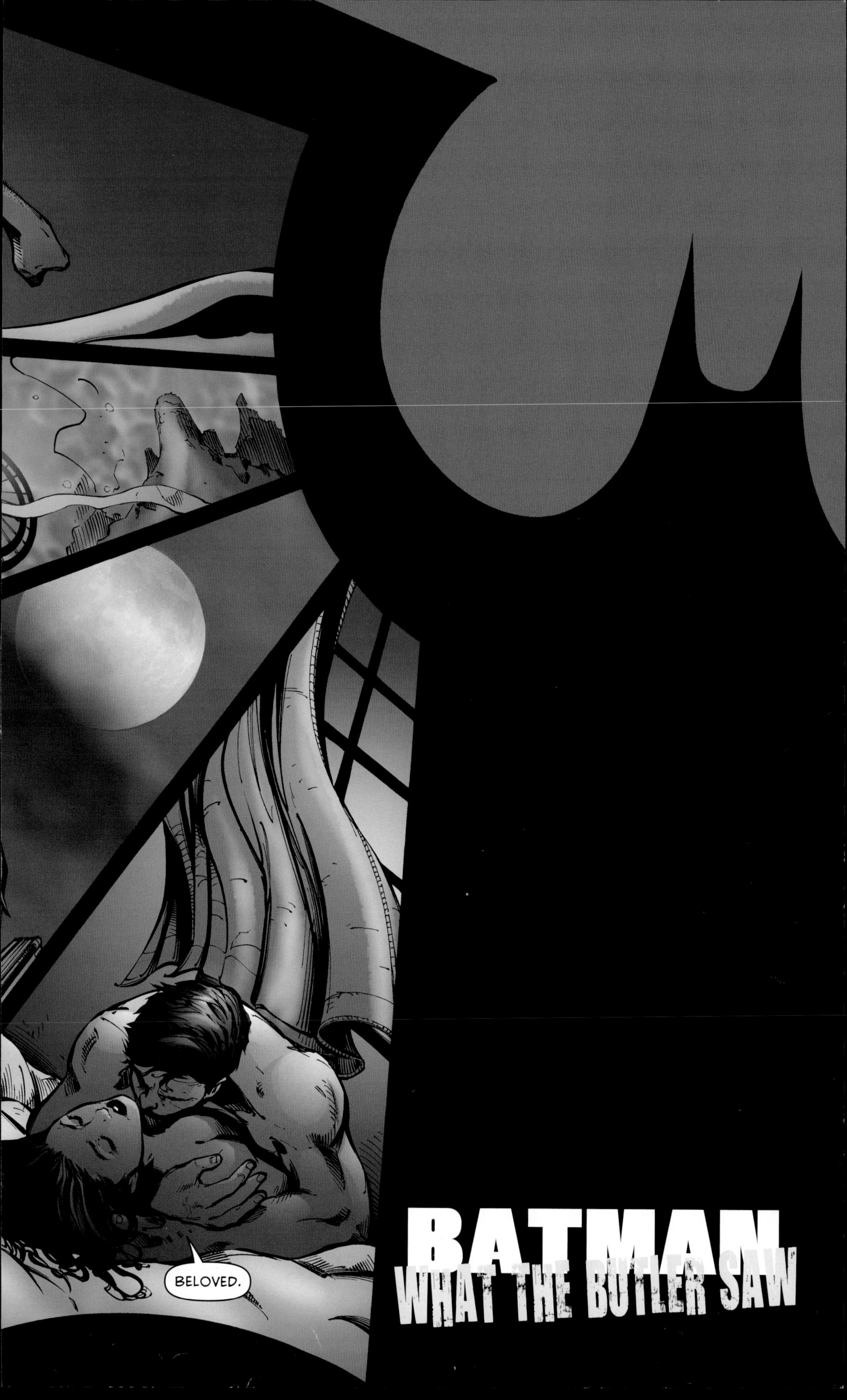
BELOVED.
BATMAN
WHAT THE BUTLER SAW

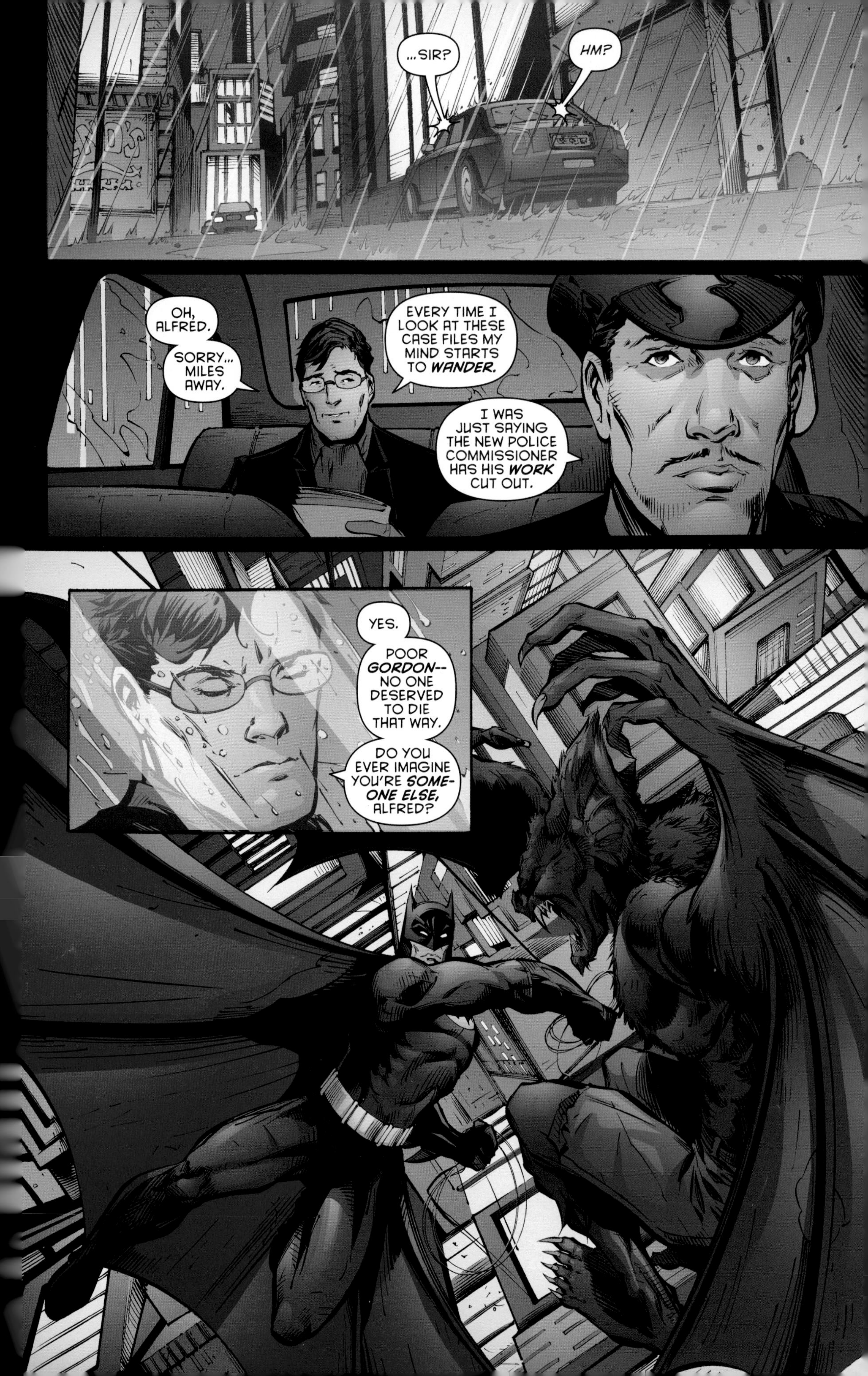
...SIR?
HM?
OH, ALFRED.
SORRY... MILES AWAY.
EVERY TIME I LOOK AT THESE CASE FILES MY MIND STARTS TO *WANDER.*
I WAS JUST SAYING THE NEW POLICE COMMISSIONER HAS HIS *WORK* CUT OUT.
YES.
POOR *GORDON*-- NO ONE DESERVED TO DIE THAT WAY.
DO YOU EVER IMAGINE YOU'RE *SOMEONE ELSE,* ALFRED?

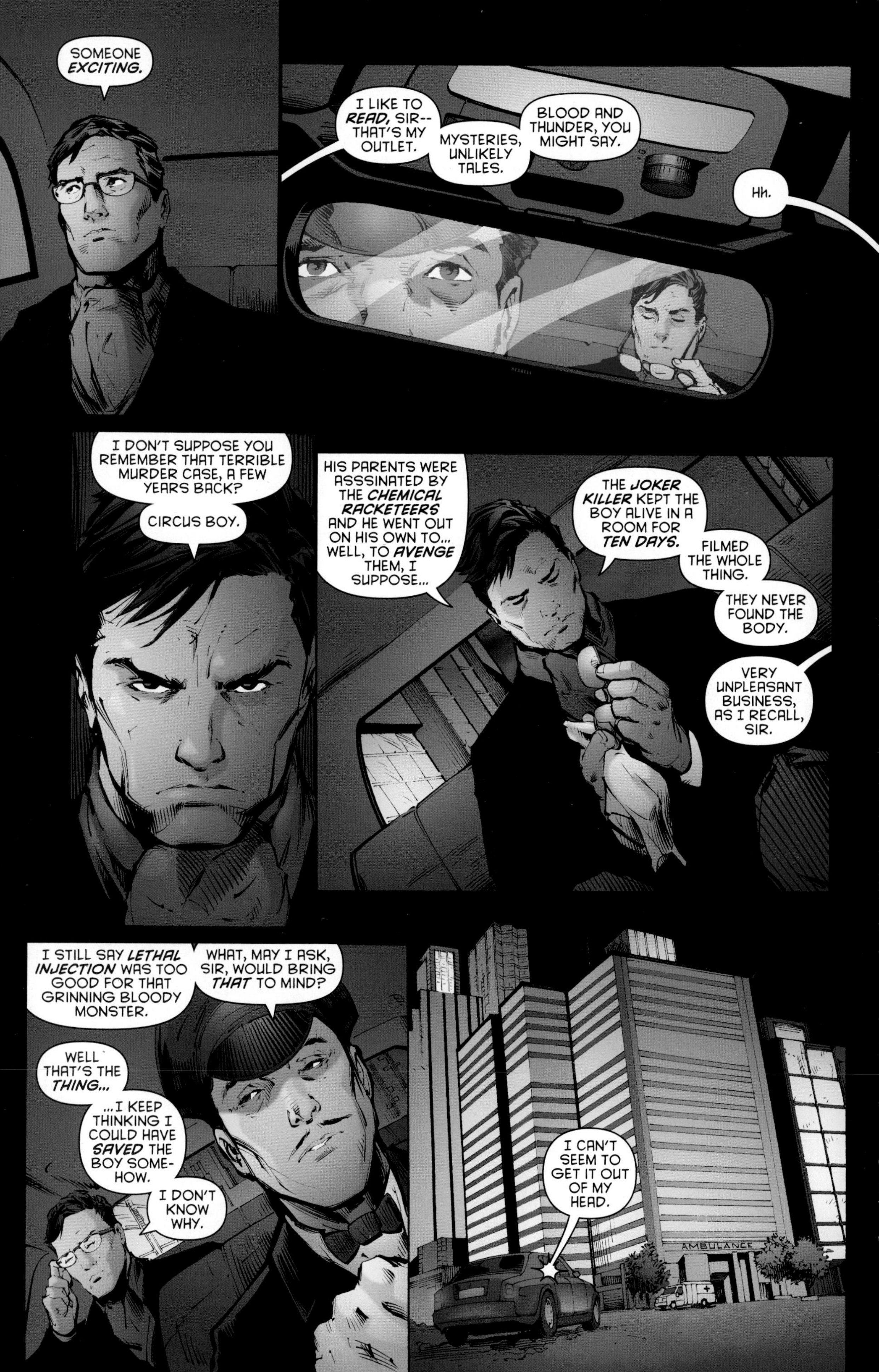

SOMEONE EXCITING.
I LIKE TO READ, SIR-- THAT'S MY OUTLET.
MYSTERIES, UNLIKELY TALES.
BLOOD AND THUNDER, YOU MIGHT SAY.
Hh.
I DON'T SUPPOSE YOU REMEMBER THAT TERRIBLE MURDER CASE, A FEW YEARS BACK?
CIRCUS BOY.
HIS PARENTS WERE ASSSINATED BY THE CHEMICAL RACKETEERS AND HE WENT OUT ON HIS OWN TO... WELL, TO AVENGE THEM, I SUPPOSE...
THE JOKER KILLER KEPT THE BOY ALIVE IN A ROOM FOR TEN DAYS.
FILMED THE WHOLE THING.
THEY NEVER FOUND THE BODY.
VERY UNPLEASANT BUSINESS, AS I RECALL, SIR.
I STILL SAY LETHAL INJECTION WAS TOO GOOD FOR THAT GRINNING BLOODY MONSTER.
WHAT, MAY I ASK, SIR, WOULD BRING THAT TO MIND?
WELL THAT'S THE THING...
...I KEEP THINKING I COULD HAVE SAVED THE BOY SOME-HOW.
I DON'T KNOW WHY.
I CAN'T SEEM TO GET IT OUT OF MY HEAD.
AMBULANCE

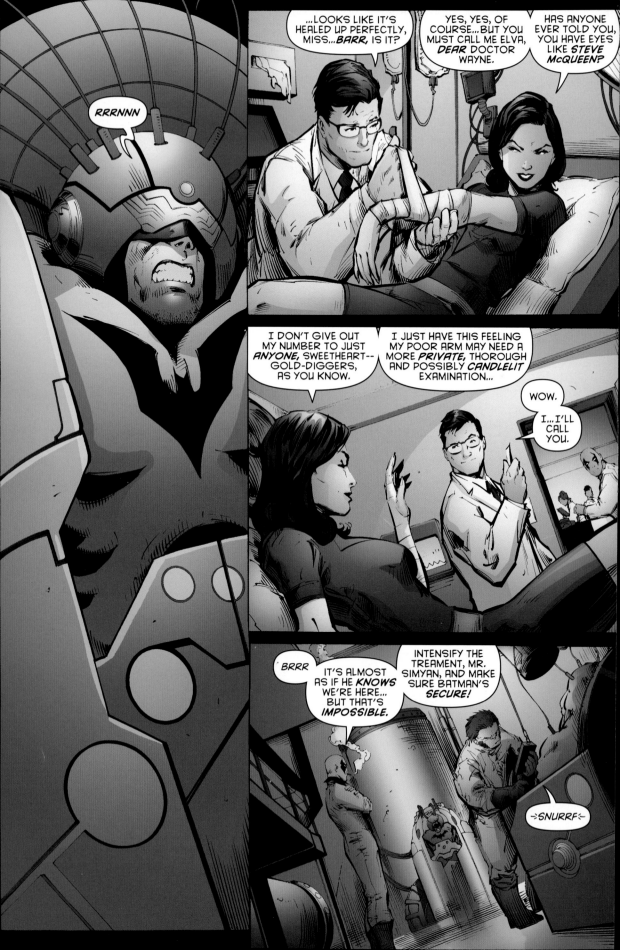

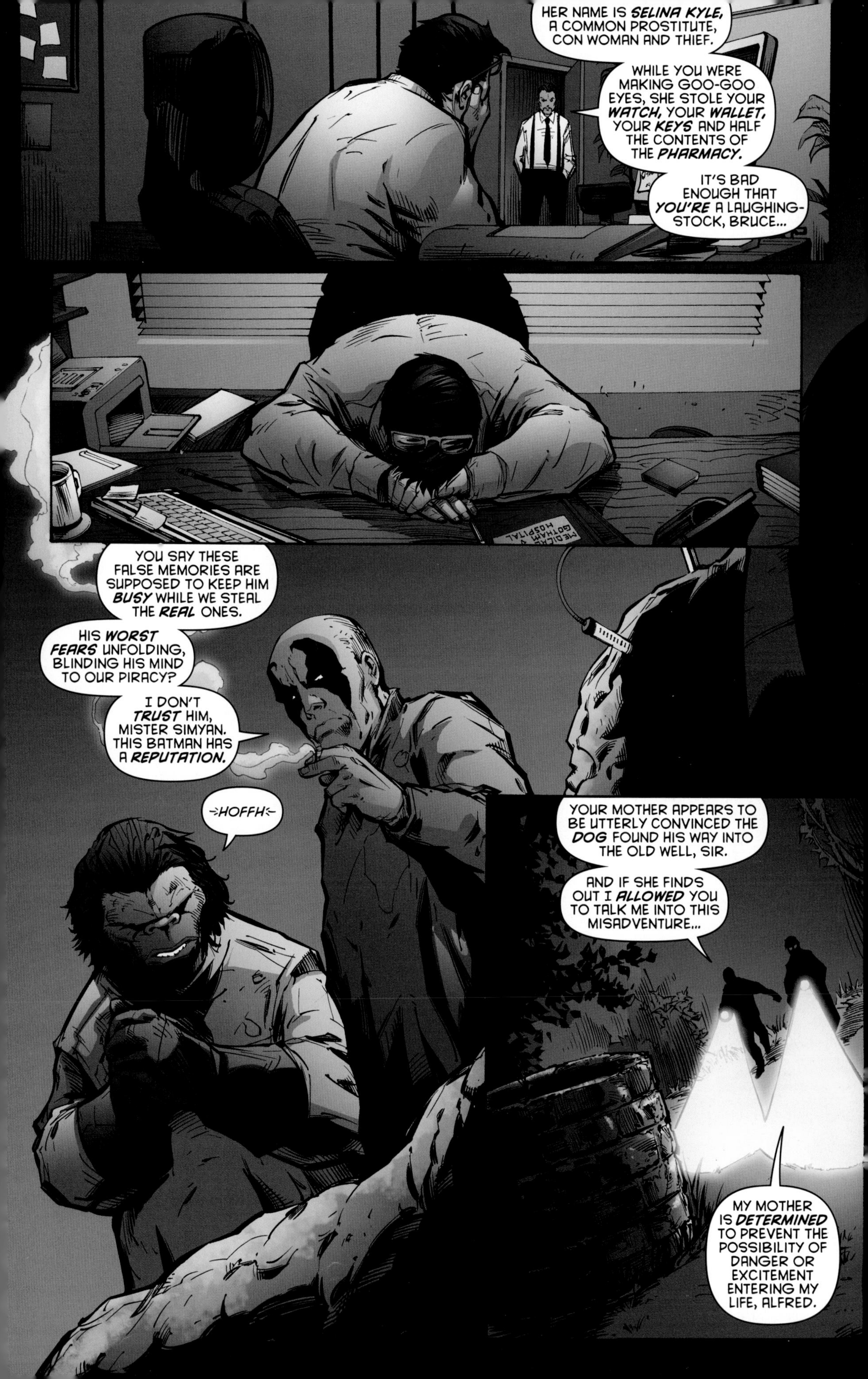
HER NAME IS SELINA KYLE, A COMMON PROSTITUTE, CON WOMAN AND THIEF.
WHILE YOU WERE MAKING GOO-GOO EYES, SHE STOLE YOUR WATCH, YOUR WALLET, YOUR KEYS AND HALF THE CONTENTS OF THE PHARMACY.
IT'S BAD ENOUGH THAT YOU'RE A LAUGHING-STOCK, BRUCE...
YOU SAY THESE FALSE MEMORIES ARE SUPPOSED TO KEEP HIM BUSY WHILE WE STEAL THE REAL ONES.
HIS WORST FEARS UNFOLDING, BLINDING HIS MIND TO OUR PIRACY?
I DON'T TRUST HIM, MISTER SIMYAN. THIS BATMAN HAS A REPUTATION.
HOFFH
YOUR MOTHER APPEARS TO BE UTTERLY CONVINCED THE DOG FOUND HIS WAY INTO THE OLD WELL, SIR.
AND IF SHE FINDS OUT I ALLOWED YOU TO TALK ME INTO THIS MISADVENTURE...
MY MOTHER IS DETERMINED TO PREVENT THE POSSIBILITY OF DANGER OR EXCITEMENT ENTERING MY LIFE, ALFRED.

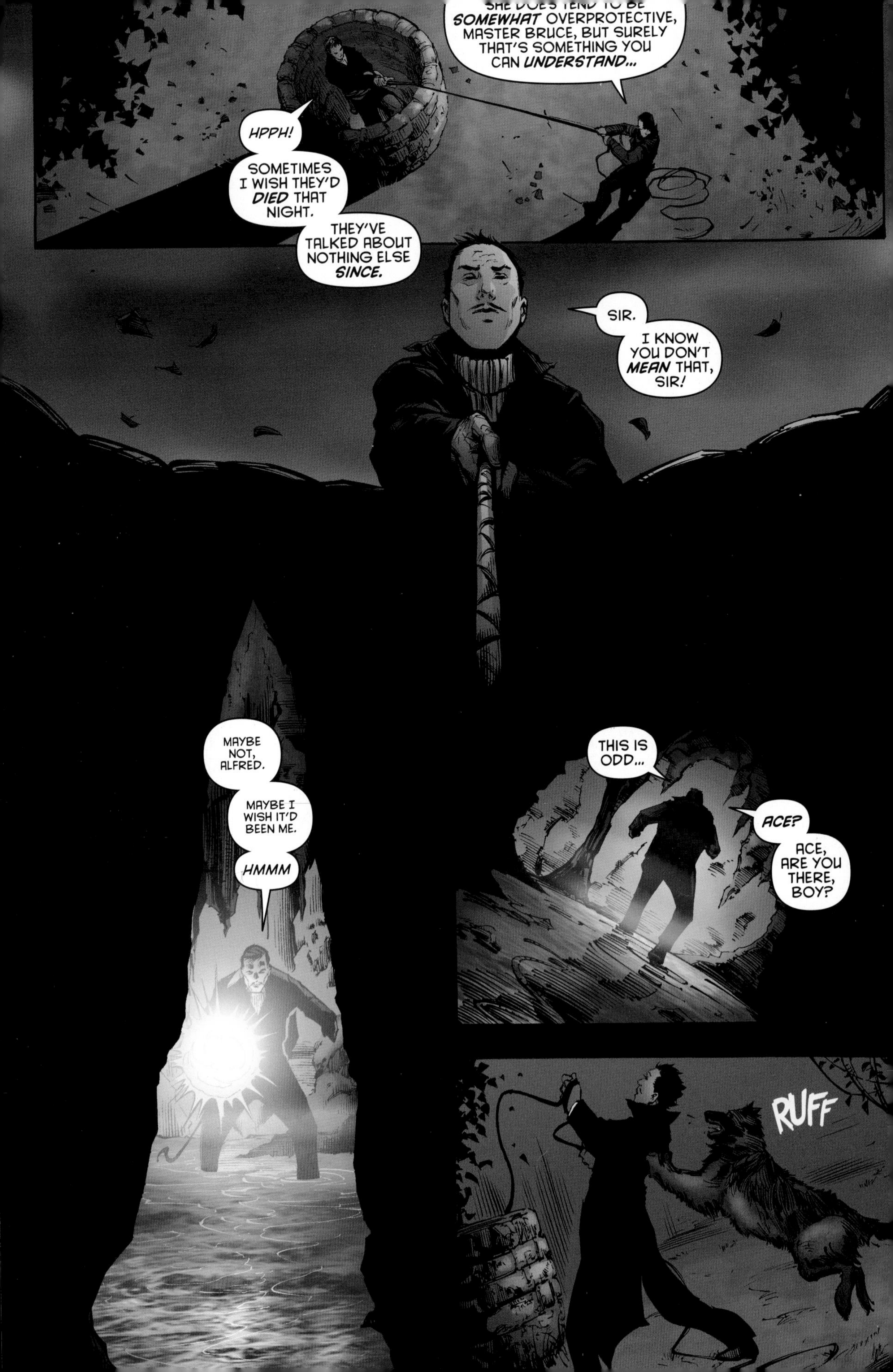

SOMEWHAT OVERPROTECTIVE, MASTER BRUCE, BUT SURELY THAT'S SOMETHING YOU CAN UNDERSTAND...
HPPH!
SOMETIMES I WISH THEY'D DIED THAT NIGHT.
THEY'VE TALKED ABOUT NOTHING ELSE SINCE.
SIR.
I KNOW YOU DON'T MEAN THAT, SIR!
MAYBE NOT, ALFRED.
MAYBE I WISH IT'D BEEN ME.
HMMM
THIS IS ODD...
ACE?
ACE, ARE YOU THERE, BOY?
RUFF

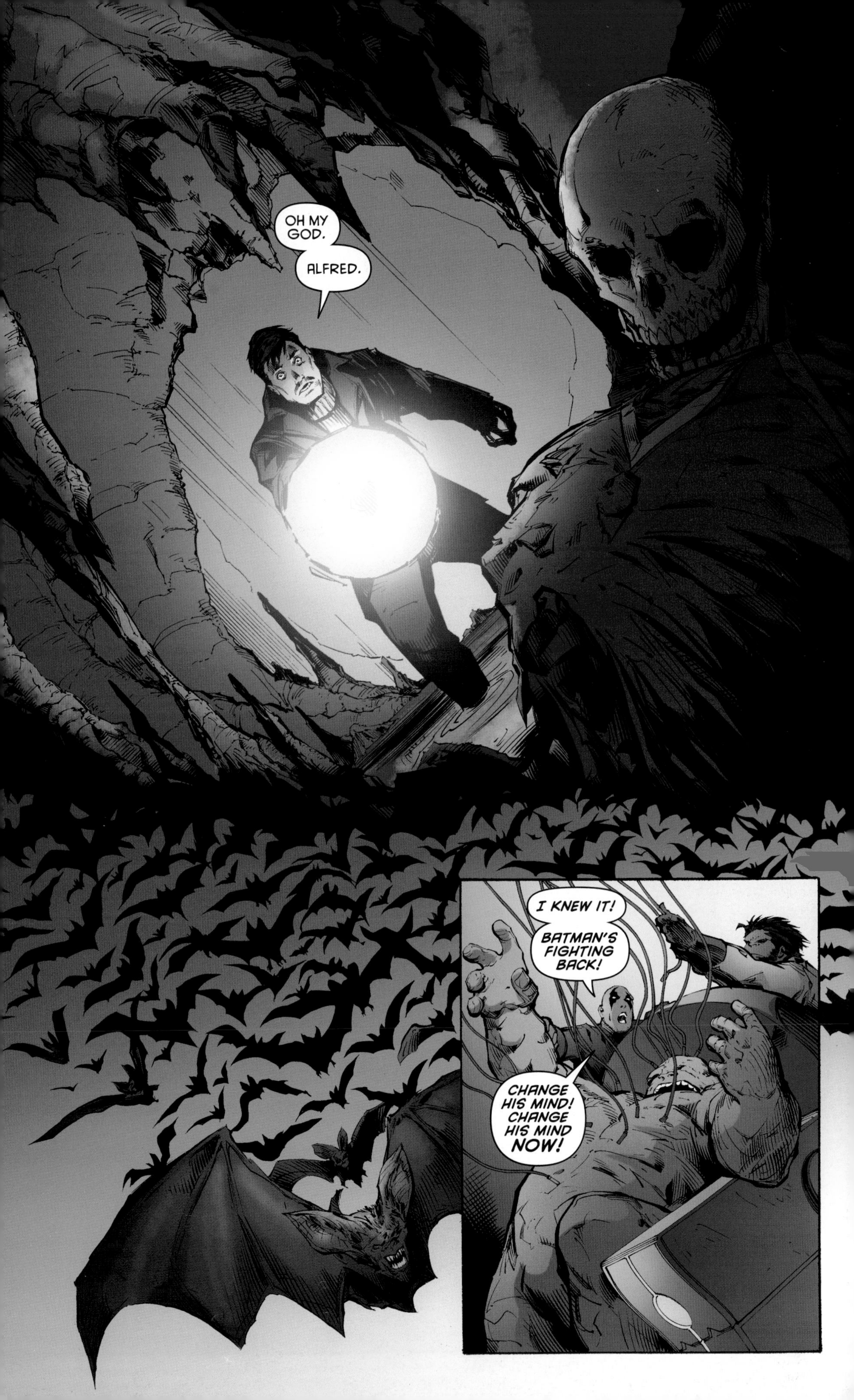
OH MY GOD.
ALFRED.
I KNEW IT!
BATMAN'S FIGHTING BACK!
CHANGE HIS MIND! CHANGE HIS MIND NOW!

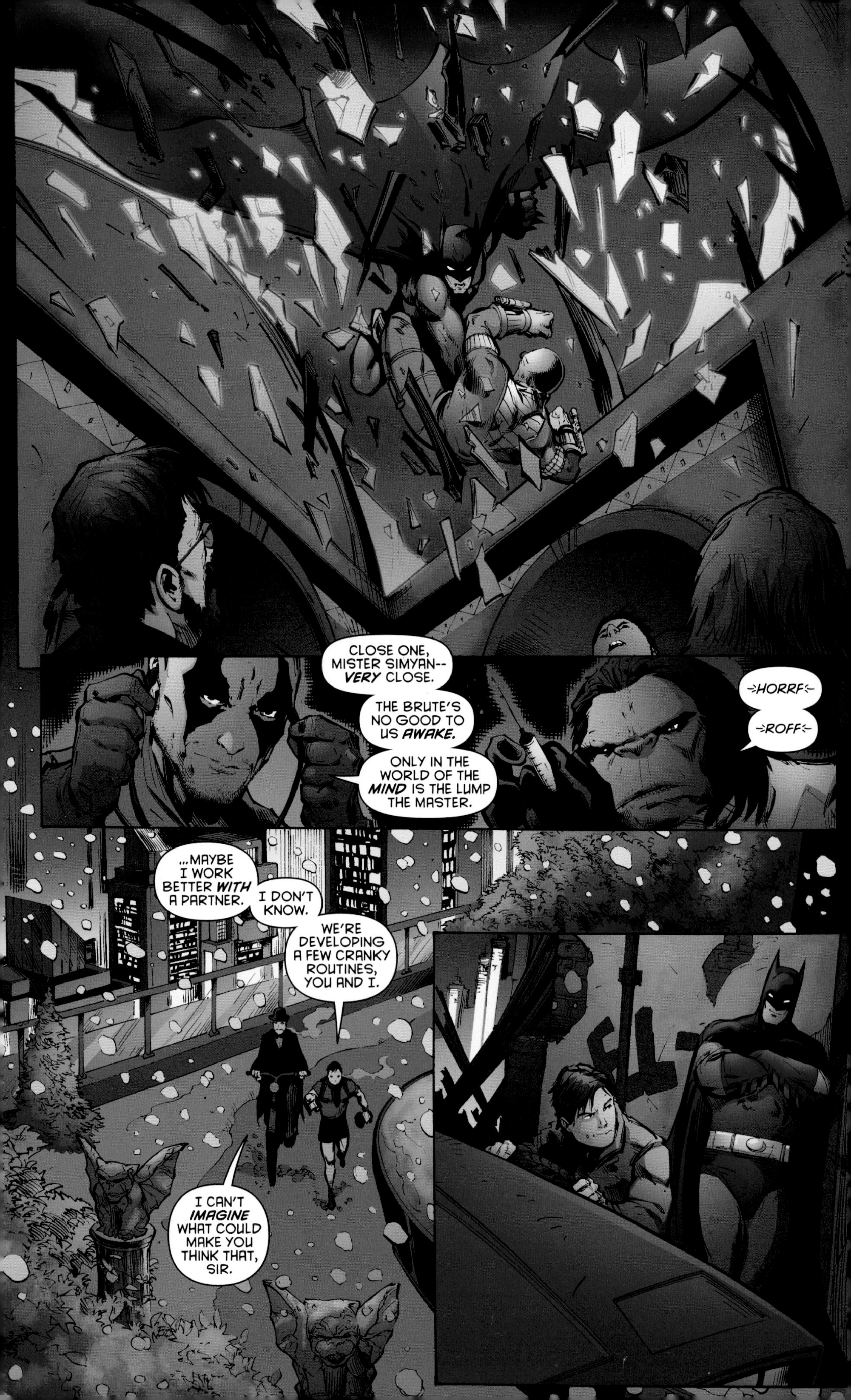
CLOSE ONE, MISTER SIMYAN-- VERY CLOSE.
THE BRUTE'S NO GOOD TO US AWAKE.
ONLY IN THE WORLD OF THE MIND IS THE LUMP THE MASTER.
HORRF
ROFF
...MAYBE I WORK BETTER WITH A PARTNER.
I DON'T KNOW.
WE'RE DEVELOPING A FEW CRANKY ROUTINES, YOU AND I.
I CAN'T IMAGINE WHAT COULD MAKE YOU THINK THAT, SIR.

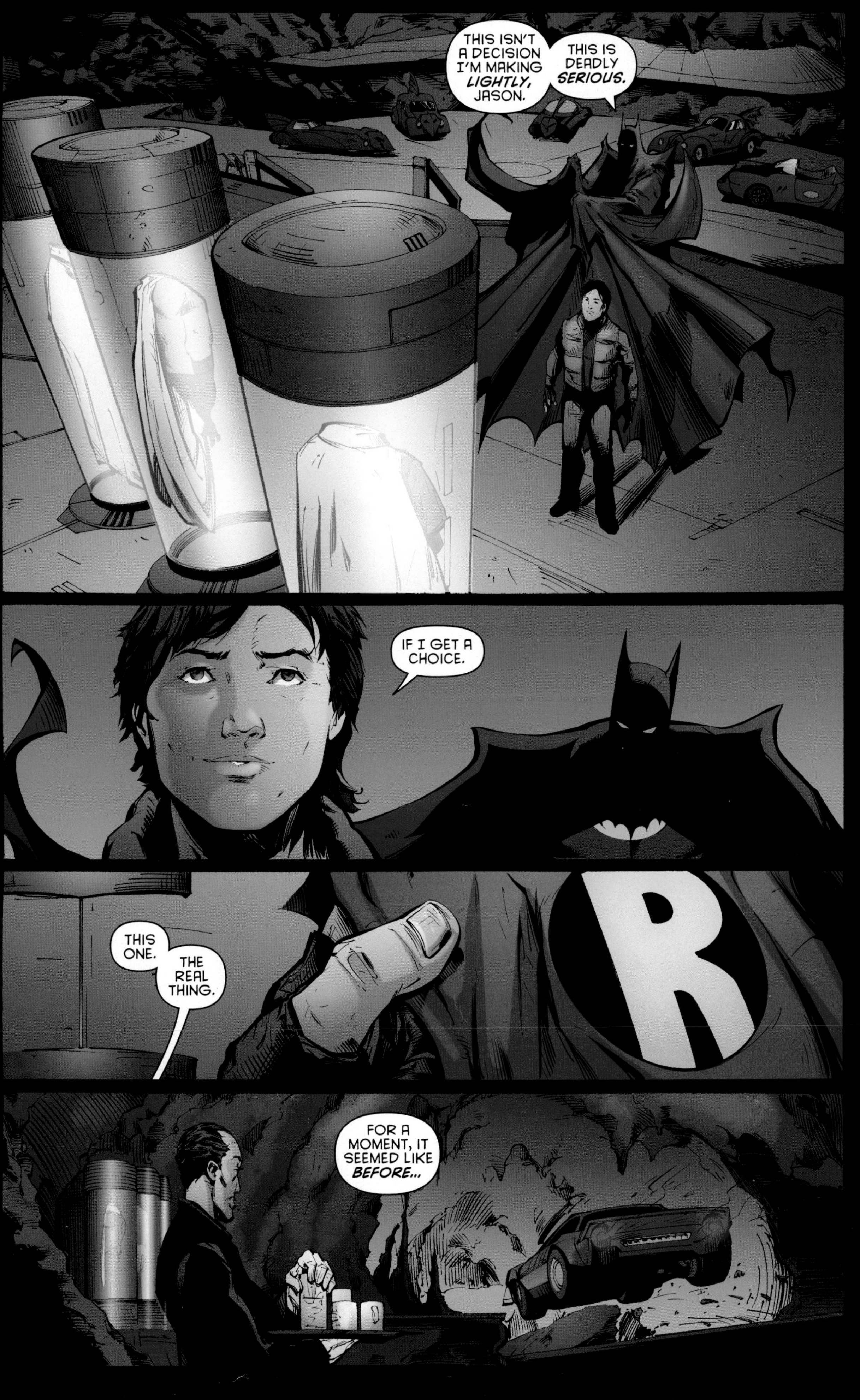
THIS ISN'T A DECISION I'M MAKING *LIGHTLY,* JASON.
THIS IS DEADLY *SERIOUS.*
IF I GET A CHOICE.
THIS ONE.
THE REAL THING.
FOR A MOMENT, IT SEEMED LIKE *BEFORE...*

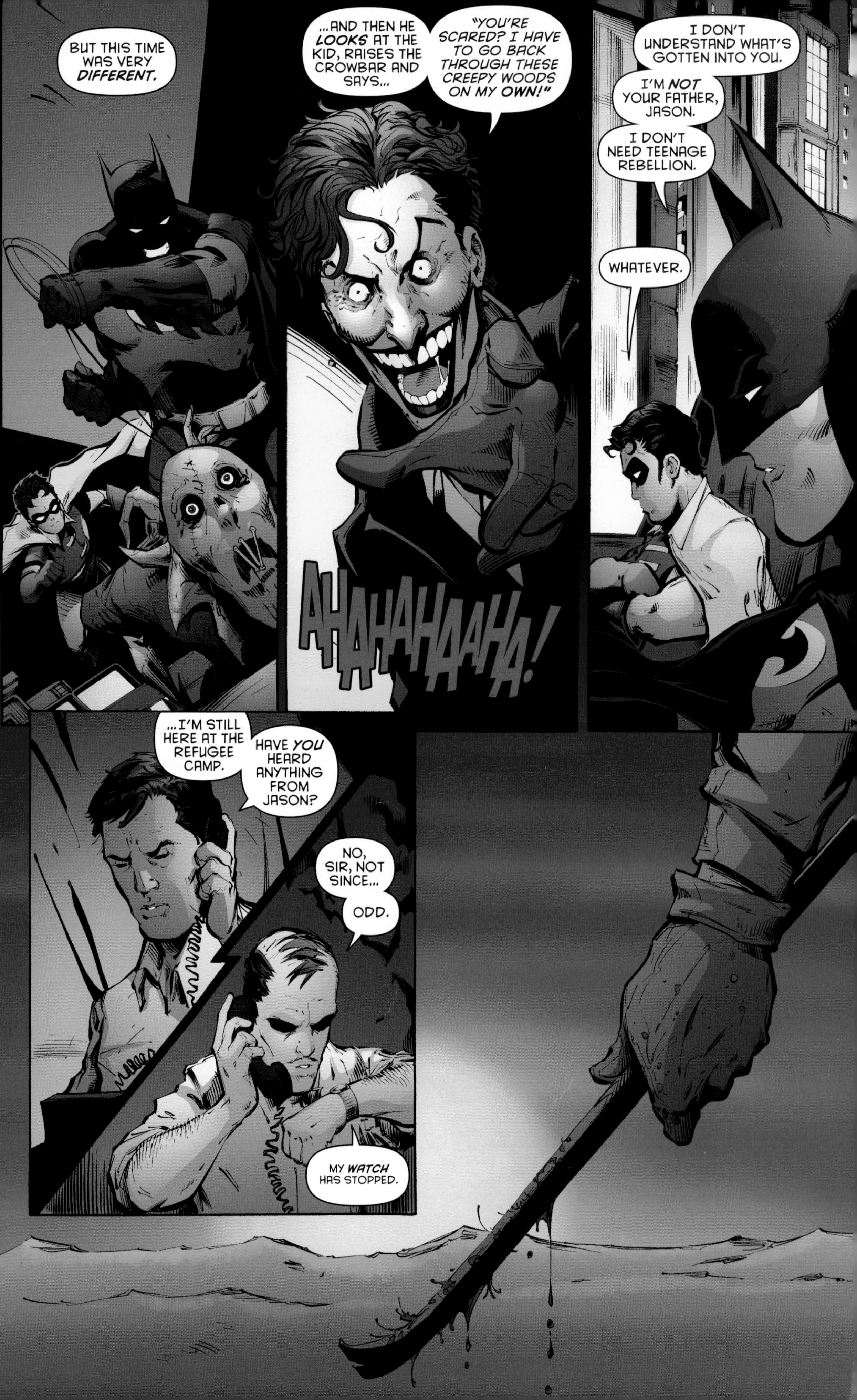

BUT THIS TIME WAS VERY *DIFFERENT.*
...AND THEN HE *LOOKS* AT THE KID, RAISES THE CROWBAR AND SAYS...
"YOU'RE SCARED? I HAVE TO GO BACK THROUGH THESE CREEPY WOODS ON MY OWN!"
AHAHAHAAAHA!
I DON'T UNDERSTAND WHAT'S GOTTEN INTO YOU.
I'M *NOT* YOUR FATHER, JASON.
I DON'T NEED TEENAGE REBELLION.
WHATEVER.
...I'M STILL HERE AT THE REFUGEE CAMP.
HAVE *YOU* HEARD ANYTHING FROM JASON?
NO, SIR, NOT SINCE...
ODD.
MY *WATCH* HAS STOPPED.

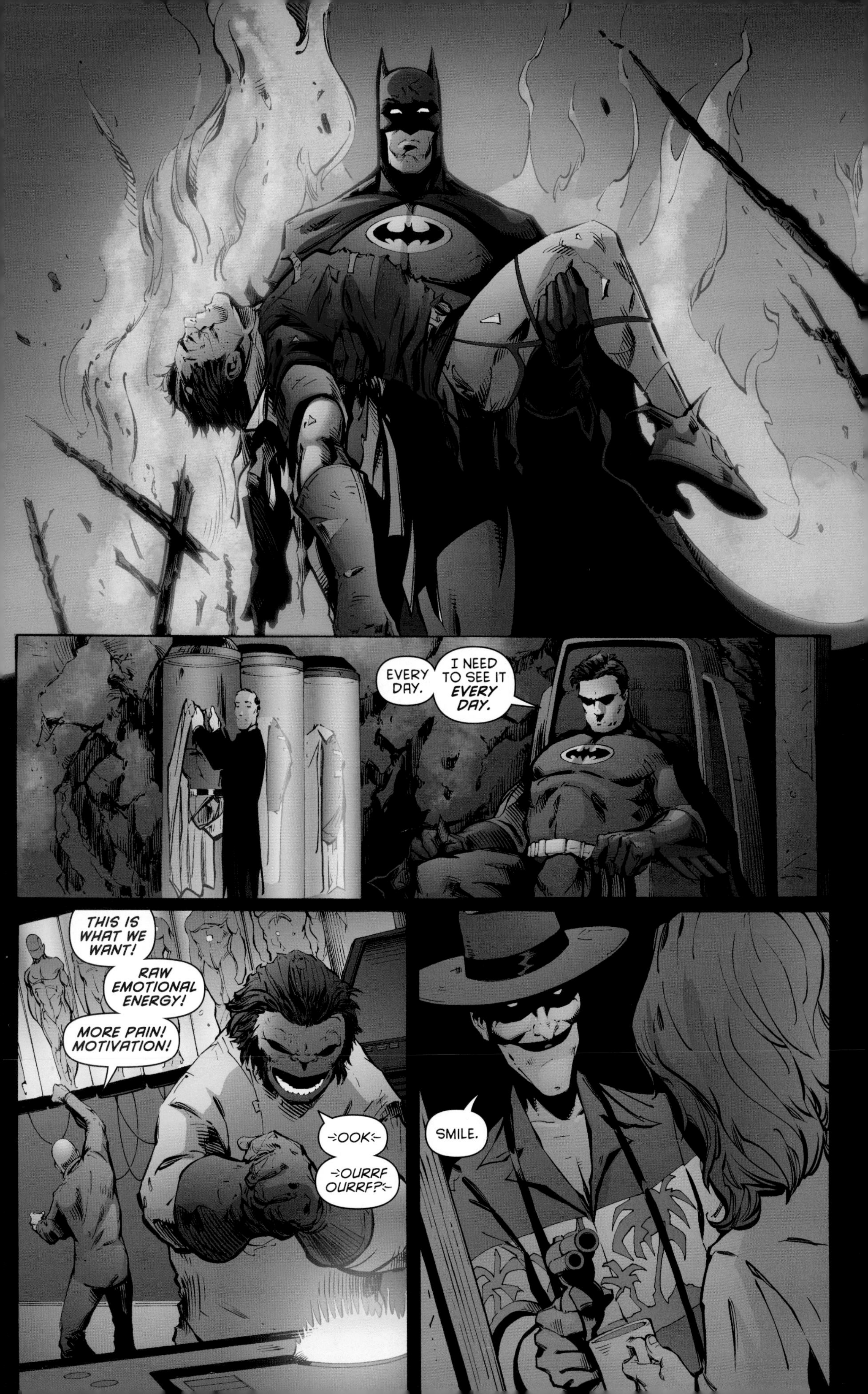
EVERY DAY.
I NEED TO SEE IT EVERY DAY.
THIS IS WHAT WE WANT!
RAW EMOTIONAL ENERGY!
MORE PAIN! MOTIVATION!
OOK
OURRF OURRF?
SMILE.

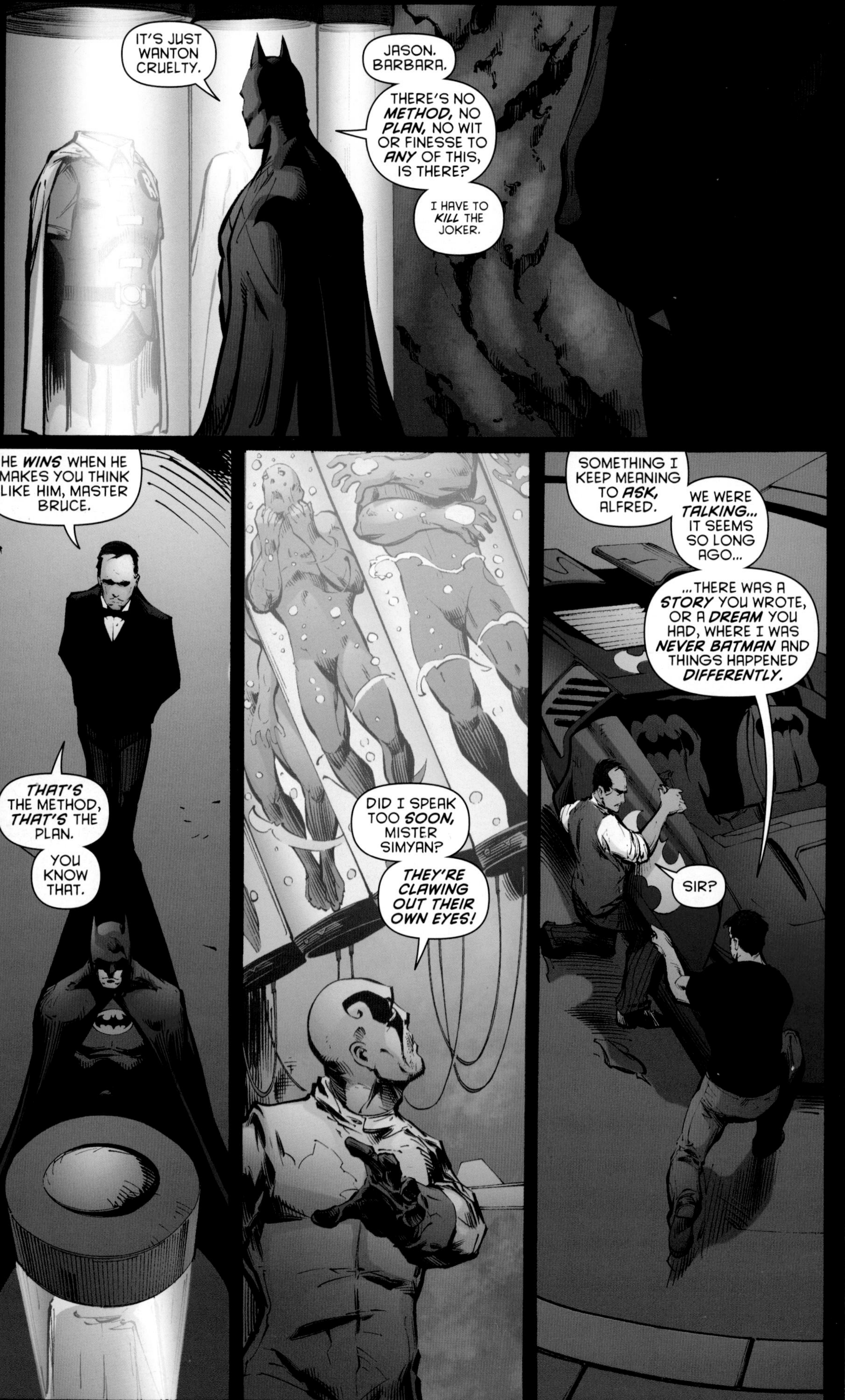

IT'S JUST WANTON CRUELTY.
JASON. BARBARA.
THERE'S NO *METHOD,* NO *PLAN,* NO WIT OR FINESSE TO *ANY* OF THIS, IS THERE?
I HAVE TO *KILL* THE JOKER.
HE *WINS* WHEN HE MAKES YOU THINK LIKE HIM, MASTER BRUCE.
THAT'S THE METHOD, *THAT'S* THE PLAN.
YOU KNOW THAT.
DID I SPEAK TOO *SOON,* MISTER SIMYAN?
THEY'RE CLAWING OUT THEIR OWN EYES!
SOMETHING I KEEP MEANING TO *ASK,* ALFRED.
WE WERE *TALKING...* IT SEEMS SO LONG AGO...
...THERE WAS A *STORY* YOU WROTE, OR A *DREAM* YOU HAD, WHERE I WAS *NEVER BATMAN* AND THINGS HAPPENED *DIFFERENTLY.*
SIR?

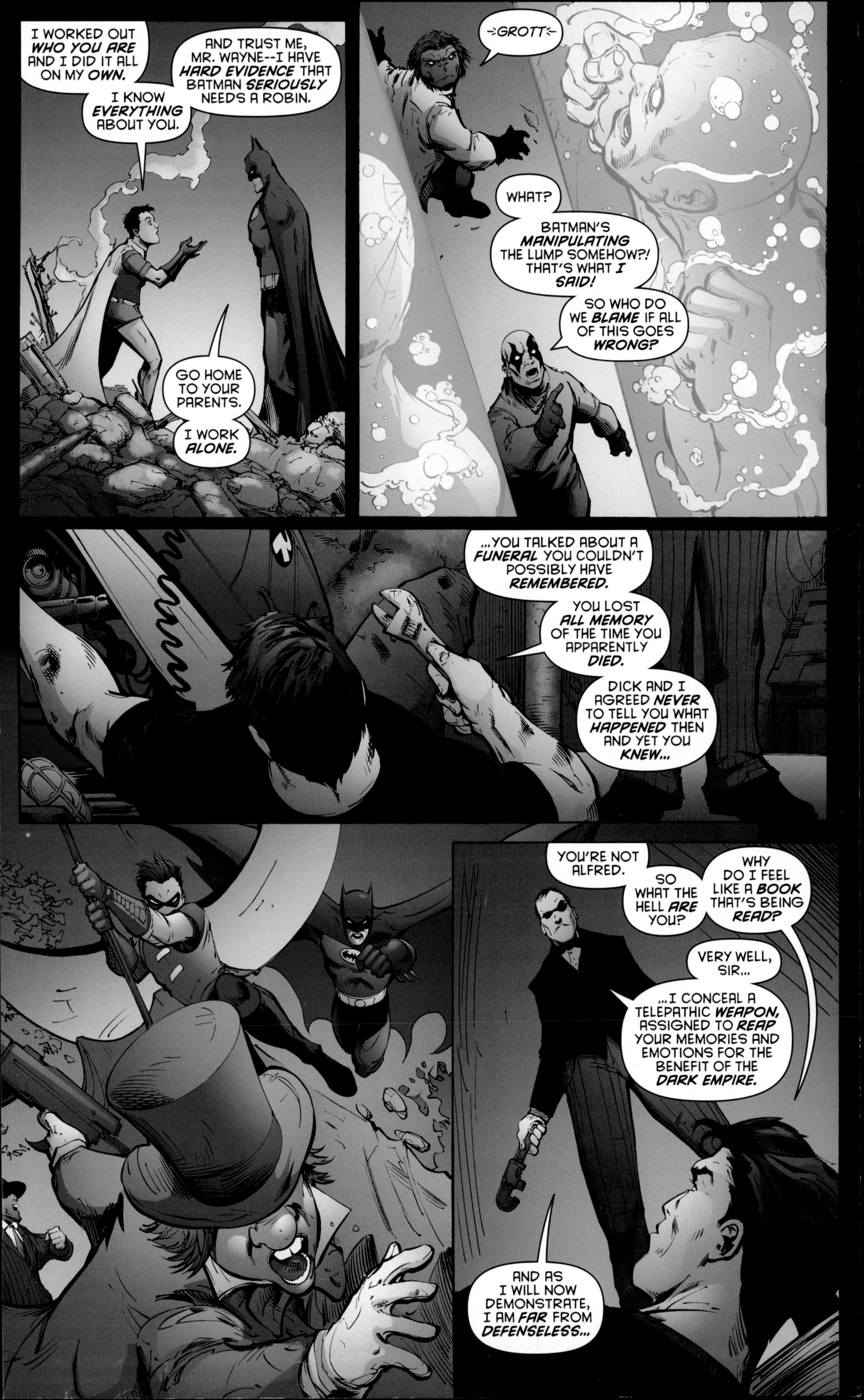
I WORKED OUT WHO YOU ARE AND I DID IT ALL ON MY OWN.
I KNOW EVERYTHING ABOUT YOU.
AND TRUST ME, MR. WAYNE--I HAVE HARD EVIDENCE THAT BATMAN SERIOUSLY NEEDS A ROBIN.
GO HOME TO YOUR PARENTS.
I WORK ALONE.
-GROTT-
WHAT?
BATMAN'S MANIPULATING THE LUMP SOMEHOW?! THAT'S WHAT I SAID!
SO WHO DO WE BLAME IF ALL OF THIS GOES WRONG?
...YOU TALKED ABOUT A FUNERAL YOU COULDN'T POSSIBLY HAVE REMEMBERED.
YOU LOST ALL MEMORY OF THE TIME YOU APPARENTLY DIED.
DICK AND I AGREED NEVER TO TELL YOU WHAT HAPPENED THEN AND YET YOU KNEW...
YOU'RE NOT ALFRED.
SO WHAT THE HELL ARE YOU?
WHY DO I FEEL LIKE A BOOK THAT'S BEING READ?
VERY WELL, SIR...
...I CONCEAL A TELEPATHIC WEAPON, ASSIGNED TO REAP YOUR MEMORIES AND EMOTIONS FOR THE BENEFIT OF THE DARK EMPIRE.
AND AS I WILL NOW DEMONSTRATE, I AM FAR FROM DEFENSELESS...

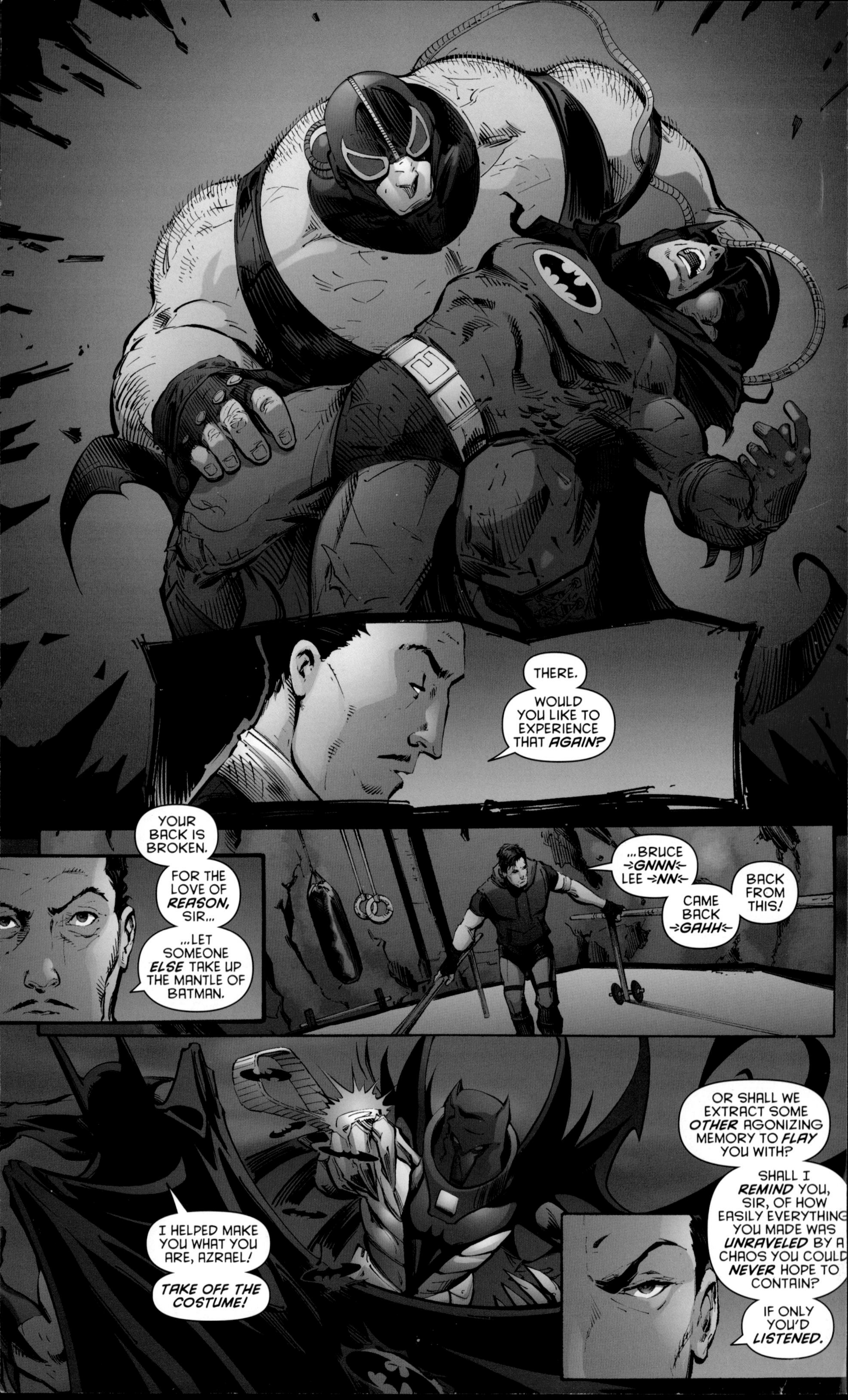

THERE.
WOULD YOU LIKE TO EXPERIENCE THAT *AGAIN?*
YOUR BACK IS BROKEN.
FOR THE LOVE OF *REASON,* SIR...
...LET SOMEONE *ELSE* TAKE UP THE MANTLE OF BATMAN.
...BRUCE -GNNN- LEE -NN-
CAME BACK -GAHH-
BACK FROM THIS!
OR SHALL WE EXTRACT SOME *OTHER* AGONIZING MEMORY TO *FLAY* YOU WITH?
SHALL I *REMIND* YOU, SIR, OF HOW EASILY EVERYTHING YOU MADE WAS *UNRAVELED* BY A CHAOS YOU COULD *NEVER* HOPE TO CONTAIN?
IF ONLY YOU'D *LISTENED.*
I HELPED MAKE YOU WHAT YOU ARE, AZRAEL!
TAKE OFF THE COSTUME!

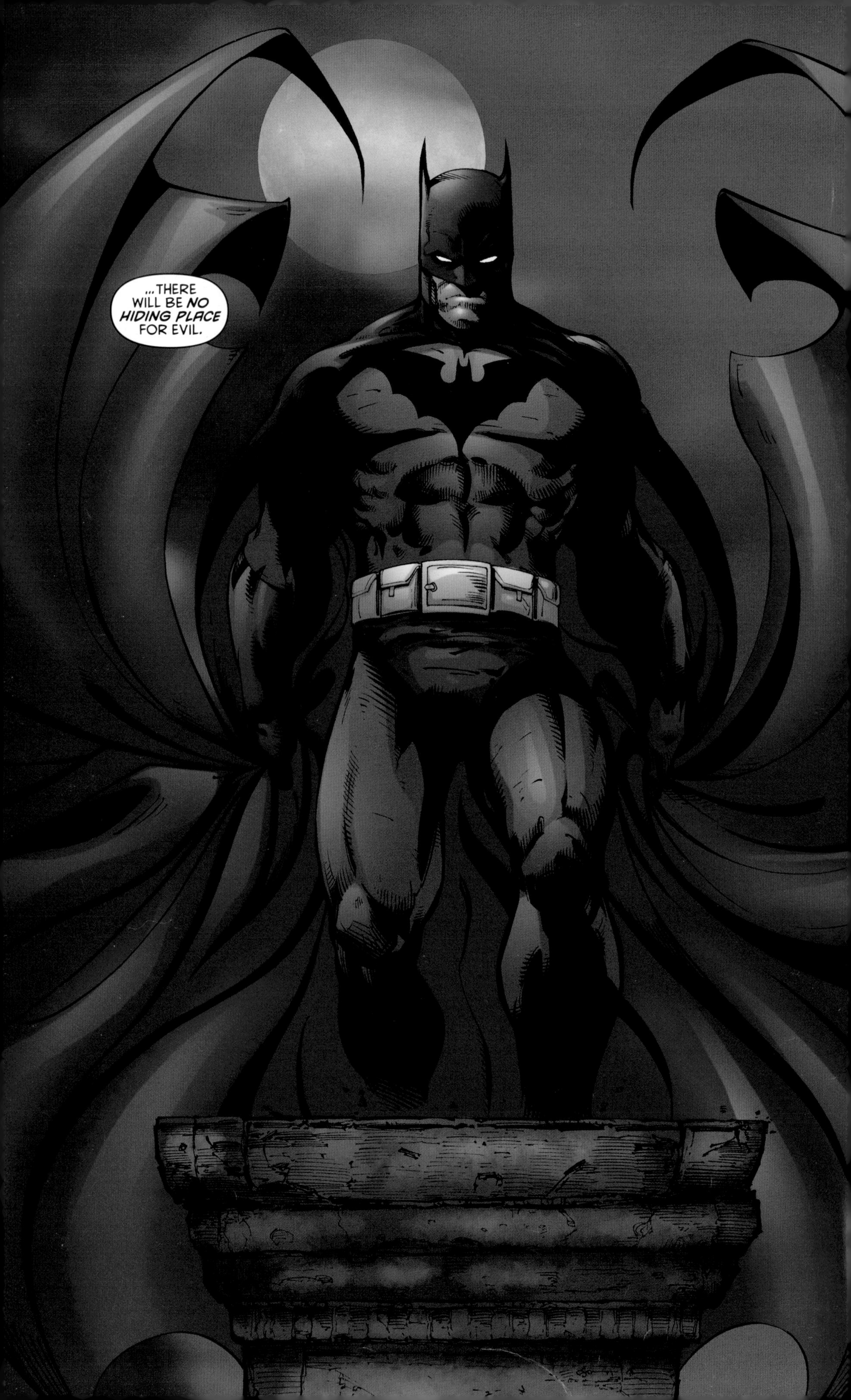
...THERE WILL BE NO HIDING PLACE FOR EVIL.

Breaking down

the

BAT

Preliminary artwork by
Tony S. Daniel
Thumbnails by
Grant Morrison

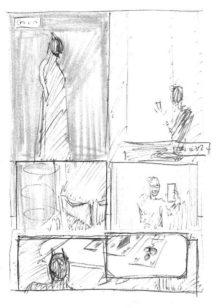

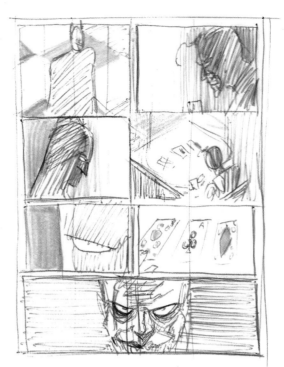

BATMAN SEQUENCE
DCU ZERO - TONY DANIEL

HI TONY - THE LAYOUT FOR
THE PAGES SHOULD BE A
LITTLE LIKE THIS - YOU
DON'T HAVE TO FOLLOW IT
SLAVISHLY AS LONG AS
THE CHECKERBOARD,
BACK + FORWARD
EFFECT WORKS.
THANKS
    GRANT

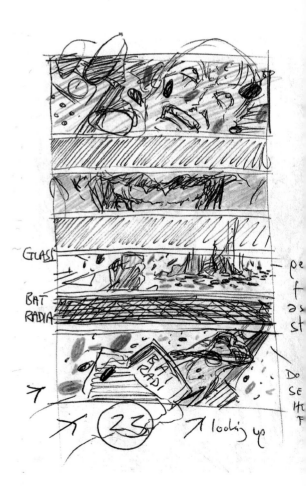

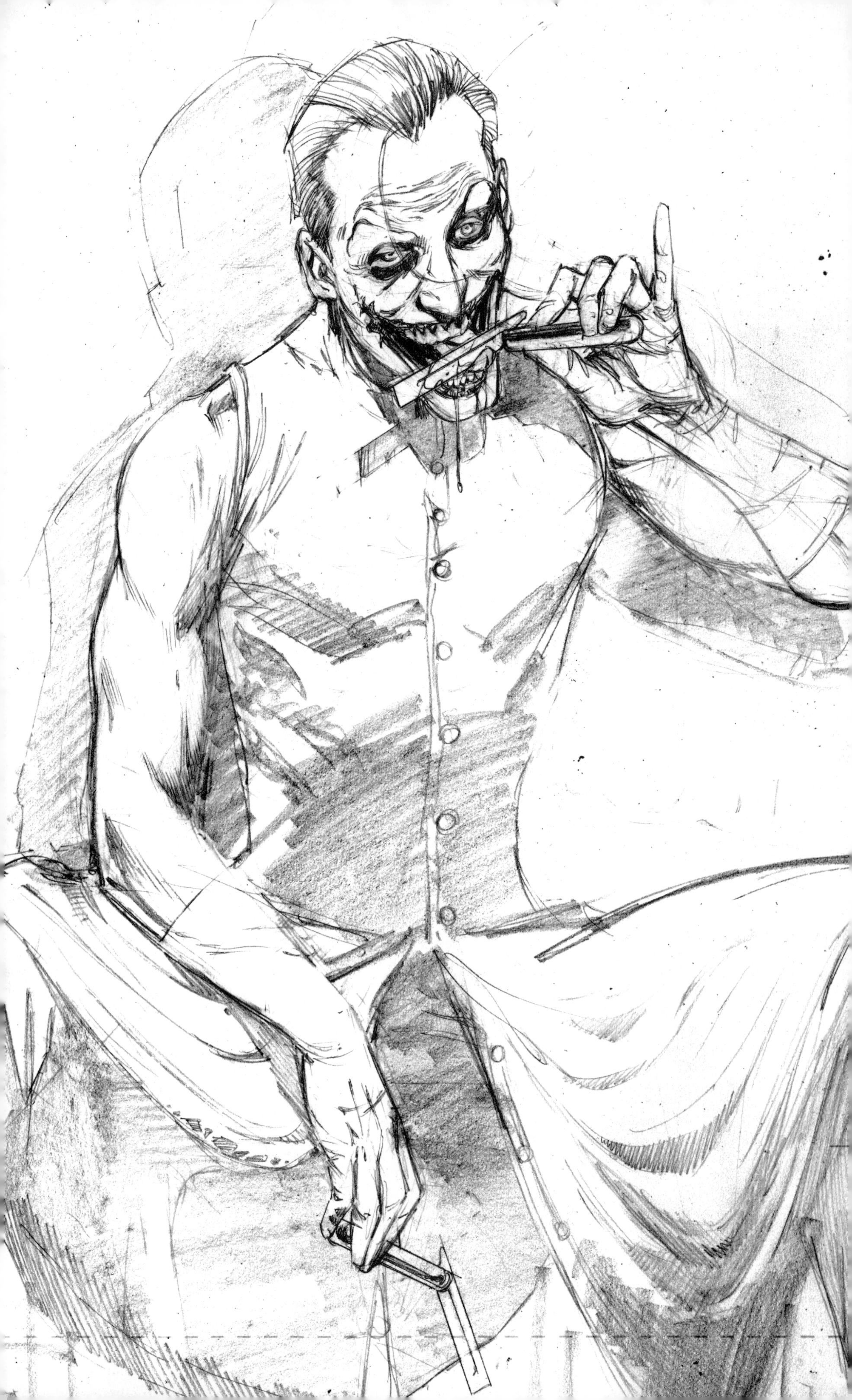

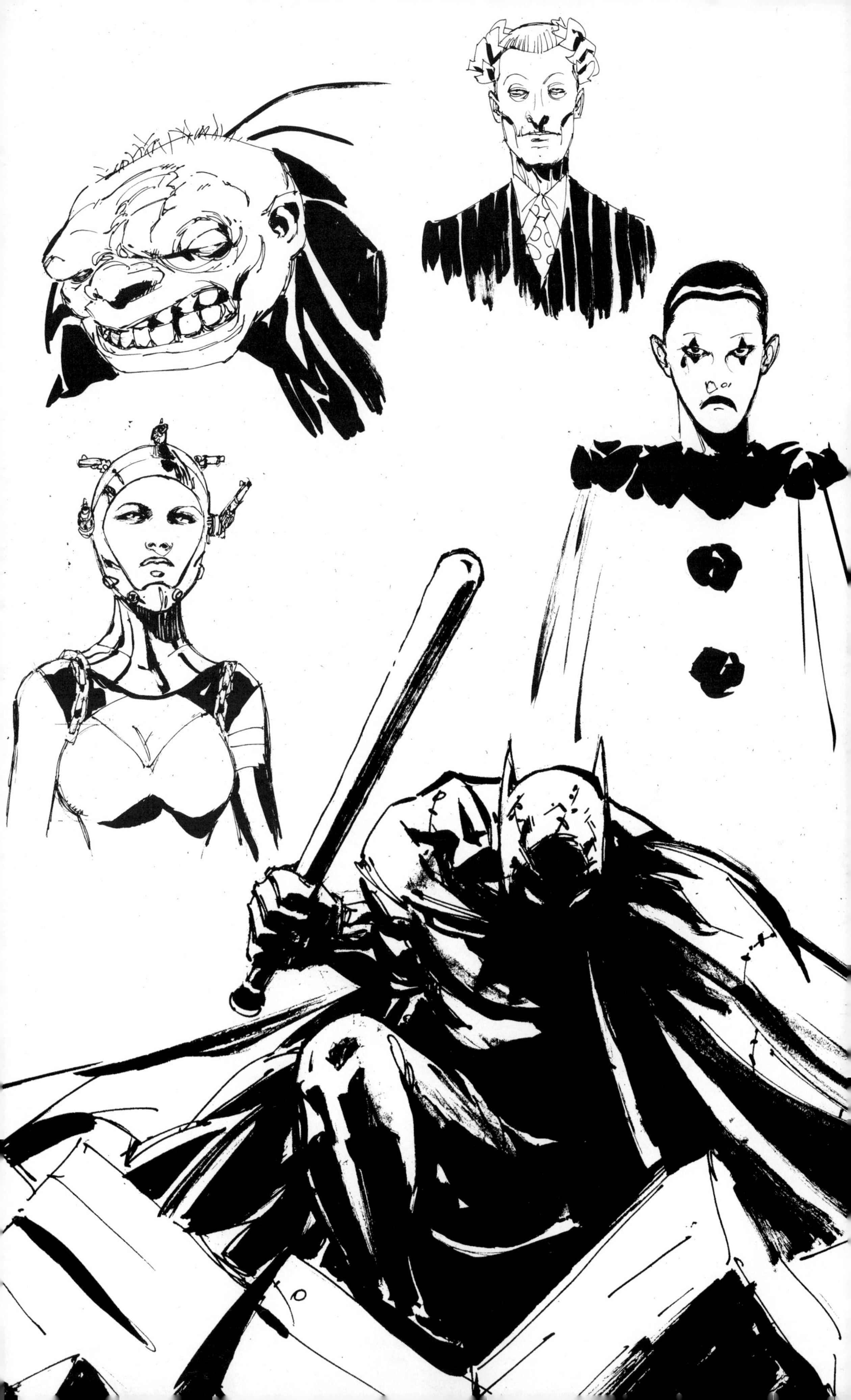

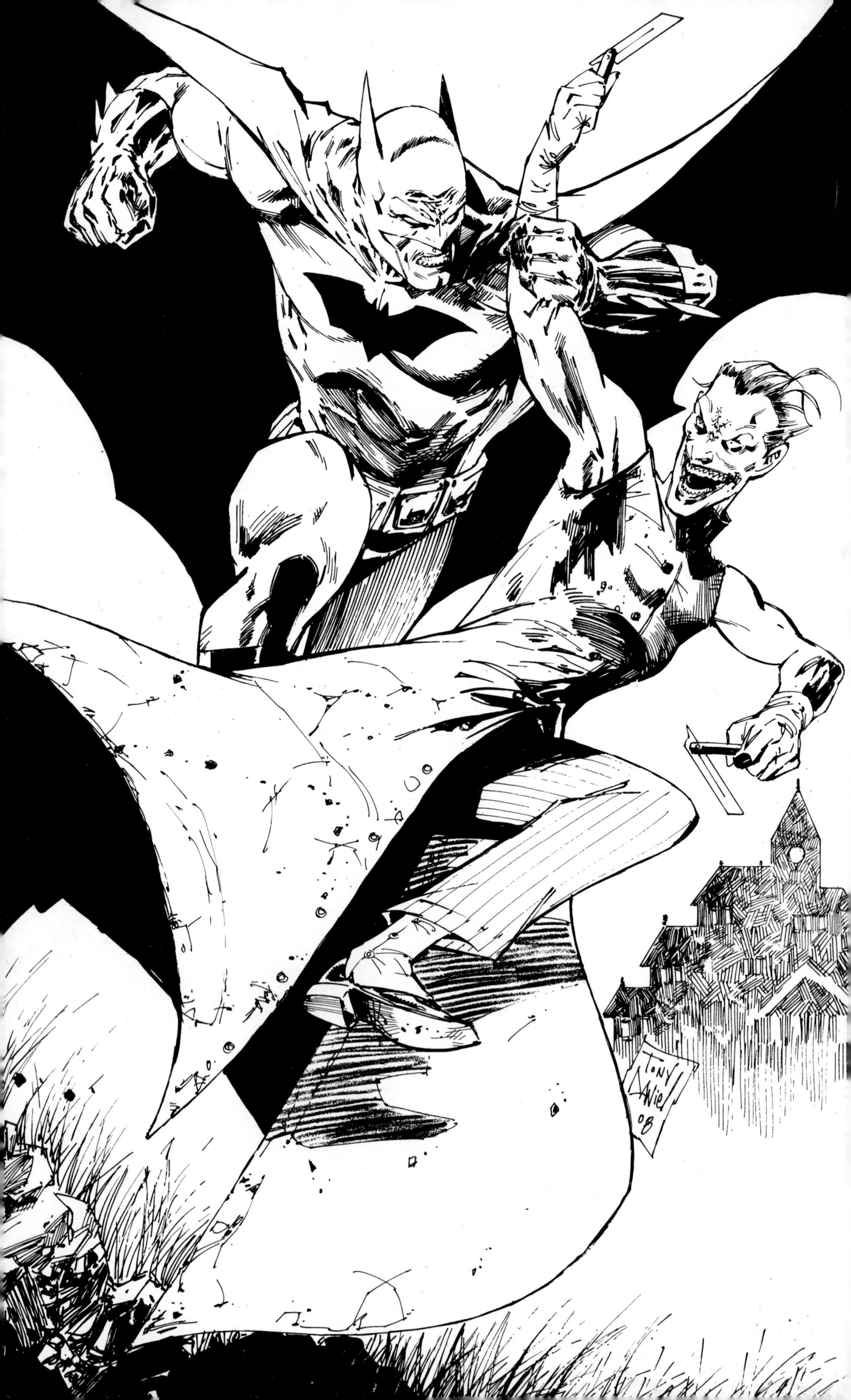
TONY DANIEL 08

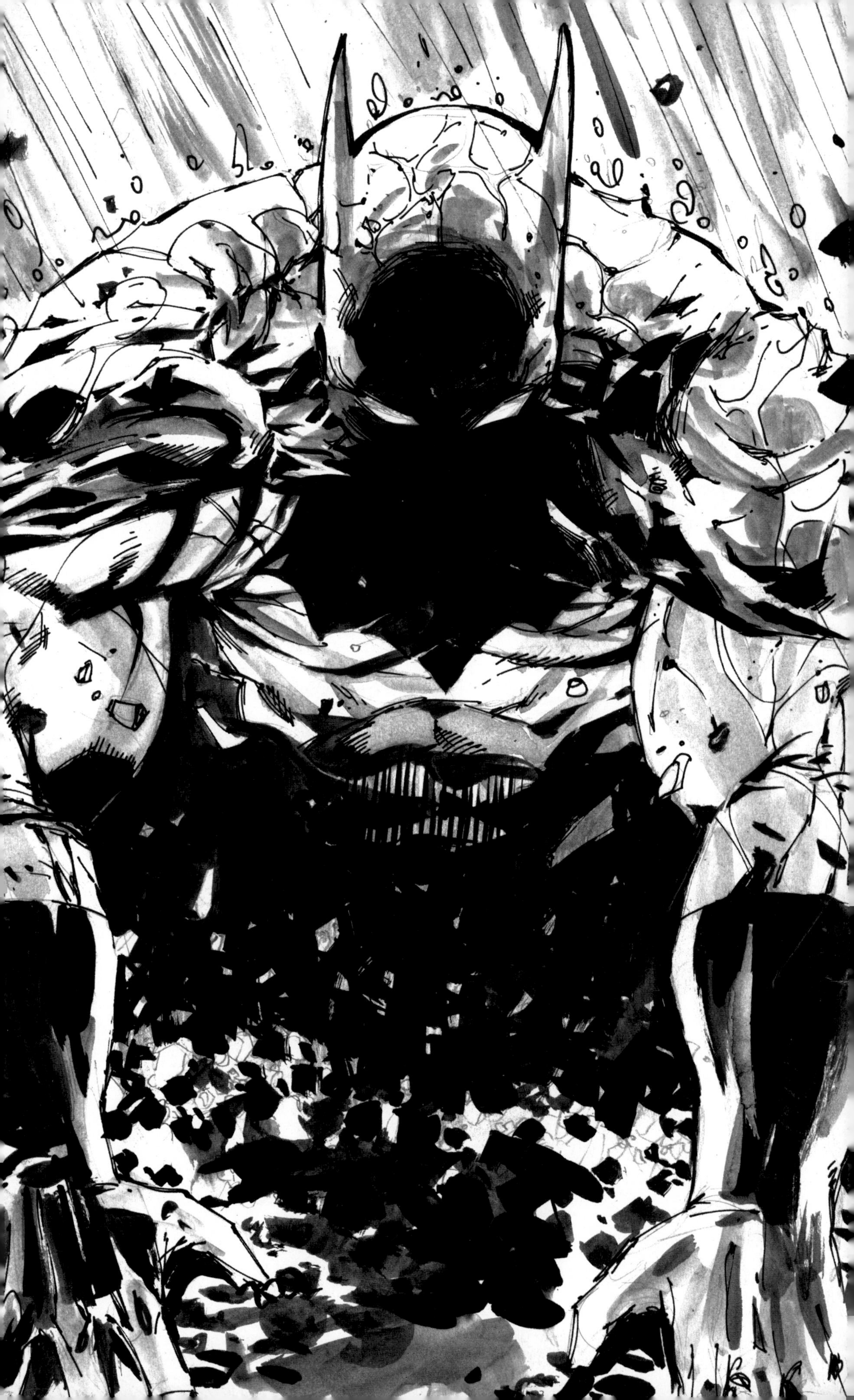

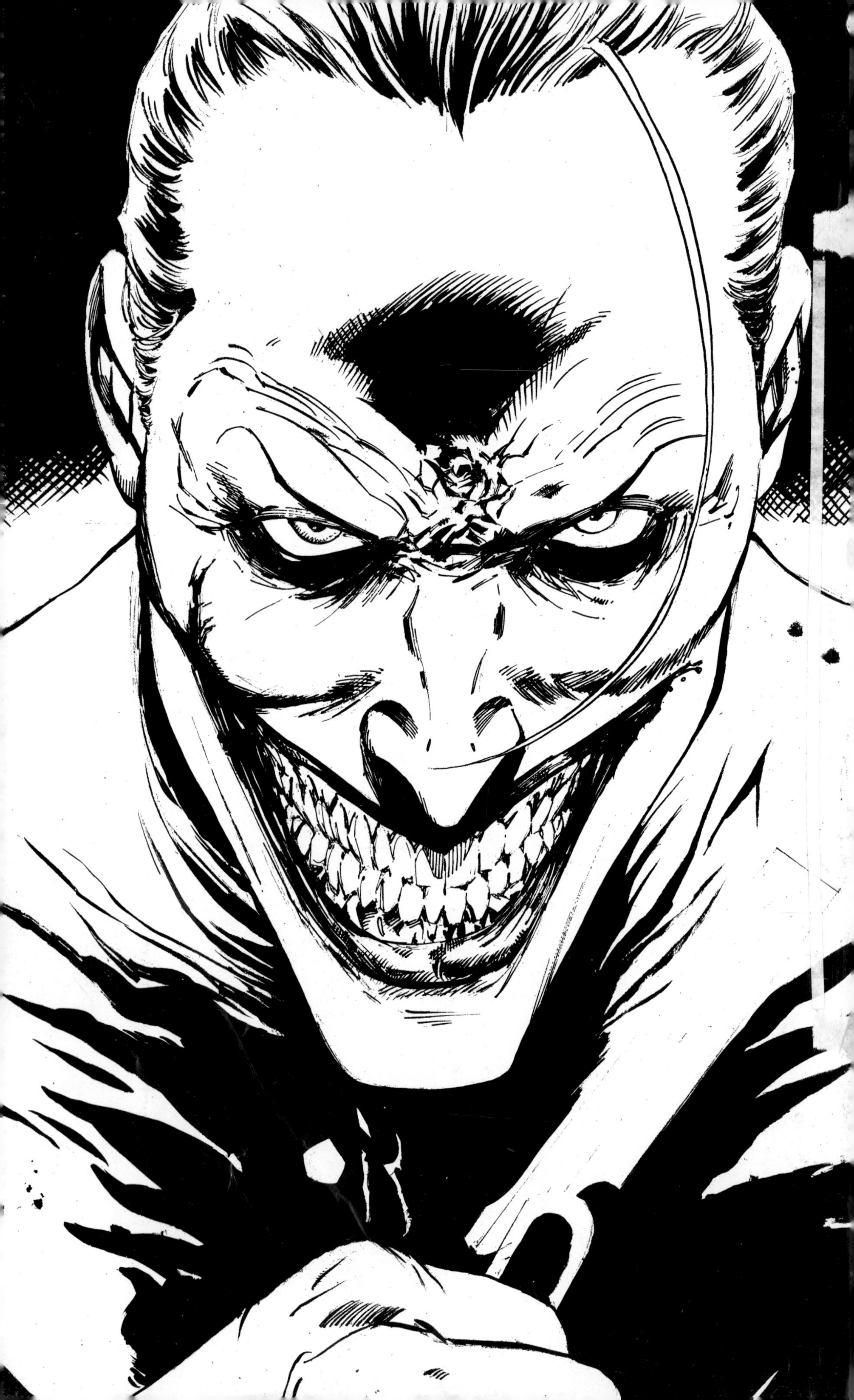